THE
RADIO YEARS

The messages preached on the radio

In Woodford county

By Randy Johnson
Cover Photo by
R Johnson

Copyright © 2015 Randy Johnson
All rights reserved.
ISBN-978-0692450512
ISBN-10-0692450513
BISAC Religion/Christian Education/ General
PACC Seminars

DEDICATION

To my wife of fifty-two years Barbara Masters Johnson and my seven lovely children. May God smile upon them continually.

To my friend Samuel I Sams who listened to the voice of God that fateful evening in May of 1972 and spoke to Barbara about the Holy Ghost. For his encouragement, companionship, and belief in me over the years.

To my friend since 1972, Rev James J Lashley who's teaching you'll see reflected in my writings. I cannot even begin to tell you of his influence on my life.

AUTHOR'S NOTES

It was 1990 when Samuel Sams and I started the Radio Ministry in Woodford County, Illinois. WCRI in Eureka wanted to open a Sunday morning broadcast and we were elected. We were to do a one-hour broadcast. We set it up with two half hour sessions with Sam first and myself second. I would pray, fast, and write every night of the week, working on revisions until the script would flow. Everything had to be right. Friday night would come quickly. Mom and I would load the kids up in whatever transportation we had and drive forty miles to Minonk to record the broadcast. Week in and week out, come rain, snow, tornados, or what ever would find us on our way to record. One winter night, we drove through a snowstorm, a whiteout that only a country living person could understand. I couldn't see twenty feet in front of me. After recording the Sunday message, I needed to drive back home to work overtime the next day. Barbara wouldn't have any part of it. I missed overtime for Saturday and Sunday a sever financial hit. Guess what? We never missed it.

The broadcasts went on for 115 weeks. Only 47 of the messages are compiled into this book. I need to locate the remaining messages and publish them also. This radio ministry was a great reward in my life. I would do it again.

The tapes and manuscripts have lain around in my file cabinet since then gathering dust. A message not preached is a job undone.

So it is with great pleasure to share some of them with you.

rjohnson@uniquecoaches.com

www.uniquecoaches.com

<u>The LORD watch between you an I while we are apart</u>.

Scripture quotations are taken from the King James Version

CONTENTS

THE GREATEST LOVE STORY EVER TOLD 08/19/1990.......9
God, out of a desire to love
HOW DOES JESUS FIT IN THE TRINITY? 09/09/1990........17
So God created man in his own image
ANCILLARY 10/07/1991.................................25
Real handy to have around
WHEN ORDINARY BECOMES EXTRAORDINARY
11/04/1990..31
The real world and the fake world
FOR PROFIT 11/11/1990.................................40
What shall a man gain?
BELIEVE 11/24/1990......................................46
Except you believe
THERE'S ROOM IN THE BOAT 12/02/1990............52
But as the days of Noe were
THE BAPTISM OF THE HOLY GHOST 12/16/1990................59
As of a rushing mighty wind
THE LESSON OF CHRISTMAS 12/23/1990..............65
A birth heralded by angels
PORTRAIT 1 01/06/1992 71
What is your portrait of Christ
PORTRAIT 2 01/20/1992 78
A Portrait of Christ
PORTRAIT 3 01/27/1991 83
Paint a portrait of Christ
PORTRAIT 4 04/07/1991 88
The spirit of the Lord is upon me
DIRECT ACCESS 02/10/1991 96
He is the most accessible God
SPEAK TO THE MOUNTAIN 02/03/1991 103
Mountains in your life
I WAS BLIND BUT NOW I SEE 02/24/1991 110
He received his sight

TOO LITTLE FOR THE LAMB   03/03/1991 117
Call your neighbors
THE PROMISE PART 1 12/08/1991 128
He's the rock
THE PROMISE PART 2   12/15/1991 138
Out of Judah arose the deliver
THE PROMISE PART 3   12/22/1991 146
But thou, Bethlehem Ephratah
THE BELLS KEEP RINGING   3/31/1991 154
The High Priest had to be truthful to himself
FIRST BELIEVE   04/07/1991 162
First believe that he is
WHERE TO FROM HERE?   04/14/1991 170
A cross, an empty tomb, an upper room
THE BIBLE   08/17/1991 177
God's Holy Word for today
WHAT SHALL A MAN GIVE?   08/25/1991 185
The burden of the Lord
MADE TO MORN   09/15/91 194
Man wasn't made to morn
MARRAGE   10/06/1991 203
Relationship between Christ and His Church
A MAJORITY OF ONE 10/20/1991 212
And I sought for a man among them
PROFOUND   10/27/1991 221
Therefore all things whatsoever
SOLD A BILL OF GOODS   11/03/1991 228
Just a bill of laden
CONVENIENT CHRISTIANITY 11/17/1991 237
Mercenary Christian
THANKSGIVING   11/24/1991 246
Feast of tabernacles
RESOLUTIONS 12/29/1991 255
Wash it clean, start with a new slate
SHAKESPEAR AS YOU LIKE IT 09/06/1992 263

There is a way which seemeth right
WASTED IS IT FOR NOTHING?   01/06/1991 .... *269*
She brake the box, and poured it on his head
CORONARY THROMBOSIS.   01/05/1992 .... *282*
Trouble on every hand
WHERE IS THE PROMISE? *291*
But of the times and the seasons
THE APOSTLES   01/26/1992 .... *300*
God's skilled craftsmen.
SALVATION   02/02/1992 .... *306*
Being justified freely by his grace
WHO CAN CONDEMN?   02/09/1992 .... *314*
The blood is for the atonement
CHRIST IS MY FRIEND   02/23/1992 .... *317*
Jesus won't let you down
HOLY GHOST   03/01/1992 .... *325*
Holy Ghost which is given unto us
THE DIVIDING LINE   02/16/1992 .... *332*
The old creation, The new creation
INADEQUATE   12/16/1992 .... *340*
We were naked and undone
THE HOPE OF THE BELIEVER 02/07/1993 .... *350*
A home that will abide for ever
DISPARE   02/21/1993 .... *360*
Do you suffer from a Lack of direction
THE LONELY GOD   02/28/1993 .... *364*
And the LORD God formed man
About The Author *369*
From The Desk *369*

THE GREATEST LOVE STORY EVER TOLD   08/19/1990

PSM 45:1 MY HEART IS INDITING A GOOD MATTER:
I SPEAK THE THINGS WHICH I HAVE MADE TOUCHING THE KING:
MY TONGUE IS THE PEN OF A READY WRITER.

There was a time, near 6000 or so years ago, when God, out of a desire to love, created a creature who had his attributes. Created in the image of God. Created with ability to reason, created with an ability to create. Created a free moral agent who would make decisions based upon a power of reason. Created with an ability to love. God would speak and the earth was formed out of nothingness. Again, he would speak and the heavens came rushing together. Speak again, and the grass and trees would appear. And again and the fish of the sea and the fowls of the air came into existence. Again, and the animals were formed. But when it came to this special creation, man, Genesis 2:7   And the LORD God formed man <of> the dust of the ground, and breathed into his nostrils the breath of life, and man became a living soul. This then, was God's ultimate creation, made just a little lower than the angels Psalms 8:5   For thou hast made him a little lower than the angels, and hast crowned him with glory and honor. This was the ultimate creation that could love and be loved. This was man.

This lonely God put together this creature for fellowship, fellowship unhampered by the walls and shackles of sin. He created him with understanding, compassion, wisdom, knowledge, and with his creative abilities so that man could understand and love God. Someone that God could love.

God sat this man, this ultimate creation, in the most beautiful garden ever created. He put this creature in the garden to dress and keep it. And the Lord God said, of every tree if the garden thou mayest freely eat: But of the tree of the knowledge of good and evil, thou shalt not eat of it: for in the day that thou eatest thereof thou shalt surely die. God created man to live forever. The brain supplied with this body would never be full.

This body we have, was designed to regenerate itself, to never grow old. Always the same physically. What causes man to age? What brings death to our door? It wasn't planned this way. It was to be eternal fellowship with our God. Walking in the cool of the day. Fellowship with the most high. God, out of compassion for his creation, said it is not good that the man should be alone, I will make him a help for him. God caused a deep sleep to come over this man Adam: and he took one of man's ribs and made a woman. From Adam's side, God took the rib. From under the arm of protection. It wasn't a bone from his foot where she could be walked on, but a rib from under Adam's arm, close to his heart.

God had set this one particular tree apart. The tree of the knowledge of good and evil. Some like to say it was an apple tree, or a pomegranate, but really it was a tree of decision. What fruit it bare was of no consequence. It was a tree of decision. One came, a serpent, that Old Devil, Satan saw in Eve's heart bitterness, Bitterness at the fact all the trees but one were theirs'. Playing on this unhealthy desire, he said to Eve, "Yea, hath God said, ye shall not eat of every tree of the garden?" Greed, one of the most destructive lusts man can have. God had, out of love, provided life, a garden, abundance, everything plus, that Eve could ever want, but greed, the lust of the eye, the lust of the flesh, and the pride of life, wanted the forbidden. And the woman said unto the serpent, "We may eat of the fruit of the trees of the garden: But the tree which is in the midst of the garden, God hath said, Ye shall not eat of it, neither shall ye touch it, lest ye die." God had told Adam not to eat of this fruit. Genesis 2:17 but of the tree of the knowledge of good and evil, thou shalt not eat of it: for in the day that thou eatest thereof thou shalt surely die. Adam told Eve what God had told him. But Eve heard Adam wrong for God didn't say a word about touching this fruit, just eating it. This was Eve's downfall. Her lust allowed Satan the wedge he needed to split Eve from fellowship with God, and once Eve, then having struck a mighty blow to the heart of Adam, Adam fell, and the kingdom fell away from him. Eve said, "ye shall not eat of it, neither shall ye touch it, least ye die." Satan then called God a liar and told the woman she wouldn't die. Why Adam ate of the fruit was never written. Did he eat it out of his love for the fallen woman? We could speculate until the end of time. Why did Adam's love for Eve surpass his love for God? Who knows, but he did. The tree was put there for a choice. Adam had to have a choice, will you love me or thee? That was Adam's choice. Adam and Eve became as gods knowing good and evil. Adam and Eve sinned. Fellowship with the Most High was broken. God cannot, will not walk with sin. Sin separates. That which was free, the unshackled fellowship with God now would cost much, cost much, cost much.

Adam and Eve tried to cover their nakedness, discovered by their new knowledge of good and evil, with fig leaves sewn together. Fig leaves could not cover their sin. It would take a blood sacrifice, an innocent life 4000 years in the future to cover their sin, the sinless sacrifice of Jesus Christ. And they heard the voice of the LORD God walking in the garden in the cool of the day. Nothing could have been more beautiful than to hear the voice of God in the cool of the day. Nearly every time God spoke to man from here on it would be in judgment or in the heat of the battle. Not until Jesus Christ came would God speak out of love. And Adam and his wife hid themselves from the presence of the LORD God amongst the trees of the garden. Sin has caused shame to put up a wall between you and your God. Adam and Eve trying to hid from the omnipresent God. Omniscient God. Everywhere, all knowing, all-powerful God. Go ahead and hide Adam! Hide yourself Adam, because you sure can't hide your sin from God. The mind of man rationalizes nearly every wrong we do. Putting your finger on sin is as elusive as killing flies with your bare hands. What have you done Adam? Why the fig leaves? We were naked God. Who told you that you were naked? Did you eat of the tree? The woman you gave me sheeeeeeeeeee----. God gave Adam a chance to confess his sin. Eve was deceived but Adam was not. God knew what Adam did, He was asking Adam if Adam knew. Adam just rationalized. Then the axe fell. And the LORD God called unto Adam, and said unto him, where art thou? Do you know where you are Adam? Do you really know the state of your soul? Death came by the sin of Adam and death reigned supreme until Moses was given the law of sacrifice pointing to Jesus Christ that was yet to come. The consequences of this act were far reaching, the ground was cursed, thorns and thistles came into being, man must sweat to earn his bread, and death was pronounced upon mankind. Romans 5:12-19 Wherefore, as by one man sin entered into the world, and death by sin, and so death passed upon all men, for that all have sinned: For until the law sin was in the world: but sin is not imputed when there is no law. Nevertheless, death reigned from Adam to Moses, even over them that had not sinned after the similitude of Adam's transgression, who is the figure of him that was to come. (Jesus) But not as the offense, so also <is> the free gift. For if through the offence of one many be dead, much more the grace of God, and the gift by grace, <which is> by one man, Jesus Christ, hath abounded unto many. {16} And not as <it was> by one that sinned, <so is> the gift: for the judgment <was> by one to condemnation, but the free gift

<is> of many offences unto justification. {17} For if by one man's offence death reigned by one, much more they which receive abundance of grace and of the gift of righteousness shall reign in life by one, Jesus Christ. Therefore as by the offence of one <judgment came> upon all men to condemnation, even so by the righteousness of one <the free gift came> upon all men unto justification of life. {19} For as by one man's disobedience many were made sinners, so by the obedience of one shall many be made righteous.

But the worst consequence was that man was cut off from the presence of God. He ejected man from the Garden of Eden to till the earth by the sweat of his brow. God, heartbroken at the decision of Adam, then made coats of skins to cloth the nakedness of his Beloved creation. Innocent blood now shed to cover their sins. "I wouldn't have done that. I would have done what God said to do." Yet each day your given a choice, just as Adam, and day after day you fail. "How, Bro Johnson, do I fail? How can you make such a blanket statement? Examine yourselves, I say. Have you done what God has told you to do? Do you put other things ahead of God? Are there things in your life that displaces God? Adam made a decision that he would be a god to himself. Instead of trusting God to tell him right from wrong, he decided to do his own telling. Of all the creatures that walk, fly, crawl, or swim, man is the only one out of tune with God. Think on this. Does God provide the birds with food? The deer in the timber? The fish in the river? Do they do as God directs them? Sure, they do, and God gets glory from this order. But when man, his perfect creation, decides to follow the will of God, the pleasure God gets from this is immeasurable. Just think, here is a creature with a will of its own, surrendering to God. Matthew 6:25-34 Therefore I say unto you, Take no thought for your life, what ye shall eat, or what ye shall drink, nor yet for your body, what ye shall put on. Is not the life more than meat, and the body than raiment? {26} Behold the fowls of the air: for they sow not, neither do they reap, nor gather into barns, yet your heavenly Father feedeth them. Are ye not much better than they? {27} Which of you by taking thought can add one cubit unto his stature? {28} And why take ye thought for raiment? Consider the lilies of the field, how they grow, they toil not, neither do they spin: {29} And yet I say unto you, That even Solomon in all his glory was not arrayed like one of these. {30} Wherefore, if God so clothe the grass of the field, which to day is, and to morrow is cast into the oven, <shall he> not much more <clothe> you, O ye of little faith? {31} Therefore take no thought, saying, what shall we eat? Or, what shall we drink? Or, Wherewithal shall we be clothed? {32} (For after all these things do the

Gentiles seek:) for your heavenly Father knoweth that ye have need of all these things. {33} But seek ye first the kingdom of God, and his righteousness, and all these things shall be added unto you. {34} Take therefore no thought for the morrow: for the morrow shall take thought for the things of itself. Sufficient unto the day <is> the evil thereof.

God, with love abounding, set a plan in action whereby man could be justified in God's sight and therefore be in his presence without being consumed. God announces the Great Plan. And I will put enmity between thee and the woman, and between thy seed and her seed, it shall bruise thy head, and thou shalt bruise his heel. What will this enmity be? It shall be the savior of the world, Jesus Christ.

On and on time went, God continued to deal with man, hoping for those that would return His love. From time to time there were those who loved God beyond life itself. Moses, soon to be pharaoh of all of Egypt, refused to be called the son of Pharaoh's daughter, choosing rather to suffer affliction with the people of God, than to enjoy the pleasures of sin for a season, Hebrews 11:24-26 By faith Moses, when he was come to years, refused to be called the son of Pharaoh's daughter, {25} Choosing rather to suffer affliction with the people of God, than to enjoy the pleasures of sin for a season, {26} Esteeming the reproach of Christ greater riches than the treasures in Egypt: for he had respect unto the recompense of the reward. Job served God without reward, Job 1:8-9 And the LORD said unto Satan, Hast thou considered my servant Job, that <there is> none like him in the earth, a perfect and an upright man, one that feareth God, and escheweth evil? {9} Then Satan answered the LORD, and said, Doth Job fear God for nought? Job served God for no reward. Satan took everything that Job had, yet when Job's wife told him to curse God and die out of the pain in her heart for her husband, Job said, Job 2:9-10 "Then said his wife unto him, Dost thou still retain thine integrity?" [Curse God, and die]. But he said unto her, "Thou speakest as one of the foolish women speaketh. What? Shall we receive good at the hand of God, and shall we not receive evil?" In all this did not Job sin with his lips. he went on to say in another place, "Though he slay me, yet will I trust in him, I will maintain mine ways before him." Daniel, Shadrack, Meshech, and Abendigo, four who served God with integrity, righteousness and suffered persecution for it. Daniel suffered under three different kings. One would have him eaten by the lions. You know the story of how God suffered the lion's mouths to be stopped. Shadrack, Meshech, and Abendigo wouldn't bow their knees to this new social world order.

They were put into a furnace seven times hotter then normal. God preserved them in the fire, not even the smell of smoke was upon them. God preserves and preserved those who love him. Trials come, no doubt. Lives are lost, no doubt. A story comes to me of twelve who were native witnesses for Christ in an Asian country. Eleven lost their heads for Christ. Persecution still exists yet today. Very few countries have the freedom we enjoy. A man I met at ICC was from a country called Morocco. A Christian. I asked him if he were going back to witness, to share this with the people he knew in Morocco. "Their religion will make them kill me if I go back."

Divine love reaches across the gulf of sin and plucks from hell the person who would love God with all their heart, mind, soul, and strength. God then sets them on their feet, clothes them in garments of righteousness, and sets a new heart in place of an old stony one. He then writes his laws upon the tablets of their hearts. The Old heart, full of murder, lies, dissimulation, and evil is gone. Fellowship with divinity is restored. Fellowship with God just as Adam had in the beginning.

Would you desire to know God as Adam did? You can. Really, you can. It's God's desire to establish His love in you. What is love, you say. Love is not fulfilling the lusts of the flesh. This love is divine. This love is a passion to give, not get. By what sign would all men know that we are his disciples? It's not a cross that is worn around our neck. No bumper sticker can declarer it. No voice can utter it. It's because you have love one for another. 1 Corinthians 13:1-10 Though I speak with the tongues of men and of angels, and have not charity, I am become <as> sounding brass, or a tinkling cymbal. {2} And though I have <the gift of> prophecy, and understand all mysteries, and all knowledge, and though I have all faith, so that I could remove mountains, and have not charity, I am nothing. {3} And though I bestow all my goods to feed <the poor>, and though I give my body to be burned, and have not charity, it profiteth me nothing. {4} Charity suffereth long, <and> is kind, charity envieth not, charity vaunteth not itself, is not puffed up, {5} Doth not behave itself unseemly, seeketh not her own, is not easily provoked, thinketh no evil, {6} Rejoiceth not in iniquity, but rejoiceth in the truth, {7} Beareth all things, believeth all things, hopeth all things, endureth all things. {8} Charity never faileth: but whether <there be> prophecies, they shall fail, whether <there be> tongues, they shall cease, whether <there be> knowledge, it shall vanish away. {9} For we know in part, and we prophesy in part. {10} But when that which is perfect is come, then that which is in part shall be done away. This kind of love cannot be demonstrated except in the Holy Ghost. God established his laws so that man could see just how impossible it was for man to be good enough to walk with God. Thou shalt, thou shalt not, on and on the list goes. Read Exodus, Deuteronomy. The offerings one had to bring, the sacrifices that had to be offered. No man was justified by the law. The law was not unto life but death. The sacrifices simply, simply? Pushed their sin forward in time until the perfect sacrifice would come. The sinless one, Jesus, Jehovah Savior. Time and time again God offered fellowship to his people. Time after time, they decided to make their own decisions. God established a priesthood to go between the people and Him. He set up a tabernacle in the wilderness, with a holy place and a holiest of holies. There being a middle wall of separation, a veil, between the two. Hebrews 9:1-7 Then verily the first <covenant> had also ordinances of divine service, and a worldly sanctuary. {2} for there was a tabernacle made, the first, wherein <was> the candlestick, and the table, and the showbread, which is called the sanctuary. {3} And after the second veil, the tabernacle which is called the Holiest of all, {4} Which had the golden censer, and the ark of the covenant overlaid round about with gold, wherein <was> the golden pot that had manna, and Aaron's rod that budded, and the tables of the covenant, {5} And over it the cherubim of glory shadowing the mercy seat, of which we cannot now speak particularly. {6} Now when these things were thus ordained, the priests went always into the first tabernacle, accomplishing the service <of God>. {7} But into the second <went> the high priest alone once every year, not without blood, which he offered for himself, and <for> the errors of the people: Hebrews 10:1-14 For the law having a shadow of good things to come, <and> not the very image of the things, can never with those sacrifices which they offered year by year continually make the comers thereunto perfect. {2} For then would they not have ceased to be offered? Because that the worshippers once purged should have had no more conscience of sins. {3} But in those <sacrifices there is> a remembrance again <made> of sins every year. {4} For <it is> not possible that the blood of bulls and of goats should take away sins. {5} Wherefore when he cometh into the world, he saith, Sacrifice and offering thou wouldest not, but a body hast thou prepared me: {6} In burnt offerings and <sacrifices> for sin thou hast had no pleasure. {7} Then said I, Lo, I come (in the volume of the book it is written of me,) to do thy will, O God. {8} Above when he said, Sacrifice and offering and burnt offerings and <offering> for sin thou wouldest not, neither hadst pleasure <therein>, which are offered by the law, {9} Then said he, Lo, I come to do thy will, O God. He taketh away the first, that he may establish the second. {10} By the which will we are sanctified through the offering of the body of Jesus Christ once <for all>. {11} And every priest standeth daily ministering and offering oftentimes the same sacrifices, which can never take away sins: {12} But this man, after he had offered one sacrifice for sins for ever, sat down on the right hand of God, {13} From henceforth expecting till his enemies be made his footstool. {14} For by one offering he hath perfected forever them that are sanctified. There is no substitute for fellowship with God. Sin has pleasure of a truth, but it is fleeting, only for a season. Never, I say, never will you find sin fulfilling. Trying to fill the emptiness in your soul with things of this world is like trying to fill a mason jar completely full of sand. No matter how fine the sand, there's always room for water. Empty spaces in your life. That emptiness is God shaped and can only be filled with His Spirit, the Holy Ghost. Adam's sin put that emptiness there, but your sin keeps it there. Our Father who art in heaven. The prayer we prayed on our knees as a child. Hallowed is thy name. Holy. Easy to say but the Old Testament people wouldn't even utter the name of God. They used YHWH. Just the initials least they desecrate God's name by misspelling. Thy kingdom come. Not my kingdom come. On earth as it is in heaven. How? What God says, goes in heaven. Thy will be done. Not my will nor the will of Adam, but thy will be done on earth as it is in heaven.

HOW DOES JESUS FIT IN THE TRINITY? 09/08/1990

PSM 45:1 MY HEART IS INDITING A GOOD MATTER:
I SPEAK THE THINGS WHICH I HAVE MADE TOUCHING THE KING:
MY TONGUE IS THE PEN OF A READY WRITER.

The last two lessons covered, the principles of Bible study
1. The Bible never contradicts itself
2. No scripture is of any private interpretation
3. No single scripture is to stand-alone

The second lesson covered Who Jesus is.
> He's our salvation, our friend, our strength, our hope, our life, our light, Jesus is sufficient for any need. I say, any need.

Third in this three part series,
> How does Jesus fit in this thing called the trinity?

The greatest created problem the Christian and Jewish community have, is to do with doctrine is the trinity.
How do you explain the trinity? You can't because it's not logical.
The word "GOD" defines the supreme entity and cannot be multi-person
I myself had, in times past, and a great deal of difficulty explaining, defining, or even understanding the trinity, There simply isn't a triune godhead.

While pouring over Old and New Testament alike and come across a scripture like, Genesis 1:26 And God said, Let us make man in our image, after our likeness: Then run across a scripture not one verse further, Genesis 1:27 So God created man in his own image, in the image of God created he him, male and female created he them. And again, Isaiah 44:24 Thus saith the LORD, thy redeemer, and he that formed thee from the womb, I am the LORD that maketh all things, that stretcheth forth the heavens alone, that spreadeth abroad the earth by myself, And Isaiah 40:13-14 Who hath directed the Spirit of the LORD, or being his counselor hath taught him? With whom took he counsel, and who instructed him, and taught him in the path of judgment, and taught him knowledge, and showed to him the way of understanding?   Then turn to Deuteronomy 6:4   Hear, O Israel: The LORD our God is one LORD: And even the TEN COMMANDMENTS say Exodus 20:3   Thou shalt have no other gods before me.   Then turning to Isaiah 12:2   Behold, God is my salvation, I will trust, and not be afraid: for the LORD JEHOVAH is my strength and my song, he also is become my salvation.   No wonder the Jews took up stones to stone Jesus in the book of John 10:33   The Jews answered him, saying, For a good work we stone thee not, but for blasphemy, and because that thou, being a man, makest thyself God.

The whole book of Isaiah is inundated with verses similar to those just read.   The whole Old Testament speaks of God becoming our salvation.   Is it any wonder then that the Jews of Jesus' day could not accept the fact that Jesus was indeed God manifest in the flesh?   1 Timothy 3:16   And without controversy great is the mystery of godliness: God was manifest in the flesh, justified in the Spirit, seen of angels, preached unto the Gentiles, believed on in the world, received up into glory.   Who was received up into glory?   Mark 16:19   So then after the Lord had spoken unto them, he was received up into heaven,   Luke 24:51 .... He was parted from them, and carried up into heaven.

God was manifest in the flesh.   What flesh?   Jesus Christ.   Who was justified in the spirit?   Jesus Christ.   Who was seen of the angels?   Jesus Christ.   Who preached unto the gentiles?   Jesus Christ.   Who was believed on in the world?   Jesus Christ.   John 1:1-3   In the beginning was the Word, and the Word was with God, and the Word was God.   The same was in the beginning with God.   All things were made by him, and without him was not any thing made that was made.   Doesn't this prove the trinity without a doubt?   Yet looking at a verse in Isaiah or Nehemiah or Psalms and become more and more confused of this trinity.   Isaiah 44:24   Thus saith the LORD, thy redeemer, and he that formed thee from the womb, I am the LORD that maketh all things, that stretcheth forth the heavens alone, that spreadeth abroad the earth by myself,   Nehemiah 9:6   Thou, even thou, art LORD alone, thou hast made heaven, the heaven of heavens, with all their host, the earth, and all things that are therein, the seas, and all that is therein, and thou preservest them all, and the host of heaven worshippeth thee.   Psalms 102:25   Of old hast thou laid the foundation of the earth: and the heavens are the work of thy hands. Genesis 1:1   In the beginning God created....   Psalms 33:6-7   By the word of the LORD were the heavens made, and all the host of them by the breath of his mouth.   {7} He gathereth the waters of the sea together as an heap: he layeth up the depth in storehouses.   And Psalms 95:5   The sea is his, and he made it: and his hands formed the dry land.

Then Psalms 104:2-35 who stretchest out the heavens like a curtain: verse 5: Who laid the foundations of the earth, verse 6 thou coverest it with the deep.... 7: at thy rebuke they fled, 13: he watereth the hills from his chambers: 14: he causeth the grass to grow for the cattle, and herb for the service of man: 19: he appointeth the moon for the seasons: the sun knoweth his going down. 29: thou hidest thy face, they are troubled: thou takest away their breath, they die, and return to their dust. 30: Thou sendest forth thy spirit, they are created: and thou renewest the face of the earth. I encourage you to read the whole 104th chapter of Psalms. Isaiah 40:28 everlasting God, the LORD, the creator of the ends of the earth... Isaiah 48:12 I am he, I am the first, I also am the last."

<u>Remember the principles of Bible study from the first lesson?</u>

1. The Bible never contradicts itself.

    Seeming contradictions are due to a carnal lack of scriptural understanding.

2. No scripture is of any private interpretation.

    No man has an exclusive understanding of the word of God.

3. No single scripture stands alone.

    The Bible supports it's self. Scripture interprets scripture. If
    We base our lives upon one scripture standing alone, we are in
    Jeopardy, for the Bible can then be made to say anything.
    Matthew 18:16 says, in the mouth of two or three witnesses every
    Word may be established. Also in 2 Cor 13:1, Num 35:30, Deut 17:6,
    19:15, 1 Tim 5:19, Heb 10:28 Always keep these principles in mind
    And you will never be led astray, even in this day of confusion.

Thinking then on these things and trying to reconcile some of the traditions handed down by our forefathers is sometimes like trying to mix oil and water, it simply doesn't work. I determined in my heart that this Godhead was understandable and I didn't have to just believe something told me. Remember our faith is based upon an understanding of the Word of God. Romans 10:17 Faith cometh by hearing, and hearing by the Word of God. And 2 Timothy 3:16-17 tells us that: All scripture is given by inspiration of God, and is profitable for doctrine, for reproof, for correction, for instruction in righteousness: {17} That the man of God may be perfect, thoroughly furnished unto all good works. And then Matthew 13:11 tells you ."it is given unto you to know the mysteries of the kingdom of heaven,"
Deuteronomy 5:4 Hear O Israel: The Lord our God is one LORD.

The Old Testament is dogmatic, explicit: There is but one God. All the scriptures at the first of the lesson indicate this. Yet you can walk into a church even today and hear the people sing: Holy..Holy..Holy! Merciful and mighty! God in three persons, blessed trinity! God in three persons? That's the "Blessed Trinity." The churches since 350 AD have doggedly insisted three individuals make up the Godhead, stating, "The Father is God, The Son is God, and the Holy Ghost is God." Then turn and say, "There are not three separate gods, but one single God." "Neither confounding the persons, nor dividing the substance." "The creed of Athanasius". Notice this wasn't a scriptural reference but some thing written to explain the trinity. Hard to understand? Definitely. Even impossible. I do not see three Gods. Do not expect to see three sitting on the throne in heaven. Rev 4:2 ..."and behold, a throne was set in heaven, and one sat on the throne." Verse 9 "And the beasts give glory and honor and thanks to him that sat upon the throne." Not them. Rev 5:1 "And I saw in the right hand of him (not them) that sat on the throne." Rev 20:11 "And I saw a great white throne, and him that sat on it," There are many more verses reading this way. While in the body, that is on this earth, I see God revealed as the Father, the Son, and the Holy Ghost and all three functioning at once. This has only to do with this earthly program. This is one God dealing with man in three different and distinct roles. By operating in different roles, all three can appear as different personalities and do no violence to the Godhead. One of the fundamental attributes of God is omnipresence. God fills all heaven and earth. 1 Kings 8:27 ...."Behold, the heaven and heaven of heavens cannot contain thee", present in all places at once, so God can be present in the Son, in the Holy Ghost, and still fill all heaven and earth. Matthew 3:16 proves this Matthew 3:16 "And Jesus, (the son) when he was baptized, went up straightway out of the water: and, lo, the heavens were opened unto him, and he saw the Spirit of God (the Holy Ghost) descending like a dove, (not a dove, but like a dove) and lighting upon him:" All three manifest at the same time, Jesus the son, coming up out of the water, The Spirit as a dove, and the voice of God. One God performing all three roles simultaneously. This is not difficult when your omnipresent. There's no balking at accepting that the Holy Spirit is God. But when it comes to the deity of Jesus Christ, the people begin to hesitate. How can Jesus be God?

The first thing is the dual nature of Jesus' birth. The Holy Ghost overshadowed Mary, as is shown in Luke 1:35 "And the angel answered and said unto her, The Holy Ghost shall come upon thee, and the power of the Highest shall overshadow thee: therefore also that holy thing which shall be born of thee shall be called the Son of God."

Jesus didn't have a natural father like you or me, but God was the father of this holy thing in Mary's womb. So Jesus had two natures: One, Mary provided him with flesh and bones body and a human nature. While the Holy Ghost made him the son of God and gave him a divine nature. The Father was present in the fetus yet not contained in the fetus. After all, God fills all heaven and earth. Jesus then entered the world by natural birth the same as you or me. This natural birth limited Jesus to the physical body and the same five sense all men have. It limited his mind in that he was restricted to the brain that came with the body. He was limited to the five senses and cut off from a conscious awareness of his Father. Why? So that he would suffer all things just as you and I do. What good is a sinless sacrifice if the sacrifice didn't have the ability to sin. Hebrews 4:15 "For we have not an high priest which cannot be touched with the feeling of our infirmities: but was in all points tempted like as we are, yet without sin." The great temptations that Jesus was victorious over. After his forty day fast, his hunger returned with fierceness unquenchable. It has been told that after the third or fourth day of fasting, hunger no longer haunts your every waking hour. This continues until your body has used up all the excess fat. Once this has taken place, the body begins to use the muscle tissue. At this point hunger unquenchable takes control. I'm told, you can eat until your full, then eat more and more yet your hunger is not slaked. It was at this point of starvation that the Devil came to Jesus, tempting, jeering, saying, "If thou be the Son of God, command that these stones be made bread." Jesus sat him straight, "Man shall not live by bread alone but by every word that proceededth out of the mouth of God. " The Devil used every device he had on Jesus. The lust of the eye, the lust of the flesh, and the pride of life. "If thou be the Son of God, cast thy self down: for it is written, he shall give his angels charge concerning thee:" Jesus again rebuked him with: "It is written again, Thou shalt not tempt the LORD thy God." I'm telling you, any devil can take just one scripture and cause you to jump off of a high tower if you don't follow the rules of Bible study. Then the devil showed Jesus all the kingdoms of the world, and the glory of them, And saith unto him, "All these things will I give thee, if thou wilt fall down and worship me." "Get thee hence, Satan: for it is written, Thou shalt worship the Lord thy God, and him only shalt thou serve."

Why temptation? Hebrews 4:15 For we have not an high priest which cannot be touched with the feeling of our infirmities, but was in all points tempted like as we are, yet without sin. and Hebrews 2:16 For verily he took not on him the nature of angels, but he took on him the seed of Abraham. 1 Timothy 3:16 ....God was manifest in the flesh,

2 Corinthians 8:9 though he was rich, yet for your sakes he became poor, that ye through his poverty might be rich. Jesus was, God gift wrapped in the flesh. How much flesh was he? He had to grow in wisdom and stature. Luke 2:52 And Jesus increased in wisdom and stature, and in favor with God and man. Jesus grew up just like any other human being. Did you ever wonder if he would have liked to find him some nice Jewish girl, settle down and raise a family? Maybe buy a little piece of land. Is that blasphemy? He had the same desires as you and me. Did you ever think of him as a man? I mean, as a man. Jesus was a man of prayer. Mark 1:35 And in the morning, rising up a great while before day, he went out, and departed into a solitary place, and there prayed. Luke 6:12 And it came to pass in those days, that he went out into a mountain to pray, and continued all night in prayer to God. Often, he spent entire nights in prayer. I'm convinced that if we want a power walk with God, doing miracle as He did, then we'll have to walk in obedience as Jesus did. Jesus said, John 14:12 He that believeth on me, the works that I do shall he do also, and greater works than these shall he do, because I go unto my Father. And "If you have the faith as a grain of mustard seed, ye shall say unto this mountain, remove hence to yonder place, and it shall remove, and nothing shall be impossible unto you." The big difference between Jesus and us is, He was a man of faith. We are of little faith. Matthew 6:30 Wherefore , if God so clothe the grass of the field, which to day is, and to morrow is cast into the oven, shall he not much more clothe you, O ye of little faith? Jesus had to pray for strength to go to the cross. Not once but three times and not just a little while. see Matthew 26:37-44 He himself said he could do nothing on his own. John 5:30 I can of mine own self do nothing: as I hear, I judge: and my judgment is just, because I seek not mine own will, but the will of the Father which hath sent me. John 12:49 For I have not spoken of myself, but the Father which sent me, he gave me a commandment, what I should say, and what I should speak. verse 50: And I know that his commandment is life everlasting: whatsoever I speak therefore, even as the Father said unto me, so I speak. Jesus was under orders, doing the job as a servant. Philippians 2:7-8 But made himself of no reputation, and took upon him the form of a servant, and was made in the likeness of men: {8} And being found in fashion as a man, he humbled himself, and became obedient unto death, even the death of the cross. He depended on God for everything. Jesus had nothing more going for him than you or I have, except, he had faith and relied upon God for everything. If it were any other way

how could you or I follow him? He is our example. Doesn't Christian mean Christ like? 1 Peter 2:21 For even hereunto were ye called: because Christ also suffered for us, leaving us an example, that ye should follow his steps: Is it possible to follow someone who has an advantage over you? He was God living by faith just as you and I are expected to live. He could do nothing on his own. John 5:19 Then answered Jesus and said unto them, Verily , verily, I say unto you, The Son can do nothing of himself, but what he seeth the Father do: for what things soever he doeth, these also doeth the Son likewise.

Jesus' favorite title for himself was the Son of Man. He could have called himself the Son of God, but he was aware of his role as a man. Until his baptism and the confirming voice of God, I don't think he was fully, I say fully, aware of his total identity. When he was twelve years old he said in Luke 2:49 I must be about my Father's business? But he couldn't have totally known, at this time.

Jesus came as a man. Did his job as a man. Died as a man. Though completely faithful in everything he did, He had to leave this world in disgrace. Galatians 3:13 Christ hath redeemed us from the curse of the law, being made a curse for us: for it is written, Cursed is every one that hangeth on a tree: And Deuteronomy 21:22-23 And if a man have committed a sin worthy of death, and he be to be put to death, and thou hang him on a tree: {23} His body shall not remain all night upon the tree, but thou shalt in any wise bury him that day, (for he that is hanged is accursed of God,) that thy land be not defiled, which the LORD thy God giveth thee for an inheritance. But God doesn't intend for it to always be that way. Jesus earned a super reward as a man. He will return as the KING OF KINGS, AND LORD OF LORDS and inherit the whole world as His eternal kingdom. Revelation 11:15 And the seventh angel sounded, and there were great voices in heaven, saying, The kingdoms of this world are become the kingdoms of our Lord, and of his Christ, and he shall reign for ever and ever. But he is coming back as a man! Acts 1:11 Which also said, Ye men of Galilee, why stand ye gazing up into heaven? this same Jesus, which is taken up from you into heaven, shall so come in like manner as ye have seen him go into heaven. and John 14:2-3 In my Father's house are many mansions: if it were not so, I would have told you. I go to prepare a place for you. {3} And if I go and prepare a place for you, I will come again, and receive you unto myself, that where I am, there ye may be also. You and I are going to be, no we are, Joint heirs with Christ Romans 8:14-17 For as many as are led by the Spirit of God, they are the sons of God. {15} For ye have not received the spirit of bondage again to fear, but ye have received the Spirit of adoption, whereby we cry, Abba, Father. {16} The Spirit itself beareth witness with our spirit, that we are the children of God: {17} And if children, then heirs, heirs of God, and joint-heirs with Christ, if so be that we suffer with him, that we may be also glorified together. How can Jesus be an heir unless he returns in the role as the son? Jesus' 1000 year reign on earth, Revelation 20:6 Blessed and holy is he that hath part in the first resurrection: on such the second death hath no power, but they shall be priests of God and of Christ, and shall reign with him a thousand years. This is Jesus' reward for a faithful sonship. But what happens to the sonship or the son role after the earthly reign ends? John 1:1 says "In the beginning was the Word" remember the word "beginning" is a finite term and we are dealing with eternity.

Eternal things have neither beginnings or endings. This is hard to grasp because we are finite in thought and have never known the infinite. Even the term "I am the Alpha and Omega" are finite. Jesus was present in the beginning, but only as God. Now consider 1 Corinthians 15:24 Then cometh the end, when he shall have delivered up the kingdom to God, even the Father, when he shall have put down all rule and all authority and power. (What rule, authority, and power?) Revelation 20:7-9 And when the thousand years are expired, Satan shall be loosed out of his prison, And shall go out to deceive the nations which are in the four quarters of the earth, Gog and Magog, to gather them together to battle: the number of whom is as the sand of the sea. And they went up on the breadth of the earth, and compassed the camp of the saints about, and the beloved city: and fire came down from God out of heaven, and devoured them. 1 Corinthians 15:24-28 Then cometh the end, when he shall have delivered up the kingdom to God, even the Father, when he shall have put down all rule and all authority and power. For he must reign, till he hath put all enemies under his feet. The last enemy that shall be destroyed is death. For he hath put all things under his Feet. But when he saith all things are put under him, it is manifest that he is excepted, which did put all things under him. {28} And when all things shall be subdued unto him, then shall the Son also himself (here's where the sonship is put down) be subject unto him that put all things under him, that God may be all in all. After the eternal family had been screened out of earth's billions, what would be the point if the son role? The Holy Ghost role, the Father role? Jesus said: Search the scriptures for in them ye think ye have eternal life: and they are they that testify of me."

ANCILLARY   10/07/1991   2799

PSM 45:1 MY HEART IS INDITING A GOOD MATTER:
I SPEAK THE THINGS WHICH I HAVE MADE TOUCHING THE KING:
MY TONGUE IS THE PEN OF A READY WRITER.

I ran across this word in a book describing a particular piece of equipment. Ancillary, auxiliary.

Real handy to have around. Like a pocket on a shirt.

Like a portable generator for when the power goes out.

No lights ? just turn the generator on.

Ancillary: it's not really necessary, just handy to have. A help, when you need it.

To some, that's their description of God. Ancillary. Like a pocket on a shirt. Real handy, when you need Him. Just put God on a shelf like some extra tool that you might need sometime, somewhere.

God isn't like that. He's not a spare tire. He'll be all or nothing. There's no second string God.

Men throughout ages have found strength and comfort in God. But they had made him their God. Not their tool. Men have tried to use God. And God will let you use Him to the saving of your own soul. To God, the all-important thing is, your soul. God will totally bankrupt the whole heaven, if that's what it takes to save your soul. How do I know that? "Though he was rich, yet for your sakes he became poor, that ye through his poverty might be rich." 2 Cor 8:9 Who? God. He bankrupted heaven by coming, gift wrapped in the flesh as Jesus Christ, that your salvation might be secured. Jesus Christ gave what you or I cannot give, a sinless life. Jesus Christ was the only one ever that could give up his life. Our lives are already forfeited by the first sin you or I ever committed. I must die for my unrepented sins. Romans 6:23 "For the wages of sin is death," You mean I have to pay for the sins I've committed? Do you have to pay for the food you eat? The entertainment you enjoy? The work you have someone else do? Do you have to pay to get into an amusement park and ride the rides? Well friend, such is the law of cause and affect. The ball that goes in the air must come down. Who says so? Why the laws of physics say so. Why then must I pay for my sins? The law of God says so. Where? In the book of Gen 2:17 "....But of the tree of the knowledge of good and evil, thou shalt not eat of it: for in the day that thou eatest thereof thou shalt surely die." But that was God speaking to Adam, you say. And the voice of God comes ringing across the hills of old Judea, "Adam where art thou." The question applies to your life today. Do you know where you are? Don't you realize that the same sin Adam committed is still in the world today? What sin? the sin of putting self-first and God second, and some put God second to none. So what is that you ask. That my friend is Idolatry. That's the sin of self-worship. Me, my, Mine. Don't you know that I is the center of sin. It's also the center of Pride. Pride goeth before a fall.

Have you ever heard anyone say, "It's hard to be humble when you're so good." I'm afraid they've already lost the battle. It's over. Pride has already got them hooked.

Pride has caused the downfall of so many interpersonal relationships that only God knows the total number.

Denny and Judy were such a lovely couple. They went to high school together for three years. The Vietnam war took Denny away for several years. But love endured the separation, and on his return, marriage soon followed. Later, Judy found out that Denny was unfaithful during his absence and she wouldn't forgive Denny's past indiscretions. Soon a full battle raged in their marriage. Denny was a loving husband totally dedicated to making Judy happy, while Judy was dedicated to making Denny grovel. Forgiveness couldn't be found in her heart. Why? Because of Pride. Jesus said that Moses gave the law of divorcement because of the hardness of the people's hearts. God didn't give it, Moses did. What will people think of me if I forgive this worm. Divorce soon followed. Both were heart broken. Both still loved each other yet because of pride, because of pride, they stayed divorced. I remember Denny saying, I still love her. I remember his actions actually showing his love for Judy. I remember Judy and her actions showing a continuing love for Denny, yet because of foolish pride, because of foolish pride, because of foolish pride, they remained divorced.

But of the tree of the knowledge of good and evil, thou shalt not eat because in the day that thou eatest thereof thou shalt surly die. Ezek 18:4"....The soul that sinneth, it shall die." Romans 6:23 "For the wages of sin is death," What is sin? Please define sin for me. Make a list that I might not sin against God. Perhaps, just perhaps I haven't sinned. Give me this list please. Well, the list is short, The Book gives me the list. Read the list in 1 John 5:17 "All unrighteousness is sin." Well you say, I'm righteous, I've done no harm to any man. Once you've accomplished this then read Isaiah 64:6 "But we are all as an unclean thing, and all our righteousness are as filthy rags," or Matthew

5:20 "Except your righteousness exceed the righteousness of the scribes and Pharisees, ye shall in no case enter into the kingdom of heaven." Jesus said in Rev 3:17-18 "Because thou sayest, I am rich, and increased with goods, and have need of nothing, and knowest not that thou art wretched, and miserable, and poor, and blind and naked: I counsel thee to buy of me gold tried in the fire, that thou mayest be rich, and white raiment, that thou mayest be clothed, and that the shame of thy nakedness do not appear, and anoint thine eyes with eye salve, that thou mayest see." what then is this white raiment? Rev 19:8 "And to her was granted that she should be arrayed in fine linen, clean and white: for the fine linen is the righteousness of saints." Our righteousness is spotted with the will of the flesh. Torn and tattered, spotted with the sins we have worked through the years. This is not proper clothing to wear in the presence of the King of Glory. Mom always taught her children to dress properly for the occasion. You can't wear the jeans with the knees out to go to grandma and grandpa's house. Why then, do you think you can stand in the presence of God with your garments, your righteousness, soiled with the works of yourself? How then can I have this righteousness that you are speaking of? Romans 8:10 "And if Christ be in you, the body is dead because of sin, but the Spirit is life because of righteousness." How then can Christ be in Me? John 14:17 "Even the spirit of truth, whom the world cannot receive, because it seeth him not, neither knoweth him: but you know him, for he dwelleth with you, and shall be in you." Who? The spirit of truth. Who is the spirit of truth? John14:6 "Jesus said I am the way the truth and the life: no man cometh unto the Father, but by me." Jesus said "I will not leave you as orphans: I will come to you. How can I receive this Spirit of Truth this Comforter Jesus was speaking of? Going to the 2nd chapter of the Book of Acts and read how the disciples of Jesus received this Comforter. Acts 2:38 "Then Peter said unto them, repent, and be baptized every one of you in the name of Jesus Christ for the remission if sins, and ye shall receive the gift of the Holy Ghost. For the promise is unto you, and to your children, and to all that are afar off, even as many as the Lord our God shall call". Then you'll be clothed in garments of righteousness. Then you'll have the righteousness of God covering you and you'll be fit for the presence of the King.

The fact is that God wants to be all in all in your life. Aren't you sick of just things? Have you found what you're looking for in life? I never could find what I was seeking after, until I met Jesus while in prayer one night. Since then I've looked no farther for the thing that satisfies. Jesus has satisfied the longing in my soul. The thrill of a roller coaster is but fleeting seconds of fun. Racing a car down a drag strip is but seconds of substitute fulfillment. Being with friends only last as long as they are near you, even that can turn sour. But life with Jesus is never ending joy. Fulfillment as it was meant to be. God fellowshipping with you in the cool of the day. Are you down in the mouth? Talk to Jesus. Everything going wrong around you? Talk to Jesus. Will he make it all go away? No, but you'll sure look at the troubles different. From a different perspective. He'll put a different set a values in your mind. I'm serious. He will. He'll put compassion in your heart like you've never known before. I'm talking about a complete life change. The cliché of the times is "Born Again". If you really get it you'll know born again. This relationship that you'll have with God won't be a part time thing that you get off the shelf when ever you need help, because the love that will be in you will long for continual fellowship with divinity. Do you know what it is like not to worry about tomorrow? Jesus said Luke 18:17 "Verily I say unto you, Whosoever shall not receive the kingdom of God as a little child shall in no wise enter therein." or except you become as a little child in faith, you'll never enter the kingdom of God. Have you ever seen a little child worry about tomorrow? These are few and far between. Don't be fearful of tomorrow. Read Luke 12:22-32 verse 32 says "Fear not little flock, for it is your Father's good pleasure to give you the Kingdom." Don't worry about it. Depend upon God. Don't be fearful of tomorrow and what it shall bring. Trust in God. Make Jesus the still point of your life. Just as the earth rotates around the poles, the still points, Jesus wants your life to revolve around him. Why? What's the advantage of this? Well, human nature is such that when we have ourselves as a pivot point the center is constantly changing. Have you ever seen a lopsided ball being thrown? Or those plastic jumping beans we enjoyed as children. Because the center of gravity continually changed the bean appeared to jump and the ball appeared to gyrated, vibrated, and skew through the air. When we are the center of our lives, our center of gravity continually changes from day to day, from hour to hour, from minute to minute, from crisis to crisis, causing our lives to vibrate and skew as we try to work out our troubles, cares, and anxieties. How to stop such a life. Make Jesus the still point and cause your life to rotate around him. No second string commitment, for He isn't a second string God working with second-string people. The hunger within you requires a total, complete, commitment to God. 1 John 5:21 "Little children, keep yourselves from idols." Don't fall pray to self-worship. Don't put any thing before God, if you do, it becomes your god, and if that, then an idol.

Christianity is not some accomplishment that you can add to your resume of life. It is your life. Totally, completely, all in compassing, all fulfilling, everything. When God comes into your life He becomes your life. He's my armor when the battles of life rage. Romans 13:12 "The night is far spent, the day is at hand: let us therefore cast off the works of darkness, and let is put on the armor of light." Ephesians 6:11 "Put on the whole armor of God, that ye might be able to withstand in the evil day, and having done all, to stand. Stand therefore, having your loins girt about with truth, and having on the breast plate of righteousness, and your feet shod with the preparation of the gospel of peace, Above all, taking the shield of faith, wherewith ye may be able to quench all the fiery darts of the wicked. And the helmet of salvation, and the sword of the spirit, which is the word of God:" He's my rock in a weary land: Isa 32:1-2 "Behold a king shall reign in righteousness, and princes shall rule in judgment. And a man (who? Jesus) shall be as an hiding place from the wind," (the winds of the plains were said to drive people crazy, always blowing and never stopping, continually blowing. Or the winds that destroyed a lot of the east coast this summer. These people I'm sure, desired a hiding place from the wind.) and a covert (a hiding place) from the tempest, as rivers of water in a dry place, (there is no better analogy for Christ), as the shadow of a great rock in a weary land (distressed, desert like, barren, hot, weary).

Oh for a shadow in the desert. Oh for a river in a dry land. Oh for a shelter from the winds and storms of life. There's no stronger foundation to build on than the rock.

Christianity is a mandate, the way of life. Jesus Christ set the pace 2000 years ago. With terse poignant statements to those around him he directed the footsteps of those that should follow him. Simple but deep were his requests of you and me. Matthew 11:28 "Come unto me, all ye that are heavy laden, and I will give you rest. Take my yoke upon you, and learn of me, for I am meek and lowly in heart: and ye shall find rest unto your souls. For my yoke is easy, and my burden is light." and " If any man will come after me, let him deny himself, and take up his cross and follow me" then again " For what shall is a man profited, if he shall gain the whole world, and lose his own soul? Or what shall a man give in exchange for his soul?" Or "No man can serve two masters: for he will hate the one, and love the other, or else he will hold to one, and despise the other. Ye cannot serve God and mammon." on and on the rules of life go. Jesus came to seek and save a lost and dying world. Adam where are you? Like a child lost in a department store. You're just not tall enough to see over the displays. Perhaps mom is just on the other side. Even this is not a good analogy for most people continue to wander through life like an unconcerned child playing in the toy department of life. Busy with our own concerns and interest until life brings us up short with the stop signs along the way. Much like the security guard who has spotted the parent-less child happily playing in the middle of a pile of new toys. "Adam, where art thou?" comes ringing across the isles of toys. God is not neglectful of his children. He knows just where we are. His big project is to make us realize where we are. His question to us is, "Do you know where you are?" With tears coursing down our cheeks, checked only by the sobs of brokenness, "Jesus, Help me I'm lost." Oh I would that you would know Him as a caring parent. As a father to confide in. As a comforter to dry your tears. As a rock of stability in this world of shifting sands. Lost and dying, battered and bleeding, you lie upon the road of life. Casualties of a society built upon the gods of self. Kneeling at the gods of self-fulfillment, your soul is bruised and bleeding, unfulfilled by the great and small successes you enjoy from life. Why? Why are you bruised and bleeding? Simply because you have not made Jesus a total commitment of your life. "Take my yoke upon you." cries Jesus from the hills of old Judah. Instead, you labor in the yoke of self-will. "I will build myself a kingdom. I will, I will ,I will." Yet on Calvary stands an old rugged cross that point to a savior who cried in a Garden long ago, " Not my will but thine be done."

WHEN ORDINARY BECOMES EXTRAORDINARY   11/04/1990

PSM 45:1 MY HEART IS INDITING A GOOD MATTER:
I SPEAK THE THINGS WHICH I HAVE MADE TOUCHING THE KING:
MY TONGUE IS THE PEN OF A READY WRITER.

In the natural world there are substitutes for almost everything. There's artificial sweetener, decaf coffee, salt substitute, synthetic insulin, plastic, textured soy protein, fake bacon, sausage, eggs, margarine, even a substitute margarine, on and on it goes. Yet experience has shown that a substitute doesn't do as good of a job as the real. I still like real butter on my baked potato. I still like sugar in my coffee. I like real coffee with caffeine. Wood has a warmth that plastic can't imitate. And nothing wears like wool. Types and anti-types. The real world and the fake world. Types and shadows.

Tekel, a native preacher in Ethiopia, went to a small village where a great tree stood in the middle. Tekel was well known to the villagers, those who worshiped this great tree. Human sacrifices were even offered in the name of this tree, this tree god that they worshipped. Of course no one was allowed to touch this sacred tree. The punishment was death, with no recourse. As Tekel approached this village the worshipers gathered around this great tree as to protect it from this preacher.

The thought of this people was to kill this man. They swarmed around Tekel, ready to kill, yet, none could harm him. Tekel asked them which was greater the tree or the ground it grew in? A great hush came over these people. One spoke, perhaps the leader of the village, "Why we suppose the ground would be greater for it is bigger than the tree." "Which then is greater," Tekel asked again, "the ground or the sky that is overhead?" "Why we suppose the sky for it covers the ground." "Well," said Tekel, "I worship the God that made the ground the tree and the sky." Reason overtook their desire to kill Tekel and the worshiping of the great tree. "Let us worship the God of the preacher Tekel." Many were filled with the Holy Ghost that day because they could see the foolishness of worshiping a substitute god. Don't get caught up in worshiping a tree, a substitute god, the creation rather that the creator. Worship the LORD God Almighty.

Just look up in the heavens, they declare the glory of God. Look at the earth, it declares His handiwork. Look at your hands, they declare His glory. No other creature is made like you. No other creature can touch his fingers with his thumb. No other creature can play the piano. Appreciate beauty. Be a virtuoso on a musical instrument. Build a skyscraper. Make a road or paint a picture. You want to see the Glory of God? Look in a mirror. Tell me how you see? How is color perceived? Tell me how you can shift your focus from one object to another as quickly as you do? Make me a camera that will do that. How is it that you can hear? Do you know? How was that assembled? What happens to a seed that you put in the ground? Why does it grow? What is gravity? Why can I breath air but not see it? The questions are unending. And the answer is God. God works, God works, God works.

While working in the central region of South Dakota a number of years ago, we passed a small country church on a back road. You know the kind, White clapboard, with a bell tower and steeple, stained glass windows and a cemetery around back. Curiosity behooves us to deviate from our pre-planed path and investigate this facility. This day was a Tuesday afternoon, so no one was around to guide us through this place of worship. Doors are kept unlocked in this land of integrity, so entrance was not denied us, nor did we feel that to enter into this sanctuary would be trespass. The light oak pews had been padded and upholstered with a blue broad cloth material. Dark Blue cut pile carpet covered the floor and platform. On the front pew sat a Spanish guitar and several guitar songbooks. The light oak pulpit had a royal blue covering down the front. This covering was bordered with gold threads and fringed with the same. There was something Holy about the way the sun shown through the stained glass windows casting it's multicolored light pictures on the pews and the pulpit. Beauty radiated from this holy place. We ventured to the basement that had been made into a fellowship area. Folding tables were here and there about the basement in orderly arrangements. On one wall was a glass display case with pictures of the congregations of this assembly down through the years. Ten maybe fifteen different pictures over the past sixty or so years. Notable was the difference in these congregations. In the beginning, dressed in the best they had, clean bib overalls, pretty smock dresses, and bonnets, each man, woman, and child of reading age, had a Bible under their arm or in their hand. Each had a Holy smile on their faces. These were a Holy people who loved their God. You could see it. You could tell it. There was no doubt about it. In the next picture, perhaps 5 or 6 years latter, a few evidently had forgotten their Bibles. Some of the smiles were missing. Perhaps it was just a bad day to take a picture. Maybe it was raining out. Who knows. The next picture reveals that, less and less had their Bibles yet more and more wore Sunday finery. Suits, and Fancy dresses, new shoes, all shined. It looked a lot like an Easter service or something similar to that. Smiles were fewer and fewer and the only one that sported a Bible was the preacher. The next picture had everyone in finery, no Bibles and the preacher in a robe. The robe must have cost him a fortune, even to his Bible, for it sure wasn't present. The next picture had everyone in robes, the preacher now had a collar and sash and no Bible. Some were smiling, some not but the absence of holiness was evident. Toward the end of this montage, only the preacher had a robe on, the rest had shorts, levis, and other forms of casual dress. The total absence of Bibles in these last pictures was conspicuous. The last picture consisted of only older people as the young had sought for something real, not just church attendance. From all appearances, the only thing they had was a nice building. But you see, the cemetery had moved indoors. Didn't they realize that their robes and trappings couldn't take the place of God's anointing? Didn't they realize they had nothing but an organization? Didn't they realize that the ordinary, that Holy thing the true church had in the beginning, the true anointing of God, had become extraordinary, it didn't even exist in their congregation anymore. Ichabod, the glory had departed from this church.

There was a time when the ark of the covenant, the place where the Glory of God dwelt between two covering cherubim. This symbol, that God was among His people, had been taken by the enemy of Israel, the Philistines. This happened because the sins of the sons of Eli the high priest, were not purged. This happened because Eli had allowed his sons to become vile and in their vileness, to cause the people of God to sin also. You can't handle the Holy things of God with defiled hands.

Eli when he heard that the Philistines had killed his sons, and the Ark of the Covenant was taken from Israel, fell over backwards and broke his neck and died. One of Eli's daughters in law was great with child, near the time of delivery, but when she heard that the ark of the covenant was taken, and that her father in law and her husband were dead, fell into travail and gave birth. As she was dying, she was told not to fear not for she had given birth to a son. And in passing away, named the child Ichabod saying, The glory is departed from Israel: because the ark of God was taken, and because of her father in law and her husband. 1 Sam 4:1-22

Because the glory had departed from this church, from this congregation, it's name was Ichabod. Without the glory, without the anointing of God, it was just a meetinghouse. Just another fraternal organization. Without God, Ichabod.

What was ordinary had become extraordinary. For a miracle to occur in this church would have been a miracle it's self. There was no life in this building. It looked Holy. It seemed Holy yet the glory had departed from it. Ichabod. God hadn't moved in this place since 1944. How do you know that? The pictures don't lie. The proof is there, there on the wall, for all to see. Can't you see it? There, right there. Under the glass. On the back wall. There's the evidence. There's the evidence. This church wasn't born dead. Time had wore on the people and complacency had taken the place of fervor. Trappings took the place of Godly Holiness, and works took the place of faith and death came upon a church. It didn't have to. They let it happen.

Throughout the Bible there are types and shadows. The Old Testament revealed a Passover lamb whose blood was put upon the doorposts of the house to ward off the death angel that wandered throughout Egypt. The death angel was a curse the pharaoh had brought upon himself by not letting the people of God go free. You know the story, The Ten Commandments with Charleston Heston as Moses. In the New Testament though, Jesus Christ is spoken of as our Passover lamb. One without spot. One without sin. After the Exodus from Egypt, in the wilderness, there was a tent that God's presence dwelt in. The tabernacle of God. Now though, the tabernacle of God is your body, the dwelling place of the Holy Ghost. At least it is supposed to be if you'll let the Holy Ghost in your kingdom. 1 Corinthians 6:19 "What? Know ye not that your body is the temple of the Holy Ghost which is in you, which ye have of God, and ye are not your own?" Of course only one can sit on the throne of your life. God or you. The good man searched the scriptures to see why it was that some had power with God while others did not, for God is no respecter of persons. Romans 2:11. He could only come up with one scripture that would indicate why. James 2:19 " thou believest that there is one God, thou doest well: ....." To say you believe and to believe is two different matters. How many gods do you worship? To be effective in the kingdom of God, God must sit on the throne of your life. All the kingdoms of our lives must be under His dominion. Not one corner left yet undone. This then, is the answer to a power walk with God. Is it me or thee, LORD?

There are then tree worshipers, the river worshipers, the worshipers of devils, worshipers of those long since dead who's bones are with us today, worshipers of money, cars, people, rock groups. People who live for praise, the thrill of the moment, the day, and the hour. Worshipers of self, another, or other things. There are those who say they worship no gods, atheists, agnostics, yet they themselves are on the throne. You will worship some god. There's no Switzerland in this thing called life. There's no neutral ground. The teachers of today teach human secularism. "Man is his own god." "Man is improving as time goes on." "You can do all things." "There is the power within you to be what you want to be." Yet to maintain a breath of life within themselves they are powerless. You have strength within yourself? Don't die then. That's the whole thing. Those who originated this doctrine of self are long since dead. Why couldn't they hold back the march of the death angel? Because, God said, "For it is appointed unto men once to die,..."Hebrews 9:27 and Psalms 90:10 "The days of our years are threescore and ten,...." Psalms 102:11 "My days are like a shadow that declineth, and I am withered like grass." Psalms 103:15 "As for man, his days are as grass: as a flower of the field, so he flourisheth. For the wind passeth over it, and it is gone, and the place thereof shall know it no more." James 4:14 "For what is your life? It is even a vapour, that appeareth for a little time, and then vanisheth away." Job 7:6 "My days are swifter than a weavers shuttle,.." Isaiah 38:12 "My dwelling is removed, and is carried away from me as a shepherd's tent, I have rolled up, like a weaver, my life, he will cut me off from the loom: From day even to night wilt thou make and end of me."

The pleasures of sin are just an anti-type the devil has place for the fulfillment of the desires of the flesh. Just a sugar substitute for the in filling of the Holy Ghost. Just a margarine to smooth the way of life. Just to get you past the desire to live for God. A substitute for the anointing oil of the Holy Ghost. Pure corn oil. Just so much corn the devil is handing you. He's just blowing smoke. And the smoke he's blowing is the rising smoke of your torment.

Life in Christ is Joy unspeakable and full of glory. The devil knows it and wants to keep you from it. He'll give you any pacifier it takes to quiet the screaming hunger of your soul. He did it to that little church in South Dakota, He's done it to multitudes throughout the ages. Read with me in the book of Revelations how God spoke to those who had let other things come into their lives.

Seven churches throughout Asia. Churches which had been established by the apostles on their missionary journeys to the lost and dying world. As these scripture are read, think of the types and shadows spoken of earlier in this message. The seven churches are stages that some churches go through, They can be periods that a Christian goes through in his life. These may have been written for your strengthening for, "All scripture is given by inspiration of God, and is profitable for doctrine, for reproof, for correction, for instruction in righteousness: That the man of God may be perfect, thoroughly furnished unto all good works." 2 Timothy 3:16

The book of Revelation of John the Divine, written by John the apostle while on a rocky and desolate isle in the Aegean sea, called the Isle of Patmos. Banished to this isle for his witness for the Word of God and his testimony of Jesus Christ. Notable is the fact that this banishment hurt his devotion to God not one wit. Revelation 1:10 "I was in the spirit on the Lord's day, and I heard behind me a great voice, as of a trumpet," Perhaps if we were to get in the Spirit on the Lord's day, God would speak to us.

Revelation 2:1 "Unto the angel of the church of Ephesus write, these things saith he that holdeth the seven stars in his right hand, who walketh in the midst of the seven golden candlesticks, I know thy works, and thy labour, and thy patience, and how thou canst not bear them which are evil: and thou hast tried them which say they are apostles, and are not, and hast found them liars: And hast borne, and hast patience, and for my name's sake hast laboured, and hast not fainted. Nevertheless I have somewhat against thee, because thou hast left thy first love. "

This is where the Ichabod church was in the second picture under glass. They were strong in good works, in labors, and in patience and all for the name of the Lord. But He had somewhat against them for they had let other things creep in displacing their total love of God.

Rev 2:5-6 "Remember therefore from whence thou art fallen, and repent, and do the first works, or else I will come and remove thy candlestick out of his place, except thou repent. But this thou hast, that thou hates the deeds of the Nicolaitans, which I also hate.

These were a part of this church, not some outside force, which was thought to try to establish a priestly order trying to model the New Testament church after the Old Testament order of priest, Levites, and common people. "Niko" to conquer, to overthrow, and "Laos" the people or laity. The object was to establish a Holy Order of Men and place them over the laity, which was foreign to the New Testament church and call them not Pastors but Clergy, Bishops, Archbishops, Cardinals, Popes. Apostolic succession, the separation of the Clergy from the laity. The church of Ephesus hated it, God hates it, and the true church has no recourse but to hate it. How can the shepherd know what is wrong with the sheep unless he is close to them. The Basque people make the best shepherds because they stay with the sheep.

John 10:11 "I am the good shepherd: the good shepherd giveth his life for the sheep. But he that is an hireling, and not the shepherd, who's own the sheep are not, seeth the wolf coming, and leaveth the sheep, and fleeth: and the wolf catcheth them, and scattereth the sheep. The hireling fleeth, because he is an hireling, and careth not for the sheep."

Revelation 2:7 " But he that hath an ear, let him hear what the Spirit saith unto the churches, To him that overcometh will I give to eat of the tree of life, which is in the midst if the paradise of God."

"And unto the angel of the church of Smyrna write, These things saith the first and the last, which was dead, and is alive, I know thy works, and thy tribulation, and poverty, (but thou art rich) and I know the blasphemy of them which say they are Jews, and are not, but are of the synagogue of Satan. Fear none of those things which thou shalt suffer: behold, the devil shall cast some of you in prison, that ye may be tried, and ye shall have tribulation ten days: be thou faithful unto death. and I will give thee a crown of life."

Perhaps this is where you are in your life and walk with God. Persecuted by those who say they are the same as you yet they wear not the same garments. The greatest persecution comes from within.

In each of the seven letters, the people are admonished to return to their first works.

Ephesus, "I have somewhat against thee, because thou hast left thy first love. ..Remember therefore from whence thou art fallen and repent, and do the first works,."..

Smyrna, "Persecuted from with in. Be thou faithful unto death, and I will give thee a crown of life."

Pergamos, "I have a few things against thee, because thou hast there them that hold the doctrine of Balaam, who taught Balac to cast a stumbling block before the children of Israel,....So hast thou also them that hold the doctrine of the Nicolaitans, which thing I hate. Repent, or else I will come unto thee quickly, and will fight against them with the sword of my mouth."

Thyatira, "I have a few things against thee, because thou sufferest that woman Jezebel, which calleth herself a prophetess, to teach, and to seduce my servants to commit fornication, and to eat things offered to idols. .... Behold, I will cast her into a bed, and them that commit adultery with her into great tribulation, except they repent of their deeds."

Sardis, "I know thy works, that thou hast a name that thou livest, and art dead. Be watchful, and strengthen the things which remain, that are ready to die: for I have not found thy works perfect before God. Remember therefore how thou hast received and heard, and hold fast, and repent. If therefore thou shalt not watch, I will come on thee as a thief, and thou shalt not know what hour I will come upon thee. Thou hast a few names even in Sardis which have not defiled their garments, and they shall walk with me in white: for they are worthy. He that overcometh, the same shall be clothed in white raiment, and I will not blot out his name out of the book of life,"

Philadelphia, "I know thy works: behold, I have set before thee an open door, and no man can shut it: for thou hast a little strength, and hast kept my word, and hast not denied my name. ... Behold I come quickly: hold fast which thou hast, that no man take thy crown."

Laodica, "I know thy works, that thou art neither cold nor hot: I would thou wert cold or hot. So then because thou art lukewarm, and neither cold nor hot, I will spew thee out of my mouth.

Behold, I stand at the door and knock: if any man hear my voice, and open the door, I will come in to him, and will sup with him, and he with me. To him that overcometh will I grant to sit with me in my throne, even as I also overcame, and am set down with my Father in his throne. He that hath an ear, let him hear what the Spirit saith unto the churches."

Laodica, rich increased with goods, you have need of nothing. That's where we're at today. I have all that I need. I'm warmly housed. My belly is full. I have friends to comfort me. Almost all my needs are met. What need have I for God? Is this where you are at today?

Do you have on the robes of self-righteousness? Look again at this letter to this tepid indifferent church called Laodica. Do you read any commendation in the words written here? I think not. God said," I'll spew you out of my mouth." "Because thou sayest I am rich, and increased with goods, and have need of nothing, and knowest not that thou art wretched, and miserable, and poor, and blind and naked." You think you are rich, and you well may be with the goods of this world, but the Spirit looks not at the outward man, but at the heart. You may have a great poverty of the soul. God was not talking to church organizations here. Hear what the spirit says to you. "Behold, I stand at the door and knock. If any man hear my voice, and open the door, I will come in to HIM, and sup with him and he with me." Jesus Christ is to much of a gentleman to break your door down, You must invite Him in. Behold He stands at the door of your heart and softly knocks. Open the door to him. There's nothing better in life than to sup with the LORD of Glory.

Repent of your sins. Ask God to forgive you of the things you have done wrong. Let the blood of Jesus Christ cover these sins. He died for you. For the sins that you have committed, the ones that would send you to the place of eternal torment, hell. Be baptized in the name of the one that died for you, Jesus Christ. And He will fill you with the Holy Ghost.

Why is it that a church in Africa can have God working mightily in the live of the people there? Why is it that miracles and wonders are a common occurrence in the churches of Asia? Why is it that you have to ring a bell to stop the worship of the Lord God Almighty in South America? Why is it that in Central America people will walk for miles just to hear the word of God preached? They need God. Do you?

Why is it that a TV evangelist can fall by the roadside? Why is it that another can do some ungodly immoral thing for the eyes of the whole world to see? Why is it that you can't get a person who only lives a few blocks away to come and worship God? Simple. They are rich, and increased with goods and have need of nothing. Yet you will sit in the darkness of your room and wonder at the futility of life. You are naked, and undone, retched and poor and you full well know it. What hinders your taking the first step? Say it. Go ahead and say it. Jesus, I need you. That's right. Go ahead. Jesus I need you. I'm naked and undone. I'm poor and retched. I need you. Fill my life with your glory. I'm yours.

It has been brought to my attention that in the last weeks 80 of the churches that were established in Ethiopia were burnt to the ground, the pastors destroyed and the missionaries run out of the country. But God still does a great work among those who will worship Him. Better than 150,000 souls have been filled with the Holy Ghost as a result of Bro Teklemariam's ministry. This kind of persecution is not foreign to this man of God. But God supplies his needs.

FOR PROFIT   11/11/1990

PSM 45:1 MY HEART IS INDITING A GOOD MATTER:
I SPEAK THE THINGS WHICH I HAVE MADE TOUCHING THE KING:
MY TONGUE IS THE PEN OF A READY WRITER.

For what shall it profit a man if he gain the whole world but lose his soul? Or what shall a man give in exchange for his soul?

This is no Daniel Webster story with souls all wrapped up in a carpetbag. No fast talking lawyer will ever talk the devil out of your soul. No man can bargain with the devil for his own soul. That's a devil's lie to make you think you have some say so about your own soul. Man feels he is the owner of his own soul.

What is the price of your soul? Is it the riches of the world or just the price of a little fling? Who owns your soul? Do you think that you have control over your own soul? If that were true then you would have control over your destiny and destination. Well you do have some control over your final destination, but not your destiny. Who owns your soul? You do know or you will know before long. Again there is no neutral ground in this battle for your soul. You belong to one or the other. No mans' land, no safe zone, no area of cease-fire, this is all out war for your soul. God set the pace six thousand years ago in the garden of Eden. Man had sold out his kingdom to the enemy. And the soul of man went along with this auction. The devil has taken the option on your soul, friend. But Jesus Christ has paid the price. Jesus Christ has offered you a blank check, signed, and waiting for your acceptance. Do you believe? Then receive what he has done for you.   Oh God that their eyes might be opened to the great battle that is going on for their soul. Oh that they might understand the final destination of the soul. Oh that they might come to a day of brightness, a day of illumination, a day of restoration, a day of purchase. The purchase of their souls by the Lord God Almighty. Oh that understanding would snap them out of this sleep unto death. Oh that somehow, this message might move them unto you. There is within man an emptiness. A void. A desire for something that is unknown to him. Throughout his life, various thing are tried and rejected. The pathway of your life is littered with discarded things that you have tried to fill this void with, I know for my own was filled with such things. Tried, failed, discarded. Some barely used. Some are dented, torn, worn, without paint, wheels missing, but discarded still the same. I tried that again and again yet it left me as empty as before. Try it again, yet the same results. Well try it again, No good. Still the same thing. Once more maybe this time it will do the trick. I don't know what your favorite thing was or is. I'm not even sure I know now what my favorite thing was. But I do know what will fill that emptiness of your soul. You do too, but you choose to ignore it. Why? Is this the price of your soul? Will you be sold for so little? Is it a bowl of porridge, Isaac? Just a little something to slake your hunger today? Time and time again God has spoke to your heart. In the field, on the tractor, in your car, in times of distress, words of comfort, words of solace when no other was around. See you believe yet you stop before you reach the goal. I feel like God is speaking to you right now. Isn't he? Go ahead and reach out, Touch the hem of his garment just like that woman that pressed through the crowd to reach Jesus. Hear him say "Who touched me?" Healing is in that touch. That touch of faith. No other could cure her, no other can cure the hunger of your soul. No other can cure you. The faith reach. You've got to make it to take it. To take hold of that check that will pay the price for your soul. Sold, on an auction block. To the highest bidder. But you've been to auctions when the weather isn't right, people just don't come and the prices are low. So it is with life. Only two bidders for your soul. Just two. But you have already sold out for nada, for nothing much, going once, going twice. But along comes another with a cross on his back. The buy back price is great but not too much for him for you are someone he loves. Who is this bidder? Why it's the man from Galilee. The son of the carpenter Joseph. Look, they've put a crown of thorns on his head. Oh, look what they have done to him. He's been beaten. Why couldn't they just kill him if that's what they wanted to do? Why, why did they beat him so? Softly he looks into your eyes. Hear him when he says, "what is the price of your soul?" For what shall it profit a man if he shall gain the whole world and lose his own soul, Or what shall a man give in exchange for his soul. You can hear it echo across the hills of old Judea. You can hear it echo in your own hearts. The question is eternal. Behold, now is the day of salvation. Today, if you will not harden your hearts, this can be the day of your fulfillment, the day you find what you've been looking for.

    My mind goes to that mercenary prophet called Balaam. Look in Numbers 22: and see what the price of this prophet was. The children of Israel had camped in the plains of Moab on this side of the Jordan river by Jericho. These people had a reputation of being fighters, rather of letting God go before them and destroying the enemies of the soul. Here in the plains of Moab was a king named Balak who opposed the children of Israel. Balak had seen what the this people had done to the Amorites and he was sore afraid. Moab sent messengers to Balaam who lived near Pethor. Paraphrasing Num 22:5-6 Behold there is a people who cover the face of the earth and they abide over near me. Come over here and curse them for they are to mighty for me and if I fight against them I might win and drive them out of this land: for I know that he whom you bless is blessed and whom you curse is cursed. Of course these messengers took the rewards of divination with them for Balaam. They went to him and spake the words of Balak to him. Balaam put them up for the night while he sought the face of God. He would ask God if it was his will to curse this people. Can you picture this? Here is a man asking God if God would like to curse the very same people he was protecting. These were Balaam's people also. That's why the name of mercenary fits him well. Highest bidder.

So in seeking God about this matter God said, "What men are these with you?" God knew who these men were, I can hear God saying with incredulity "Who are these men with thee?" Well, oh Balaam wasn't daunted by this question, he just kept right on going, "Balak the son of Zippor, king of Moab, hath sent unto me, saying, Behold there is a people come out of Egypt, which coverth the face of the earth: come now curse me them, peradventure I shall be able to overcome them, and drive them out." God said unto Balaam, Thou shalt not go with them, thou shalt not curse the people: for they are blessed." Well the next morning, before breakfast was even served, there Balaam was speaking to the princes of Moab saying, "Go home, for the LORD refused to give me leave to go with you." Doesn't this sound like a cop out? Sounds to me like this man has already sold out. He didn't say, "I'm not going to go and curse this people for they are blessed." No, what came out was, Daddy won't let me go but I still want to. I may be sitting down, but on the inside I'm still standing up. The princes went back to Balak with this report. Balak sent back princes more and more honorable than they. This is what they said to Balaam. "Let nothing, I pray thee, hinder thee from coming unto me: for I will promote thee unto a very great honor, and I will do whatsoever thou sayest unto me: come therefore, I pray thee, curse me this people." Nobleness must have rose up in the bosom of Balaam for the answer was, "If Balak would give me his house full of silver and gold, I cannot go beyond the word of the LORD my God, to do less or more." But, if you will stick around for the night I'll go see if God has maybe changed his mind. Balaam had just sold out. Well, Balaam went with the chief princes and tried to curse the children of Israel but only blessings would come out. "How goodly are thy tents, O

Jacob, and thy tabernacles, O Israel! As the valleys are they spread forth, as gardens by the river's side, as trees of light aloes which the LORD hath planted, and as the cedar trees beside the waters. He shall pour the water out of his buckets, and his seed shall be in many waters, and his king shall be higher than Agag, and his kingdom shall be exalted. God brought him forth out of Egypt, he hath as it were the strength of an unicorn: he shall eat up the nations his enemies, and shall break their bones, and pierce them through with his arrows. He crouched, he lay down as a great lion: who shall stir him up? Blessed is he that blessth thee, and cursed is he that curseth thee." Balaam tried on every side to curse them . But no. Poor Balaam, He had already sold out. The auctioneer's hammer had fallen. Going once, going twice, sold to an empty promise of esteem. Balaam couldn't curse the children of Israel but, he told the king of the Midieanites how the children could curse themselves. But Balaam's reward was short for Numbers 31:8 tells us, "And they slew the kings of Midian..... Balaam also the son of Beor they slew with the sword." And verse 15, And Moses said unto them, "Have ye saved all the women alive? Behold, these caused the Children of Israel, through the counsel of Balaam, to commit trespass against the LORD on the matter of Peor." Balaam, prophet of esteem, sold out for nothing. Just a mercenary, sold to the highest bidder. For what shall it profit a man if he gain the whole world but lose his soul? Or what shall a man give in exchange for his soul? What did Balaam say? "If Balak would give me his whole house full of silver and gold, I cannot go beyond the word of the LORD my God," Great words flowing from the man, but he did cause them to be cursed. There was no record of his material reward except a sword.

Another, by the name of Achan, sold out for a wedge of gold, a goodly garment, and two hundred shekels of silver. $538.00 worth of forbidden.

This cost the lives of 36 good men plus Achan's sheep, his donkeys, his oxen, his sons, his daughters, his wife, his tent and all that he had and his life. If only he had waited. After all the battles were over, in Joshua 22:8 they divided all the spoils of their enemies. Just till the end of the year. Greed got him nothing. Achan had an ache and that cause him to sell out. For what shall it profit a man if he gain the whole world but lose his soul?

Solomon, he who spoke 3000 proverbs and wrote 1005 songs, Solomon, the wisest man that ever lived, author of the book of Proverbs, Author of the book of Ecclesiastes, Solomon the author of the Song of Solomon, a book of the Bible portraying Christ and the Church. A spiritual allegory of Christ and his Church. Solomon who built the great beautiful tabernacle unto the LORD, said, "And whatsoever mine eyes desired I kept not from them, I withheld not from my heart any joy, for my heart rejoiced in all my labour: and this was my portion of all my labour." Solomon, whom the Queen of Sheba came to see if all the reports she had heard of his wisdom and kingdom were true. King Solomon exceeded all the kings of the earth for riches and for wisdom. But king Solomon loved many strange women, together with the daughter of Pharaoh, women of the Moabites, Ammonites, Edomites, Zidonians, and Hittites, of the nations concerning which the LORD said unto the children of Israel, "Ye shall not go in to them, neither shall they come in unto you: for surely they will turn your heart after their gods: " Solomon clave unto these in love. And he had seven hundred wives, princesses, and three hundred concubines: and his wives turned away his heart. His heart was not perfect with the LORD as was the heart of his father David. For Solomon went after Astoreth the goddess of the Zidonians, and after Milcom the abomination of the Ammonites. And Solomon did evil in the sight if the LORD, and went not fully after the LORD, as did his father David. He built an high place for Chemosh the abomination of Moab and for Molech, the abomination of Ammon. Solomon sold out for women. Lots of women and they caused him to do abomination in the sight of the LORD. God never put his sanctification on more than one wife. He only made one woman for Adam, not a harem of 700. But this wasn't what caused Solomon's downfall. No it was the wives that he took that caused him to sin. I wonder why he chose the forbidden. Could it be the reason is, that he withheld nothing from himself?

    Judas Iscariot, who sold the Lord for the price of a slave. It surly couldn't have been the money. There was no prestige in what he did. Why, Judas? Why? Judas went and hung himself. For what shall it profit a man if he gain the whole world but lose his soul? Or what shall a man give in exchange for his soul?

    Barnabas had some land. He sold it and brought the proceeds and laid it at the apostles' feet. The need was great and he simply felt compelled to help the work of the early church. Many others also had done this very same thing, and no one lacked for distribution was made as the need arose. Two others saw what was going on and sold a possession but kept back a portion for their selves. They then lied to the Holy Ghost about the price of the possession and both fell over dead. They wanted the prestige of being part of this thing but they wanted to keep a part of their own. The sin was in the lie not in the keeping. Sold out for just a portion. Sold out for just a little bit. Sold out. And Peter answered her, "Tell me whether ye sold the land for so much? And she said, Yea, for so much. Behold the feet of them which have buried your husband are at the door, and shall carry thee out." And she died. Yea, for so much.

I'm sure those four words have haunted her for centuries. Yea, for so much. What shall a man give in exchange for his soul?

I do not wish to make you think that all have sold out for the material riches of this world. I do not wish to make you think that all have sold out. No, the scripture are full of those who stood fast in the face of adversity. History is rich with those who have stood fast. Even in this our day there are those who would not sell out even to death. The thing to beware of is the little prices that are offered every day. Small bids made for your soul. Not the big ones. Not the great ones, But the small foxes that spoil the vine , and thus the fruit of your walk with God. The big things, the large prices, are not terribly hard to resist but it's the everyday hum of the wheels that will destroy you. The tedium, the times that your not watching, the times that you've failed to pray for a while. The times that you lose sight of the goal the high mark the calling of the LORD, that you sell out for a bowl of porridge. Something to slake the hunger of the day. Remember. For what shall it profit a man if he gain the whole world but lose his soul? Or what shall a man give in exchange for his soul? What is the price of your soul? Will you accept the price that Jesus Christ has Paid for you? It's easy to do. Repent of the sins that you've done. Be baptized in the name of Jesus Christ for the remission of these sins, and he will give you the Holy Ghost. This is the earnest of your inheritance. This is your seal of approval of the Holy Ghost. This is Bro Randy Johnson for WE PREACH JESUS MINISTRIES PO BOX 274 EUREKA ILLINOIS

WE INVITE YOU TO ATTEND THE UNITED PENTECOSTAL CHURCH AT 3510 W. MALONE ST IN PEORIA ILLINOIS OR THE UNITED PENTECOSTAL CHURCH IN PONTIAC ILLINOIS

THANK YOU FOR LISTENING

BELIEVE 11/24/1990

PSM 45:1 MY HEART IS INDITING A GOOD MATTER:
I SPEAK THE THINGS WHICH I HAVE MADE TOUCHING THE KING:
MY TONGUE IS THE PEN OF A READY WRITER.

Here are a few pointers on how to enjoy the Word of God.

First, don't start your reading at Genesis the first book of the Bible. Begin at the Book of Acts, the history of the church of the living God. In the book of Acts you'll read of the miracles and wonders that were performed as God worked through Holy Ghost filled people. You'll read how people lay in the streets so that the shadow of one of the apostles would fall upon them and they would be healed of their sickness. You'll read of a man being bitten by a poisonous viper and not dying. You'll read of the persecution that came on the believers.

Next, read the book of John. This book is one of the four Gospels or the good news. In the book of John you'll read John's view of Jesus Christ and his ministry. John looked at Jesus through the eyes of the beloved disciple. John looks at the special aspects of the character or work of Christ in each chapter. In one, Jesus is the son of God. In another he's the son of Man. In another He's the soul winner, another, he's great Physician, in another, the divine teacher and so on through each chapter. Read Matthew as he looks at Christ as the Kingly Messiah. Read Mark, and he portrays Christ as the Wonder Worker. Luke, shows him to be the friend of sinners and outcasts. Each Gospel is as different as four separate accounts of Jesus life on earth can be. For seen through the eyes of four different witnesses there is to be similarities and differences. As you read these and study them , you'll see that they interleave. I've taken the time to put the four together in a notebook, and seen an amazing picture of the Christ. Try it. Remember there are no contradictions in the Bible. If you have any questions, just drop us a line and we'll explain it to the best of our knowledge.

For a real treat then read the Book of Revelations, the last book in the Bible and the only book that gives a blessing to those that read and those that hear this book of prophecy. Next, are the epistles or the Letters to the Churches throughout Asia. Remember these are written to churches not people that have not yet received salvation.

Moving to the Old Testament, read the book of Proverbs for instruction in day to day living. Next, I would recommend reading the book of Psalms. Next, read The Song of Solomon, thinking of Jesus Christ and his church. Then go to Genesis, Exodus, then go to Joshua. Read from here to Psalms. Now go to the prophets beginning with Isaiah. Have fun.

What does it take to believe? Or what does believing require of me?
- John 7:38 He that believeth on me as the scripture hath said, out of his belly shall flow rivers of living water.
- Mark 16:16 He that believeth and is baptized shall be saved, he that believeth not shall be damned.
- John 3:15 That whosoever believeth in him should not perish, but have eternal life.
- John 20:31 But these things are written, that ye might believe that Jesus is the Christ, the son of God, and that believing ye might have life through his name.
- Ephesians 2:8 For by grace are ye saved through faith, and that not of yourselves: it is a gift of God.
- Romans 10:43 To him give all the prophets witness, that through his name whosoever believeth in him shall receive remission of sin.

There are 300 new testament scriptures on believing. Is believing important? There are 300 reasons why believing is important. Romans 10:14 says "How shall they call on him in whom they have not believed? and how shall they believe in him of whom they have not heard? Jesus said at the feast of Tabernacles "He that believeth on me as the scriptures hath said, out of his belly shall flow rivers of living water." Rivers, not streams. not river but Rivers... Wouldn't you like to feel that rivers of living water were flowing out of your inner most being? Totally unimaginable Bro Johnson. Yes but it is for you...

John 7:38 "He that believeth on me, as the scripture hath said, out of his belly shall flow rivers of living water. (But this spake he of the spirit, which they that believe on him should receive: for the Holy Ghost was not yet given, because that Jesus was not yet glorified.)" Jesus said that whosoever believeth upon him would receive the Mighty Baptism of the Holy Ghost. Mark 16:16 states "He that believeth and is baptized shall be saved, but he that believeth not shall be damned. and these signs shall follow them that believe, In my name shall they cast out devils, they shall speak with new tongues, They shall take up serpents, and if they drink any deadly thing, it shall not hurt them, they shall lay hands on the sick, and they shall recover." Poignant, terse, to the point, statements, They shall, They shall, They shall. No wonder some of the denominational world, for years, has been trying to take this set of verses out of the Bible. You don't like a verse of the Bible? Then cut it out. Jehobakid king of Judah did because he didn't like what the LORD had written through the pen of Jeremiah the prophet. In fact, he even burnt the missal. But the LORD simply had Jeremiah write another to replace it. But the new letter contained many other words even harder to bare. Read it in Jeremiah 36. Well, you can cut the scriptures to shreds but you'll still be judged from the Books. The Master has a master set in heaven. An archive copy if you please.. You can't ignore scripture. your salvation depends on ever word of God. Not just the ones you want to believe. Every word of God. 2Tim 3:16 "All scripture is given by the inspiration of God and is profitable for doctrine, for reproof, for correction, for instruction in righteousness: that the man of God may be perfect, thoroughly furnished unto good works." Ignorance of the law is of no excuse, willful ignorance of the Word of God won't hold water when you stand before Him. Do you think that you can be willingly ignorant and get off scott free? You can't use that argument when you stand before a judge in this world, do you think that you'll be able to use ignorance for an excuse, when you stand before the heavenly judge?

Romans 1:16 "For I am not ashamed of the gospel of Christ: for it is the power of God unto salvation to every one that believeth, to the Jew first, and also to the Greek. For therein is the righteousness of God revealed from faith to faith: as it is written, the just shall live by faith. For the wrath of God is revealed from heaven against all ungodliness and unrighteousness of men, who hold the truth in unrighteousness, Because that which may be known of God is manifest in them, for God hath shewed it unto them. For the invisible things of him from the creation of the world are clearly seen, being understood by the things that are made, even his eternal power and Godhead, so that they are without excuse: Because that, when they knew God, they glorified him not as God, neither were thankful, but became vain in their imaginations, and their foolish heart was darkened. professing themselves to be wise, they became fools".....Psalms14:1 "The fool hath said in his heart, there is no God." They have become unbelievers.

Acts chapter 10 "There was a certain man in Caesarea called Cornelius, a centurion of the band called the Italian band, A devout man, and one that feared God with all his house, which gave much alms to the people, and prayed to God alway." Was this man saved? Sure sounds like it to me. Here was a man that had his whole household respecting and loving God with all they had. He gave much money to the people. He prayed always. The scripture says, He was a devout man. I'm sure that he believed. His life seemed to show it. Yet. "He saw a vision evidently about the ninth hour of the day an angel coming in to him, and saying to him, Cornelius. And when he looked on him, he was afraid, and said, What is it Lord?" Two things are notable here, <u>One</u>, When your in the presence of the Lord or his angels, a holy fear, an awesomeness, is present. <u>Two</u>, The angels of the LORD bare with them the authority of the LORD God Almighty. No angel of the LORD will ever tell you something that is contrary to the written Word. Beware of the messenger that tells you otherwise. He's a messenger of Satan, not God.

Look at Galatians 1:8 "But though we, or an angel from heaven, preach any other gospel unto you than that which we have preached unto you, let him be accursed."

"And he said unto him, Thy prayers and thine alms are come up for a memorial before God." Don't think that God hasn't seen the things that you've done, both good and bad. Santa Claus isn't the one who knows what you've been doing, God is. "And now send men to Joppa, and call for one Simon, whose surname is Peter: He lodgeth with one Simon a tanner, whose house is by the sea side: he shall tell thee what thou oughtest to do." God knows right where you live. On a recent trip, flying at 30000 feet the roads look like heavy lines on paper, the houses are just small squares. You can't see anyone walking around, they are just too small, after all, you're over 5 miles in the air. Yet, while watching the ground a flash of light catches the eye, perhaps it is the sun off of the windshield of a car or truck. The thought comes to mind, this is the same way it is with God when you pray. It's like a flash of light pointing you out to God. It's a hand raised in a crowd. it's a red blazer in a field of blue. God knows right where you are.

Cornelius sent for this man called Peter. Isn't this what believing is all about? Cornelius could have just believed. After all if God would have sent an angel to Cornelius with this message, couldn't he have just told Peter to go to Cornelius?

Believing requires something of each of us. Yes, God could have sent Peter to them. As a matter of fact, He appeared to Peter in a trance, and spoke to him, telling him that the men from Cornelius were on the way. As Peter thought on this vision, the Spirit said unto him, "Behold, three men seek thee. Arise therefore, and get thee down, and go with them doubting nothing: for I have sent them." Then Peter went down to the men which were sent unto him from Cornelius, and said, "Behold, I am he whom ye seek: what is the cause wherefore ye are come?" God didn't tell Peter why they were there.

And they said, "Cornelius the centurion, a just man, and on that feareth God, and of a good report among all the nations of the Jews, was warned from God by an holy angel to send for thee into his house, and to hear words of thee." Believing calls for action. Look how this man that believed worked.

And on the morrow after they entered into Caesarea. And Cornelius waited for them, and he called together his kinsmen and near friends. He wanted them to hear what this man called Peter would say to him concerning salvation. And as Peter was coming in, Cornelius met him, and fell down at his feet, and worshiped him. But Peter took him up, saying, "Stand up, I myself also am a man." And as he talked with him, he went in, and found many that were come together. Cornelius wanted to share the good news with as many as would come. He believed. Peter went on to say, "Therefore came I unto you without gainsaying, (I have came without fee) as soon as I was sent for: I ask therefore for what intent ye have sent for me?" God didn't tell Peter why he was to go with these men. Just that he was to go. Listen to this. "And Cornelius said, Four days ago I was fasting until this hour, and at the ninth hour I prayed in my house, and behold, a man stood before me in bright clothing." Not only was he a giving, believing, praying man. But he was a fasting man, a man who knew what it was to purposely go without food so that he could keep his fleshly desires under control. Was this believer saved? Peter said in chapter 11:14 That Cornelius said that the angel told him to send to Joppa and call for Simon Peter, "Who shall tell thee words, whereby thou and thy house shall be saved."

How was this man called Cornelius and his house to be saved? Read on as Peter preached the word of God. 34: Then Peter opened his mouth, and said, "Of a truth I perceive that God is no respecter of persons: But in every nation he that feareth him, and worketh righteousness, is accepted with him. The word which God sent unto the children of Israel, Preaching peace by Jesus Christ: (he is lord of all:) That word, I say, ye know which was published throughout all Judah, and began at Galilee, after the baptism which John preached: How God anointed Jesus of Nazareth with the Holy Ghost and with power: who went about doing good, and healing all that were oppressed of the devil, for God was with him. And ye are witnesses if all things which he did both in the land of the Jews, and in Jerusalem, whom they slew and hanged on a tree: Him God raised up the third day, and showed him openly, Not to all the people, but unto witnesses chosen before of God, even to us, who did eat and drink with him after he rose from the dead. And he commanded us to preach unto the people, and to testify that it is he which was ordained of God to be the judge of quick and dead. To him give all the prophets witness, that through his name whosoever believeth in him shall receive remission of sins." While Peter yet spake these words, the Holy Ghost fell on all them which heard the word." How do you know it was the Holy Ghost, Peter? I heard them. What did you hear? Read on. " For they heard them speak with tongues, and magnify God." What's next Peter? What should the active believer do? "Can any man forbid water, that these should not be baptized, which have received the Holy Ghost as well as we?" And he commanded them to be baptized in the name of the Lord. Believing is receiving. Believing demands action. There is no stagnant, none working believism in the Christian Faith. Believing requires action. Hebrews 11:1,6 "Now faith is the substance of things hoped for, the evidence of things not seen. verse 6, But without faith it is impossible to please him: For he that cometh to God must believe that he is, and that he is a rewarder of them that diligently seek him. "

The man walked a tight wire across the great Niagara falls. The crowd cheered as he stepped from the wire onto the finish platform. As he raised his hands for their silence, he asked, "who believes that I can push this wheel barrow across the falls on this wire?" A great cheer rose from the crowd. Again, If any one believes I can do this stunt, let him stand out." Far in the back one man raised his hand. Come up here. The tight wireman commanded. The man came to the front as was requested. The crowd was silent. The walker asked again. "Do you believe that I can push this wheel barrow across the falls on this wire?" "O, yes" came the reply. Again a cheer rose from the crowd. "Then if you believe, get in the wheel barrow."

You see, believing requires action. It is easy to say that you believe but when the chips are down, what will you do? He that believeth on me as the scriptures hath said, out of his belly shall flow rivers, rivers of living water.

How, Jesus, must I believe? Acts 2:38 "Repent and be baptized every one of you in the name of Jesus Christ, for the remission of your sins, and ye shall receive the Gift of the Holy Ghost. For the promise is unto you and your children, and to all that are afar off, even as many as the Lord our God shall call."

Maybe your like Cornelius. Your a good man, giving alms to those who are in need, helping your friends and neighbors. Reading your Bible and praying every day. Perhaps you even fast. You believe. But have you relieved the Baptism of the Holy Ghost yet? This is the earnest of your inheritance. Just a token of that which is waiting for you latter on. It's yours why not receive it.

This is Bro Randy Johnson for We Preach Jesus Ministries

THERE'S ROOM IN THE BOAT   12/02/1990

PSM 45:1 MY HEART IS INDITING A GOOD MATTER:
I SPEAK THE THINGS WHICH I HAVE MADE TOUCHING THE KING:
MY TONGUE IS THE PEN OF A READY WRITER.

Genesis 6:5 "And God saw that the wickedness of man was great in the earth, and that every imagination of the thoughts of his heart was only evil continually."

Matthew 24:37 "But as the days of Noe were, so shall also the coming of the son of man be. For as in the days that were before the flood they were eating and drinking, marrying and giving in marriage, until the day that Noe entered into the ark, And knew not until the flood came, and took them all away, so shall the coming of the Son of man be."

We live in a time unparalleled by any other, except by the days of Noah.

Genesis 6:5 "And God saw that the wickedness of man was great in the earth, and that every imagination of the thoughts of his heart was only evil continually." What can be said to a verse such as this? I ask you, what generation has Adult bookstores on their main streets? Stores without windows where sin is done in the darkness by men and women that have a mind continually toward evil. If there wasn't a market for this filth then the stores would close. The evil is deeply ingrained in the heart of those that frequent these dens of inequity. What generation has the "Adults only" back rooms in the video stores? What generation has no definition of pornography? What generation, does in the open what it used to do in the back room and dark corners? This is that untoward generation Peter spoke about in the book of acts. What is the answer? Acts 2:40 "Save yourselves from this untoward generation," this Christ crucifying generation where evil men and seducers become worse and worse. Where every man who takes the time to say hello to a small child is looked on with suspect. Children are a delight, but don't dare give them attention for fear of being thought to be a pervert. Suspect is cast at any one who gives extra attention to children. Why? Because this is a wicked and perverse generation where the pictures of missing children are put on the milk cartons and signboards throughout our land. This is a generation that sacrifices it's babies on the alters of pleasure. If it feels good do it. That's the motto of today.

2 Timothy 3:1 " This know also, that in the last days (when? In the Last days) perilous (dangerous) times shall come. (Why?) For men shall be lovers of their own

selves, (never has there been such a self centered generation of me, my, mine) covetous (desiring what is someone else's), boasters, proud, blasphemers, disobedient to parents, unthankful, unholy, without natural affection, trucebreakers, false accusers, incontinent, (no control over their appetites, unchaste) fierce, despisers of those that are good, traitors, heady, high-minded, lovers of pleasures more than lovers of God, Having a form of godliness, but denying the power thereof: from such turn away. For of this sort are they which creep into houses, and lead away silly women laden with sins, led with divers lusts, Ever learning, and never able to come to the knowledge of the truth." What generation is this scripture talking about? The last generation... "But as the days of Noah were, so shall also the coming of the Son of man be." What does this mean? Jesus is coming back for his church. When? In such a time as this when wickedness is in such proportion in our world as it was in the days of Noah. Yes, I said world. This is a global, not just the United States of America.

"And it repented the LORD that he had made man on the earth, and it grieved him at his heart. And the LORD said, I will destroy man whom I have created from the face of the earth, both man, and beast, and the creeping thing, and the fowls of the air, for it repenteth me that I have made them. But Noah found grace in the eyes of the LORD." How? By being righteous before the LORD. "Noah was a just man and perfect in his generations, and Noah walked with God." The earth also was corrupt before God, and the earth was filled with violence. Does this sound familiar? Not a day goes by that you don't read of some one being mugged, raped, or killed on the streets of our fair cities. Can you take a subway in New York without jeopardizing your life? Can you walk through the parks of our cities at night without fear? Can you?

God looked down at a world populated with people much like today and said, " The end of all flesh is come before me: for the earth is filled with violence through them: and behold, I will destroy them with the earth." Why? Because their way is continually evil. There is no chance of ever recovering them. There is no hope of reversal of this total corruption. They like their adult bookstores, their buildings without windows. They like their perverted ways. They have continually rejected all that is good. All have gone astray, all have turned every one to his own way, There is none righteous, no not one. Their conscience has been seared as with a hot iron. Without natural affection. Isa 59:7 Their feet run to evil, and they make hast to shed innocent blood: their thoughts are thoughts of inequity, wasting and destruction are in their paths." Ezekiel 16: "Thou hast also taken thy fair jewels of my gold and of my silver, which I had given thee, and madest to thyself images if men, and didst commit whoredom with them," 20 "Moreover thou hast taken thy sons and thy daughters, whom thou hast borne unto me, and these hast thou sacrificed unto them to be devoured. Is this of thy whoredoms a small matter, that thou hast slain my children, and delivered them to cause them to pass through the fire for them?" Noah's generation offered their children to the gods of pleasure. Gods they themselves had created, Molek. "Make thee an ark of gopher wood, rooms shalt thou make in the ark, and shalt pitch it within and without with pitch. And this is the fashion which thou shalt make it of: The length of the ark shall be three hundred cubits, the breadth of it fifty cubits, the height of it is thirty cubits." (about 550 ft long, 92 feet wide, and 55 ft high.)

Hebrews 11:7 "By faith Noah, of things not seen as yet, moved with fear, preparing an ark to the saving of his house, by which he condemned the world, and became heir of the righteousness which is by faith." Noah believed God, and moved as his belief required him. The Bible doesn't say that Noah was independently wealthy. Noah financed this venture with the sweat of his brow. Noah, his wife, his three sons, and friends built this massive structure in the middle of who knows where. You can hear the people talk as Noah cleared a large area of land to lay the keel of this tremendous structure. What in the world are you building Noah? A boat. With hand-hewn beams, hand made pegs, Noah built this ark. Years in the making, years. Some say that it took 120 years to build the ark, chopping down the trees. Hewing the beams into usable members. Boring the holes for the pegs. Hand fitting each and every piece, using pegs for fasteners, like the oak beams in the older barns that still stand throughout this land. Every board had to be hand made. There wasn't a lumberyard down the street. No nails screws or bolts, just pegs. I'm sure he had the help of friends and neighbors at first. Maybe they had a boat raising or two. Just for the fun of it. People rally to the sound of the beat of drums. But in the long run, when the day gets long, they go home to the comfort of their own dwellings. Many have come to build the ark, the vessel that will carry us through the up and coming storm that waits on the horizon, held in check by the hand of God, until we finish the ark, the church , the body of Christ for the salvation of your soul. Jesus and 12 others began this ark two thousand years ago in an upper room in Jerusalem. He had help. Some 500 started out to build the ark yet at the laying of the keel there were only 120 souls there. 1990 years this ark, the church, has been in the building. Almost 2000 years. With hand-hewn beams, carried to a hill outside of the city, Jesus lay the keel. With nails driven through his hands he set the pace for the construction of his church. The ark now has a name that is above every name. It's registered in the Port of God. It's the ol ship of Zion. The church.

For years, this faithful man built the ark. Everything he had went into the construction of the ark. There are those who build the little churches in nondescript towns and villages throughout this land, they sit on broken down couches with the springs poking through. Humble people in humble dwellings. They are the Noah of today. They have put every thing they have in to the work of God. Why? Because their home is on the other side. Their home is in heaven, They realize that everything that we have here is just for a while then is not. It's just for a season. But everything we have in heaven is for time without end. This earthly system is temporal, but the other is heavenly and eternal. You can't take it with you but you sure can send it on ahead. Lay up treasures where moth nor rust can corrupt. Mat 6:20 Noah knew that this world was going to be covered with water and every living thing destroyed. His only salvation was in the construction of the ark. Why build a great house only to have it destroyed by flood?

THESE ARE PREACHING NOTES

Build a great work unto the LORD

No record of Noah rich

Must provide for family

Provide for the ark

What you doing tonight Noah?

Working on the ark

Probably became joke

Ask ol Noah what he's going to do with the ark that far from water

Preaching

Going to rain

What is rain

Dew watered the land

What is the rapture

never heard of catching away.

End near? Ha!

Noah=eccentric

off deep end

Noah's folly

Preaching preaching preaching

Spending all his money on that ol ark. Noah's folly

Neglecting his children's need

They wanted for nothing

Neighbors thought children needed a Nintendo

Ought to take a vacation Noah.

No time, the LORD is coming

Hammering sawing, chipping away at the logs

Preaching preaching every time someone would listen

first drew crowd

Come see Noah's folly

Have you been to Noah's folly yet?

topic of conversation everywhere laughter

It's going to rain. It's" It's" It's"

JESUS IS COMING JESUS IS COMING JESUS IS COMING

Year after year. Year after year Year after year

Been working on the ark, the church, since 1972

18 years sawing hammering preaching

Noah didn't need deprogrammed

Noah preached the truth

Sons or daughters saved

Don't like their holiness

radical

Salvation is radical

Sin is radical

Eyes of LORD no difference in sin no degrees

sin kills

Only human's degrees of sin

No sin in lives makes parents condemned

Holy Joes need to be deprogrammed

Like a lily in an onion patch

Don't condemn get in the ark

At least you know where their at

Did you before they got saved?

Judge yourselves

Are you happy with your life?

Really happy?

Noah's ark not Chris Craft

No teak Walnut or brass

Hand hewn boards with tar caulking pegged

size and proportion given by God

one window one door

only one door to the church Christ you must enter in through

his sacrifice

how?

No engine no Cat

no compass or charts

No deck stewards no purser no cruise ship

No sail no rudder God was the pilot of this ship

God is the pilot of the ship of Zion the church

No water where Noah was to float this boat

But a boat ordained of God to the salvation of souls

Noah preached salvation by an ark who's plans were provided by God

Built by Noah, three sons, wives and Noah's wife

Eight souls out of a multitude

Say anything to you?

Not built for eight but for whomever will

empty rooms in the ark

God designed Noah built for many

Can you see the similarity ?

Noah's ark and Gods church

There is a rain coming the likes of which you've never seen before.

That rain is a time of trouble the such as the world has never seen

Reserved for fire.

Heaven and earth melt with fervent heat

Only escape Jesus' ark the church

 Salvation is predicated on your belief that God is able to save your soul. That God was manifest in the flesh, walked among the people, was crucified, and rose again on the third day, that this is available to you. If only one person in the whole world were to believe that Jesus Is the Christ, the Jesus would have done it for him or her. Jesus loves you so much that he died for you. But, you say, he knew that he would rise again. Read the scripture. You'll see that crucifixion was the most ignoble death a man could ever die. Think of the beating he took for your healing, Isaiah 53:5 "But he was wounded for our transgressions, he was bruised for out iniquities: the chastisement of our peace was upon him, and with his stripes we are healed." Think of the humility that he endured. He knew that the days to come were so horrible that he prayed, "if it be possible, let this cup pass from me." He could have said, I have other things to do, turned and walked out of the garden, never to be crucified. But he saw your face, he saw the pain you have in your heart today. He prayed for you until the pain was so great, it nearly burst his heart . I think that you understand where he was. I think that you understand where I'm coming from.

    Jesus laid the keel but now is the day of your salvation.

    Get you a room in the ark.

    The vacancy sign still hangs by the door.

    Acts 2:38 --

THE BAPTISM OF THE HOLY GHOST   12/16/1990

PSM 45:1 MY HEART IS INDITING A GOOD MATTER:
I SPEAK THE THINGS WHICH I HAVE MADE TOUCHING THE KING:
MY TONGUE IS THE PEN OF A READY WRITER.

AND SUDDENLY   ACTS 2:1-4 "AND WHEN THE DAY OF PENTECOST WAS FULLY COME, THEY WERE ALL WITH ONE ACCORD IN ONE PLACE. AND SUDDENLY THERE CAME A SOUND FROM HEAVEN AS OF A RUSHING MIGHTY WIND, AND IT FILLED ALL THE HOUSE WHERE THEY WERE SITTING. AND THERE APPEARED UNTO THEM CLOVEN TONGUES LIKE AS OF FIRE, AND IT SAT UPON EACH OF THEM. AND THEY WERE ALL FILLED WITH THE HOLY GHOST, AND BEGAN TO SPEAK WITH OTHER TONGUES AS THE SPIRIT GAVE THEM UTTERANCE."

In the past, a great interest has been aroused in the churches throughout the land. The subject? The baptism of the Holy Ghost. Almost all denominations study, discuss, or argue about the baptism of the Holy Ghost. The spirit baptism is so life changing that some churches are even divided by it.

Look at Apollos in the book of Acts 18:25 " ....instructed in the way of the LORD, and being fervent in the spirit, he spake and taught diligently the things of the Lord, knowing only the baptism of John." Most eloquent, sincere but sadly ineffective! Here was Apollos leading a group of twelve, who managed to hold their own, while another Holy Ghost baptized group was turning the world up side down. What made the difference? The Holy Ghost super power made the difference.

Why is so little significance placed on the birth of the church, the living body of Christ? We place great emphasis on Christmas, Easter, and Good Friday yet little significance is placed on the day of Pentecost, the birth of the church. The focus seems to be placed on Christ coming to be with us, Christmas, then on Christ being in us, Pentecost, the Holy Ghost Baptism. This first Church was born in a blaze of glory, evidently man has outgrown what God started. Why hasn't that neighbor of yours told you about the goodness of God? Perhaps he received the silent Baptism of the Holy Ghost. His witness is mute. Well the Church wasn't born in a corner. Jesus Christ was out in the open about everything he preached. When He lay the foundation of the church 2000 years ago, it wasn't done in a closet or behind closed doors.

What really happened to that group of 120 that stayed in that upper room waiting for the promise of the Father? 5000 started out to serve Him yet by the time the seventh week came to pass, only 120 remained. Jesus said Acts 1:4-5,8 "... Should not depart from Jerusalem, but wait for the promise of the Father, which, saith he, ye have heard of me. For John truly baptized with water, but ye shall be baptized with the Holy Ghost not many days hence........ye shall receive power, after that the holy Ghost is come upon you: and ye shall be witnesses unto me both in Jerusalem, and in Judea, and in Samaria, and unto the uttermost part of the earth"

120 believers assembled together. Ignoring the feast days. Only one thing was on their minds, The promise of the Father. When would it come? The third hour, nine o'clock in the morning, they were all of one mind and one accord, their minds were on God, thinking of the events of the last month or so. Waiting, wondering. Then there was a sound like a rushing mighty wind, and it filled all the house where they were sitting. Look to the streets where there were gathered men and women from all the known earth, gathered for the feast of Pentecost. This roaring must have sent all scurrying for shelter. This wind burst into the room where the 120 were gathered together. It filled all the house where they were at. As this wind subsided, there appeared a great ball of fire, it hung in the center of the room, While the 120 stared transfixed, small flames resembling tongues, streaked across the room and suspended themselves above each member of the group. Not a hair was singed, not one piece of clothing was scorched. Inside each was felt a churning and burning. The feeling defying description. Thrills and chills up and down your spine. Relaxing, the presence of God soaking, submerging, flooding your soul. "In the last day, that great day of the feast, Jesus stood and cried, saying, if any man thirst, let him come unto me, and drink. He that believeth on me, as the scripture hath said, out of his belly shall flow rivers of living waters...." "For by one spirit are we all baptized into one body, whether we be Jews or Gentiles, whether we be bond or free, and have been all made to drink in to one Spirit." 1 Cor 12:13 The Spirit of God, invisible but real, the very real presence of God came down upon each and every believer. Completely surrounded, enveloped, immersed in Him. Baptized. Inwardly, individually, they drank the presence and power of the Holy Ghost. Freely, flowing through them, like rivers of living water. "The fountains of the great deep were broken up, and the windows

of heaven were opened." Gen 7:11 This quote may have been for Noah's day but salvation of today is brought the same way.

This baptism of the Holy Ghost bathed them from head to foot. Such thrills, such bliss, never had they experienced any thing the likes of this. Their chins began to quiver, trembling and shaking all over, their tongues quit cooperating with their minds, instead of normal speech, unintelligible sounds came forth. The Spirit of God formed the words in their minds.

Some were dancing, some were leaping for joy, some swaying, some screaming, turning in circles, even a few prostrate on the floor. The Word of God said of the people in the streets, Acts 2:13 "And they were all amazed, and were in doubt, saying one to another, What meaneth this? Others mocking said, These men are full of new wine." New wine was made by soaking dried grapes in the old wine and then pressing them a second time. Powerful, intoxicating, producing wild delirious emotions. Gibberish by drunkards, was the label. 17 nations said, "And how hear we every man in our own tongue, wherein we were born? Behold, are not all these Galileans?" Isaiah caught a glimpse of the effect of the Holy Ghost on the tongue 700 years back: Isaiah 28:10-12 For with stammering lips and another tongue will he speak to this people. To whom he said , this is the rest wherewith ye may cause the weary to rest, and this is the refreshing: yet they would not hear." Ezekiel said it this way 600 years earlier: Ezekiel 11:19-20 "And I will give them one heart, and I will put a new spirit within you: and I will take the stony heart out of their flesh, and I will give them an heart of flesh: that they may walk in my statutes, and keep mine ordinances, and do them: and they shall be my people, and I will be their God."   The prophet Joel had forecast this happening eight centuries before. Joel 2:28-29 "And it shall come to pass afterward, that I will pour out my spirit upon all flesh, and your sons and your daughters shall prophesy, your old men shall dream dreams, your young men shall see visions: and also upon the servants and upon the handmaidens in those days will I pour out my spirit." John the Baptist knew there would be better coming: Matthew 3:11 "I indeed baptize you with water unto repentance: but he that cometh after me is mightier that I, whose shoes I am not worthy to bear: he shall baptize you with the Holy Ghost, and with fire."

Jesus said it this way: "If any man thirst..." Those 120 in the upper room were thirsty for the Holy Ghost, they waited, and they got it.

Peter stood, Acts 2:14 "...lifted up his voice, and said unto them, "Ye men of Judaea and all ye that dwell at Jerusalem, be this known unto you, and harken to my words: For these are not drunken, as ye suppose, seeing it is but the third hour of the day. But this is that which was spoken by the prophet Joel," The blood of Jesus Christ was laid upon their hands by Peter's preaching. Conviction settled upon their hearts and they cried out. "Men and brethren what shall we do? Then Peter said unto them, Repent, and be baptized every one of you in the name of Jesus Christ for the remission of sins, and ye shall receive the gift of the Holy Ghost. For the promise is unto you, and your children, and to all that are afar off, even as many as the LORD our God shall call." then they that gladly received his word were baptized: and the same day there were added unto them about three thousand souls.

The Spirit that submerged those three thousand one hundred and twenty souls was and is invisible, yet it manifest it's self in such a way that the disciples could determine later if a believer had received an identical experience. Jesus compared it to the wind in John 3:8 "The wind bloweth where it listeth, and thou hearest the sound thereof, but canst not tell whence it cometh, and whither it goeth: so is everyone that is born of the Spirit" The effects of the wind can be seen and heard yet it is invisible. Acts 2,33 "Therefore being by the right hand of God exalted, and having received of the Father the promise of the Holy Ghost, he (Jesus) hath shed forth this, which ye now see and hear." Paul spoke of his own ministry in 1 Corinthians 2:4 " My speech and my preaching was not with enticing words of man's wisdom, but in demonstration of the Spirit and of power." The Holy Ghost produces the effects that are perceived by the physical senses of the listener. Uninhibited worship, tears flowing freely, hands raise toward heaven, speaking and singing in languages never learned. God blessing his people. Filling them with His Spirit. Peter went to preach to Cornelius and his household in Acts 10:44 "While Peter yet spake these words, the Holy Ghost fell on all them which heard the word. And they of the circumcision which believed were astonished, as many as came with Peter, because that on the Gentiles also was poured out the gift of the Holy Ghost. For they heard them speak with tongues, and magnify God." Peter said "And as I began to speak, the Holy Ghost fell on them, as on us at the beginning." Acts 11:15 How did you know that, Peter? "I heard them speak with tongues just like we did when we received the Holy Ghost." Paul was at Ephesus, a city near the west coast of Turkey, only ruins now, the seat of the temple of the goddess Diana, preaching to a group of converts, Acts 19:6 " And when Paul had laid his hands upon them, the Holy Ghost came on them, and they spake with tongues, and prophesied." The Holy Ghost came on them and they spake with tongues.

Born again. God taking out the heart of stone and putting in a heart of flesh, a heart that is moved with the natural affections of life. Not the heart that can't be moved to compassion. One that feels the agony of others. One that can feel a widow's sorrow and grief over the passing of her husband. A heart that is in tune with God.

John 3:3-7 "Except a man be born again, he cannot see the kingdom of God. Nicodemus saith unto him, How can a man be born when he is old? Can he enter the second time into his mother's womb, and be born? Jesus answered, Verily, verily, I say unto thee, Except a man be born of water and of the Spirit, he cannot enter into the kingdom of God. That which is born of the flesh is flesh, and that which is born of the Spirit is spirit. Marvel not that I said unto thee, Ye must be born again." Belief requires something of you. To believe is good but not enough. Remember, Noah believed what God said, but that wouldn't keep him dry, the ark did, the result of his belief. The devils believe there is one God but that won't save them. Except a man be born of the water and Spirit he cannot enter into the kingdom of God. Pretty precise. Leaves absolutely no room for doubt. Jesus said it, better believe it.

How to be born of the water? Repentance of your sins grants you forgiveness, water baptism remits your sins and initiates you into the family of God. The baptism of the Holy Ghost is the Spirit Baptism that changes your heart, turns you around and heads you in the right direction. It takes away our sinful nature. No longer are you bound by sin. Not under the law of sin. No longer a slave to sin. Something happens to us that we could never, never accomplish. God's righteousness becomes our own. Romans 3:22 "Even the righteousness of God which is by faith of Jesus first unto all and upon all them that believe..." Exalted to a position of joint heirs with Jesus Christ. Restored Harmony with God. As though we had never committed and wrong. As innocent as a newborn babe. Born again.

A new life. Clean, pure, Holy, and righteous. The Spirit is present within to help us retain this righteousness. Directing our footsteps day to day. It is now possible to understand God's spiritual truths, to obey them, and to please God.

When something as powerful as this is available to believers, why would anyone not teach it? Not understanding it, they would rather not discuss that they don't know. For this they are willingly ignorant of, "If I don't know it, it's not worth knowing. " Remember what was said on the very first broadcast? 2 Peter 1:20 "No scripture is of any private interpretation." No man has an exclusive on the scriptures. It is for whosoever will. To enter into God's kingdom, to obtain all the benefits, and beauties, we must come according to the Scriptures, by birth of water baptism and the baptism of the Holy Ghost. But, you say, is it really for me today? Acts 2:39 "For the promise is unto you, and your children, and to all that are afar off, even as many as the Lord our God shall call." God has not changed the divine plan. There is nowhere in the scripture that indicates a change of plans. The gift of the Holy Ghost is every believer's birthright privilege. Wise men brought gifts to the baby Jesus, but little did they realize what a gift he had for them. Wise men and women still seek Jesus today. Receive the gift of the Holy Ghost, it's for you today.

THE LESSON OF CHRISTMAS   12/23/1990

PSM 45:1 MY HEART IS INDITING A GOOD MATTER:
I SPEAK THE THINGS WHICH I HAVE MADE TOUCHING THE KING:
MY TONGUE IS THE PEN OF A READY WRITER.

Christmas, a time of trees and decorations, the smell of pine in the house, baking cookies, of relatives, of good cheer, a time of good feeling, Christmas, a time of giving. Throughout the land people will be gathered together giving to one another gifts from the heart. The best gift a person can give is a gift that he or she wants for theirselves. For this is giving a part of themselves to the other. Isn't that what Christmas is all about? Giving.
Christmas is a very special time of the year for my family and myself. I'm sure you feel the same. Would you please allow me to tell you what Christmas means to me and mine.

The time of the year that Jesus was born isn't really known, but tradition has put the King's birth at this time, So laying aside all that is not worship let us worship the savior for who we have this time set aside. Jesus Christ, born a king in the city of David, a savior, Christ our Lord. A birth heralded by angels. Heralded by the heavens themselves, Rejoice greatly, O daughter of Zion, shout, O daughter of Jerusalem: behold thy King cometh unto thee: and he is just, and having salvation,....

Oh if that innkeeper would have, could have known who it was that lay in his stable. If only he would have known. It would have been the honeymoon suite for Mary and Joseph and not the stable. Christ wouldn't have been born in a manger. But it was meant to be this way. For the honeymoon suites and fine hotels represent the luxuries of this life. Jesus' ministry wasn't unto the rich but the poor and hungry, to those in need. Jesus said it was easier for a camel to pass through the eye of the needle then for a rich man to enter into heaven. The eye of the needle was a small gate entering in to the city. Though not entirely impossible for a camel to get through, but a very hard and lengthy process. A rich man trusts in his riches and not in the savior. "Because thou sayest, I am rich, and increased with goods, and have need of nothing, and knowest not that thou art wretched, and miserable, and poor, and blind, and naked:" Luke 16:20 "And he said unto them, Take heed, and beware of covetousness: for a man's life consisteth not in the abundance of the things which he possesseth. And he spake a parable unto them, saying, the ground of a certain rich man brought forth plentifully: And he thought within himself, saying, What shall I do, because I have no room to bestow my fruits? And he said, this will I do, I will pull down my barns, and build greater, and there will I bestow all my fruits and my goods. And I will say to my soul, Soul, thou hast much goods laid up for many years, take thine ease, eat, drink, and be marry. But God said unto him, Thou fool, this night thy soul shall be required of thee: then whose shall those things be, which thou hast provided?" So is he that layeth up treasure for himself, and is not rich toward God. Is it wrong to be rich? No, just as long as you know who gave it to you. Your prosperity cometh from above, you haven't done this thing yourself. David the king was rich. Solomon was rich. Job was rich. Abraham was rich. Many in the Bible were rich yet they forgot not who it was that provided for them. This life is but a stewardship, not ownership. Out west, some years back, while working in a boat shop, I met a man who had a sugar beet farm in Canada. This man had heart problems and was concerned over his children inheriting the rights to the farm. In Canada, you see, the Queen owns the land and the people just have a right to farm it. Well, when the person who holds these rights dies, the rights go back to the Queen. Well, he never made it back to Canada, he passed on. What became of the farm I don't know. But the idea is, life is just a stewardship responsibility, not a proprietary agreement. You don't own it, your just using it.

So Jesus the Christ wasn't born into an affluent society but one of austerity. Mary and Joseph weren't rich, just typical people who were blessed of God to be the parents of the Messiah, the savior of the world.

Mary and Joseph traveled to Bethlehem 5 miles s.w. of Jerusalem. Mary in her third trimester, due to give birth, traveling five miles over rugged hills, riding on an ass. There wasn't an Amtrak, No US air. No American Express to fly, just hardship. I don't know how long it took to make that five miles, but I'm sure it took quite a while. With stopping and resting, because Mary probably couldn't take much over half a mile at a time. She couldn't walk for very long I'm sure. Then, to arrive in a town that was booked up as solid as a city with three conventions, going from inn to inn, until one had compassion and said, My manger in empty, you can stay there, if you would like? Born in a manger no crib for his bed, the little Lord Jesus lay down his sweet head. Born in a manger, to his own a stranger, a man of sorrow, pain, and agony. For unto you is born this day in the city of David, a Savior, which is Christ the LORD. And this shall be a sign unto you, you shall find the babe wrapped in swaddling cloths, lying in a manger. Angels, proclaiming the birth of Christ to those who were interested. Wise men in the east, Shepherds in the fields, attending the flocks. Close to God and in love with His creation. They were listening for His voice. Meanwhile, far to the East, wise men, those who looked for His coming and understood what the scriptures meant, saw the star rise in the sky and they began their journey to greet the new King. Tradition says there were three wise men but the Bible didn't feel it was necessary to enumerate, nor even to give their names. It does say," Behold, there came wise men from the east to Jerusalem, saying, where is he that is born King of the Jews? For we have seen his star in the east, and have come to worship him. When Herod the king had heard these things, he was troubled, and all Jerusalem with him." Remember, this is the Herod that Josephus said, took the principle men of the entire Jewish nation, and ordered them shut up in the hippodrome, to be shot through with arrows at the time of his death so that there would be morning in the land over his passing away. Demented in mind, ruthless, better to be Herod's pig then his sons, because he had his own sons slain. Herod gathered together all his chief priests and scribes and demanded of them, Where should this king be born?

In Bethlehem in the land of Judea, for this it is written by the prophet "And thou Bethlehem, in the land of Juda, art thou not the least among the princes of Juda: for out of thee shall come a Governor, that shall rule my people Israel. This sent chills up and down Herod's spine for if there were to come an insurrection during his commission, Caesar would have his head. Then Herod, when he had privily called the wise men, enquired of them diligently what time the star appeared. And he sent them to Bethlehem, and said, go and search diligently for the young child, and when ye have found him, bring me word again, that I may come and worship him also. Herod had no desire to worship someone that would take over the rule of the Jews. He wanted to eliminate the competition before it grew up. When they had heard the king, they departed, and lo, the star, which they saw in the east, went before them, till it came and stood over where the young child was. One thing is evident in this verse. The star hadn't been shining when they went in to see Herod. So God would announce to the Jews, through the scribes and priest, that the messiah, the anointed one, Jesus the Christ, had indeed been born. The star could have led the wise men directly to the child Jesus but it evidently wasn't shinning for the scripture says, "And, Lo, the star, which they saw in the east, went before them. When they saw the star, they rejoiced with exceeding great joy. Think on this verse for a moment. Savior the content. Let your mind wander a bit. Here were men who had traveled for days, months, perhaps years to get to this place. The scripture doesn't say how far east they were. Perhaps just a few days journey. East is east. But, they rejoiced with exceeding great joy over the star. The scripture is not laced with superlatives, and this verse is indeed loaded with superlatives. Exceeding great joy. Why did they go to Herod? Well, there wasn't any star to guide them. Evidently it had been taken away. So they went to where a king would have been born to inquire about the newborn king. When they came out from the inquiry, and When they saw the star, they rejoiced with exceeding great joy. Messiah has come, shall we rejoice?

Wise men, seeking after the baby Jesus. The king. The Messiah, the anointed one, the savior of the world, he that would come and free his people from the hard bondage that enslaved their souls. Oh, they looked for one that would cause insurrection and overthrow the bondage of the Romans. They looked for one to be born in King's houses. They looked for a deliver, a Moses or a Joshua, maybe even a David. One clothed in fine linen, purple, scarlet, and a crown. Who would look for a babe in a manger? And when they were come into the house, they saw the young child with Mary his mother, and fell down, and worshipped him: and when they had opened their treasures, they presented unto him gifts, gold, frankincense, and myrrh. Gifts fit for a King! Gold the noble metal, incorruptible, the symbol of deity, Frankincense, pure incense, the symbol of pure prayers, myrrh, a sweet smelling savior, used for incense, medicine, the symbol of humanity and divinity united.

There in the manger lay God, gift wrapped in the flesh. 1 Tim 3:16 "And without controversy great is the mystery of godliness: God was manifest in the flesh, justified in the Spirit, seen of angels, preached unto the gentiles, believed on in the world, received up into glory." Who was? God was. It took a tiny little baby to set the whole world on its ear. Never, had the life of one so affected history. No king, martyr, or wise man has ever made such an impact on this world. Even time itself is divided by his birth. BC before Christ AD anno domini in the year of our lord CE common event.

Then Herod, when he saw that he was mocked of the wise men, was exceedingly wroth, and sent forth, and slew all the children that were in Bethlehem, and the coasts thereof, from two years old and under, according to the time which he had diligently enquired of the wise men. Genocide. The Devil has tried to stop the deliver coming from the time of Adam and Eve. He's tried to stop the promise of God, Genesis 3:15 " And I will put enmity between thee and the woman, and between thy seed and her seed, it shall bruise thy head, and thou shalt bruise his heel." His, was the guiding hand that helped Cain kill Abel. Stop the lineage of the Christ. That was the battle cry of the Devil. When Joseph's brothers sold him into slavery, that was the hand of the evil one. When the king of Egypt told the mid wives to slay the sons of Israel, that was the hand of the evil one. When he cause conditions to be such as to cause Rahab to become a harlot, that was the hand of the evil one. When he cause Ruth to lose her husband, that was the hand of the evil one, Stop the lineage. Stop the lineage. On and on it goes, throughout the Old Testament, time after time, stop the lineage of the messiah, the deliver. But, Romans 11:26 says "And so all Israel shall be saved: as it is written, There shall come out of Sion the Deliver, and shall turn away ungodliness from Jacob: For this is my covenant with unto them, when I shall take away their sins." God had for warned Joseph in a dream, given by an angel, to flee into Egypt, for Herod would seek the life of the young child. There was no hesitation in the steps of Joseph for "When he arose, he took the young child and his mother by night, and departed into Egypt." And was there until the death of Herod: that it might be fulfilled which was spoken of the Lord by the prophet, saying Out of Egypt have I called my son." More than 300 prophecies were fulfilled on that eventful day 1990 years ago. Twenty writers living in different times in history and under greatly varying circumstances penned the scriptures pointing to this very day. Thousands waited expectantly for the messiah to come. They knew the time. You could feel it in the air. Much like today. Something is going to happen. Something is in the air. Could it be that this could be the day that starts eternity? Are you waiting to see the coming of the LORD of Glory?

Luke 2:25 "and, behold, there was a man in Jerusalem, whose name was Simeon, and the same man was just and devout, waiting for the consolation of Israel: and the Holy Ghost was upon him. And it was revealed unto him by the Holy Ghost, that he should not see death, before he had seen the Lord's Christ. And he came in the Spirit into the temple (that is, he was led by the Holy Ghost to come to the temple): and when the parents brought in the child Jesus, to do for him after the custom of the law, Then took he him in his arms, and blessed God, and said, Lord, now lettest thou thy servant depart in peace, according to thy word: For mine eyes have seen thy salvation, (God will reveal, to those who want to see, His salvation, Jesus Christ.) Lord, now lettest thou thy servant depart in peace, according to thy word: For mine eyes have seen thy salvation, Which thou hast prepared before the face of all the people, (God cause the babe to be born at a time when all the people would know, because of the star, that Jesus indeed had been born. The priests, the scribes, and the Pharisees knew when the Deliver was to be born.

The scriptures are very plain on this time.) For mine eyes have seen thy salvation, which thou hast prepared before the face of all the people, a light to lighten the Gentiles, and the glory of thy people Israel. And Joseph and his mother marveled at those things, which were spoken of him. And Simeon blessed them, and said unto Mary his mother, Behold, this child is set for the fall and rising again of many in Israel, and for a sign which shall be spoken against, (Yea, a sword shall pierce through thy own soul also,) that the thoughts of many hearts may be revealed." Then there was one called Anna, a prophetess, great with age, a widow of 44 years, who served God continually with prayers and fasting, And she coming in that instant gave thanks likewise unto the LORD, and spake of Him to all them that looked for the redemption in Jerusalem." Think for a minute. What thoughts must have went through Mary's heart. This child is set for the fall and rising again of many in Israel, yea, a sword shall pierce through my soul also? She knew it was a miracle birth. But what was this child? She knew he was the messiah, but like every other mother, she had her ideas plans, and expectations for his life. But a sword shall pierce through my soul also? Her mind races back to the comforting words of the angel, "Fear not, Mary: for thou hast found favor with God." Surely, she consoled herself with these words many times over the next 33 years. You can console yourself with these words. Fear not friend, thou hast found favor with God. You look for the Consolation of Israel, a light to lighten the Gentiles. Jesus the Christ. He is your savior. For unto you is born this day in the city of David a Savior, Which is Christ the Lord. Why don't you let the Morning Star rise in your hearts. Allow Jesus to be your savior. Make this a Christmas to remember. The star on top of your tree could lead you to the savior. Let the angels rejoice over the birth of a newborn babe in Christ. The angels rejoice over one sinner that comes to Jesus.

    Under your tree, sits gifts that you've sacrificed to give to your loved ones, wrapped in the prettiest paper, foils, and ribbons you could find. Nothing, is too good for your friends and loved ones. Then how much greater is your Father in heaven? He knows how to give the greatest gift ever known to the whole universe, The Holy Ghost, God's Spirit dwelling in you, in your life, He becomes your life. Repent of the sins you've committed against God, those sins of self. The sins of wrong doing. And be baptized in the name of Jesus Christ of the remission of these sins. And you shall receive the gift of the Holy Ghost. For this promise is unto you.... ***This essay was adapted from a sermon by Dr James Allan Francis in "The Real Jesus and Other Sermons" © 1926 by the Judson Press of Philadelphia (pp 123-124 titled "Arise Sir Knight!").***

PORTRAIT 1   01/06/1991

PSM 45:1 MY HEART IS INDITING A GOOD MATTER:
I SPEAK THE THINGS WHICH I HAVE MADE TOUCHING THE KING:
MY TONGUE IS THE PEN OF A READY WRITER.

Christmas is past for another year. Lingering yet behind are the memories of wrapping paper, ribbons, and decorated trees. There remains yet, the invigorating feeling from having spent the special days with loved ones. Lingering in the house remains the smell of pies, cookies, and turkey. Past is New Year's Eve with it's attending celebrating. New Year resolutions have been made and broken. The thing that needs to be changed is the I can't to I won't. Put in a proper perspective, they become easier to deal with. Philippians 4:13 "I can do all things through Christ which strengtheneth me." Christian, there are no I can't in your life concerning sin. You are no longer bound by the chains and fetters of sin. Your problem is I won't. God has given you the victory over sin. Receive it, use it. Cast off those self-imposed limitations, those things you've decided you can't do. Remember: "I can do all things through Christ which strengtheneth me." Hebrews 12:4 tells you "Ye have not yet resisted unto blood, striving against sin." The road from Calvary is anointed with the blood of the martyrs. Faithful men and women that have resisted sin unto death. Jesus said to the church of Smyrna "Be thou faithful unto death, and I will thee a crown of life." In America, we do not have to fight the battles against sin unto death. Our persecution comes from between our ears. In our own mind. Loose that new man and let him go.

What is your portrait of Christ? What picture of Jesus do you hold in your minds eye? Is it something Michael Angelo painted? Effeminate, weak looking, a regular Casper Milquetoast. Maybe it's something drawn by Hook. Young Jesus, rugged, bearded, robed with a look of peace and love about him. Descriptions. Describe someone you know in 75 words or less. Try it. How about this one? This tanned, slight built, rugged Jewish man is a builder of fine furniture, and has a hobby of making pottery. He is totally unpretentious in manner and dress, and yet not indifferent to his appearance and report. He is a man of complete honesty, and a totally faithful friend who has taught me a great deal about myself. Or this one: He had wavy brown hair and compassionate dark eyes. He spoke with a strong voice that commanded your complete attention. Perhaps it was the authority with which he spoke, nonetheless, you were compelled to listen to his words of wisdom on the foundational basics of life. He lived exactly what he taught.

How do you boil down what you know about a person into a consommé' of thoughts and words?

"Jesus: born in an obscure village. The son of a peasant woman. He grew up in another village, where he worked as a carpenter in his father's shop until he was thirty. Then for three years, he was an itinerant preacher. He never wrote a book or held an office. He never had a family or owned a house. He didn't go to college or some seminary. He never visited a big city or traveled over two hundred miles from the place where he was born. He did none of the things one usually associates with greatness. He had no credentials but himself. He was only thirty-three when the tide of public opinion turned against him. His friends left him when He was turned over to his enemies to go through the mockery of a trial. He was nailed to a cross between two thieves and while he was dying, his executioners gambled for the only property he had on earth, his clothing. When he was dead, he was laid in a borrowed tomb of a friend.

Nineteen centuries have come and gone, and today he is the central figure of the human race and leader of mankind's progress. All the armies that ever marched, and all the navies that ever sailed, all the parliaments that ever sat, and all the kings that ever reigned, put together, have not affected the life of man on this earth as much as that one solitary life. Written by, I don't know who, this discourse aptly describes the life, but not the person, of one called Jesus of Nazareth, the carpenter." JAMES ALLAN FRANCIS, *One Solitary Life,* pp. 1–7 (1963).*

Galatians 5:22 " but the fruit of the Spirit is love, joy, peace, longsuffering, gentleness, goodness, faith, meekness, temperance, against such there is no law. And they that are Christ's have crucified the flesh with the affections and lusts. If we live in the Spirit, let us also walk in the Spirit. Let us not be desirous of vain glory, provoking one another, envying one another."

The fruit of the Spirit is love, joy, peace, longsuffering, gentleness, goodness, faith, meekness, and temperance. The Spirit of Christ. The Holy Ghost dwelling in you. If then this is the Spirit of Christ, and indeed it is the Spirit of Christ, then this is what Christ was like when he walked the face of the earth. What then was his personal appearance? Isaiah 53:2 says "For he shall grow up before him as a tender plant, and as a root out of dry ground: he hath no form nor comeliness, and when we shall see him, there is no beauty that we should desire him. He is despised and rejected of men, a man of sorrows, and acquainted with grief: and we hid as it were our faces from him, he was despised, and we esteemed him not. Surely he hath born our grief's, and carried our sorrows: yet we did esteem him stricken, smitten of God, and afflicted." Does this scripture refer to his personal appearance? For years, it has been used to infer that Jesus had no personal beauty. Could it be, that to propagate a plant, a portion of the root must be up out of the ground. Israel was a plant that was long dry, it bore no fruit, it abode in dry ground. He was despised and rejected of men. What men? Israel, the Jews, his own.

      Psalm 45:2 speaks of the beauty of the Lord God Almighty Gift wrapped in the flesh. "Thou are fairer than the children of men: grace is poured into thy lips: therefore God hath blessed thee for ever." Born the second man Adam, this man was the sum total of perfection and beauty. The only sinless child that was ever born into the world, surely, he had a perfect body. Those who listened to his teachings but loved their sins were angered by them and saw in him no beauty that they should desire him. Beauty, not the effeminate beauty of Michael Angelo but the rugged beauty of a man. A real man. Despised and rejected, a man acquainted with sorrows, the picture of humility and compassion.

      Luke 3:40 "And the child grew, and waxed strong in spirit, filled with wisdom: and the grace of God was upon him.-- And Jesus increased in wisdom and stature, and in favor with God and man." Before Jesus' three year ministry began, he was accepted where ever he went, Luke 2:46 "And it came to pass, that after three days they found him in the temple, sitting in the midst of the doctors, both hearing them, and asking them questions. And all that heard him were astonished at his understanding and answers." A young man, twelve years old, astonishes the doctors of the law with his understanding of the scriptures. What were the questions these learned men asked of Jesus? Were they questions concerning the messiah? Maybe they asked him, "Who is it the prophet spoke of in Isaiah? "He is despised and rejected of men, a man of sorrows, and acquainted with grief: and we hid as it were our faces from him, he was despised, and we esteemed him not." Or maybe, Who is this? "For unto us a child is born, unto us a son is given: and the government shall be upon his shoulder: and his name shall be called Wonderful, Counselor, The mighty God, The everlasting Father, The prince of peace. Or: "Behold a king shall reign in righteousness, and princes shall rule in judgment. And a man shall be as an hiding place from the wind, and a covert from the tempest, as rivers of water in a dry place, as the shadow of a great rock in a weary land." His answers to their probing questions were to provoke these learned men to stop and think about the messiah. They knew what time it was according to scripture. They all waited for the consolation of Israel. For this anointed one, the messiah. Jesus the Christ. Perhaps he read them this verse and that from the scrolls, then asked them who the writer spoke of. Or maybe he read another from the Psms. "They weren't the questions, like he asked latter on of those that had already rejected him. The questions that couldn't be answered without commitment one-way or the other. Who are you? They asked. I'll tell you who I am if you will tell me one thing. The baptism of John was it of God or man? Answer it one way and you've rejected the council of God against yourself. Answer in the other way and you've compromised your position. Questions like this are not asked to allow you to save face but to shake you into reality.

The main point being that until he began his ministry, he was easily accepted in their midst, He was in favor with his townsmen. These might well have been those that crucified him latter on.

Have you ever been around someone that was extremely easy to get along with? The kind of person that you just like to be around. One that was easy to carry on a conversation with. A good listener. One that never seemed to resent your intruding in their life. They always have an ear for your troubles. Such a one is Jesus the Christ. Our succor. Our rock. Our strong tower. Our help in time of need. But the fruit of the Spirit is: love, joy, peace, longsuffering, gentleness, goodness, faith, meekness, temperance, against such, there is no law. Love: it covers a multitude of sins. Joy: is cheerfulness, delight. Peace is quietness. Longsuffering is patience, tolerance, forbearance, balance, calmness. Gentleness is: suitableness, equity, mildness, clemency is a gentleman. Goodness is: virtue, beneficence. Faith is: assurance, belief, and fidelity. Meekness is: humbleness, a willingness to be ruled without having to concentrate on being submissive. Temperance is: self control, continence. Show me the man of these qualities. Where is he? Let me see him. There. There he is, preaching, teaching the multitude on the hillside. There he is walking down the streets of Jerusalem. There he sits, with his disciples, teaching them about the finer things of life. There he is healing the lame man by the pool. There he is healing the blind man. There he is, going to dinner with the ex tax collector. There he is raising the widow's son from the dead. There he is raising Jairus' daughter from the dead. There he is healing the Centurion's servant. Never in a hurry, always has the time to stop and listen, to talk, to heal. To minister to the people's needs. Food for the hungry. Water for the thirsty. Hope for the hopeless. Care for those without anyone to care for them. Everything to everyone. The personification of all that is, or ever will be good, Jesus the Christ. And yet: "He (is) despised and rejected of men, a man of sorrows, and acquainted with grief: and we hid as it were our faces from him, he was despised, and we esteemed him not. Surely he hath born our grief's, and carried our sorrows: yet we did esteem him stricken, smitten of God, and afflicted."

Jesus said in Luke 7:9 " Full well ye reject the commandment of God, that ye may keep your own tradition." John 12:48 "He that rejecteth me, and receiveth not my words, hath one that judgeth him: the word that I have spoken, the same shall judge him in the last day. For I have not spoken of myself, but the father which sent me, he gave me a commandment, what I should say, and what I should speak." John 15:22 "If I had not come and spoken unto them, they had not had sin: but now they have no cloak for their sin. He that hateth me hateth my Father also. If I had not done among them the works which none other man did, they had not had sin: but now have they both seen and hated both me and my Father." They esteemed him stricken of God. It's God's judgment come down upon him, because he, being man, hath made himself to be God. No man can forgive sin. God alone can forgive sins. Jesus ask them, which is easier, to forgive sin or to heal this lame man? Questions that can't be answered without admitting that he indeed is the Christ, the Anointed one. They esteemed him to be under the judgment of God. They had to or admit that he was God manifest in the flesh. But they wouldn't. Why wouldn't they admit that he was the Christ? If they admitted he was the messiah, it would interrupt the whole political system of the priesthood. Yes, I said the political system of the priesthood. The priesthood had degenerated to the place that priest were appointed by the Herod and not by God. It had become a political position to control the Jews. A tool. They were known for their religious zeal, so the best way to keep them under control was through their religion. A ministry controlled by Rome was the answer. John 11:47 "Then gathered the chief priest and the Pharisees a counsel, and said, what do we? For this man doeth many miracles. If we let him thus alone, all men will believe on him, and the Romans shall come and take away both our place and nation. And one of them, named Caiaphas, being high priest that same year, said unto them, Ye know nothing at all, nor consider that it is expedient for us, that one man should die for the people, and that the whole nation perish not."...From that day forth they took counsel together for to put him to death.

From the time that Jesus came back from Egypt until the event in the temple at twelve years of age are not recorded in the Word of God. Then from this incident until Jesus' baptism by John twenty-eight years latter are lost to history. What of his childhood? How about the years as a teenager and a young man? Men have tried to place Jesus in this region or that, but no hard facts are to be found. If it were important to our salvation, they would have been placed in the Bible. But to no avail, such was not the case. Some say that Joseph had died while Jesus was a youngster. We know that he was alive when Jesus was twelve, Luke 2:41 "Now his parents went to Jerusalem every year at the feast of the Passover. And when he was twelve years old, they went up to Jerusalem after the custom of the feast." But what happened after is not told. No mention is made of Joseph in Jesus' ministry. Somewhere, sometime, Joseph must have passed away. This left Jesus, the eldest son, to provide for his mother and his brothers. Later, as Jesus hung on the cross he told His mother that John was to be her son and that she was to be John's mother. John 19:26 " When Jesus therefore saw his mother, and the disciple standing by, whom he loved, he saith unto his mother, Woman, behold thy son! Then saith he to the disciple, behold thy mother! And from that hour that disciple took her unto his own home." Hanging on the cross, in the very throws of death, in pain unknown to you and me, His concern is for the welfare of his mother. Faithful even unto death. A true gentleman.

Jesus became our high priest at the age of thirty. Jesus was baptized, not for the remission of sins, for he was without sin, but to fulfill all righteousness. The high priest was initiated into his office by washing and anointing. He was washed of John in the river Jordan and anointed by God with the Holy Ghost. Baptized into the priesthood.

Jesus was such a magnetic personality that he could walk past a man named Phillip and say simply to him follow me and Phillip did.

The day after Jesus was baptized of John, he was walking past John and two of John's disciples. John spoke up and said of Jesus, Behold the lamb of God. The two disciples hearing him speak such, followed after Jesus. Blessed is the one that doesn't hesitate to follow. He who hesitates is lost. No hesitation in the actions of these two. Jesus turned and said, "What seek ye?" This is graciousness in action. To prevent the two from being embarrassed in addressing him, after hearing the character John had given him, Jesus turned and gave them a chance to explain themselves. Jesus still asks this question today. What do you seek in the company you keep? What do you seek in the conversations you engage in? What do you seek in the works you do? Do you seek humiliation, illumination, justification, edification, or sanctification of your soul? Or do you just seek self-gratification?

"Rabbi, where dwellest thou?" Teacher, where do you live so that we may come and learn from you? We know that you are a teacher sent from God. He sayeth unto them, Come and see. Jesus does not dwell in the tumult of worldly affairs, nor in worldly pleasures, nor in carelessness or indolence but in a humble and contrite spirit, in the spirit of faith, of forgiveness, of obedience. Jesus can be found dwelling in the praises of his people. He dwells in the handclaps and in the hallelujahs. He can be found wherever two or three are gathered together in his name. To you, dear friend, he says Come and see.

One of these men was Andrew, who ran and found his brother Simon Peter, and said, "We have found the messiah the Christ." The next day Jesus went into Galilee, and findeth Phillip, and sayeth unto him, "Follow Me." Simple, not a long protracted plea, just simply, follow me. Men work their lives through to win to the LORD a few followers. Working day and night, teaching, pleading, begging, trying to show others the simplicity that is in Christ, yet multitudes will reject the only thing that will give them relief. Jesus the Christ. But Jesus said just a simple, "Follow Me." The whole key is that these men were looking for the messiah. Phillip findeth Nathanael, and saith unto him, we have found him of whom Moses in the law, and the prophets did write, Jesus of Nazareth, the son of Joseph. And Nathanael said unto him, can there any good thing come out of Nazareth? Phillip saith unto him, "Come and see."

"Come and see." The universal call. Come and see the Lord Jesus Christ. Psalms 34:8 "O taste and see that the Lord he is good: blessed is the man that trusteth in him."

PORTRAIT 2   01/20/1990

PSM 45:1 MY HEART IS INDITING A GOOD MATTER:
I SPEAK THE THINGS WHICH I HAVE MADE TOUCHING THE KING:
MY TONGUE IS THE PEN OF A READY WRITER

As I write this message for this Sunday, war has broken out in the Middle East. My son is in St. Louis taking his physical, reactivated by the Marines after serving four years of active duty. Many of you are in the same boat. My prayers are for your sons and husbands also. I feel, we are witnessing a time of the fulfilling of a great prophecy. I do not believe in Christian wars. I do not believe there has ever been a Christian war fought on the level of mankind. Christian wars are fought in the spiritual battles of life not with guns and killing. I am not a pacifist, I believe in defending what is mine. I believe in defending my wife and children, my home, those things that were given to me for a stewardship responsibility. I believe the Bible supports that view. Sadam Hussan may say that this is a holy war if he wishes, I do not know what his religion teaches, I do know what the Word of God says and teaches. There are no Protestant and Catholic wars. There are no Moslem and Christian wars. For if the two sides knew what the title they take upon themselves teaches they wouldn't be fighting in the streets as they have been. We are living in a time unparalleled in history except in it's corruption. My breath is held in anticipation of the next step, the next scripture to be fulfilled. I've had the baptism of the Holy Ghost for nearly nineteen years and never, I say never have I seen so many backsliders coming home to Jesus. Young men and women, older folks, children, hundreds, no thousands coming back to the Father's house. This is revival folks. I don't want to be pictured as one of these nuts that walk up and down the streets with a sandwich sign saying, "The end is near." However, folks the feeling is in the air. If anyone attacks Israel, the blood will run to the horse's bridle and this is the time of the end. Look up your redemption draweth nigh. Ezekiel 38, 39 Read it. Ezek 37:21,22 read this also. Ezek 38:20 ...And the mountains shall be thrown down, and the steep places shall fall, and every wall shall fall to the ground. Verse 22, And I will plead against him with pestilence and with blood, and I will rain upon him and upon his bands, and upon many people that are with him, an overflowing rain, and great hailstones, fire, and brimstone. Zechariah 14 read this one. After this or during this war that will or is taking place right now, Daniel 8:23- "And in the latter time of their kingdom, when the transgressors are come to the full, a king of fierce countenance, and understanding dark sentences, shall stand up. And his power shall be mighty, but not by his own power:(the incarnate Satan) and he shall destroy wonderfully (wondrously), and shall prosper, and practice, and shall destroy the mighty and holy people (the Jews). And through his policy, also he shall cause craft to prosper (by the mark of the beast rev 13:17) in his hand, and he shall magnify himself in his heart, (2 Thes 2:3-4) and by peace shall destroy many: he shall also stand up against the Prince of princes,(Jesus) but shall be broken without hand. 2 Thes 2:3-4 "Let no man deceive you by any means: for that day shall not come except there come a falling away first, and the man of sin be revealed, the son of perdition, Who opposeth and exalteth himself above all that is called God, or that is worshipped, so that he as God sitteth in the temple of God, shewing himself that he is God." All of this above scriptures means that what is happening in the middle east, what is happening with the Jews returning to Israel, what is happening to the united Europe, all of Europe is uniting together in a common market scheduled to happen on Jan 1 1993 It's called EEC92. They have their own currency, policies, laws, on and on it goes, the whole world is aligning themselves with this common market. The Japanese are buying into every European business they can before the doors close. EEC92, and look what is happening in the churches throughout the land, all these things are the fulfillment and the preparation of the fulfillment of scriptures. It is the end time. How easy it is for the person that doesn't know the scriptures to bury their head under the protection of their wing and forget the daystar shines bright out side of their windows. Go ahead and ignore the signs, the Jews did when Jesus came the first time.

    Two weeks ago, we began a series on A Portrait of Christ. The only basis we have of forming a portrait of Jesus Christ is the written word of God. By searching the scriptures, we can form a word picture of the Man Jesus Christ. Looking in the book of Galatians 5:22 gives the description of Jesus Christ. The Spirit spoken of here is the Spirit of Christ, which the believer shall receive, according to Acts 2:38, when he repents and is baptized in the name of Jesus Christ for the remission of his sins.

    Spoken of was Isaiah 53:2 for he shall grow up before him as a tender plant, and as a root out of dry ground: he hath no form nor comeliness, and when we shall see him, there is no beauty that we should desire him. He is despised and rejected of men, a man of sorrows, and acquainted with grief: and we hid as it were our faces from him:" Does this scripture refer to his personal appearance? I think not. Spoken of was the love and compassion that Jesus had even though he hung on the cross in the throws of death. His concern was for the welfare of his mother. While he hung on the cross he spoke to the thief beside him, "Today thou shalt be with me in paradise." Who is this man of compassion called Jesus? What is your mind's image of him? Do you fancy him as one easily rode over? Someone to walk on and take advantage of? Someone to be delt harshly with then discarded? Of no consequence? Just a man that was abused then hung for the whole world to gape at? You don't know him then. This week we shall take a tour through the Word of God and see more of the compassionate Christ.

John 21:25 "And there are also many other things which Jesus did, the which, if they should be written every one, I suppose that even the world itself could not contain the books that should be written. "

Galatians 5:22 The Fruit of the Spirit is love, joy, peace, longsuffering, gentleness, goodness, faith, meekness, temperance. The picture of Christ as he walked the face of the earth. Greater love hath no man then this that a man lay down his life for his friends.

There is no greater feeling in the world then to have all these fruits working in your life at the same time. Surely you've had one or two or many of these things working in your life but have you had all of them working at the same time? In this person is no malice. There is absolutely no hard feeling for anyone in your heart. You believe whatever anyone tells you. You do not loose your temper at anyone. On and on this list goes. Only with the Holy Ghost alive and well in your life can you live this kind of life. How would it feel if you didn't have that hard feeling for that man at work? How about when you were ripped off at the garage the last time you had your car worked on. Well you felt like you got ripped off anyway. Lets look at compassion in the works when we look at the life of one called Peter. Impetuous Peter, the apostle with the shoe shaped mouth. Peter, a fisherman, the son of a fisherman. Naturally impulsive, tenderhearted, full of contradictions, presumptuous yet timid, self sacrificing yet self seeking, Gifted with spiritual insight yet dense and slow to apprehend the deeper truths at times, this man became the rock and foundation of mans' faith after his conversion or baptism with the

Holy Ghost. Peter, full of failures, full of denials of Christ, full of self-seeking, is like the story of many of your lives. Just can't seem to make the grade that you have set for yourselves. You think that you are unworthy of any consideration by Jesus Christ. Well, do you think that he came to seek and save those that didn't need any help? The worst thing that could have ever been said was the statement that "God helps them that help themselves." If you can help yourself then why do you need God? A drowning man cannot be saved until he is utterly exhausted and ceases to make the slightest effort to save himself." Only when you quit struggling in your own power and rely upon the Lord will he help you out of your troubles. Your troubles. The hardest part is to realize that the greater part of the troubles that you have are created by yourself. We've been taught throughout our lives that, you got yourself into trouble, get yourself out. You broke it you fix it. we're responsible for our own actions. That's adulthood we're told. I have an adult children who are responsible for their actions, but I wouldn't hesitate to help them out of their troubles. Would you hesitate to help your children? We give pleasure to our Heavenly Father too. He is more careful about His children then we could ever be. Why don't you just lean back into His arms and let Him take over?

Jesus had told the disciples to get into a ship and to go to the other side of the sea while he, Jesus, sent the multitude away. Mat 14:23 "But the ship was now in the midst of the sea, tossed with the waves: for the wind was contrary. And in the fourth watch of the night, Jesus went unto them, walking on the sea. And when the disciples saw him walking on the sea, they were troubled, saying It is a spirit, and they cried out for fear. But straightway Jesus spake unto them saying, be of good cheer, it is I, be not afraid. And Peter answered him and said, Lord, if it be thou, bid me come unto thee on the water. And he said, Come. and when Peter was come down out of the ship, he walked on the water, to go to Jesus. But when he saw the wind boisterous, he was afraid, and beginning to sink, he cried, saying, Lord save me. And immediately Jesus stretched forth his hand, and caught him, and said unto him, O thou of little faith, wherefore didst thou doubt?" Just think there were twelve on that boat but only impetuous Peter got out and walked on the water. There's something to be said for just doing without figuring out if it will happen or not. I think there was a grin on Jesus' face when he rebuked Peter. I don't think that was a real severe rebuke. Jesus was happy that Peter got out of the boat. Another point is that the second that Peter began to sink, Jesus grabbed him. Get the point. If your walking on the waters by faith and you begin to sink, Jesus will rescue you. The only thing that keeps you from walking by faith is your unbelief. You either don't believe that God will regard your prayers, or you simply don't think God hears you. I understand I've been there. Unworthy of consideration. Unworthy of a second glance. Unworthy of forgiveness. Unworthy of Calvary. Unworthy of the Master's touch. The song goes *"Just as I am without one plea, but that thy blood was shed for me and that thou bidd'st me come to thee*

just as I am and waiting not to rid my soul of one dark blot to thee whose blood can cleanse each spot

just as I am though tossed about with many a conflict, many a doubt fighting fears within, without

Just as I am poor wretched blind, sight, riches, healing of the mind Yea all I need in thee I find

Just as I am thou wilt receive, wilt welcome, pardon, cleanse, relieve Because thy promise I believe" Charlotte Elliot 1835

Friend, It's not because we're worthy of the blood of Christ. It's not because we deserve salvation. It's not because of righteousness of our own doing. No, It is simply because of the Grace of God. Grace, not worthiness. Grace, not because we deserve it. Grace, free grace. Anything other than free grace isn't grace at all. You fell. You've slipped. You were Christian and you've sinned. Well, while your laying face down in the mud crying about your failure, think how it would be if every child that ever tried to walk, stayed down when he fell. No one would walk would they? Push yourself up to your knees, ask God to forgive you for your indiscretion. Get up and carry on. Who cares what that dude you work with thinks. He may call you a hypocrite, but you know your forgiven. He'll find out after a while that your true blue. Wouldn't you rather go to heaven forgiven though scorned by that man, then to wind up in hell? Look, time is very short. The rapture is at hand. The master says "Arise, my love, my fair one, and come away." the winter of your desolation is past Christian friend. Reach out like that woman with the issue of blood, all her money spent on a cure, now reaching out to touch the hem of the garment of the Master. Healing is in that touch. Lift up the hands that hang down, and the feeble knees, and make straight paths for your feet.

PORTRAIT 3   01/27/1991

PSM 45:1 MY HEART IS INDITING A GOOD MATTER:
I SPEAK THE THINGS WHICH I HAVE MADE TOUCHING THE KING:
MY TONGUE IS THE PEN OF A READY WRITER

<u>**Sometimes**</u> it is difficult to put into words the mind picture you have of someone. The last two weeks we have attempted to bring you a word picture of Jesus Christ. Last week, by using the apostle Peter, one or more of the attribute of Christ was presented. the week before the Scripture given in Galatians was used to show the Spirit of Christ and his attributes. Last week, war was spoken of and how there never has been a Christian war. That those calling themselves Christian, make war on other religions. Be sure the word Christian was used not religious. Religion crucified Christ, not embraced him.

Oh that I could paint a portrait of Christ so appealing that no one listening could resist coming to know him. Have you ever had a friend that you just loved to be around? I know, sooner or later the fun of it wears off and you fray each other's nerves. Jesus Christ never will, I say Never be presumptuous. He will never take advantage of a relationship. He is a true friend that sticketh closer than a brother. He won't let you down no matter how many times you may let him down. Mat 18:21 "Then came Peter to him, and said, Lord, how oft shall my brother sin against me, and I forgive him? Till seven times? Jesus saith unto him, I say not unto thee, until seven times: but until seventy times seven." If Jesus Christ expects you to forgive 70 times 7, then how much do you think he will forgive you? He won't even keep track. You've failed? Get up, dust yourself off. Ask Christ to forgive you and forgive yourself. Repent of it. That means, you won't do it again.

I'll tell you how wonderful Jesus is, Psms 103:13 " Just as a father has compassion on his children, so the Lord has compassion on them that fear Him." He takes our sins and puts them as far away as the east is from the west. Psm 103:12 " As far as the east is from the west , so far hath he removed our transgressions from us." Don't think that this is a license to sin because Galatians 5:13 says "..ye have been called unto liberty, only use not liberty for an occasion to the flesh, but by love serve one another." and 1 Pet 2:16 "As free, and not using your liberty for a cloak of maliciousness, but as the servants of God." Let the Word teach you how that Christ has freed us from the bondage of the law and of sin. Luke says that, Jesus stood in the synagogue on the Sabbath day and there was brought a book, the book of Isaiah, for him to read, and when he had opened the book and found the place where it was written in Isaiah Luke 4:18 "The spirit of the Lord is upon me, because he hath anointed me to preach the gospel to the poor, he hath sent me to heal the broken hearted, to preach deliverance to the captives, and recovering of sight to the blind, to set a liberty them that are bruised, to preach the acceptable year of the Lord. And he closed the book, and gave it again to the minister, and sat down. And the eyes all of them that were in the synagogue were fastened on him. And he began to say unto them, This day is this scripture fulfilled in your ears." He had stopped reading Isaiah at a comma, and not a period. And that was the reason they all looked at him. But when he said, "today is this scripture fulfilled in your ears." Then he proclaimed himself to be the messiah, the Christ.

The rest of the scripture in Isaiah read, "and the day of vengeance of our God, to comfort all that mourn, To appoint unto them that mourn in Zion, to give beauty for ashes, the oil of joy for mourning, the garment of praise for the spirit of heaviness, that they might be called trees of righteousness, the planting of the LORD, that he might be glorified." They waited for Jesus to finish the scripture reading they all knew so well. But instead, he spoke, "This day is this scripture fulfilled in your ears."

Jesus Christ came to heal the brokenhearted, The last part of the verse is for his second coming. He closed the book because the rest of the Scripture would have carried us into the second coming after this present age had come to an end. Now is the acceptable time. Now is the day of salvation. Jesus came to heal the broken hearted. Are you suffering today? To set a liberty them that are bruised. Are you beaten and bruised by the trials of today and by sin? To preach deliverance to the captives. Are you a slave to sin? are you a slave to what and who you are? To preach the acceptable year of the Lord. Every fiftieth year was the year of Jubilee. The year that every man received his possessions back and every man was returned to his own family. Those that had been sold into slavery for payment of a debt were set free. The land that had to be sold went back to it's original owner, there wasn't such a thing as a foreclosure. God had given the land, not man, and God set it up so that a few wouldn't wind up with all. Fifty years and everything was restored to it's original owners. It was the great emancipation every fifty years. The acceptable year of the Lord. Jesus came to restore those that were sold into sin by the desires of the flesh. Sold on the auction block of desire. Remember that

Romans 6:23 says "For the wages of sin is death," Sin has a price, a high price, a very high price. Death. Eternal death. Forever death. I'm telling you, A Man can't bargain to sell his soul to the Devil, more than likely, it's already been bought for some meager price that would embarrass the tar out of every one of us. The acceptable year of the Lord. The year of your life that could very well be the greatest year you have ever known, if. Child of God, to you he says, "The night is far spent, the day is at hand: let us therefore cast off the works of darkness, and let us put on the armor of light. Let us walk honestly, as in the day, not in rioting and drunkenness, not in chambering and wantonness, not in strife and envying, but put on the Lord Jesus Christ, and make not provision for the flesh, to fulfill the lusts thereof. Gal 5:1 "Stand fast therefore in the liberty wherewith Christ hath made us free, and be not entangled again with the yoke of bondage."

"The spirit of the Lord is upon me, because he hath anointed me to preach the gospel to the poor, he hath sent me to heal the broken hearted, to preach deliverance to the captives, and recovering of sight to the blind, to set a liberty them that are bruised, to preach the acceptable year of the Lord. To set at liberty them that are bruised," Mat 12:20 says "A bruised reed shall he not break, and a smoking flax shall he not quench, till he send forth judgment unto victory." A reed, A single reed, signifies weakness. A bruised reed must signify a weakness, or a state of weakness that borders on total spiritual death. Life plays us some very hard lessons.

Most are to the heart, to the depth of our very soul. Some are killing wounds that take the life out of us, but they don't have to be. Jesus was despised and rejected of all men, yet he was victorious. You see he had nothing to prove to anyone. We try to prove our worthiness to others thus leaving ourselves open for devastating blows to the ego. You do not need acceptance from others, you need acceptance into the family of God the body of Christ. You need to please God and not man. If indeed you do please God, then no man can point a finger of accusation at you and cluck their collective tongue at the wrongs you do in trying to please man. Who do you serve? God or man? Whose servant are you? Please God and not man. The Lord Jesus wants you to succeed in all your endeavors. He will not break or crush you, He will gently, ever so gently heal your bruises. And a smoking flax shall he not quench. Flax was used as the wick in oil lamps. But after all the oil had been burnt out of the lamp, used up, the flax would continue to smoke. The lamp is your lamp to light the way for others to see Christ in you. The oil is the Holy Ghost which you receive when you repented of your sins and was baptized in to that Name above all names, Jesus Christ. If you've let the oil run out of your life, your flax will smoke, and Jesus won't put out your small smoking flame, He'll encourage you to seek the addition of more oil of the Holy Ghost by compassionate wooing. Jesus won't quench even the slightest amount of desire you have for salvation, friend. He will treat you with greatest tenderness you have ever known, encouraging you to seek after him. "A bruised reed shall he not break, and a smoking flax shall he not quench," "The spirit of the Lord is upon me, because he hath anointed me to preach the gospel to the poor, he hath sent me to heal the broken hearted, to preach deliverance to the captives, and recovering of sight to the blind, to set a liberty them that are bruised, to preach the acceptable year of the Lord. But the fruit of the Spirit is Love, joy, peace, longsuffering, gentleness, goodness, faith, meekness, temperance: against such there is no law. And they that are Christ's have crucified the flesh with the affections and lusts. Does that say anything to you?

    The apostle Peter, close to the Lord, part of the inner circle, one that was quick to let the Lord know that he would stand with him even to death. Good ol Peter, Cephus, the rock, the one that got out of the boat to walk on the water. The fisherman. Good ol Peter. Jesus said, "Whom do men say that I am?" Peter said, "Thou art the Christ." later "Peter answered and said unto him, though all men shall be offended because of thee, yet will I never be offended. Jesus said unto him, "Verily I say unto thee, That this night, before the cock crow, thou shalt deny me Thrice. Peter said unto him, Though I should die with thee, yet will I not deny thee. That night, the very same night, Peter slept while Jesus prayed, And he cometh unto the disciples, and findeth them asleep, and saith unto Peter, "What, could ye not watch with me one hour?" He then went back to prayer And he came and found them asleep again: for their eyes were heavy. And he left them, and went away again, and prayed the third time, This was the night Jesus was taken in the Garden. The most castigating scripture is in Mat 26:56 "Then all the disciples forsook him, and fled. And they that had laid hold on Jesus led him away to Caiaphas the high priest, where the scribes and the elders were assembled. But Peter followed him afar off unto the high priests palace, and went in, and sat with the servants, to see the end....Now Peter sat without in the palace: and a damsel came unto him, saying, Thou also wast with Jesus of Galilee. But he denied before them all, saying, I know not what thou sayest. And when he was gone out into the porch, another maid saw him, and said unto them that were there, This fellow was also with Jesus of Nazareth. And again he denied with an oath, I do not know the man. And after a while came unto him the that stood by, and said to Peter, Surely thou also art one of them, for thy speech betrayed thee. Then began he to curse and to swear, saying, I know not the man. And immediately the cock crew. And Peter remembered the word of Jesus, which said unto him, Before the cockcrow, thou shalt deny me thrice. And he went out, and wept bitterly." Have you ever failed Jesus to the point that you've went and wept bitterly? Thoroughly discussed with yourself? Discouraged by your actions? I think that Peter probably spent the next three days with his face hidden from all. Later, after Jesus was resurrected and seen of Mary Magdalene and the other Mary, the young man in the sepulcher, and the angel said to them to go and tell the disciples and Peter what they had seen. The next time you read of Peter was on the first day of the week in Luke 24:12 "Then arose Peter, and ran unto the sepulcher, and stooped down, and beheld the linen clothes laid by themselves, and departed, wondering in himself at that which was come to pass. Later in John, Peter, Thomas, Nathaniel, the sons of Zebedee, and two other disciples went fishing. Fished all-night and caught nothing. When morning was come, Jesus stood on the shore: but the disciples knew not that it was Jesus. then Jesus saith unto them, Children have ye any meat? They answered No. And he said unto them, Cast your net on the right side if the ship, and ye shall find." The first to recognize that it was Jesus was Peter. He didn't walk on the water this time. He dove in and swam to the Lord of Glory. After they were done eating the fish that Jesus had prepared for them, Jesus turned to Peter, Simon, "son of Jonas, lovest thou me more than these? Yea Lord, thou knowest that I love thee. Feed my sheep. He saith it him again the second time, Simon sin of Jonas, lovest thou me? Yea lord, thou knowest that I love thee. He saith unto him, Feed my sheep He saith unto him the third time, Simon son of Jonas, lovest thou me? Peter was grieved because he said unto him the third time Lovest thou me? Lord thou knowest all things: thou knowest that I love thee. Feed my sheep. Verily verily I say unto thee, when thou wast young thou girdest thyself, and walkest whither thou wouldest: but when thou shalt be old, thou shalt stretch forth thy hands and another shall gird thee, and carry thee whither thou wouldest not. Peter turned and saw John asking Jesus which is he that betrayeth thee? And what shall we do with him?" Jesus said "If I will that he tarry till I come, what is that to thee?" Peter denied, bitterly denied Jesus yet Jesus delt with him with compassion that is unheard of in our lives. "Peter, lovest thou me more than these?" I don't know what that does to you friend but I want to weep. Peter denied Christ with swearing cussing if you please. yet he was forgiven.

PORTRAIT 4   04/07/1991

PSM 45:1 MY HEART IS INDITING A GOOD MATTER:
I SPEAK THE THINGS WHICH I HAVE MADE TOUCHING THE KING:
MY TONGUE IS THE PEN OF A READY WRITER

Another Easter has come and gone. The tomb is empty. The Cross-no longer holds the savior. Still, there are some that see the crucified savior still on the cross. He said destroy this temple and in three days I will raise it up. Crucifixion, the most horrible death one could ever die. Yet, he went willingly that we might be free from sin and have life everlasting. Is it something that I am worthy of? I think not. I'm worthy only of death. Is it something that I can earn? No, there is only one price to pay and that is acceptance of the sacrifice that Jesus accomplished. Can I, by doing great works, by paying a great homage, by walking on my knees upon broken glass, earn or be worthy of this great salvation? Even if you were to give your body to be burned, you couldn't even earn one splinter from the tree that Jesus died on.

Have you ever had a friend that you just loved to be around? Jesus Christ will never take advantage of a relationship. He is a true friend that sticketh closer than a brother. Jesus won't let you down no matter how many times you may fail him. Mat 18:21 "Then came Peter to him, and said, Lord, how oft shall my brother sin against me, and I forgive him? Till seven times? Jesus saith unto him, I say not unto thee, until seven times: but until seventy times seven." Remember the 490 from last week? If Jesus Christ expects you to forgive 70 times 7, then how much do you think he will forgive you? He won't even keep track. You've failed? Get up, dust yourself off. Ask Christ to forgive you and forgive yourself. Repent. That means, you won't do it again.

I'll tell you how wonderful Jesus is, Psms 103:13 " Just as a father has compassion on his children, so the Lord has compassion on them that fear Him." He takes our sins and puts them as far away as the east is from the west. Psm 103:12 " As far as the east is from the west , so far hath he removed our transgressions from us." This is not a license to sin. Galatians 5:13 says "..ye have been called unto liberty, only use not liberty for an occasion to the flesh, but by love serve one another." and 1 Pet 2:16

"As free, and not using your liberty for a cloak of maliciousness, but as the servants of God." Let the Word teach you how that Christ has freed us from the bondage of the law and of sin. Luke says that, Jesus stood in the synagogue on the Sabbath day and there was brought a book, the book of Isaiah, for him to read, and when he had opened the book and found the place where it was written. Luke 4:18 "The spirit of the Lord is upon me, because he hath anointed me to preach the gospel to the poor, he hath sent me to heal the broken hearted, to preach deliverance to the captives, and recovering of sight to the blind, to set at liberty them that are bruised, to preach the acceptable year of the Lord. And he closed the book, and gave it again to the minister, and sat down. And the eyes all of them that were in the synagogue were fastened on him. And he began to say unto them, This day is this scripture fulfilled in your ears." He had stopped reading Isaiah at a comma, and not a period. And that was the reason they all looked at him, waiting for him to finish the scripture reading. But, he said, "today is this scripture fulfilled in your ears." He proclaimed himself to be the messiah, the Christ.

The rest of the scripture read, Isa 61:2 "and the day of vengeance of our God, to comfort all that mourn, To appoint unto them that mourn in Zion, to give beauty for ashes, the oil of joy for mourning, the garment of praise for the spirit of heaviness, that they might be called trees of righteousness, the planting of the LORD, that he might be glorified." They were waiting for Jesus to finish the scripture reading. They all knew it so well. Instead, he spoke, "This day is this scripture fulfilled in your ears."

Jesus Christ came to heal the brokenhearted, The last part of the verse is for his second coming. He stopped at a comma because the rest of the Scripture would have carried us into the second coming of Christ, after this present age had come to an end. Now is the acceptable time. Now is the day of salvation.

Jesus came to heal the broken hearted.

Are you suffering?

To set a liberty them that are bruised.

Are you beaten and bruised by the trials and tribulations of today and by sin?

To preach deliverance to the captives.

Are you a slave to sin?

Are you a slave to what and who you are?

To preach the acceptable year of the Lord.

Every fiftieth year was the year of Jubilee. The year that every man received his possessions back and every man was returned to his own family. Isn't it strange that

Pentecost is fifty days from the Passover, from Easter? The Holy Ghost was given on the day of Pentecost. The only liberty that has ever been given is the spiritual liberty given by the Holy Ghost. In the year of the Jubilee, those that had been sold into slavery for payment of a debt were set free. The land that had to be sold went back to it's original owner, there wasn't such a thing as a foreclosure. God had given the land, not man, and God set it up so that a few wouldn't wind up with all. Fifty years and everything was restored to it's original owners. It was the great emancipation every fifty years. The acceptable year of the Lord. Jesus came to restore those that were sold into sin by the desires of the flesh. Sold on the auction block of sin. Romans 6:23 says "For the wages of sin is death," Sin has a price, a high price, a very high price. It's Death. Eternal death. Forever death. I'm telling you, A Man can't bargain to sell his soul to the Devil, more than likely, it's already been bought for some meager price. The acceptable year of the Lord. This year could very well be the greatest year you have ever known, if. Child of God, to you he says, "The night is far spent, the day is at hand: let us therefore cast off the works of darkness, and let us put on the armor of light. Let us walk honestly, as in the day, not in rioting and drunkenness, not in chambering and wantonness, not in strife and envying, but put on the Lord Jesus Christ, and make not provision for the flesh, to fulfill the lusts thereof". Gal 5:1 "Stand fast therefore in the liberty wherewith Christ hath made us free, and be not entangled again with the yoke of bondage."

"The spirit of the Lord is upon me, because he hath anointed me to preach the gospel to the poor, he hath sent me to heal the broken hearted, to preach deliverance to the captives, and recovering of sight to the blind, to set a liberty them that are bruised, to preach the acceptable year of the Lord. "To set at liberty them that are bruised," Mat 12:20 says "A bruised reed shall he not break, and a smoking flax shall he not quench, till he send forth judgment unto victory." A reed, A single reed, a weak bruised reed. A state of weakness that borders on total spiritual death. Life deals us some very hard lessons.

Most are to the heart, to the depth of our very soul. Some are killing wounds that take the life out of us, but they don't have to be. Jesus was despised and rejected of all men. I've never known that feeling, have you? You see though, Jesus had nothing to prove to anyone. We try to prove our worthiness to others and in doing so, we leave ourselves open for devastating blows to the ego. You don't need the acceptance of others, you need acceptance into the family of God. The body of Christ. You need to please God and not man. If indeed you do please God, no man can point a finger of accusation at you. None can cluck their accusing tongue at you. God or man? Whose servant are you? Please God and not man. The Lord Jesus wants you to succeed in all your endeavors. He will not break or crush you. He will gently, ever so gently heal your bruises. And a smoking flax shall he not quench. Flax was used as the wick in oil lamps. But after all the oil had been burnt out of the lamp, used up, the flax would continue to smoke. The lamp is your lamp to light the way for others to see Christ in you. The oil is the Holy Ghost which you receive when you repented of your sins and was baptized in to that Name above all names, Jesus Christ. If the oil has run out of your life, your flax will smoke, but Jesus won't put out your small smoking flame. He'll encourage you to seek the oil of the Holy Ghost by compassionate wooing. Jesus won't quench even the slightest amount of desire you have for salvation, friend. He will treat you with greatest tenderness you have ever known encouraging you to seek after him. "A bruised reed shall he not break, and a smoking flax shall he not quench," "The spirit of the Lord is upon me, because he hath anointed me to preach the gospel to the poor, he hath sent me to heal the broken hearted, to preach deliverance to the captives, and recovering of sight to the blind, to set a liberty them that are bruised, to preach the acceptable year of the Lord. But the fruit of the Spirit is Love, joy, peace, longsuffering, gentleness, goodness, faith, meekness, temperance: against such there is no law. And they that are Christ's have crucified the flesh with the affections and lusts. Does that say anything to you?

    The apostle Peter, close to the Lord, part of the inner circle, one that was quick to let the Lord know that he would stand with him even to the end. Good ol Peter, Cephus, the rock, the one that got out of the boat to walk on the water. The fisherman. Jesus said, "Whom do men say that I am?" Peter said, "Thou art the Christ." later "Peter answered and said unto him, though all men shall be offended because of thee, yet will I never be offended. Jesus said unto him, Verily I say unto thee, That this night, before the cock crow, thou shalt deny me Three times. Peter said unto him, Though I should die with thee, yet will I not deny thee. : That night, the very same night, Peter slept while Jesus prayed, "And he cometh unto the disciples, and findeth them asleep, and saith unto Peter, What, could ye not pray with me one hour?" He then went back to prayer And he came and found them asleep again: for their eyes were heavy. And he left them, and went away again, and prayed the third time," it was this night that Jesus was captured in the Garden of Gethsemane. Then, all the disciples forsook him and fled. And they that had laid hold on Jesus led him away to Caiaphas the high priest, where the scribes and the elders were assembled. But Peter followed him afar off unto the high priests palace, and went in, and sat with the servants, to see the end....Now Peter sat without in the palace: and a damsel came unto him, saying, Thou also wast with Jesus of Galilee. But he denied before them all, saying, I know not what thou sayest. And when he was gone out into the porch, another maid saw him, and said unto them that were there, This fellow was also with Jesus of Nazareth. And again he denied with an oath, I do not know the man. And after a while came unto him the that stood by, and said to Peter, Surely thou also art one of them, for thy speech betrayed thee. Then began he to curse and to swear, saying, I know not the man. And immediately the cock crew. And Peter remembered the word of Jesus, which said unto him, Before the cockcrow, thou shalt deny me thrice. And he went out, and wept bitterly. " Have you ever failed Jesus to the point that you've went and wept bitterly? Thoroughly discussed with yourself? Discouraged by your actions? I think that Peter probably spent the next three days with his face hidden from all. Later, after Jesus was resurrected and seen of Mary Magdalene and the other Mary, the young man in the sepulcher. And the angel said to them to go and tell the disciples and Peter what they had seen. The next time you read of Peter was on the first day of the week in Luke 24:12 "Then arose Peter, and ran unto the sepulcher, and stooped down, and beheld the linen clothes laid by themselves, and departed, wondering in himself at that which was come to pass." Later in John 21:2 Peter, Thomas, Nathaniel, the sons of Zebedee, and two other disciples went fishing. Fished all-night and caught nothing. When morning was come, Jesus stood on the shore but the disciples knew not that it was Jesus. then Jesus saith unto them, Children have ye any meat? They answered No. And he said unto them, Cast your net on the right side if the ship, and ye shall find. The first to recognize that it was Jesus was Peter. He didn't walk on the water this time. He dove in and swam to the Lord of Glory. After they were done eating the fish that Jesus had prepared for them, Jesus turned to Peter, Simon, son of Jonas, lovest thou me more than these? Yea Lord, thou knowest that I love thee. Feed my sheep. He saith it him again the second time, Simon son of Jonas, lovest thou me? Yea lord, thou knowest that I love thee. He saith unto him, Feed my sheep. He saith unto him the third time, Simon son of Jonas, lovest thou me? Peter was grieved because he said unto him the third time Lovest thou me? Lord thou knowest all things: thou knowest that I love thee. Feed my sheep. Verily verily I say unto thee, when thou wast young thou girdest thyself, and walkest whither thou wouldest: but when thou shalt be old, thou shalt stretch forth thy hands and another shall gird thee, and carry thee whither thou wouldest not. Peter turned and saw

John asking Jesus "which is he that betrayeth thee? And what shall we do with him? " Jesus said "If I will that he tarry till I come, what is that to thee?" Peter denied, bitterly denied Jesus yet Jesus delt with him with compassion that is unheard of in our lives. Peter, lovest thou me more than these? I don't know what that does to you friend but I want to weep. Peter denied Christ, yet he was forgiven. Backsliders, Come home to Jesus. Young men and women, Older folks, children, come back to the Father's house. This is revival folks. Isaiah 53:2 "For he shall grow up before him as a tender plant, and as a root out of dry ground: he hath no form nor comeliness, and when we shall see him, there is no beauty that we should desire him. He is despised and rejected of men, a man of sorrows, and acquainted with grief: and we hid as it were our faces from him:"

John 21:25 "And there are also many other things which Jesus did, the which, if they should be written every one, I suppose that even the world itself could not contain the books that should be written. "

Galatians 5:22 "The Fruit of the Spirit is love, joy, peace, longsuffering, gentleness, goodness, faith, meekness, temperance". In this person there is no malice. There is absolutely no hard feelings for anyone in your heart. You believe whatever anyone tells you. You do not loose your temper at anyone. On and on this list goes. Only with the Holy Ghost alive and well in your life can you live this kind of life. How would it feel if you didn't have any hard feelings? Peter, full of failures, full of denials of Christ, full of self-seeking, is like the story of many of our lives. Just can't seem to make the grade that we have set for ourselves. You think that you are unworthy of any consideration by Jesus Christ. Well, he didn't come to seek and save those that didn't need or want him. That didn't need his help. The worst thing that could have ever been said was the statement that "God helps them that help themselves." If you can help yourself then why do you need God? Only when you quit struggling in your own power and rely upon the Lord will he help you out of your troubles. It's hard to realize that the greatest part of the troubles we have are of our own creation. We've been taught throughout our lives that you got yourself into trouble, get yourself out. Some times it's like chewing fat, the more you chew the bigger it gets. Troubles are that way, They just keep growing the more we worry over them. Responsibility, you broke it you fix it. All our lives we've been taught, your responsible for your own actions. You broke it, you fix it. That's good, we must be responsible to live in society. It's necessary to be responsible for your actions. What kind of society would it be if we were to blame everyone else for our own ignorance? One where every thing you buy has a disclaimer of responsibility for misuse on it. "Do not intentionally concentrate fumes." "May be hazardous to your health." "Do not place hands or feet under mowing deck." "Cigarette smoking may be hazardous to your health." "The manufacture cannot take responsibility for any misuse intended or accidental". We must have responsibility for our own actions. You'll stand before God and give an account for your actions. You'll have no one to argue your case then. But with our own children, now, today, we wouldn't hesitate to help our children out of trouble. Or maybe, it should be put, Help them while they are in their troubles. Give them support, counseling, encouragement. We are a delight to our heavenly Father. He is more careful about His children then we could ever be. Why don't you just lean back into His arms and let Him take over? Let him strengthen you in your time of trouble. He wants to.

Jesus had told the disciples to get into a ship and to go to the other side of the sea while he, Jesus, sent the multitude away. Mat 14:23 "But the ship was now in the midst of the sea, tossed with the waves: for the wind was contrary. And in the fourth watch of the night Jesus went unto them, walking on the sea. And when the disciples saw him walking on the sea, they were troubled, saying It is a spirit, and they cried out for fear. But straightway Jesus spake unto them saying, Be of good cheer, it is I, be not afraid." The storms of life have your ship about ready to sink? Darkness is all about you? You think that you're in the boat alone? Then the voice comes soft and sweet, "Be of good cheer, it is I." And Peter answered him and said, "Lord, if it be thou, bid me come unto thee on the water. And he said, Come." When the storms of life rage, then will come the times of closeness with Jesus, when you of your own will and intent could never do what Jesus would help you to do. Mat 14:25 "Master if it be thou, bid me come unto thee on the water. And when Peter was come down out of the ship, he walked on the water, to go to Jesus. But when he saw the wind boisterous, he was afraid, and beginning to sink, he cried, saying, Lord save me. And immediately Jesus stretched forth his hand, and caught him, and said unto him, O thou of little faith, wherefore didst thou doubt?" Just think there were twelve on that boat but only Peter got out and walked on the water. Was Peter impetuous, or doubting his own ability, or just in love with the Savior? We need some of that out of the boat faith in Christ. There's something to be said for just doing, just trusting to the Lord, without figuring if it will happen or not. I know there was a grin on Jesus' face when Peter got out of the boat. Like a father with a child's first step. Wherefore dist thou doubt? Jesus was happy that Peter got out of the boat. Peter began to sink, Jesus grabbed him. Get the point. If your walking on the waters by faith and you begin to sink through self-doubt, I can't, I can't, Jesus will rescue you, your there by faith in the operation of God.   But the only thing that keeps you from walking by faith is your unbelief, your doubt in your ability to trust in God. You either don't believe that God will regard your prayers, or you simply don't think God hears you. I understand that I've been there. Unworthy of consideration. Unworthy of a second glance. Unworthy of forgiveness. Unworthy of Calvary. Unworthy of the Master's touch. "Just as I am without one plea, but that thy blood was shed for me and that thou bidd'st me come to thee" Charlotte Elliott 1835

      just as I am Friend, It's not because we're worthy of the blood of Christ. It's not because we deserve salvation. It's not because of righteousness of our own doing. No, It is simply because of the Grace of God. Grace, not worthiness. Grace, not because we deserve it. Grace, free grace. Anything other than free grace isn't grace at all. You fell. You've slipped. You were Christian and you've sinned. Well, while your laying face down in the mud crying about your failure, think how it would be if every child that ever tried to walk, stayed down when he fell. No one would walk would they? Push yourself up to your knees, ask God to forgive you for your indiscretion. Get up and carry on. Look, the time is very short. The rapture is at hand. The master says "Arise, my love, my fair one, and come away." the winter of your desolation is past, spring is here, life has come again to you. Reach out like that woman with the issue of blood, all her money spent on a cure, now reaching out to touch the hem of the garment of the Master. Healing is in that touch. Lift up the hands that hang down, and the feeble knees, and make straight paths for your feet. Jesus wants to be your ever-present help in time of need. Your rock in a weary and desolate land. Your rose of Sharon. Your lily of the valley of your life. "Yea though I walk through the valley of the shadow of death.". Life is that valley. Let the shepherd of your soul guide you around the thorns and rocky places of life. Jesus loves you like no other person could ever love you. Lift up your hands right now and call on him. Jesus, Jesus, Jesus. He needs no explanation. He knows. Just acknowledge him. Master, if it be thou, bid me come. Help master I'm drowning. Feel his hand slip into yours. Feel the load being lifted? Jesus I love you.

DIRECT ACCESS   02/10/1991

PSM 45:1 MY HEART IS INDITING A GOOD MATTER:
I SPEAK THE THINGS WHICH I HAVE MADE TOUCHING THE KING:
MY TONGUE IS THE PEN OF A READY WRITER

What can be said about Christ that would make you love him?

What can be said about Jesus that would make you realize your need for him? He is the most accessible God you could ever know. There was a time when it wasn't so, but now he has taken down the middle wall of partition, making access to the Holiest of Holies for all. You need no middleman no intercessor. Why do some think they must go through another god, saint, or person to access the most High? The Bible clearly says in Hebrews 4:13 "Let us therefore come boldly unto the throne of grace, that we may obtain mercy, and find grace to help in time of need." and in 10:19 "Having therefore, brethren, boldness to enter into the holiest by the blood of Jesus. By a new and living way, which he hath consecrated for us, through the veil, that is to say, his flesh: and having a high priest over the house of God, let us draw near with a true heart in full assurance of faith, having our hearts sprinkled from an evil conscience, and our bodies washed with pure water." Jesus Christ the accessible God.

After the creation of man, the age was known as the dispensation of innocence. Man existed on the face of the earth under the most favorable conditions ever known. The land was a veritable garden of luxuriant verdure. Sin was unknown to man. Eastward in Eden were two trees known now to nearly all mankind, the tree of life and the tree of the knowledge of good and evil. You all know the story about the fall of man. This fall brought sin and sin brought death and a wall of separation between God and man. No longer could man boldly walk with God in the cool of the day. It would be near 2500 years before God gave the law of sacrifice to Moses and Romans 5:14 says "Death reigned from Adam to Moses even over them that had not sinned after the similitude of Adam's transgression," Occasionally a man or two had found grace in the eyes of God and God communicated with them. Few though they were. Man in general did not have free access to God. The beginning of the giving of the law and salvation through sacrifice began with the Passover in Egypt. Later God initiated this as a perpetual feast, as a memorial to His bringing them out of Egypt, which is the picture, the representation of sin. Jesus Christ being our Passover lamb whose blood protects us from the death angel, having brought us out, and bought us out of sin by his sinless death on the cross. Being made sin for us. Remember that death entered by one man's sin, Adam's, so life entered by one man's sinless life, Jesus'.

Still, direct access was not permitted.

Laws, laws, laws, page after page of laws governing the conduct of the priests, the people, the offerings, the tribes, the land, everything. Laws, laws, and more laws. In one place a man was stoned for picking up sticks on the Sabbath, in another, because the people murmured against Moses, deadly snakes bit the complainers. After many died and repentance was on their heart, a way of redemption was made by having the bitten people look by faith upon a brazen serpent. It was harsh laws but they were stiff necked people.

Exo 20:22-24 "And the LORD said unto Moses, thus shalt thou say unto the children of Israel, ye have seen that I have talked with you from heaven. Ye shall not make with me gods of silver, neither shall ye make unto you gods of gold. An alter of earth thou shalt make unto me, and shalt sacrifice thereon thy burnt offerings, and thy peace offerings, thy sheep, and thine oxen: in all places where I record my name I will come unto thee, and I will bless thee. "

Exo 21:15 "And he that smiteth his father, or his mother, shall be surely put to death.(some of these laws would be good for today) And he that curseth his father, or his mother shall surely be put to death."

Exo21:24 "Eye for eye, tooth for tooth, hand for hand, foot for foot, burning for burning, wound for wound, stripe for stripe. If a man shall steal an ox, or a sheep, and kill it, or sell it, he shall restore five oxen for an ox, and four sheep for a sheep."

Exo 22:25 " If thou lend money to any of my people that is poor by thee, thou shalt not be to him as a usurer, neither shalt thou lay upon him usury."

Lev 4:27-29 "And if any one of the common people sin through ignorance, while he doeth somewhat against any of the commandments of the LORD concerning things which ought lot to be done and be guilty, Or his sin, which he hath sinned, come to his knowledge: then he shall bring his offering a kid of the goats, a female without blemish, for his sin which he hath sinned. And he shall lay his hand upon the head if the sin offering, and slay the sin offering in the place of the burnt offering."

Burnt offerings, sacrifices, thou shalt, thou shalt not, and still, only the High priest had access to God and that,

Hebrews 9:7 "…only once a year, but not without blood which he offered for himself, and for the errors of the people."

Man, continually sinning had caused this breach in the fellowship with God. Man's sin caused all the laws to be implemented.

1 Tim 1:9 Hebrews 7:19 Gal 3.24 "Knowing this, that the law is not made for a righteous man, but for the lawless and disobedient, for the ungodly and for sinners, for unholy and profane, for murders of fathers and murders of mothers, for manslayers, for whoremongers, for them that defile themselves with mankind, for men stealers, for liars, for perjured persons, and if there be any other thing that is contrary to sound doctrine," The law is for the lawless, them that are a law unto themselves do not need the law. They behave themselves.

Mat 22:36 Master which is the greatest of the commandments? Jesus said, Love the LORD thy God with all thy heart, and with all thy soul, and with all thy mind, and with all thy strength: this is the first commandment. and the second is like, namely this, Thou shalt love thy neighbor as thyself. There is none other greater commandment than these." Jesus said on these two hang all the law and the prophets." These two are the basis for all that was written in the law and the prophets. The golden rule. Do unto others as you would have them do unto you. Not the distorted perverted "Do unto others and split" or "Them that has the gold makes the rules." But Love God totally and your neighbor as yourself. There's not one of us that doesn't pamper the flesh. We love ourselves. The greatest concern we have is for creature comfort. Air conditioning, heating, soft ride, the smell of a new car, fine homes, on and on. I'm not condemning them, just illustrating a point. How do you treat your neighbor? As you treat yourself? Let's start next door.

The law is for the lawless.

Hebrews 7:19 "For the law made nothing perfect, but the bringing in of a better hope did, by the which we draw neigh unto God." Perfection was not in the law, for no man, save Jesus, could fulfill all the law. Jesus said he came to fulfill the law not to destroy it. The law was a school master to bring us to Christ, that we may be justified by faith. Galatians 3:24 "For if there had been a law given which could have given life, verily righteousness should have been by the law. And if then by the law by works." Then we would have had no need for Christ to have died for us. His suffering would have been in vain, just the same as if the blood of bulls and goats could have imparted salvation to us. No, it's not by our own righteousness but by the righteousness of Jesus Christ that we have access to God. Direct Access.

Jesus always had time for everyone. Be it the leper in Matthew 8:2 or a child in luke 18:15. He still has time for you and me.

Zacchaeus in a tree, a rich man, chief among the publicans, sought to see Jesus but could not because of the crowd. Zacchaeus ran forward of the crowd where they soon would pass. Climbing up a sycamore tree, a rich man of considerable stature among the publicans, to catch a glimpse of Jesus. Jesus saw him and what it was Zacchaeus was doing. And when Jesus came to the place, he looked up and saw him and said unto him, "Zacchaeus, make haste, and come down, for today I must abide at thy house." Zacchaeus made haste and came down and received him joyfully. And Zacchaeus stood and said unto the Lord, Behold, Lord, the half of my goods I give to the poor, and if I have taken any thing from any man by false accusation, I restore him fourfold. (the tax collectors had to turn in the tax that the Romans levied, but anything they could extort extra was theirs) And Jesus said unto him, This day is salvation come to this house, forasmuch as he also is a son of Abraham. Zacchaeus the tax collector had found the direct access to God through worship and repentance. Zacchaeus was in a tree but now in the arms of the Lord.

Blind Bartimaeus in Mark 10:47-52. Sat by the highway begging. "And when he heard that it was Jesus of Nazareth, he began to cry out, and say, Jesus, thou son of David, have mercy on me. And many charged that he should hold his peace, but he cried the more a great deal, Thou son of David, have mercy on me. And Jesus stood still, and commanded him to be called. And they call the blind man, saying unto him, Be of good comfort, rise, he calleth thee. And he casting away his coat rose and came to Jesus. Now Jesus knew what it was that this blind man wanted of him but he wanted the blind man to speak it. What will thou that I should do unto thee? The blind man said unto him, Lord, that I might receive my sight. Go thy way thy faith hath made thee whole. And immediately he received his sight, and followed Jesus in the way." Worship, the key to direct access. Bartimaeus called him the Son of David, the messiah, the Christ. Then he called him Lord. Worship stopped the savior in his coarse of the day. Worship opened the way to healing. Worship gave faith. Worship gave direct access to the most High.

And it came to pass, as he went into the house of one off the chief Pharisees to eat bread on the Sabbath day, that they watched him. And, behold, there was a certain man before him which had the dropsy. And Jesus answering spake unto the lawyers and

Pharisees, saying, Is it lawful to heal on the Sabbath day? And they held their peace. and he took him, and healed him, and let him go.

The dead were raised: Luke 8:41 "And behold, there came a man named Jairus, and he was a ruler of the synagogue (this man was second only to the over seer or bishop of the congregation, he was the one that chose who would read the scroll , the book of law, that day. Could this be the same man that brought the scroll of Isaiah to Jesus that fateful day when Jesus read from the Book in Luke 4:18 proclaiming himself to be the Christ?) And behold, there came a man named Jairus,(direct access requires you to come the Master) and he was a ruler of the synagogue: and he fell down at Jesus' feet(second request is to worship him). and besought him greatly(thirdly, you have to lay your wants out in the open) that he would come into his house:(if the master would just come and lay his hands on her she would be healed. Ask in faith believing) For he had one only daughter, about twelve years of age, and she lay dying. But as he went the people thronged him."

Luke 9:43-49 And a woman having an issue of blood twelve years, which had spent all her living upon physicians,(she had exhausted her resources. Why do we wait until we're totally spent to ask Jesus for our needs?) And a woman having an issue of blood twelve years, which had spent all her living upon physicians, neither could be healed of any. Came behind him, and touched the border of his garment: (this was a faith move on her part) and immediately her issue of blood stanched. And Jesus said," Who touched me? When all denied, Peter and they that were with him said , Master, the multitude throng thee and press thee, and sayest thou, Who touched me? And Jesus said, somebody hath touched me: for I perceive that virtue is gone out of me. And when the woman saw that she was not hid, she came trembling, and falling down before him, (here's worship again) she declared unto him before all the people for what cause she had touched him, and how she was healed immediately. And he said unto her, daughter be of good comfort: thy faith hath made thee whole, go in peace. (I well imagine, by this time, Jairus was fit to be tied. His daughter sick unto death and Jesus taking time for everyone that came along.) Then, while he yet spake, there cometh one from the ruler of the synagogue's house, saying too him, Thy daughter is dead, trouble not the master. But when Jesus heard it, he answered him, saying, fear not: believe only, and she shall be made whole. And when he was come into the house, he suffered no man to go in save Peter and James and John, and the father, and the mother of the maiden. And all wept, and bewailed her: but he said, weep not, she is not dead, but sleepeth. And they laughed him to scorn, (or they grinned a ghastly smile showing the contempt they felt for his person and knowledge, ridiculing the truths they couldn't comprehend nor love. No not Jairus nor his wife I'm sure, but the others gathered there.) And they laughed him to scorn, knowing that she was dead. And he put them all out, and took her by the hand, and called, saying, maid arise. And her spirit came again, and she arose straightway: and he commanded to give her meat.

Worship, praise, and prayer are the keys to direct access with God. He's no farther away than one simple word, Jesus. While at work one day, the crane I was using had buttons to make it move in all directions. I hadn't been there very long so I wasn't very familiar with the operation of this piece of machinery. The case the crane was hooked to weigh near 500 pounds. The fixture for the attachment of this piece was chest high. I wanted to lift the structure off the fixture but instead I was trolleying the hoist toward a solid wall. The case began to move at rapid speed as I had the trolley stretched way out, there was a lot of pressure on the cables. The case came toward me, sliding on the fixture, threatening to crush me between the case and the wall. I screamed the only thing that would help, Jesus. I'm telling you, the case stopped. It stopped dead. I praised God for a while you can be sure. There's power in that name. A friend of ours was driving when a car ran into a tank truck in front of her. The truck overturned, and she didn't have time to steer clear of the truck. Collision was inevitable. She shielded her face with her hands and screamed Jesus. When the car came to rest, she hadn't hit the tanker at all. Later the officer at the scene congratulated her on her skillful avoidance of collision with what would have been a fatal accident. She told the officer just what I have reported here. What a mighty God we serve. Folks I'm telling you, Jesus watches over you just as a faithful father would over his children. Who among you wouldn't protect your children?

I've cried out when the pressures of life have just about overcome my strength, Jesus was already on the scene waiting for my cry. Strength would come flowing from the fountainhead of strength, Jesus.

"Behold, I stand at the door and knock", says Jesus in the book of Revelations, "If any man hear my voice and open the door, I will come in to him, and will sup with him, and he with me." Don't be like the one in Solomon's Song Son 5:2 "I sleep, but my heart waketh: it is the voice of my beloved that knocketh, saying, open to me , my sister, my love, my dove, my undefiled: for my head is filled with dew, and my locks with the drops of the night. I have put off my coat, how shall I put it on? I have washed my feet, how shall I defile them? My beloved put in his hand by the hole of the door, and my bowels were moved for him. I rose up to open to my beloved, and my hands dropped with myrrh, and my fingers with sweet smelling myrrh, upon the handles of the lock. I opened to my beloved, but my beloved had withdrawn himself, and was gone: my soul failed when he spake: I sought him, but I could not find him, I called him, but he gave me no answer.

To know the presence of the Most High is truly a good feeling, but to know He came, knocked, and whispered only to be rejected, does not set well with one's soul.

Jesus Christ has an open door policy. We have direct access into the Holiest of Holies where dwells the shekhinah glory of God. Some cannot accept this, cannot accept this as fact. They must use others to make intercession for them. But I'm telling you, You, need to talk to Him yourself, direct. Don't rely on the prayers of others. Tell Jesus what it is that you want him to do in your life. Repent baptize Holy Ghost.

SPEAK TO THE MOUNTAIN   02/03/1991

PSM 45:1 MY HEART IS INDITING A GOOD MATTER:
I SPEAK THE THINGS WHICH I HAVE MADE TOUCHING THE KING:
MY TONGUE IS THE PEN OF A READY WRITER

2 Peter 3:3- " **Knowing this first**, that there shall come in the last days scoffers, walking after their own lusts, and saying, Where is the promise of his coming? for since the fathers fell asleep, all things continue as they were from the beginning of the creation."

Verse 9 " The Lord is not slack concerning his promise, as some men count slackness, but is long suffering to us-ward, not willing that any should perish, but that all should come to repentance. But the day of the Lord will come as a thief in the night, in the which the heavens shall pass away with a great noise, and the elements shall melt with fervent heat, the earth also and the works that are therein shall be burned up. Seeing then that all these shall be dissolved, what manner of persons ought ye to be in all holy conversation and godliness, looking for and hasting unto the coming of the day if God, wherein the heavens being on fire shall be dissolved, and the elements shall melt with fervent heat? Nevertheless we, according to his promise, look for new heavens and a new earth, wherein dwelleth righteousness."

2 peter 3:8 "But, beloved, be not ignorant of this one thing, that one day is with the Lord as a thousand years, and a thousand years as one day."

Psalms 90:4 "For a thousand years in thy sight are but as yesterday when it is past, and as a watch in the night."

Matthew 24:3 "And as he sat upon the mount of Olives the disciples came unto him privately, saying, Tell us, when shall these things be? and what shall be the sign of thy coming? and the end of the world?"

Three questions were asked here.

1. "When shall these things be?" That is, The destruction of the temple which was accomplished by the Roman general Titus in 70 ad
2. "What shall be the sign of thy coming?" Or, How can we tell when you are coming back?

3. "When shall be the end of the world?" The consummation of this age?

xxxxxxxxxxxxxxxxxxxx

Mark 11:22-23 "Have faith in God. For verily I say unto you, That whosoever shall say unto this mountain, be thou removed and be thou cast into the sea, and shall not doubt in his heart, but shall believe that those things which he saith shall come to pass, he shall have whatsoever he saith."

xxxxxxxxxxxxxxxxxxxxx

We are not concerned with what men and women say nor are we concerned with what the agnostic says. We are concerned with what thus sayeth the Lord. David said, "thy word is forever settled in heaven oh Lord." Jesus said, "not one jot or title shall pass away till it all is fulfilled. " Just because men and women doubt the Word of God does not take away from its voracity. People, it's possible in our carnal mind to lose confidence in the word of God. One reason for this doubt, is because of a lack of love for the Word. If you don't love the word, you're not going to receive the strength that is in it for you. Another reason for doubt, is because so many never hear the Word of God. It's hard to love something that your not acquainted with. It's hard to love a person you never did see.

I've heard of folks that had an old fashioned love at first sight. But sight was an important factor. It was with me, I like to see what I am going to love. I think that a lot of time we get to thinking that God's Word is old fashioned and for old fogies, way off some where. It belongs to another age. And we are trying to drag it up here some two millenniums removed from Calvary and make it work. Well, it was built to work today.

We're not trying to take some word from another day and remold it to fit today. This was built for then and now. God is God. God does not have to improve, He is. You need to bring back your strong feelings and faith in the word of God and to stand therein. God's word shall not pass away. It is alive and real today. The word of God is not what you say it is, Nor what anyone says it is. But the word of God is the Word of God.

xxxxxxxxxxxxxxxxxxxxxxxxx

When shall these things be? and what shall be the sign of thy coming? and the end of the world? Jesus went out and departed from the temple: and his disciples came to him for to show him the buildings of the temple. The temple was built of green spotted marble according to Lightfoot. Josephus said some of the stones were fifty feet long, twenty-four broad and sixteen thick. When shall this temple be put into utter destruction? Jesus said, "Many shall come in my name saying I am the Christ, and deceive many. And ye shall hear of wars and rumors of wars: Nation shall rise against nation and kingdom against kingdom: famines, pestilences, and earthquakes, in divers places. Luke adds that there shall be fearful sights and great signs from heaven. Before the Roman general took Jerusalem, these signs were given:

1. A star hung over the city like a sword and a comet continued in the sky for a whole year.

2. At the feast of the unleavened bread, at the ninth hour of the night, a great light shone about the alter and the temple, and this continued for half an hour.

3. At the same feast, a cow led to be sacrifice brought forth a lamb in the midst of the temple.

4. The eastern gate of the temple which was made of solid brass, and very heavy, and could hardly be shut by twenty men, and was fastened by strong bars and bolts, was seen the sixth hour of the night to open of it's own accord.

5. Before sun setting there were seen, over all the country, chariots and armies fighting in the clouds, and besieging cities.

6. At the feast of Pentecost, when the priests were going into the inner temple by night to attend their service, they heard first an motion and noise, and then a voice, as a multitude, saying, let us depart hence.

7. One man, a country fellow, four years before the war began, and when the city was in peace and plenty, came to the feast of the tabernacles, and ran crying up and down the streets, day and night: "A voice from the east! A voice from the west! A voice from the four winds! A voice against Jerusalem and the temple! A voice against the bridegrooms and the brides! A voice against the people!" The magistrates tried by stripes and tortures to restrain him, yet he still cried, with a mournful voice, "Woe, woe, to Jerusalem!" And this he continued to do for several years together, going about the walls and crying with a loud voice: "Woe, woe to the city, and to the people, and to the temple" and as he added "Woe, woe to myself!" a stone from some sling of engine struck

him dead on the spot! Josephus Wars of the Jews book 6 chapter 5 verse 3 and 4.

Josephus was a Jewish historian.

Another Tacitus an Roman Historian gives nearly the same account.

These are not scripture but the history of the fulfillment of scripture. Not one stone was left upon another. Destruction was total. You've seen the remains. The Dome of the Rock sits there now. Most wrongly call it the Mosque of Omar.

All these are the beginning of sorrows. The beginning of travailing pains. These are only the first throws of what was to come. On and on goes the prophecy. Now we stand a at time of the fulfillment of the ultimate of prophecies: Jesus' second coming. Many look to what is going on in the Gulf as the fulfillment of the end time prophecies. It looks like it. It feels like it. It seems to concur with the scriptures. Never has there been a time such as now. We've talked about the EEC. The one world government. The New World Order. These are sign posts along the way for the Christian. Now is the appointed time. Today is the day of salvation. The Book of Revelation speaks of the terrible tribulation that is to come. the Book of Ezekiel says concerning Gog, Magog, Meshech, Tubal, Persia, Ethiopia, Libya, Gomer, And Togarmah and many people with them. This is nearly the whole world. Ezekiel 39:2-4 "Thou shalt ascend and come like a storm, thou, and all thy bands, and many people with thee. And I will turn thee back, and leave but the sixth part of thee,(seventeen out of every hundred) and will cause thee to come up from the north parts, and I will bring thee upon the mountains of Israel: And I will smite thy bow out of thy left hand, and will cause thine arrows to fall out of thy right hand. Thou shalt fall upon the mountains of Israel, thou, and all thy bands, and the people that is with thee: I will give thee unto the ravenous birds of every sort, and to the beasts of the field to be devoured. This is for a time at the end. " Not yet, but soon. The build up in the middle east looks like the time spoken of here. Never has this group of nations been assembled in this area. So this looks like that spoken of by Ezekiel.

Wars and rumors of wars. Never will there be a war like this war. This is a war to end all wars. So spoke the people in the early 1900s. WW1 The end of all wars. WW2, most terrible of wars. Now we stand at the brink of what could well be another major war. Every war had it's thunder preachers saying this man or that is the antichrist, This is the end time, The end is near, and so on. Wars and rumors of wars, earthquakes in various places, pestilence and famine, evil men and seducers growing worse and worse. On and On the prophecies go. But the real object, the real subject is, where do you stand in Christ? Or where do you stand with Christ?

There is always going to be troubles until the end of this age. No man knoweth the day nor hour, but we're not to be ignorant of His coming. How much time is left? I don't know. Surly the day is set before God circled in red. Every day brings us closer. How far do we have to go yet dad? Just a little farther down the road son. Seven days are in the creation week. Six days the Lord God worked on the earth and mankind, The seventh He rested. 2 peter 3:8 "But, beloved, be not ignorant of this one thing, that one day is with the Lord as a thousand years, and a thousand years as one day."

Four thousand years of old testament history, four days. 1991 years of the new testament age has already been spent. That's five thousand nine hundred and ninety one years according to our calendar. That's five days and 23 hours and 48 minutes according to the figures. Twelve minutes of the last day. Nine years till the end of the century. Revelations tells us there are seven years of tribulation that is to come. Subtract that from the nine years and that gives two. It's not coincidence that the EEC comes in to power on January the 1st 1993, seven years before the end of the century. Revelations 13:17 Speaks of a mark that all must have to buy or sell, The EEC, the commonwealth of nations may not use anything but the trade dollar among themselves. A unified Europe. The whole world is aligning with her. There will be no trade except you use the trade dollar. They already have it. All the nations of the EEC must give up their sovereignty. It reigns supreme. A bolt, nut or nail cannot depart from the design authorized by the cartel. No one nation can have an advantage over the next, This is not something from George Orwell, and this is now brother, now. This is not the United States of Europe this is different, this is not a democracy or a republic, you draw the assumptions. Where are you in Christ? Jesus has a job for you. He knows you and has a plan for your life. It don't matter how young or what age you are. There is no retirement in Christ. Not until the end. Then the benefits are out of this world. What is the overcoming sin in your life? The one that keeps knocking you down? Hebrews 12:1 Says, "Let us lay aside every weight, and the sin which doth so easily (easily, not with guile or force but easily) beset us (knock us off course), and let us run with patience the race that is set before us, looking unto Jesus the author and finisher of our faith, who for the joy that was set before him endured the cross, despising the shame, and is set down at the right hand of the throne of God." Romans 12:1 "I beseech you therefore, brethren, by the mercies of God, that you present your bodies a living sacrifice, holy, acceptable, unto God, which is your reasonable service."

Sacrifice, not the blood of bulls and goats not some lamb slain for your sins but present your selves and a living, continuing, ongoing, sacrifice, holy, acceptable, unto God, How? through day by day service, through worship, through loving with a Godly love the body of Christ, His church which he bought with his blood when he died on that tree two thousand years ago. Oh that Besetting sin, you've tried and tried to conquer it. Many time it has cast you down like the snare of the fowler a trap set in your way. It's a pit dug in the way, the road of your life. Disguised, covered over with leaves, twigs, and dust. Set to trip you up the first time your not looking. These are mountains in your life that you can't seem to climb. Well, hear the word of faith, Mark 11:22-23 "Have faith in God. For verily I say unto you, That whosoever shall say unto this mountain, be thou removed and be thou cast into the sea, and shall not doubt in his heart, but shall believe that those things which he saith shall come to pass, he shall have whatsoever he saith."

What do you mean by that Bro Johnson? Look at Mark the 11th chapter. Jesus and the disciples had just came from Bethany and went past a fig tree that had no figs upon it for the time of figs was not yet. Jesus then cursed the fig tree and it died from the roots. He took care of business in Jerusalem and past by the fig tree on the way back. Peter called to remembrance the fig tree saying "Master, behold the fig tree which thou cursed is withered away. Have faith in God. For verily I say unto you, That whosoever shall say unto this mountain, be thou removed and be thou cast into the sea, and shall not doubt in his heart, but shall believe that those things which he saith shall come to pass, he shall have whatsoever he saith." I think that Jesus cursed a perfectly good fig tree for a spiritual application. The time of figs was not yet. But the fig tree had leafed out. Yet there were no figs on the tree. The mountain was the subject of this conversation not the fig tree. Whosoever shall say unto this mountain, be thou removed and be thou cast into the sea, and shall not doubt in his heart, but shall believe that those things which he saith shall come to pass, he shall have whatsoever he saith. You have spiritual mountains in your life that you can't overcome, speak to that mountain. Cast it into the sea. Have faith in God, doubting nothing, cast away that mountain in your life. In the late 1800s two men were prospectors in Alaska. Long had they been together through long winters and short summers. Inseparable, would describe the relationship between the two. One early spring morning, after twenty years together, Sam died. Charley was devastated. Charley performed the necessary rituals by himself as there wasn't anyone else around. He dug the grave deep and straight, near the stream the two had worked for so many years together. Covering Sam with his Hudson blanket, putting his gold pan over Sam's face. Charley covered him up. With sorrow, turning to the cabin they had shared for so long together, heart broken, lost, desolate. In the corner, the dark corner sat Charlie till long after the sun had gone down. Dragging himself off to bed exhausted. Only to sleep in his cloths on the covers, for who cared. The first light of morning coming through the eastern window hit Charlie in his closed eyes. Rising, wiping the sleep from his sorrowful eyes, he shuffled to the stove to make coffee. grabbing the pot he turned to the water, catching a glance of Sam, sitting in his rocker, wrapped with his Hudson bay blanket, stone cold dead. Is my mind going? Ran through his mind. Shuffling over to where Sam sat, he reached out and touched him. Oh God what is going on? Picking Sam up again he shuffled back to the grave only to perform that same ritual over again. Twice, to bury a friend is twice devastated. Charlie shuffled back to the cabin for some hope of solace. The day was long, when friends are gone. Charlie did what he could to keep busy. Night and then the morning came and Sam was again in his rocker, Charlie performed the same ritual again. Another night and morning and the same. Sam again in the rocker. Burial night and morning and Sam again. Charlie had lost it, every night he would go out and dig Sam up, bring him inside and sit him in the rocker. Charlie had lost all reality over the death of his friend. Some of you are like that. Take that sin, bury it deep. Put a marker on top of it, "Here lies the sin that so easily beset me," or Fred Jones or what ever your name is. And leave it buried. Speak to that mountain. Cast it far from you. Let it be said of you as it was of Jesus " The zeal of His Fathers house hath eaten him up." No better testimony could be said of you than this. Set your mind and course with a laser like intensity. No man can serve two masters. Bury that sin deep in the waters of salvation. Repent of your sin be baptized in the name of Jesus Christ for the Remission of your sins, and you shall receive the gift of the Holy Ghost. Speak to the Mountains in your life.

I WAS BLIND BUT NOW I SEE   02/24/1991

PSM 45:1 MY HEART IS INDITING A GOOD MATTER:
I SPEAK THE THINGS WHICH I HAVE MADE TOUCHING THE KING:
MY TONGUE IS THE PEN OF A READY WRITER

John 9:25 ....."One thing I know, that whereas I was blind, now I see."

Did it ever strike you how wonderfully calm and collected our Lord must have been at this time? He had been preaching in the temple, talking to a multitude of Jews. They were furious with him, a number of stones which were used in repairing the temple were lying about on the floor, and they took up these stones to cast at him. He, by some means, forced a passage, or simply went out, and escaped out of the midst of them, and when he came to the gate of the temple with his disciples, who seem to have followed him in the way in which he was able to make it through the throng of his foes, he saw this blind man, and, as if there had been no bloodthirsty foes at his heels, he stopped, stopped as calmly as if an attentive audience had been waiting upon his teachings, to look at the blind man. The disciples stopped too, but they stopped to ask questions about the blind man. How much they were like us today! Always ready to talk. How unlike the Jesus! He is always ready to act. The disciples wanted to know how the man came to be blind, but the Master meant to deliver the man from this blindness. They were very apt at entering into the speculative theories about the origin of sin or the cause of certain strange providences, But Christ is ever for seeking out, not the cause, but the remedy, not the reason for the disease, but the way by which the disease can be cured. The blind man is brought to him. But Christ asks no questions, makes no statements, spitting down on the dust, he stoops, picks up some dust, and works it into mud, when he has done this, he applies the clay to the eyeholes of the man (for I believe, there were no eyes there) and plasters them up so that the spectators can look on and see a man with clay upon where his eyes should be. "Go, says Jesus, to the pool of Siloam, and wash." Some kind friends, no doubt, led the man, who was only too glad to go. The blind man was glad enough to avail himself of any divine remedy. He went, he washed the clay from his eyes, and he received his sight, a blessing he had never known before. No doubt with rapture he gazed upon the trees! With pleasure he beheld the costly, stately appointing of the temple, with what interest and pleasure he would look into the face of Jesus, the man who had given him sight. Father Adam put out our spiritual eyes some 5991 years ago. The natural man cannot see spiritual things. He does not have the spiritual eye, that has gone, gone for ever. We are born with out it. Born blind. Christ brings the beautiful message of salvation into this world, and his gospel is less then nothing in men's eyes. They esteem it even as spittle, spittle mixed with clay. The mere thought of Christianity thoroughly disgusts most them. The yuppies and puppies turn on their pompous heels and will have nothing to do with it, Pomp and glory all say that the gospel is a contemptible and a base thing. But Christ puts the gospel on the blinded eyes, the eyes of those who know they are blind, a gospel which, like clay, seems as if it would make men more blind than before.

But it is through the foolishness of preaching that Christ saves them that believe. 1 Cor 1:21 "Where is the wise? where is the scribe? where is the disputer of this world? Hath not God made foolish the wisdom of this world? For after the wisdom of God the world by wisdom knew not God, it pleased God by the foolishness of preaching to save them that believe." The Holy Spirit is like Siloam's pool. We go to him, or rather he comes to us, the convictions of sin, the blindness caused by sin, the sins are wash away by the cleansing influences of the Divine Comforter, by baptism in His name. And behold, we who were once so blind that we could see no beauty in divine things, and no excellence in the crown jewels of God, begin to see things in a clear and heavenly light. Brightness has dawned in our lives, the Son has shined in, and the Day star has shown into our hearts, giving life to the dead, sight to the blind and healing for our souls. And we rejoice exceedingly before the Lord.

No sooner do we see, then we are brought before our adversaries, and the text of this message is a part of the testimony in our defense of the healer who had wrought this miracle upon us, whom, as to this particular time, have not yet understood Him to be the messiah. "One thing I know, that, whereas I was blind, now I see." This is the unanswerable argument. I was blind, but now I see. You can't argue against this? There have been, in times past, when impostors who say they are the Christ, the Anointed one sent from God, have led the people around by the nose. Men would believe anything, and any crazy maniac, man or woman, who might stand up and proclaim themselves to be the Messiah, would be sure to have some followers. I think this time we live in now with all of it's attending faults, is not so credulous as that time which we have just spoken of. There is a great deal of questioning, questioning by men in high places, in official positions, and who long ago ought to have had their faith established, or to have renounced their positions, they have ventured to question the very things they have sworn to defend. There is questioning everywhere, but to my mind it seems, that we need not be afraid. If the gospel of God is true, and without a doubt it is true, it can stand any quantity of questioning. I am more afraid of the deadness and lethargy of the public mind about true Christianity than any sort of enquiry or controversy about it. As silver tried in the furnace is purified seven times, so the Word of God, and the more it is put into the furnace, the more it will be purified, and the more beauteous the pure ore of revelation will glitter in the sight of the faithful. Never be afraid of a questions. Questions gender study of God's word, and study of God's word genders true answers. The weapons of our warfare are not carnal. Go ahead and arm yourself with the word of God. Go armed with your testimony. Go armed with this argument, the argument which this former blind man used, Whereas I was blind, but now I see. Though you may be unarmed in every other respect, if you know how to wield these two, you may, through grace, come off more than a conqueror. It's forcible. It's irrefutable because it is a personal argument.

I heard a person, the other day, use a similar argument. I had been laughing at a certain system of getting rich, and really it seems to me pardonable to laugh at all these systems, for I believe they are all almost equally as good or bad as the others. The person in question said," Well I can't laugh at it." "Why?" I asked. "Because," said he, "It's made me rich." I had no further answer. If this person had really become rich by such and such a system, it was to him an unanswerable argument, and to me, could he produce any other cases, it would be one that I would not wish to answer. The fact is, the personality of the thing gives it power. It's first person singular. And It says, "I bear eye witness for God that, in my case, this thing has been true. "I will not blush nor stammer to say, I bear my personal witness to the truth of Christ's gospel in my own case." I've been lifted up from sin, I've been delivered from bondage, I've been delivered from doubt, from fear, from despair, from intolerable agony, I've been lifted up to joys unspeakable, and into the service of my God, I bear my own testimony, and I believe. That's your force in the world. And it will be mightily increased if you constantly make your witness for Christ a personal one. I dare say Bro. Sams in Minonk, can tell what God has done for him. But to me, to my own soul, what grace has done for me will be more of an establishment to me for my faith than what Christ has done for this person or that person, it may do well, but, if I can say, "I myself have proved it," here is an argument which drives the nail in a sure place, and then clinches it over too. I believe you must prevail with a personal testimony to the value of Christianity in your own case, for that which you despise yourself you can never persuade others to value.

"I believe, therefore I have spoken,"

Man will never move the world who lets the world move him. But the man that stands firm and says, "I know, I know, I know Christ can change you because it is burnt into my own inner consciousness," such a man's very appearance becomes an argument to convince others.

The scripture says of Jesus," The zeal of his father's house hath eaten him up." Jesus was totally consumed by the job he had to do. We need to be totally consumed by faith. Totally consumed by grace. Then, and only then, will we have irresistible arguments for Christianity.

This ex-blind man's argument was an appeal to men's senses, nothing is more forcible than this. "I was blind, You saw what I was, some of you saw me at the gate of the temple, I was blind, now I see. You can all see that I have eyes, or else I could never see you." He was appealing to their senses.

You ask, "what is that? this Holy Living of the Child of God. The person filled with the Holy Ghost and fire." That's the change the Holy Ghost makes in men's lives. This is the best argument that can be made for the Gospel, the good news. When this precious truth was first preached in Jamaica, people objected to it greatly. They preferred to leave the native Jamaicans ignorant of this Holy thing. The missionaries asked of the plantation owners, "What has been the effect of this Holy Ghost infilling on your workers?" "Well, some were constantly drunken before, some were thieves and liars , and some were all three. But now, they are all different. they don't drink, lie or steal. " "Well, if the gospel has made such a change on your workers, don't you think you ought to put your total influence behind it?"

When a common whore can be filled with the Holy Ghost and made chaste, when a drunkard that spends all his family's living on booze, a total fiend in human form, who makes his families life a living hell when he came home from drinking, who's children would literally hide under the bed from fear, when this kind of person can be made sober, Look at him, see him now, his lovely wife greets him, welcomes him home, his children run to meet him. He sings louder the praises of God, now then what he used to cuss, Glory be to God. When the bum that has given up on life and could care less, can be made steady and dependable, the man that cared not one whit for God, has been made to worship God with his whole heart mind, soul and strength, and has put his total confidence in Jesus Christ, I think then these are arguments that the world cannot answer.

If indeed this that we preach does no more in the world than any system, religion or creed, well then, go ahead and despise it. If men receive the Gospel of Christ and the Holy Ghost and continue to live as they did before. Then you have every right to despise it. But we bring forward to you proofs. There are thousands no hundreds of thousands that have received the Baptism of the Holy Ghost, that have been baptized in Jesus name, that were at one time the off scouring of the earth. Now they are loyal, trustworthy, dependable citizens of their community. They have an unanswerable argument.

And the man said, "If any would have told me three months ago, that I should be living for God I would have knocked his block off. If any would have said that I should testify of the goodness of Christ I would have called him every name in the book. I'd have laughed him to scorn But grace has change me. My whole life is changed, All things have passed away, all things have become new." Those that hate this truth cannot help but notice. They hate Christianity, they say, but if Christianity does things like this, this life changing, the more the better.

Now, in the streets, in the shopping malls, in the places of business, at work, in our every day life, there has got to be an argument against which there is no answer, that, whereas was blind, but now I see, whereas I was sinful, now virtuous, whereas I despised God, but now I fear Him, Respect Him as God. This is the best answer for this age. A living personal witness of what divine grace can do in your life.

"One thing I know, that, whereas I was blind, now I see."

The desire of knowledge is almost universal, but the attainment of it is indeed rare. The Bible says that men are ever learning but are not able to come to the knowledge of the truth. But if a man should attain the knowledge of Christ, he may take a high degree in the gospel, a totally satisfactory degree, a master's degree which shall land him safely in heaven, put a palm branch in his hand, and the eternal song in his mouth. this is a whole lot more honor than any earthly degree will ever bestow upon him. I am only an unlettered Christian. I do have the Masters degree and I have a something in here, in my heart, that answers all your arguments, whatever they may be. I don't know what geology saith, I may not understand all about history, I may not comprehend all the strange things that are daily coming to light, but one thing I know, it is an absolute matter of consciousness to me, it's clear to me, that I, who was once blind, have been made to see. Once when I looked at a Bible, it was a dull dry book, that when I thought of prayer, it was a dreary piece of work done only in monasteries and on high mountains, but now, the Bible a honey comb full of honey, Prayer is my vital breath, communion with the Most High God. Life is now full.

This change, this undoubted change, this supernatural work in my innermost parts, will stand in the stead of all the arguments that can be drawn from all the sciences, Whereas, I was blind, but now I see.

One man says, I don't see how that can be. I say, I have received the Holy Ghost just as the first church did some 1900 some years ago. Twenty people come up to me and say, "There is no such thing available to you today that just ushered in this new thing." We don't believe in it. One proves that it isn't so to themselves in Latin, another proves that it isn't so to themselves mathematically, and eighteen others prove it in one way or the other to themselves. Well, I can't answer your arguments to me in Latin, mathematics, or eighteen other ways, but one thing I can say, Whereas I was Blind, and now I see. I received that thing you say is unavailable to me today, the Holy Ghost, just like the Apostles did. I read it in the Word of God. God never took it away. Romans 11:29 "The Gifts and calling of God are with out repentance". God is not capricious. He will never take the gifts away until the end of this age. One thing I know, that which cannot be beaten out of me, which cannot be hammered out of mine own consciousness, out of my mind, that, whereas I was blind, but now I see.

Do you see the beauty of Christ? Do you see the loveliness of the gospel? Do you perceive the excellence of being in Christ, of receiving the Holy Ghost? Can you read you personal title to mansions in the skies? Are you a total stranger to these holy things? Is your soul in the darkest of nights, without a star, without a ray of knowledge or comfort? Without sight? Without hope?

Listen. Jesus is passing by. HE stops. HE makes clay of the dust and spittle and packs it upon your eyes. Go wash in the pool called shalom. Be baptized in my name, the name of Jesus Christ. Be immersed in the Holy Ghost and filled with his delight. Once I was blind, but now I see. Your sight is restored. Empty eye sockets are filled. The word of God becomes an open Book sweeter than honey.

This blind man, when he found his eyes, came boldly before his neighbors, and before Christ's enemies, and said, One thing I know, whereas I was blind, now I see. He came forward, dressed in the garment of righteousness given to him by Jesus Christ, and confessed his testimony before all men. He had never seen the light of day. I said, he had never seen the light of day. He had never seen a bird, a star, the dust swirl up the street. He had never seen his Mother, his sisters, his brothers, his father. He had never seen those who were his benefactors those who gave to him as he begged at the temple gate. But now, but now he could be all. He could see. No man could deny it. It wouldn't do any good. Here he stood, seeing. He had boldness to stand before all. They said, This man that healed thee is a sinner. Whether he be a sinner or no, What difference does it make He healed me. I was blind, but now I see.

The man comes before the church,

Brethren, I have come to unite with you. I know the Greek Testament, I have also read a good deal in Latin, I understand the vulgate, I can now, if you please, give you the 1st chapter of Mark in Greek, or the second chapter of Exodus in Hebrew. I have also from my youth up given myself to the study of natural and applied sciences. I am a master of rhetoric, and am able to reason logically. on and on this man goes. The old man in the congregation stood up and asked, "Did you ever feel yourself to be a sinner? Did you ever feel that Christ is a precious savior? Are you putting your trust in him? Have you received the Holy Ghost since you believed?" All the knowledge, wisdom, skills, intelligence, or speaking ability is nothing compared to the knowledge of the excellency of Christ. There are many that don't even know that they're blind. Jesus said, "you say you see but you're blind. For if you were blind you would see." Paradox? I don't think so. but to know that you're blind is a good thing, but not enough. You don't have a lease on life. Your option could be pulled and any moment. The silver cord could be loosed, the pot broken at the well. Repent of the sins that have held you in check. Repent of all of your sins. Wash away those sin buy being baptized in the name of Jesus Christ. Receive your spiritual sight by receiving the Holy Ghost. Then you can say as the ex blind man, "where as, I was blind, but now I see." Receive Ye the Holy Ghost. This is Bro. Randy Johnson for the We Preach Jesus Ministries.

TOO LITTLE FOR THE LAMB   03/03/1991

**PSM 45:1 MY HEART IS INDITING A GOOD MATTER:
I SPEAK THE THINGS WHICH I HAVE MADE TOUCHING THE KING:
MY TONGUE IS THE PEN OF A READY WRITER**

THERE IS IN THIS TIME FRAME MUCH CONSTERNATION OVER WHERE WE ARE IN PROPHECY, WHAT WILL BE DONE IN THE NEXT FEW DAYS, WEEKS OR YEARS. This should not be the concern of the lost and dying. Their attention should focus on where they are in their relationship to God. Lost means that you don't have a proper aspect on where you are. That you must locate a reference point. Lost means that you must call out and locate your spiritual leader. Your shepherd. The one that cares for your soul. The one that knows exactly where you are and will let you know the reference point, Jesus the Christ. Don't be a cast sheep, helplessly laying on your back unable to move because your wool is so full of mud that it weighs you down. Unable to get up on your feet again. Cry out. The sheep follow the shepherd and know his voice, but the goats have a mind of their own. Which are you?

Lord Jesus, help us to have the right attitude towards the spiritual leadership, the local shepherds, of the body of Christ, the church which you bought with your own blood. Lord you purchased us with your life giving, sin covering blood on the cross at cavalry. You bought us with your blood and saved us from death, hell and the grave. You gave to us life everlasting and more abundant. Help us to follow your teachings in the Word of God. Help us to become more and more like you, Help us to become totally Christian. Lord you've shown to us thorough your word, the pathway of life. You've given to us the key to peace, Joy, happiness, life, and truth, help us to apply it to our lives daily. In Jesus name we pray for these things that will glorify you in our daily transactions and manner.

The Old Testament was our schoolmaster to lead us to Christ. In it are types and shadows of that which has or will come.

The Easter holiday is fast approaching. We all know that Easter is a time that we celebrate Christ rising from the grave. His resurrection is indeed important but please remember how Jesus got there and what he accomplished by being there. There is a feast of the Jews which occurs at about this same time, the feast of the Passover.

All the feasts of God are types and shadows of the real (the heavenly spiritual). The tabernacle plan that God gave Moses on top of Mt. Sinai is a type or shadow of the church and how that we approach Christ thru repentance, baptism and the infilling of the Holy Ghost. The laws given were a shadow of the work that the Holy Ghost would do in our lives, and so on and on. the type and shadow that we are concerned with in this message, is the feast of the Passover.

The Bible begins with the creation. Soon Adam and eve had sinned, they were expelled from the Garden of Eden. Cain had killed Able and a mark had been put on him identifying him as a slayer of men. Jacob had stolen the birthright from Esau although God has already given it to Jacob. He had bargained with Laban for Rachel and wound up with Leah, worked seven more years for Rachel, had his wages changed so many times it's hard to keep track, Fed up, he drug up, and headed for his father's house. Reconciled with Esau through a life-changing struggle with an angel, no longer Jacob but now Israel because as a prince he had power with God. Time had passed and twelve sons born only to have one favorite son sold by his own brothers, into Egyptian slavery. Joseph was made to be the head of Potipher's household. Potipher's wife had an eye for this virtuous young Joseph but Joseph would not fulfill her lustful dreams. He was lied upon by Potipher's wife and put in prison only to be brought up some time latter to interpret a dream that pharaoh had. He found favor and was made the second man in the whole kingdom. A great famine was upon the land and through a series of events, the whole family was reconciled and given the fairest of the land in honor of Joseph. The Israelites prospered, grew into great numbers, Joseph had died and a new pharaoh who knew not Joseph or the story rose up and put the Jews into slavery for fear of them. Years passed and God hearing the cry of his children rose up a deliver, Moses. Moses went into pharaoh time and again saying, thus sayeth God, "Let my people go that they might worship me." Pharaoh paid no heed to this request so God sent the gods they worshiped to them in droves. Flies, frogs, locusts, darkness, blood time after time pharaoh hardened his heart until Go told Moses that he would strike dead the first born throughout the land, from the firstborn of Pharaoh's house to the firstborn of the sheep. To stay, to stop the hand of the death angel, God instituted the feast of the Passover: Exodus 12:5 "Your lamb shall be without blemish, a male of the first year: ye shall take it out from the sheep, or from the goats: and ye shall keep it up until the fourteenth day of the same month: and the whole assembly of the congregation of Israel shall kill it in the evening. And they shall take of the blood, and strike it on the two side posts and the upper doorpost of the houses, where in they shall eat it. And they shall eat the flesh in that night, roast with fire, and unleavened bread, and with bitter herbs they shall eat it. Eat not of it raw, or sodden at all with water, but roast it with fire, his head with his legs, and with the purterance thereof. And ye shall let nothing of it remain until the morning: and that which remaineth of it until the morning ye shall burn with fire. And thus shall ye eat it, with your loins girded, your shoes on your feet, and your staff in your hand, and ye shall eat it in haste: it is the LORD's Passover."

Then and only then did the death angel pass over their house. Salvation was brought to their house by the blood of the Lamb. Salvation is brought to your house by the blood of Jesus Christ, the Lamb of God sent to take away the sins of the world.

Exodus 12:3,4 "They shall take to them every man a lamb, according to the house of their fathers, a lamb for an house: and if the household be too little for the lamb, let him and his neighbor next unto his house take it according to his eating shall make your count for the lamb."

The Passover lamb wasn't killed just to be looked at It was killed to be eaten. Our Lord Jesus Christ wasn't slain just so we may hear about him, think and talk about him, but that we may feed upon him. Everything that has to do with Christ's work is of real practical and vital consequence to believers. He's food for our souls. It is in faith that we receive him. It is in love that we embrace him and in hope we rejoice in him.

The lamb of the Passover was not to be eaten just in part and some to be left, and some to be divided at the feast. The whole lamb was to be eaten. And, in like manner, the whole of Christ is to be spiritually received by us. We must receive all that he is, and all that he did, with an open and grateful heart. There cannot be any picking and choosing among the good things of Christ, but all his attributes must be accepted. We are all sinners saved by grace, and we all need the savior, and we need the sum total of the savior.

So, as the whole Passover lamb was to be eaten, I think that it can be said, that all the power to save, which is in Christ, is meant to be exercised. He is able to save to the uttermost all them that come to him. That uttermost power of his was not intended to lay idle. He is able to save all those who are at the very end of the earth, and that power to save the outcasts and the off scouring was not intended to be left unused. The whole lamb was meant to be eaten at once. None was to be kept until the morning. As with the manna, there was to be no storing for future use. They were to eat it the manna then and there. The members of Christ's Body the Church, should always look to the present use of the Lamb of God and all that is in him. We can delight ourselves and each other with the anticipation of the rapture and the millennium reign of our Christ, the Glory that is to dawn yet upon this earth. But we had better concern ourselves with the needs of this present age, with the necessities of those who are perishing, because of the lack of the knowledge of Christ. Christ is meant for this present time, this present use. Whatever he may do a thousand years from now is of no concern to us right now. Christ is for today. Christ is the I AM. Not the I will be, nor the I have been, but the I Am. Now. Today, if you will hear his voice, harden not your hearts. Today! Now! Even now he is ready to mightily save. Now by his blood, to deliver his people from the avenging angel, and by his flesh to be the continual food of their souls, and we are to see to it that we do not project ourselves into a future age, being negligent of the present use of the ever present Savior who is with us always, even to the end of this age.

The Passover lamb was meant to be eaten, to be all eaten, and to be all eaten there and then, And Christ is meant to be used, meant to be altogether used, and to be used just now. Right now.

They shall take to them every man a lamb, according to the house of their fathers, a lamb for a house. True Christianity begins in the home. Are you searching your heart to know what you have to do with Christ personally? In your own relationship? In your own individuality? Don't be taken with some delusion, a fatal delusion, that you can get to heaven by being carried along with the force of the crowd. You, You must come to Christ personally. You must receive the Holy Ghost Personally. You must repent of your sins personally. You must be baptized in the name of Jesus Christ for the remission of your sins, personally. It's a personal faith, a personal repentance, a personal baptism, and a personal baptism of the Holy Ghost. It's a personal Lamb without spot or blemish. You must apply the blood of the lamb to the doorposts and lintels of your life. You must personally feed on the Lamb. It is no use for you to go and talk of the Lamb to your neighbor until you have made the Lamb yours. You must be personal partaker of the Lamb. Ask yourself, have I applied the blood of Jesus Christ to my life? Have I fed upon the Lamb of God? This is not a question of church membership. This is not a question of heritage, of natural birth. This is a question of and about yourself. How is it with your soul brother? Even Christians of long standing need to ask this question. The mind is extremely tricky and you may have kept up an unknown sham conversion for a long time. Perhaps even this soul searching will not pull the mask off some eyes, only the hand of death will reveal the terrible truth to some, much too late.

It was the unspeakable mercies of God that a Lamb was provided for our Passover. We deserved to die for our sins.

A lamb for a house. We should have Christ for our whole family. There was to be a paschal lamb for all the members of the family, "A lamb for a house." All those in the family were to share the blessings, which the lamb brought. The man or woman that has a partner in Jesus Christ is a privileged person. Beyond compare, are the blessings of worshiping the Lord together. There's no greater joy than to see your children follow in your own footsteps. Bro Sams has no greater joy than to see his son Matthew, before a congregation, preaching the word of God. I have no greater joy than to see my daughter Jessica, teaching Sunday school. The wife of a minister of God. All my daughters are living for God. My wife lives for God. It's a joy to my heart. I know that some of you also have this blessing. Your house is a little bit of heaven. Women, you don't have to fight an uphill battle when your husband is the Lord's servant. Husbands, you don't have to fight an uphill battle when your wife is of the Lord. Children, when your parents are God fearing people you have ever right to be happy. You others, trust in the Lord with all your heart, lean not upon your own understanding. God will give you grace in the day of adversity. Have you this blessing? I know that some of you do. But, how is it with your soul though brother? Keep the praises constantly going up towards heaven for the grace that has been given you brother. Pour out praise and honor to him that has so favored you with the baptism of the Holy Ghost..

Maybe some your children are still little. You're looking forward to the hope that the Lamb of God will still be available to your whole house. How can you be assured of this? The scripture answers this dilemma. You, yourself cannot save your children. This is far beyond your power. This is a divine work of grace, and has to be done by the Holy Ghost. You have only this scripture, "Train up a child in the way he should go, and when he is old, he will not depart from it." You know that the training a child receives affects their adult life. We must add something to our training to make it effectual. There must be constant prayer to make the training effectual. There must be constant prayer and fasting where the training appears to fail, for we must pray for those children who are past the age where we can influence their lives through training. Remember, the effectual fervent prayer of a righteous man availeth much. I don't think we'll have to plead long for our sons and daughters without seeing our prayer-hearing God stretching out his hand to save them. If we do, if we must look upon the delay as a trial of our faith and we mist intensify our prayer and fasting until it becomes agony, and in that agony we can lay hold upon the covenant angel, as Jacob did, and cry,"

I will not let thee go unless thou bless me and my seed also." So choice a gift as this may be reserved for something more earnest than the prayer to which we have yet attained, and when the Lord shall have flung us upon our faces, shall have brought us to self despair, shall have made us see, in the rebellious character of our children, a picture of our own rebelliousness, and made to see, in our own agony,, a reflection of the agony in the heart of Jesus over our wanderings, then, perhaps, he will speedily listen to us, and our children shall, be sheltered beneath the blood of the Lamb.

Our children should not be left untaught about salvation. I'm surprised at how many young people appear to know little or nothing about the Holy Ghost. Few even know who Jesus is, other than as swear word. Many have been to a Sunday school students for years. It's strange how quickly they forget what they have learned. That which is learned by rote, and has not been taught at all, is brushed easily from the memory, a young person seldom forgets the teachings, moistened with a mother's tears. There is a wonderful power about a mother's voice, when she talks to her children about Jesus and his love. It stamps itself upon the heart, and friend, the heart is a far better place for truth than the brain can ever become. We forget what we only learn with the head, but we don't forget what we learn with the heart, experientially. Parents, teach your children this, let them, from their youth, know the Holy Scriptures, which are able to make them wise unto salvation, let them be early acquainted with the precious truths of the gospel of Jesus Christ. Do you know the Word of God? Bro Sams and Myself will gladly give you a home bible study course in the comfort of your home. Twelve lessons of one hour a week each. Just drop us a card.

But above all things if we are to have our family feed upon Jesus Christ, we must set a good example. too severe or cold of training, where the example isn't good, will not train up a child in the way he should go. Now if you pray with your lips in one way, and live in another way, your lives will win the day, and your children will be like you are not what you ask then to be. It is a great pity when men are great in the prayer room, and bad at home. When those that a show great kindness to their Christian friends and seem to have given away all their honey to strangers outside the walls of their own homes, and have no sweetness left for their own children. We need to set such an example that will be safe for our sons and daughters to follow, and then there will very rarely be found any instance where training, teaching, prayer, and a good example have gone together, where the blessings of God has failed to come. God grant to you at any rate the grace to attend to all these matters, and then if you should prove to be the father of an Ishmael, or the mother of an Esau, you will not have to say, "I've kept the vineyards of others, but mine own vineyard have I not kept," but you will feel that you did use such means as were within your reach, even though the blessing of God did not come to your children.

I pray that it may be your privilege to have the Lamb of God that is without spot or blemish, for your whole household. And that you may joyfully, from the youngest to the oldest, partake of all the benefits of the common sacrifice, which is provided for all.

Exodus 12:3,4 "They shall take to them every man a lamb, according to the house of their fathers, a lamb for an house: and if the household be too little for the lamb, let him and his neighbor next unto his house take it according to his eating shall make your count for the lamb."

There's nothing said about if the lamb was too little for the family. Just not sufficient to feed the household. Here, the silence concerning such a contingency as to the insufficiency of the Passover lamb, for the household is meant to teach us an important lesson. The lamb was never too little for the household. The Jews say that the Passover was never meant to be eaten with the intent on feasting, only a small portion was eaten by each person. There were, no doubt, large families, but there was always sufficient lamb for each one to have a small portion. We do not come to the Lord's Supper merely to eat and drink, Paul said "Have ye not houses to eat and drink in?" but we come there for a religious observance, and a small portion of bread and a sip of wine is sufficient. There may have been as many as twenty persons in one house who would partake of the Lamb, and in the Lord's case, at the last supper, he sat down to the Passover with the twelve, making thirteen including himself, but the possibly of there not being enough lamb is not covered in the Scripture. It merely states if the household be too little for the lamb. Friend, there is sufficient lamb for the proper observance of the Passover feast.

And now, using the spiritual type, rest assured there never can happen that there wouldn't be enough of Jesus Christ to feed all our families. "Well", we're a very large family. The children need a large table when they all sit down to gather. Yes, and no doubt some of those Jewish families were as large as that, yet they all fed upon the paschal lamb, and there is enough in Christ for all your family, and there would be enough even if it consisted of twenty persons, or even twenty thousand. If any of them perished, it would not be because Christ was insufficient for them, but because they had not received him, not believed on him. Don't let the number of your household hold back your praying or working for them, and don't rest until, by God's grace, all of them shall know and trust in Christ.

But our family is more peculiar than that, you say. We are a family of godless sinners. It does happen, that a man who, in the past, was a unsurpassed offender, is filled with the Holy Ghost. Being filled with God's spirit he now is like a great speckled bird to all the rest of his family. He simply don't fit in. His brother is a drunk, his sister is totally godless, his mom and dad despise Christianity, and as he lives around them, he can only wonder in his head, how it was that Devine grace should have ever selected one out of such a family as his. He doesn't remember any of his relation who ever received the Holy Ghost. They've been the devils as far back as his mind can trace. Well friends, if it is so with any of your family, don't hesitate, for a single minute, in your prayers or in your efforts for them, under such a wicked, dishonoring notion as that, perhaps, your family is just too bad for Christ to save. too wicked for the lamb. Their sins are too many for his blood to wash away, and their necessities too great for him to relieve. That just can't be. You have an all-sufficient Savior to talk of, to rely upon, and to bring before them. Go to him in prayer for all your family, beseeching that all the members of your family may participate in the blessings procured by the Lamb of God. The apostle Paul wrote to Timothy, "I exhort therefore, that, first of all, supplications, prayers, intercessions, and giving of thanks, be made for all men." Meaning that, all ranks, conditions, and all sorts of men. The only person we are told not to pray for, is the one that has committed the unpardonable sin, Blasphemy of the Holy Ghost. Calling the Holy Ghost of the Devil. Never should we look a child of ours in the face and feel that to speak of Christ to that child would be useless, for he cannot be saved." Never give up hope that your child can be saved. Never doubt the possibility of salvation for anybody. Never doubt the feasibility of salvation for anyone. There is no grade of sin in God's eyes. Sin is sin. Thee are no levels of sin. There are no levels of salvation. Sin is sin. No maybe sins.

No half sins anymore than there is a half-truth. A half-truth is a lie. Any true statement structured to deceive is a lie. You can go to hell for that as quick as for murder.

Don't relax your efforts to save. Don't suffer your hopes to be dampened. Lead on. Plead on. Pray on, brother, till your whole household has been brought to feed upon the Passover lamb, Jesus Christ. At the King's banquet table of mercy, there will never be a failure of foods. Look at how the tables groan with the weight of the oxen and the fatlings for the great gospel supper, the wine and milk are poured out with an free hand. There shall be enough to satisfy the hunger and thirst of all who will ever come to that table as long as time shall last. Ten thousand and thousands of thousands could come flocking to the house of bread, there will always be found enough to spare for all who come.

If the household be too little for the lamb, let him and his neighbor next unto his house take it according to the number of the souls." My household and my father's household, rejoice to know that we can feed upon the Lamb of God, but our households are much too little for the Lamb. Our household is much too little to sing the praises of Jesus, the Lamb of God, by ourselves. We need Christ to be revealed to thousands, no tens of thousands, and unnumbered millions of souls. for the attributes of Christ to be revealed only in my family would not be enough. The Lamb is too large for just our family. A great multitude must sing, " Worthy is the Lamb." Our household is too little to do all the work that is to be done in this end time. The task is too great for a few to reach the untold millions that haven't heard this precious message of salvation. I asked a friend, onetime, what she must do to make it to heaven. "Obey the Ten Commandments," she said. Have you kept them, No, she answered. She was totally ignorant of the plan of salvation, The Passover lamb. She had been going to a Christian church for ten years listening to the social gospel. How many do you know that do not know the path that leads to salvation. How many are dying, untold about the Passover Lamb that taketh away the sins of the world? How many feel it would be great to be a missionary to the dark continent of Africa, or go maybe to Tahiti, to bask in the sun and spread the gospel to the natives? How many feel a calling on their lives to go to some strange far away place and teach others about Christ? Too little for the Lamb? Go first to your neighbors. There are untold millions that haven't heard this truth that live within 100 miles of here. Where will the missionary come from to tell them? Maybe Tahiti, or Africa? No, from your house to your neighbor's house to his neighbors house to his neighbors house. From house to house they, the early church, preached the gospel. Spreading the good news. Your household is too little for the Lamb. Until the knowledge of the Lord shall be spread as the waters cover the sea, until then, we shall still feel that the household is too little for the Lamb. Look then, after the neighbor, after the man who is near to you, and if you do this, you'll not have so far to go as to Africa.

Your neighbor is the person who is most likely to be influenced by you. A total stranger would need more time to introduce himself, but your neighbor already knows something about you, and if he sees that you are a consistent Christian that will materially assist you in delivering the message of Christ to him. If you are living as you ought to live, your neighbor knows something about the effect the gospel has had upon your life. You are the man that can give him a living example as well as the written word. 2 Cor 3:2 "ye are our epistle written in our hearts, known and read of all men."

Do you need to know the Lamb of God that taketh away the sins of the world? He's not difficult to know. Drop a card to the We preach Jesus ministries PO box 274 Eureka, Ill and we will come and tell you about the Lamb. You see, our household is too little for the lamb. This is Bro Randy Johnson for the we preach Jesus Ministries.

Here is a man, whose household is too little for the lamb, and he has called in his next-door neighbor to share the feast with him. "Come in, friend," he says, "I have a wife and two children, and our household is too little for the lamb. You have a wife and one child, come in, and we will keep this Passover together." Sweet fellowship. They feed on the same Lamb, and in doing so, they would come to know each other as they had never done before. They would talk together concerning the divine plan of sacrifice by which they were being saved while Egypt was being destroyed. They would talk to each other about that day when there was darkness over all the land of Egypt except in the houses of the Israelites. They would talk about the flies, the frogs, the locusts, how the hand of God was stretched forth to save them. Happy that they could meet under one roof and eat this Passover together. A pleasant time for all of them, and I can tell you that, if you are bringing any souls to Jesus, those you bring to Him, by the power of the Holy Ghost, are the best companions you have ever had. You will talk together of all that the Lord has done for you. Like two, that might only have smoldered alone, you will burn and blaze when you are put together.

Together that night, sheltered under the same blood, sharing the same lamb, partaking of the same bitter herbs, and each one with his loins gird about and with his staff in his hand, these families would never be at enmity against one another. Very near kin to one another. Cemented by the cross of Christ. Where we love each other for Christ's sake, and love Christ as we see him revealed in one another, such love, as that will outlast our earthly life, and will reach on into eternity, and be sweet even in heaven. Both families would have sweet memories. Sweet memories to share with one another in the years that were to come down the road of life. A new communion, two families ready to help each other, to cheer each other in the future. They that fear the Lord, when they speak often one to another concerning him, are sure to be mutually helpful to one another, and I think that this bringing in of other

THE PROMISE PART 1   12/08/1991

PSM 45:1 MY HEART IS INDITING A GOOD MATTER:
I SPEAK THE THINGS WHICH I HAVE MADE TOUCHING THE KING:
MY TONGUE IS THE PEN OF A READY WRITER

Have you ever wondered why Jesus was born, crucified, and rose again on the third day?

All my life I had heard of this man called Jesus, saw the dioramas of the manger scene, heard of the three wise men that came to see the baby Jesus, yet until I came to know him in a way that is hard to relate to you, I thought he was just, just the son, a human being that God had sent to take care of a job that God couldn't do himself. My first encounter with a serious effort to attend church, brought aggravation. I wanted to learn of God not some second in command. All they taught about was this man called Jesus. I didn't think that Jesus had power to heal, comfort, or work miracles. I had been raised all my life to believe in divine healing. I was seventeen years old before I ever had received a shot. This group believed all sickness was cause by metaphysical reasons and if you would get yourself in harmony your sicknesses would be cured. I didn't know this, I simply believed that God is, and he would reward faith. Faith in the operation of God.

The Jews have waited almost six thousand years for the promised deliver to come. Six thousand years of patience. Six thousand years of graves along the path of history. The graves of those who have gone before never having received the promised messiah. To the Wailing Wall to pray, to stick their written prayers in the cracks of the eastern wall of the temple. Hopefully, expectantly, waiting for the deliver. Every year at the feast of the Passover they put what is known as the Elijah cup on the table. Every year, they opened the door at a certain time of this feast. Who for? That prophet Elijah that must first come before the Messiah would appear. Gal 4:4 "But when the fullness of the time was come, [God sent forth] his Son, made of a woman, made under the law," Rejected and despised of men. 1 Cor 2:6-8 Howbeit we speak wisdom among them that are perfect: yet not the wisdom of this world, nor of the princes of this world, that come to naught: {7} But we speak the wisdom of God in a mystery, <even> the hidden

<wisdom>, which God ordained before the world unto our glory: {8} Which none of the princes of this world knew: for had they known <it>, they would not have crucified the Lord of glory."

How can I explain to you what is the purpose of Jesus Christ? What can I say to prick your curiosity into digging deeper into this hunger you have within you? Every year you set up a beautiful smelling tree in you living room, you nearly bankrupt yourself buying presents for friends, relatives, and your children. Yet the one that Christmas is all about is thought of as a baby in a manger not the savior of the world. Jesus Christ had a tree alright, but it was a rugged wooded cross decorated with his own body that stood on a bald hill that day.

I love the sights and sounds of Christmas. My mind is full of memories of shopping when downtown Peoria was full of stores. I love the sights and sounds and smells of Christmas. On every street corner stood the red kettle with someone in blue uniform ringing a bell. A band of four or five would be playing Christmas carols by the kettle. Block and Kohl's had an automated display in their window. I would, as a child, stand and watch this display while my mom patiently waited for my curiosity to be filled. I would wonder how this display worked. But alas, no longer do the blue uniformed men and women ring the bells in the streets. No longer are the bells large and melodious. Now the bells are small and tinny sounding. Why, I asked my wife, do you think the bells are so small? She didn't know. "Why don't the church bells ring on Sunday mornings, cutting the cold December air with their call to worship?" I asked her. Could it be, just could it be that same spirit that caused the people to reject Christ the first time he came is still working in this world today? The fire sirens go off so loud that it's impossible to stand near, without holding your ears, yet no one complains. After all, there's a fire to put out. On the corner stands a small church, white and old. Bell tower still standing with bell intact, yet it remains silent. Silent because the neighbors can't sleep in on Sunday with this infernal banging and clanging of the bell. So the bells are silent throughout the land, no longer proclaiming, no longer calling anyone to worship the Savior that was born two thousand years ago. Despised and rejected among men. Yet at the end, every knee shall bow and every tongue confess that Jesus is Lord. What proclaims the need of salvation throughout the land? Is it a fire siren-calling volunteers to a fire? Is it the small bells that ring on the street corners of the land? Is it the sound of the silence of the bells that hang still in the bell towers of the land? Is it the wind blowing around the eves on a cold winter night? Whispering of the freezing cold wind that drives the snow across the plowed fields. I think not. It's the heart inside of a man that hungers for the savior that was born in the shadow of a cross. One with a mission upon his head. One that only time would show forth the glory of God. It's a cross not a manger. It's an empty tomb not a babe in swaddling cloths. It's a small lad named Jesus, saying to his parents, Luke 2:49 "How is it that ye sought me? wist ye not that [I must be] about my Father's business?" It's God manifest in the flesh hanging on an old rugged cross, crying out Mark 15:34 ...." [Eloi , Eloi], lama sabachthani?........ My God, my God, why hast thou forsaken me?"

    XMAS, XMAS did you ever wonder why Christ was taken out of Christmas? Perhaps it's the algebraic expression of someone who didn't know who Jesus is. X for the unknown factor. A variable named X. Ah friend of mine Jesus is not a variable, he's the rock upon which we may base our lives. The word of God says that he is truth, 2 Cor 1:20 "For all the promises of God in him <are> yea, and in him Amen, unto the glory of God by us." James 1:17 "Every good gift and every perfect gift is from above, and cometh down from the Father of lights, with whom is no variableness, neither shadow of turning." Jesus Christ is not the X factor but the law by which we can base our entire lives upon. He's the precept, He's the rock of ages cleft for me. When the winds of the storms of life get to blowing hard and strong he puts me in the cleft of the rock and puts his hand over me. The storms cannot harm me for I'm sheltered in the rock.

    Luke 2:11 "For unto you is [born this day] in the city of David a Savior, which is Christ the Lord." The promised one. In the form of a baby. Was it not the priest that said Luke 2:29 "Lord, now lettest thou thy servant depart in peace, according to thy word: For mine eyes have seen thy salvation, which thou hast prepared before the face of all people, a light to lighten the Gentiles, and the glory of thy people Israel." He knew who this small babe was. He had read the three hundred some prophecies concerning this baby. A promise spoken of by twenty of the Old Testament writers. Here, in this small town, lay a baby that would change the course of the whole world. Time itself would be separated by this event. BC and AD. From the beginning of time the Devil has tried to stamp out the lineage of Christ. Time and again, time and again. The genealogy of Christ reads with some of the strangest, the most common people that ever lived. A blue blood? I hardly think so. Not by this lineage. But truly the Lion of Judah. Gen 49:10 "The scepter shall not depart from Judah, nor a lawgiver from between his feet, until Shiloh come, and unto him <shall> the gathering of the people <be>." Prophecy after prophecy painting a picture of the anointed one that should come. The son of David,

The eternal king of David's throne, the righteous branch of David, Jehovah our righteous one, Jehovah's anointed one, the promised seed, Jehosua, Jehovah had become my salvation, Jesus.

Satan had put a wall up between God and his creation by causing Adam and Eve to sin. Because of this God cursed the serpent and said, Gen 3:15 I will put enmity between thee and the woman, and between thy seed and her seed, it shall bruise thy head, and thou shalt bruise his heel. The seed of a woman was to bruise the head of the serpent. Not the seed of a man but the seed of a woman. Promises to Abraham, Isaac and Jacob. Promises to Moses and sixteen others. On and on the painting goes until it would seem to be as clear as a portrait hanging upon a wall. Yet when the time came, conflicting ideas, preconceived notions cause the Jewish nation to miss the messiah. What preconceived ideas do you have about Christmas and the Christ child?

When Cain slew Abel the Devil thought that he could stop the lineage of Christ. By rising up in Cain, by the same sin that struck down Eve, he used Cain as a weapon, to slay his brother and by the same stroke, kill the possibility of God ever using Cain in the lineage of Christ. He didn't realize that God had already chosen one not yet born to be the branch Christ would come out of. Gen 4:25 "And Adam knew his wife again, and she bare a son, and called his name Seth: For God, <said she>, hath appointed me another seed instead of Abel, whom Cain slew." Gen 4:26 "And to Seth, to him also there was born a son, and he called his name Enos: then began men to call upon the name of the LORD." Seth had taught his Son about God and had taught him well. Access to the most high God is the most important thing you could ever learn. From Seth to Noah the lineage of Christ was relatively unhindered. But during this time, the wickedness of man grew worse and worse. Gen 6:5 "And God saw that the wickedness of man <was> great in the earth, and <that> every imagination of the thoughts of his heart <was> only evil continually." God told Noah that "The earth also was corrupt before God, and the earth was filled with violence." Gen 6:13 "And God said unto Noah, The end of all flesh is come before me, for the earth is filled with violence through them, and, behold, I will destroy them with the earth." You know the story of Noah, his wife, his three son and their wives. Until Noah, until the flood, the adversary had plenty to keep him busy, but now he once again knew where the lineage of Christ would come through. There were only eight people on the ark. Just eight. So, Noah had become a vine dresser, one that raised grapes. In the course of this preserving of the juice of the vine, Noah became drunk and had passed out in his tent. Gen 9:22 "And Ham, the father of Canaan, saw the nakedness of his father, and told his two brethren without. And Shem and Japheth took a garment, and laid <it> upon both their shoulders, and went backward, and covered the nakedness of their father, and their faces <were> backward, and they saw not their father's nakedness. And Noah awoke from his wine, and knew what his younger son had done unto him. And he said, Cursed <be> Canaan, a servant of servants shall he be unto his brethren." What Ham had done isn't written in the word of God, but it was sufficient to have him and his seed cursed for all of time. Strike a blow for the adversary, the lineage wouldn't come out of Ham. It was narrowed down to just two. But God had set the lineage to come through Shem. Time and time again at every opportunity that presented itself to him, a blow was struck at this seed that would bruise his head. He was sure this would be accomplished when he had the Egyptians to kill all the man children among the Jewish slaves. Not so for God had appointed a man child whom would carry the torch of salvation through this and other dark nights. Time prevents the telling of Rahab, of Ruth, of Boaz, of David, of Solomon, on and on it goes. In captivity, in freedom, in sin, yet onward marched the lineage of the one that would come and free his people from their sins. Who is this Root of Jesse? Who is this Bright and morning star? Who is this rose of Sharon? Where is he to come from? Will it be the palaces of the Kings? In gold and finery, draped with the royal robes of majesty, circled about with droves of servants taking care of every need. For unto you is born this day in the city of David, a savior. Read the prophecies concerning this Christ.

THE MESSIAH WOULD BE THE SEED OF A WOMAN

Gen 3:15   And I will put enmity between thee and the woman, and between thy seed and her seed, it shall bruise thy head, and thou shalt bruise his heel.

Gal 4:4   But when the fullness of the time was come, God sent forth his Son, made of a woman, made under the law, (LUKE 2:7, REV 12:5)

THE PROMISED SEED OF ABRAHAM

Gen 18:18   Seeing that Abraham shall surely become a great and mighty nation, and all the nations of the earth shall be blessed in him?

FULFILLED IN

Acts 3:25   ye are the children of the prophets, and of the covenant which God made with our fathers, saying unto Abraham, and in thy seed shall all the kindreds of the earth be blessed.

PROMISED SEED OF ISAAC

Gen 17:19   And God said, Sarah thy wife shall bear thee a son indeed, and thou shalt call his name Isaac: and I will establish my covenant with him for an everlasting covenant, <and> with his seed after him.

WHICH WAS FULFILLED IN

Mat 1:2   Abraham begat Isaac, and Isaac begat Jacob, and Jacob begat Judas and his brethren,

THE PROMISED SEED OF JACOB

Num 24:17   I shall see him, but not now: I shall behold him, but not nigh: there shall come a Star out of Jacob, and a Sceptre shall rise out of Israel, and shall smite the corners of Moab, and destroy all the children of Sheth.

THIS WAS FULFILLED IN

Luke 3:34   which was <the son> of Jacob, which was <the son> of Isaac, which was <the son> of Abraham, which was <the son> of Thara, which was <the son> of Nachor,

WAS TO DESCEND FROM THE TRIBE OF JUDAH

Gen 49:10   The sceptre shall not depart from Judah, nor a lawgiver from between his feet, until Shiloh come, and unto him <shall> the gathering of the people <be>.

FULFILLED IN

Heb 1:8   But unto the Son *he saith,* Thy throne, O God, *is* for ever and ever: a sceptre of righteousness *is* the sceptre of thy kingdom.

THE HEIR TO THE THRONE OF DAVID

Isa 9:7   of the increase of <his> government and peace <there shall be> no end, upon the throne of David, and upon his kingdom, to order it, and to establish it with judgment and with justice from henceforth even for ever. The zeal of the LORD of hosts will perform this.

IT'S FULFILLMENT

Mat 1:1   the book of the generation of Jesus Christ, the son of David, the son of Abraham.

WHERE WAS HE TO BE BORN?

Micah 5:2   But thou, Bethlehem Ephratah, <though> thou be little among the thousands of Judah, <yet> out of thee shall he come forth unto me <that is> to be ruler in Israel, whose goings forth <have been> from of old, from everlasting.

THE FULFILLMENT

Mat 2:1   now when Jesus was born in Bethlehem of Judaea in the days of Herod the king,

THE TIMING WAS PERFECT THOUGH THE STUDY OF THIS WOULD TAKE AN ENTIRE WEEK OF BROADCASTS

Dan 9:25   Know therefore and understand, <that> from the going forth of the commandment to restore and to build Jerusalem unto the Messiah the Prince <shall be> seven weeks, and threescore and two weeks: the street shall be built again, and the wall, even in troublous times.

SIXTY NINE WEEKS OF YEARS UNTIL THE COMING OF THE MESSIAH TO THE DAY. THE WISE MEN KNEW IT, THE SCRIBES, THE PHARISEES AND THE PRIESTS KNEW IT. BUT THEY DETERMINED NOT TO ACCEPT JESUS CHRIST AS THE FULFILLMENT OF THE ROLL OF MESSIAH.

TO BE BORN OF A VIRGIN

Isa 7:14   Therefore the Lord himself shall give you a sign, Behold, a virgin shall conceive, and bear a son, and shall call his name Immanuel.

Mat 1:18   Now the birth of Jesus Christ was on this wise: When as his mother Mary was espoused to Joseph, before they came together, she was found with child of the Holy Ghost.

How could a woman give birth to a son when she had never known a man? Did not God create this being known as man? Why is it inconceivable that God himself would cause this ovum in the womb of this young lady to be fertilized? Mary gave Jesus his humanity but God gave him his divinity. The dual nature of Christ is that he was human and divine. We are just human. God gave with his divinity a sin free nature. Adam had this nature until he sinned. Only two ever had God as their Father, Adam and Jesus. Now, through Christ, we also may have God as our Father, but, and only, if we do his will and not our own. It's not an on again off again type of relationship. It's a relationship formed out of a love sacrifice where the individual puts aside his or her desires and actively seeks to please the savior. A true relationship between a husband and wife are forged of this same metal. Remember, that Love is a passion to give.

EVEN HEROD'S MASSACRE OF THE INFANTS THROUGHOUT THE LAND WAS FORETOLD

Jer 31:15   Thus saith the LORD, A voice was heard in Ramah, lamentation, <and> bitter weeping, Rahel weeping for her children refused to be comforted for her children, because they <were> not.

Mat 2:16   Then Herod, when he saw that he was mocked of the wise men, was exceeding wroth, and sent forth, and slew all the children that were in Bethlehem, and in all the coasts thereof, from two years old and under, according to the time which he had diligently inquired of the wise men.   Why did this man destroy all these infants? Because he heard that a king of the Jews had just been born and he was the king at the time. No one was going to take the throne away from him, he would see to it. Messiah has come shall we weep?

Did you ever wonder why the wise men came to inquire of Jesus the Messiah at the household of Herod? Jesus was foretold to be the king of the Jews. Where else would you find an infant king but in a king's house.

Mat 2:2 "Where is he that is born King of the Jews for we have came to worship him. Herod said, when you find him, let me know so that I can worship him too." We know what was in his heart for was it not revealed when he destroyed all the children of the land two years old and under? Man's inhumanity to man has went on since Cain slew Able. What possesses a man that he would do such a thing as this? What drives a man that he would even think of beating his fellow man until his back looked like hamburger? I don't understand, I just don't understand. Is human life so cheap, is man so calloused, is his heart so hard that he just don't feel any thing for his fellow man? Is it the feeling of power over another that causes one to act so? It's frightening, terribly frightening.

How did Jesus escape this massacre?

Hosea 11:1   When Israel <was> a child, then I loved him, and called my son out of Egypt.

This prophecy reflected the fact that Joseph and Mary would take the babe Jesus into Egypt and so they did.

Mat 2:13-15 "And when they were departed, behold, the angel of the Lord appeareth to Joseph in a dream, saying, Arise, and take the young child and his mother, and flee into Egypt, and be thou there until I bring thee word: for Herod will seek the young child to destroy him." Mat 2:14   "When he arose, he took the young child and his mother by night, and departed into Egypt: And was there until the death of Herod: that it might be fulfilled which was spoken of the Lord by the prophet, saying, Out of Egypt have I called my son."

Jesus ministered unto his people as Isaiah foretold in:

Isa 9:1-2   Nevertheless the dimness <shall> not <be> such as <was> in her vexation, when at the first he lightly afflicted the land of Zebulun and the land of Naphtali, and afterward did more grievously afflict <her by> the way of the sea, beyond Jordan, in Galilee of the nations. {2} the people that walked in darkness have seen a great light: they that dwell in the land of the shadow of death, upon them hath the light shined.

If you would read Matthew 4:12-16 you can see the fulfillment of this prophecy.

Mat 4:12-16   Now when Jesus had heard that John was cast into prison, he departed into Galilee, {13} And leaving Nazareth, he came and dwelt in Capernaum, which is upon the sea coast, in the borders of Zabulon and Nephthalim: {14} That it might be fulfilled which was spoken by Esaias the prophet, saying, {15} The land of Zabulon, and the land of Nephthalim, <by> the way of the sea, beyond Jordan, Galilee of the Gentiles, {16} The people which sat in darkness saw great light, and to them which sat in the region and shadow of death light is sprung up.

The Lord was not only the Messiah but also a prophet and a priest:

Deu 18:15   The LORD thy God will raise up unto thee a Prophet from the midst of thee, of thy brethren, like unto me, unto him ye shall hearken,

John 6:14   Then those men, when they had seen the miracle that Jesus did, said, This is of a truth that prophet that should come into the world.

As a priest,

Psa 110:4   The LORD hath sworn, and will not repent, Thou <art> a priest for ever after the order of Melchizedek. The fulfillment is found in,

Heb 6:20 whither the forerunner is for us entered, <even> Jesus, made an high priest for ever after the order of Melchisedec. The priesthood of Melchisedec, someday we will study what was so different about his priesthood. You see, he was not of the tribe of Levi but of Judah. None of this tribe was called to serve in the tabernacle for they were not of the proper lineage as far as the earthly flesh was concerned. Melchisedec had a higher priesthood, one of the realm of the Spiritual, or heavenly priesthood. Hebrews says it this way, without father or mother, that is, without the levitical parentage, without father of the tribe of levi and without mother of the tribe of Levi but Heb 7:4 "Now consider how great this man <was>, unto whom even the patriarch Abraham gave the tenth of the spoils." Heb 7:9 "And as I may so say, Levi also, who receiveth tithes, paid tithes in Abraham." Heb 7:10 "For he was yet in the loins of his father, when Melchisedec met him." Jesus Christ an high priest after the order of Melchisedec.

Time has slipped by us again. The study of the prophecies concerning the birth, life, death, and resurrection of our Lord of Glory will take the next two Sundays or so to complete. I hope that you've enjoyed this study and will tune in again next Sunday to hear about this Baby born in the shadow of the cross. Born to glory, honor, and praise.

THE PROMISE PART 2   12/15/1991

PSM 45:1 MY HEART IS INDITING A GOOD MATTER:
I SPEAK THE THINGS WHICH I HAVE MADE TOUCHING THE KING:
MY TONGUE IS THE PEN OF A READY WRITER

The promised one. Out of Judah arose the deliver. Out of Bethlehem, came the promise, Micah 5:2   But thou, Bethlehem Ephratah, <though> thou be little among the thousands of Judah, <yet> out of thee shall he come forth unto me <that is> to be ruler in Israel, whose goings forth <have been> from of old, from everlasting. Isa 9:7   of the increase of <his> government and peace <there shall be> no end, upon the throne of David, and upon his kingdom, to order it, and to establish it with judgment and with justice from henceforth even for ever. The zeal of the LORD of hosts will perform this. Isa 7:14   Therefore the Lord himself shall give you a sign, Behold, a virgin shall conceive, and bear a son, and shall call his name Immanuel. Gal 4:4   But when the fullness of the time was come, God sent forth his Son, made of a woman, made under the law, Gal 4:5   "To redeem them that were under the law, that we might receive the adoption of sons." As a lion, as a lamb led to the slaughter, as a king without a kingdom, as the lion of the tribe of Judah. Jesus Christ wears many coats, but the image of Him in a manger wrapped on swaddling cloths, is the most helpless scene one could imagine. Who is this babe in a manger? Why has he come? Why are the angels proclaiming his birth. Is this really the salvation of the Lord? He's so small, what can a baby do to deliver the people from captivity? he can't even feed himself how can he save others? The voice of doubt uttering the discouraging words to any and all ears that will stand to hear. The mocking, jeering crowd, shouting Crucify him, crucify him. Not all had this attitude for there was a Holy man named Simeon who came to the temple when Joseph and Mary brought Jesus to the temple on the eighth day as the law required.   Luke 2:25 "And, behold, there was a man in Jerusalem, whose name <was> Simeon, and the same man <was> just and devout, waiting for the consolation of Israel: and the Holy Ghost was upon him. And it was revealed unto him by the Holy Ghost, that he should not see death, before he had seen the Lord's Christ. And he came by the Spirit into the temple: and when the parents brought in the child Jesus, to do for him after the custom of the law,

Then took he him up in his arms, and blessed God, and said, Lord, now lettest thou thy servant depart in peace, according to thy word: For mine eyes have seen thy salvation, Which thou hast prepared before the face of all people, A light to lighten the Gentiles, and the glory of thy people Israel. And Joseph and his mother marveled at those things which were spoken of him."

Here was a nation that had been in captivity for the last 600 years. Now they were under the rule of Rome. it was a time of much distress. For four hundred years there hadn't been a prophet in the land. No one had heard from God in 400 years. They felt God forsaken. The Roman government had made the priest hood a political position and the only thing the people had was a form of religion. People were crucified, stoned, fed to the lions, fought against gladiators, and were, in general, just so much offal on the sea of life. Here was a people that were trouble makers for the Roman government. Just slaves to a far away king. Beasts of burden to be trodden down in the streets and highways of the land. To be oppressed or under bondage is near impossible for a free people to imagine. How can one that has been free all their lives imagine what it is to be in slaved? What kept this people going? What sustained them in the hard places of life? It was the Promise, Rom 11:26 "And so all Israel shall be saved: as it is written, There shall come out of Sion the Deliverer, and shall turn away ungodliness from Jacob:" Rom 11:27 For this <is> my covenant unto them, when I shall take away their sins. What did they do with verses of scripture like Isa 53:5 "But he <was> wounded for our transgressions, <he was> bruised for our iniquities: the [chastisement] of our peace <was> upon him, and with his stripes we are healed" Isa 53:4 "Surely he hath borne our griefs, and carried our sorrows: yet we did esteem him stricken, smitten of God, and afflicted." Isa 53:5 "But he <was> wounded for our transgressions, <he was> bruised for our iniquities: the chastisement of our peace <was> upon him, and with his stripes we are healed." Isa 53:6 "All we like sheep have gone astray, we have turned every one to his own way, and the LORD hath laid on him the iniquity of us all." Isa 53:7 "He was oppressed, and he was afflicted, yet he opened not his mouth: he is brought as a lamb to the slaughter, and as a sheep before her sheerer is dumb, so he openeth not his mouth." Isa 53:8 "He was taken from prison and from judgment: and who shall declare his generation? for he was cut off out of the land of the living: for the transgression of my people was he stricken." Isa 53:9 "And he made his grave with the wicked, and with the rich in his death, because he had done no violence, neither <was any> deceit in his mouth." Isa 53:10 "Yet it pleased the LORD to bruise him, he hath put <him> to grief:

when thou shalt make his soul an offering for sin, he shall see <his> seed, he shall prolong <his> days, and the pleasure of the LORD shall prosper in his hand." Perhaps they are like the Acts 8:30 "And Philip ran thither to <him>, and heard him read the prophet Esaias, and said, Understandest thou what thou readest?" Acts 8:31 "And he said, How can I, except some man should guide me? And he desired Philip that he would come up and sit with him." Acts 8:32 "The place of the scripture which he read was this, He was led as a sheep to the slaughter, and like a lamb dumb before his shearer, so opened he not his mouth:" Acts 8:33 "In his humiliation his judgment was taken away: and who shall declare his generation? for his life is taken from the earth." Acts 8:34 "And the eunuch answered Philip, and said, I pray thee, of whom speaketh the prophet this? of himself, or of some other man?" Acts 8:35 "Then Philip opened his mouth, and began at the same scripture, and preached unto him Jesus." The eunuch knew not who Isaiah spoke of, neither did the Jews for they crucified the Lord of Glory.

Isa 7:14 "Therefore the Lord himself shall give you a sign, Behold, a virgin shall conceive, and bear a son, and shall call his name Immanuel." The hope of every young woman was that she would be the one to give birth to the promised one. They prolonged their single state just to give God one more chance to use them to fulfill this promise. From that day Isaiah gave it, seven hundred or so years before, until Mary conceived, they hoped and prayed it would be them. The talk of the elders in the gates of the city revolved around this promise given by God. "Well, will it be today that God gives us a deliver? Or will it be some other time?" This went on for years and years until time wore the edges off the promise. Talk turned to other things that older people pleasure each other with. No longer did the young women think about being the one, the chosen one that would give birth to the deliver. Time had taken it's tole on the promise. Soon another ruler would rise up and oppress the people and they would cry out for God to fulfill the promise. "Oh give us a deliver oh God of Israel. Free us from the oppression and yoke of slavery." One hundred years, two hundred years, three, four, on and on it went, until the day the angel appeared to Mary: Luke 1:26-35 "And in the sixth month the angel Gabriel was sent from God unto a city of Galilee, named Nazareth, {27} To a virgin espoused to a man whose name was Joseph, of the house of David, and the virgin's name <was> Mary. {28} And the angel came in unto her, and said, Hail, <thou that art> highly favored, the Lord <is> with thee: blessed <art> thou among women. {29} And when she saw <him>, she was troubled at his saying, and cast in her mind what manner of salutation this should be. {30} And the angel said unto her, Fear not, Mary: for thou hast found favor with God. {31} And, behold, thou shalt conceive in thy womb, and bring forth a son, and shalt call his name JESUS. {32} He shall be great, and shall be called the Son of the Highest: and the Lord God shall give unto him the throne of his father David: {33} And he shall reign over the house of Jacob for ever, and of his kingdom there shall be no end. {34} Then said Mary unto the angel, How shall this be, seeing I know not a man? {35} And the angel answered and said unto her, The Holy Ghost shall come upon thee, and the power of the Highest shall overshadow thee: therefore also that holy thing which shall be born of thee shall be called the Son of God." Luke 1:38 "And Mary said, Behold the handmaid of the Lord, be it unto me according to thy word. And the angel departed from her." More than once deliverance came to Israel from a barren womb. Here was a young lady, engaged to be married to Joseph, pregnant with a child other than Joseph's. What would you think? Mary went to be with her cousin Elizabeth for three months and when she came home don't you know she showed. The end of the first trimester. Matthew says it this way, Mat 1:18-25 "Now the birth of Jesus Christ was on this wise: When as his mother Mary was espoused to Joseph, before they came together, she was found with child of the Holy Ghost. {19} Then Joseph her husband, being a just <man>, and not willing to make her a public example, was minded to put her away privily. {20} But while he thought on these things, behold, the angel of the Lord appeared unto him in a dream, saying, Joseph, thou son of David, fear not to take unto thee Mary thy wife: for that which is conceived in her is of the Holy Ghost. {21} And she shall bring forth a son, and thou shalt call his name JESUS: for he shall save his people from their sins. {22} Now all this was done, that it might be fulfilled which was spoken of the Lord by the prophet, saying, {23} Behold, a virgin shall be with child, and shall bring forth a son, and they shall call his name Emmanuel, which being interpreted is, God with us. {24} Then Joseph being raised from sleep did as the angel of the Lord had bidden him, and took unto him his wife: {25} And knew her not till she had brought forth her firstborn son: and he called his name JESUS." The promised seed had come. Born of a woman, the son of God. Who was this woman that she should be so blessed? Just a young woman that had found favor in the sight of God. Micah 5:2 "But thou, Bethlehem Ephratah, <though> thou be little among the thousands of Judah, <yet> out of thee shall he come forth unto me <that is> to be ruler in Israel, whose goings forth <have been> from of old, from everlasting."

    And the angels proclaimed the birth Luke 2:11 "For unto you is born this day in the city of David a Savior, which is Christ the Lord."

Born this day in the city of David was a light to lighten the gentiles, a minister unto his own people as was prophecies in Isaiah:

Isa 9:1-2 "Nevertheless the dimness <shall> not <be> such as <was>in her vexation, when at the first he lightly afflicted the land of Zebulun and the land of Naphtali, and afterward did more grievously afflict <her by> the way of the sea, beyond Jordan, in Galilee of the nations. {2} The people that walked in darkness have seen a great light: they that dwell in the land of the shadow of death, upon them hath the light shined. "

In Matthew 4:12-16 you can see the fulfillment of this prophecy

Mat 4:12-16 "Now when Jesus had heard that John was cast into prison, he departed into Galilee, {13} And leaving Nazareth, he came and dwelt in Capernaum, which is upon the sea coast, in the borders of Zabulon and Nephthalim: {14} That it might be fulfilled which was spoken by Esaias the prophet, saying, {15} The land of Zabulon, and the land of Nephthalim, <by> the way of the sea, beyond Jordan, Galilee of the Gentiles,{16} The people which sat in darkness saw great light, and to them which sat in the region and shadow of death light is sprung up."

Jesus Christ came also as a Prophet

Deu 18:15 "The LORD thy God will raise up unto thee a Prophet from the midst of thee, of thy brethren, like unto me, unto him ye shall hearken,"

this was fulfilled in

John 6:14 "Then those men, when they had seen the miracle that Jesus did, said, This is of a truth that prophet that should come into the world."

Jesus came As a priest,

Psa 110:4 "The LORD hath sworn, and will not repent, Thou <art> a priest for ever after the order of Melchizedek."

The fulfillment is found in,

Heb 6:20 "Whither the forerunner is for us entered, <even> Jesus, made an high priest for ever after the order of Melchisedec." The priesthood of Melchisedec, someday we will study what was so different about his priesthood. You see, he was not of the tribe of Levi but of Judah. None of this tribe was called to serve in the tabernacle for they were not of the proper lineage as far as the earthly flesh was concerned. Melchisedec had a higher priesthood, one of the realm of the Spiritual, or heavenly priesthood. Hebrews says it this way, without father or mother, that is, without the Levitical parentage, without father of the tribe of Levi and without mother of the tribe of Levi but

Heb 7:4 "Now consider how great this man <was>, unto whom even the patriarch Abraham gave the tenth of the spoils."

Heb 7:9 "And as I may so say, Levi also, who receiveth tithes, paid tithes in Abraham."

Heb 7:10 "For he was yet in the loins of his father, when Melchisedec met him." Jesus Christ an high priest after the order of Melchisedec.

Jesus was an high priest not after the earthly priesthood but one of higher origin, of a spiritual or heavenly priesthood.

The prophet Isaiah declared that he would be despised and rejected of his own people.

Isa 53:3 "He is despised and rejected of men, a man of sorrows, and acquainted with grief: and we hid as it were <our> faces from him, he was despised, and we esteemed him not."

And John says that

John 1:10 "He was in the world, and the world was made by him, and the world knew him not."

John 1:11 "He came unto his own, and his own received him not."

John 1:12 "But as many as received him, to them gave he power to become the sons of God, <even> to them that believe on his name:" John 1:13 "Which were born, not of blood, nor of the will of the flesh, nor of the will of man, but of God."

To be born of God. We all are born of the flesh, but this is speaking of spiritual things. You cannot be born of spiritual things by the will of the flesh. Jesus told Nichademius in

John 3:5-8 "Jesus answered, Verily , verily, I say unto thee, Except a man be born of water and <of> the Spirit, he cannot enter into the kingdom of God. {6} That which is born of the flesh is flesh, and that which is born of the Spirit is spirit. {7} Marvel not that I said unto thee, Ye must be born again. {8} The wind bloweth where it listeth, and thou hearest the sound thereof, but canst not tell whence it cometh, and whither it goeth: so is every one that is born of the Spirit."

When Jesus Christ stood before Pilate in judgment, Pilate asked him if he was the king of the Jews. Jesus answered with,

John 18:37 ...." Thou sayest that I am a king. To this end was I born, and [for this cause came] I into the world, that I should bear witness unto the truth. Every one that is of the truth heareth my voice."

When Jesus prayed in the Garden before he was captured he ended his prayer with John 12:27 "Now is my soul troubled, and what shall I say? Father, save me from this hour: but for this cause came I unto this hour."

John 12:28 "Father , glorify thy name. Then came there a voice from heaven, <saying>, I have both glorified <it>, and will glorify <it> again." John 12:29 "The people therefore, that stood by, and heard <it>, said that it thundered: others said, An angel spake to him."

John 12:30 "Jesus answered and said, This voice came not because of me, but for your sakes."

John 12:31 "Now is the judgment of this world: now shall the prince of this world be cast out."

John 12:32 "And I, if I be lifted up from the earth, will draw all <men> unto me."

John 12:33 "This he said, signifying what death he should die."

John 12:34 "The people answered him, We have heard out of the law that Christ abideth for ever: and how sayest thou, The Son of man must be lifted up?"

Who is this Son of Man?

They knew that Jesus had been proclaimed the messiah but couldn't understand that he had to be crucified.

Can you comprehend that one came to die for you? How is it that it is so difficult to realize that sin in our lives must be paid for? Is it that we are so temporal, so earthly that there is no comprehension of heavenly things? Heaven is so distant, yet earth is so close, that the only things that can be seen are of the world. doesn't a knowledge of the heavenly come with the package? I think so. But our faith must be exercised into believing that these things are so. How is it that you believe that there is a China, or Great Britain, or even an ocean? Have you seen these things? I've been to the ocean I know there are at least three oceans, I've walked the beaches, felt the water splash around my feet. I know about the Rocky Mountains, for I've camped high up close to the clouds, felt the electricity in the air in a mountain storm, breathed the fresh, clean, mountain air. I've seen Niagara falls in the winter time. I've ate fish at Port Dover. I know a lot of things about this ol earth, but there are more things I don't know then those things I do know. I've been to Calvary and seen Jesus hanging on the cross, I've seen his cruel torture under the whip, I've seen him on his knees, praying in the garden, I've seen the crimson flow of blood that flows for me. I've walked the lonely path of life with Jesus at my side, I've felt him as he braved the storm for me and calmed the waters. In the midst of the storm he has comforted me. I've had him feed me with the fishes and the loaves. He's my rock that I've anchored my life in. And when pressures get so great that I no longer could cope with them, he brushes away the tears. He knows where my boundaries are, What my limits are. How much I can take. I've learned to lean more and more upon him the older I get in Christ. I still venture out by myself every now and then only to find myself lost in the fogs of life. Jesus I've done it again, help me out of this mess I've got myself into please? These times are not as frequent as they used to be. I'm learning to lean upon him for all my life's substance. Like one man said, "I used to be a believer, but now I am a knower."

2 Tim 1:12 "..... for I know whom I have believed, and am persuaded that he is able to keep that which I have committed unto him against that day."

Let me persuade you to know who it is that Christmas is all about and to make him yours also. To believe and to know that he is truly the savior and that he came to seek and save those that are lost and that he came to become a perpetuation, the payment for our sins. That we may have life through his death, and in that life, life more abundantly.

Time has slipped by us again. I hope that you've enjoyed this study and will tune in again next Sunday to hear about this Baby born in the shadow of the cross. Born to glory, honor, and praise.

This is Bro Randy Johnson of the We preach Jesus Ministries
Po box 274
Eureka, Il

THE PROMISE PART 3   12/22/1991

PSM 45:1 MY HEART IS INDITING A GOOD MATTER:
I SPEAK THE THINGS WHICH I HAVE MADE TOUCHING THE KING:
MY TONGUE IS THE PEN OF A READY WRITER

Luke 2:11   "For [unto you is born] this day in the city of David a Savior, which is Christ the Lord."

Micah 5:2   "But thou, Bethlehem Ephratah, <though> thou be [little among the] thousands of Judah, <yet> out of thee shall he come forth unto me <that is> to be ruler in Israel, whose goings forth <have been> from of old, from everlasting."

Isa 9:6-7   "For unto us a child is born, unto us a son is given: and the government shall be upon his shoulder: and his name shall be called Wonderful, Counselor, The mighty God, The everlasting Father, The Prince of Peace. {7} Of the increase of <his> government and peace <there shall be> no end, upon the throne of David, and upon his kingdom, to order it, and to establish it with judgment and with justice from henceforth even for ever. The zeal of the LORD of hosts will perform this."

Dan 7:14   "And there was given him dominion, and glory, and a kingdom, that all people, nations, and languages, should serve him: his dominion <is> an everlasting dominion, which shall not pass away, and his kingdom <that> which shall not be destroyed. "

Zec 3:8-9   "Hear now, O Joshua the high priest, thou, and thy fellows that sit before thee: for they <are> men wondered at: for, behold, I will bring forth my servant the BRANCH. {9} For behold the stone that I have laid before Joshua, upon one stone <shall be> seven eyes: behold, I will engrave the graving thereof, saith the LORD of hosts, and I will remove the iniquity of that land in one day."

Isa 11:1-5   "And there shall come forth a rod out of the stem of Jesse, and a Branch shall grow out of his roots: {2} And the spirit of the LORD shall rest upon him, the spirit of wisdom and understanding, the spirit of counsel and might, the spirit of knowledge and of the fear of the LORD, {3} And shall make him of quick understanding in the fear of the LORD: and he shall not judge after the sight of his eyes, neither reprove after the hearing of his ears: {4} But with righteousness shall he judge the poor, and reprove with equity for the meek of the earth: and he shall smite the earth with the rod of his mouth, and with the breath of his lips shall he slay the wicked. {5} And righteousness shall be the girdle of his loins, and faithfulness the girdle of his reins. "

      Isa 28:16 "Therefore thus saith the Lord GOD, Behold, I lay in Zion for a foundation a stone, a tried stone, a precious corner <stone>, a sure foundation: he that believeth shall not make haste. "

      Isa 32:1-2 "Behold, a king shall reign in righteousness, and princes shall rule in judgment. {2} And a man shall be as an hiding place from the wind, and a covert from the tempest, as rivers of water in a dry place, as the shadow of a great rock in a weary land. "

      Ezek 37:21-28 "And say unto them, Thus saith the Lord GOD, Behold, I will take the children of Israel from among the heathen, whither they be gone, and will gather them on every side, and bring them into their own land: {22} And I will make them one nation in the land upon the mountains of Israel, and one king shall be king to them all: and they shall be no more two nations, neither shall they be divided into two kingdoms any more at all: {23} Neither shall they defile themselves any more with their idols, nor with their detestable things, nor with any of their transgressions: but I will save them out of all their dwelling places, wherein they have sinned, and will cleanse them: so shall they be my people, and I will be their God. {24} And David my servant <shall be> king over them, and they all shall have one shepherd: they shall also walk in my judgments, and observe my statutes, and do them. {25} And they shall dwell in the land that I have given unto Jacob my servant, wherein your fathers have dwelt, and they shall dwell therein, <even> they, and their children, and their children's children for ever: and my servant David <shall be> their prince for ever. {26} Moreover I will make a covenant of peace with them, it shall be an everlasting covenant with them: and I will place them, and multiply them, and will set my sanctuary in the midst of them for evermore. {27} My tabernacle also shall be with them: yea, I will be their God, and they shall be my people. {28} And the heathen shall know that I the LORD do sanctify Israel, when my sanctuary shall be in the midst of them for evermore. "

      Luke 2:11 "For unto you is born this day in the city of David a Savior, which is Christ the Lord."

There are hundreds of scriptures concerning the coming of The Savior, both the first time and the second. Israel read these scriptures and saw a king delivering them from the oppression of their captors. Scriptures such as those in Isa 53:1-10   Who hath believed our report? and to whom is the arm of the LORD revealed? {2} For he shall grow up before him as a tender plant, and as a root out of a dry ground: he hath no form nor comeliness, and when we shall see him, <there is> no beauty that we should desire him. {3} He is despised and rejected of men, a man of sorrows, and acquainted with grief: and we hid as it were <our> faces from him, he was despised, and we esteemed him not. {4} Surely he hath borne our griefs, and carried our sorrows: yet we did esteem him stricken, smitten of God, and afflicted. {5} But he <was> wounded for our transgressions, <he was> bruised for our iniquities: the chastisement of our peace <was> upon him, and with his stripes we are healed. {6} All we like sheep have gone astray, we have turned every one to his own way, and the LORD hath laid on him the iniquity of us all. {7} He was oppressed, and he was afflicted, yet he opened not his mouth: he is brought as a lamb to the slaughter, and as a sheep before her shearers is dumb, so he openeth not his mouth. {8} He was taken from prison and from judgment: and who shall declare his generation? for he was cut off out of the land of the living: for the transgression of my people was he stricken. {9} And he made his grave with the wicked, and with the rich in his death, because he had done no violence, neither <was any> deceit in his mouth. {10} Yet it pleased the LORD to bruise him, he hath put <him> to grief: when thou shalt make his soul an offering for sin, he shall see <his> seed, he shall prolong <his> days, and the pleasure of the LORD shall prosper in his hand.

They scratched their collective heads at Zec 13:6   "And <one> shall say unto him, What <are> these wounds in thine hands? Then he shall answer, <Those> with which I was wounded <in> the house of my friends." The birth of Christ can't be studied without looking at the cross, the tomb, and the upper room. Christ came to seek and save such as are lost. He wasn't born out of the desire of a man and wife to have offspring but the desire of God to provide a savior for the world. And he is indeed that savior.

*******The time of the year that Jesus was born really isn't known. The climate of Israel parallels our own, so of the shepherds were in the fields tending the flocks, it would stand to reason that it wasn't in the middle of winter.   But tradition has put the birth of Christ at this time, So laying aside all theoretical and theological arguments, let's worship the savior for who we have this time of the year is set aside. Jesus Christ, born a king in the city of David, a savior, Christ our Lord. A birth heralded by the angels of God, in the fields out side of ole Judeah. Heralded by the stars in the heavens themselves. "Rejoice greatly, O daughter of Zion, shout, O daughter of Jerusalem: behold thy King cometh unto thee: and he is just, and having salvation,...".

All this, in a baby, wrapped in swaddling cloths, laying in a manger. Oh if that innkeeper could have known who it was that lay in his stable. If only he would have known, he would have given to that Holy couple, his own bed. Christ wouldn't have been born in a manger. But the divine hand of God had set it in order that it should have been this way. The hotel suites and fine homes represent the luxuries of this life and Jesus was to be a man of no earthly possessions. Jesus said to a scribe that said he was willing to follow him: Mat 8:20 "The foxes have holes, and the birds of the air <have> nests, but the Son of man hath not where to lay <his> head." His ministry wasn't to the rich and prosperous of the land, But to those who were in need, the poor, the humble, and to the hungry. Mat 11:28 "Come unto me, all <ye> that labor and are heavy laden, and I will give you rest." Mat 11:29 "Take my yoke upon you, and learn of me, for I am meek and lowly in heart: and ye shall find rest unto your souls." Mark 2:17 "....They that are whole have no need of the physician, but they that are sick: I came not to call the righteous, but sinners to repentance." Jesus said it was easier for a camel to pass through the eye of the needle then for a rich man to enter into heaven. The Prov 28:11 "[The rich man] <is> wise in his own conceit, but the poor that hath understanding searches him out." A rich man trusts in riches and his own wisdom and not in Jesus Christ. "Because thou sayest, I am rich, and increased with goods, and have need of nothing, and knowest not that thou art wretched, and miserable, and poor, and blind, and naked:" Luke 16:20 "And he said unto them, Take heed, and beware of covetousness: for a man's life consisteth not in the abundance of the things which he possesseth. And he spake a parable unto them, saying, the ground of a certain rich man brought forth plentifully: And he thought within himself, saying, What shall I do, because I have no room to bestow my fruits? And he said, this will I do, I will pull down my barns, and build greater, and there will I bestow all my fruits and my goods. And I will say to my soul, Soul, thou hast much goods laid up for many years, take thine ease, eat, drink, and be marry. But God said unto him, Thou fool, this night thy soul shall be required of thee: then whose shall those things be, which thou hast provided? So is he that layeth up treasure for himself, and is not rich toward God." Is it wrong to be wealthy? Must you take a vow of poverty to serve God? No, such extreme measures are not required of you. What is required is that you realize that you have nothing that wasn't given to you by God. Your prosperity has been given to you from above. God has given you the ability to manage you finances and in this ability, riches have materialized. Many righteous men of the Bible were rich yet, not a single one forgot who it was that provided the riches for them. Life is but a stewardship given to us by God, it's not an ownership. In the state of South Dakota in 1976, while I was working in a boat shop in the town of Mobridge, I met a gentleman who was the owner of a sugar beet plantation in Canada. This gentleman had extreme heart problems and was greatly concerned over his children not being able to inherit the rights to the farm. The Queen owns the land in Canada and the people living there have the right to use it. When the person who holds these usage rights dies, the rights go back to the Queen. He never made it back to Canada and his plantation, he passed on unconcerned about his rights to a heavenly home. What became of his farm no longer troubles him, nor me for that matter. I don't know what became of the whole situation. But the point is, life is just a stewardship responsibility, not a proprietary agreement. You don't own it, your just using it.

Jesus Christ wasn't born into the affluent society of his day. Mary and Joseph weren't of the rich crowd, they were just typical Jewish people who were blessed by God to be the parents of the Messiah, the savior of the world.

Mary and Joseph began a journey of five or so miles to Bethlehem for the time of taxing was upon the land and all had to return to the area they were born in. Mary was great with child, in her third trimester, due to give birth to the Messiah. There wasn't any type of public transportation that we enjoy today. Just hardship. We are not told how long it took to make the journey, but of a surety, it took quite a while. Mary, walking and riding on the donkey, had to be extremely uncomfortable and in all probability, couldn't go much over half a mile at a time. Arriving at a city that had already seen the influx of generations of travelers, tired, weary, in need of rest, going from inn to inn in search of a room. Turned away time and again until room was found in the manger of an inn. Warm, and comfortable, but not a likely place for a King to be born. And the angel's sang out to the shepherds attending their flocks in the fields, For unto you is born this day in the city of David, a Savior, which is Christ the LORD. And this shall be a sign unto you, you shall find the babe wrapped in swaddling cloths, lying in a manger. Far to the East were the wise men, Men who looked for His coming and understood what the scriptures had said, saw the Morning star rise in the sky, and began their journey to greet the new King. The Bible doesn't say how many or even give their names, but it does say ,"behold, there came wise men from the east to Jerusalem, saying, where is he that is born King of the Jews? For we have seen his star in the east, and have come to worship him.

When Herod the king had heard these things, he was troubled, and all Jerusalem with him." This is the demented Herod that Josephus said, took the principle men of the entire Jewish nation, and ordered them shut up in the hippodrome, to be shot through with arrows at the time of his death so that there would be morning in the land over his passing away. Demented in mind, ruthless, it was said, "it is better to be Herod's pig then his sons," because he had his own sons slain. Herod gathered together all his chief priests and scribes and demanded of them, Where should this king be born?

In Bethlehem in the land of Judea, for this it is written by the prophet "And thou Bethlehem, in the land of Judah, art thou not the least among the princes of Juda: for out of thee shall come a Governor, that shall rule my people Israel." Chills ran up and down Herod's spine for if there were to come an insurrection during his commission, Caesar would have his head. And a new king of the Jews meant insurrection. Then Herod, when he had privily called the wise men, enquired of them diligently what time the star appeared. And he sent them to Bethlehem, and said, go and search diligently for the young child, and when ye have found him, bring me word again, that I may come and worship him also. This man had no desire to worship the one that could cause him to lose his head. He simply wanted to eliminate the trouble before it started. When they had heard the king, they departed, and lo, the star, which they saw in the east, went before them, till it came and stood over where the young child was. Evidently the star wasn't shining when they went in to see Herod. God would announce to the Jews, through the scribes and priest, that the messiah, the anointed one, Jesus the Christ, had indeed been born. If the star was shinning it would have led the wise men directly to the child Jesus. The scripture says, "and, Lo, the star, which they saw in the east, went before them. When they saw the star, they rejoiced with exceeding great joy. Selah, stop, think for a moment. These were men who had been traveling for days, months, perhaps years to get to this place. But, they rejoiced with exceeding great joy over the star. The scripture is not laced with superlatives, and this verse is indeed loaded. Exceeding great joy. Let me ask you, Why did they go to see Herod? Wasn't there a star to guide them. Evidently it had been taken away. They simply went to where a king would have been born. When they came out from the inquiry, and When they saw the star, they rejoiced with exceeding great joy.

Men, seeking after the baby Jesus, The king, The Messiah, the anointed one, the savior of the world. The Jews looked for one that would cause insurrection and overthrow the bondage of the Romans. They were seeking one that would be born in a King's house. They looked for a deliver, a Moses or a Joshua, maybe even a David. One clothed in fine linen, purple, scarlet, and a crown. Not a baby in a manger. And when they were come into the house, they saw the young child with Mary his mother, and fell down, and worshipped him: and when they had opened their treasures, they presented unto him gifts, gold, frankincense, and myrrh. Gifts fit for a King! Gold the noble metal, incorruptible, the symbol of deity, Frankincense, pure incense, the symbol of pure prayers, myrrh, a sweet smelling savior, used for incense, medicine, the symbol of humanity and divinity united.

There lay God, gift wrapped in the flesh.

1 Tim 3:16 "And without controversy great is the mystery of godliness: God was manifest in the flesh, justified in the Spirit, seen of angels, preached unto the gentiles, believed on in the world, received up into glory."

Never, has the life of one person so affected history. Never has there been a king, a martyr, or a wise man make such an impact on this world.

"Then Herod, when he saw that he was mocked of the wise men, was exceedingly wroth, and sent forth, and slew all the children that were in Bethlehem, and the coasts thereof, from two years old and under, according to the time which he had diligently enquired of the wise men." Genocide. Stop the Christ is the battle cry of the devil But, Romans 11:26 says "And so all Israel shall be saved: as it is written, There shall come out of Zion the Deliver, and shall turn away ungodliness from Jacob: For this is my covenant with unto them, when I shall take away their sins." God had for warned Joseph in a dream to flee into Egypt, for Herod would seek the life of the young child. There was no hesitation in the steps of Joseph, for "When he arose, he took the young child and his mother by night, and departed into Egypt.". And was there until the death of Herod: that it might be fulfilled which was spoken of the Lord by the prophet, saying Out of Egypt have I called my son." More than 300 prophecies were fulfilled on that eventful day 1991 or so years ago. Twenty writers living in different times in history and under greatly varying circumstances penned the scriptures pointing to this very day. Thousands of Jews waited for the messiah to come though time had dulled the sharpness of the prophecies of his coming. (God cause the babe to be born at a time when all the people would know, because of the star, that Jesus indeed had been born. The priests, the scribes, and the Pharisees knew when the time was right for the Deliver to be born. The scriptures are plain concerning the time.) Simeon said, "Mine eyes have seen thy salvation, Which thou hast prepared before the face of all the people, A light to lighten the Gentiles, and the glory of thy people Israel." And Simeon said to Mary, " Behold, this child is set for the fall and rising again of many in Israel," {They expected a temporal deliver, and when it wasn't so, they rejected him and he became a rock of offence and a stone of stumbling as was foretold in

Isa 8:14-15 "And he shall be for a sanctuary, but for a stone of stumbling and for a rock of offence to both the houses of Israel, for a gin and for a snare to the inhabitants of Jerusalem. And many among them shall stumble, and fall, and be broken, and be snared, and be taken." Behold, this child is set for the fall and rising again of many in Israel, and for a sign which shall be spoken against, (Yea, a sword shall pierce through thy own soul also,) that the thoughts of many hearts may be revealed." What were the thoughts that must have went through Mary's head? This child is set for the fall and rising again of many in Israel, yea, a sword shall pierce through my soul also? She knew this was a miracle birth. She knew this baby was to be the messiah, but she, like every other mother, had her plans for his life. But a sword shall pierce through my soul also? Her mind races back to the comforting words of the angel, 'Fear not, Mary: for thou hast found favor with God." She found comfort in these words many times over the next 33 years. You can console yourself in these words also. Fear not friend, thou hast found favor with God. You look for the one known as Consolation of Israel, as the light to lighten the Gentiles. For unto us is born this day in the city of David a Savior, Which is Christ the Lord. Why don't you let the this Morning Star rise in your hearts. Make this a Christmas to remember. Make the angels rejoice over your birth as a new born babe in Christ.

Under your tree, sits gifts that you've sacrificed to give to those you love. You've wrapped them in the prettiest paper, foils, and ribbons you could find. Nothing, is too good for your friends and loved ones. Then how much greater is your Father in heaven? He knows how to give the greatest gift ever known to the whole universe, The Holy Ghost, God's Spirit dwelling in you, in your life, He becomes your life. Repent of the sins you've committed against God, those sins of self. The sins of wrong doing. And be baptized in the name of Jesus Christ of the remission of these sins. And you shall receive the gift of the Holy Ghost. For this promise is unto you and your children and to those afar off, even as many as the Lord our god shall call.

THE BELLS KEEP RINGING   3/31/1991

PSM 45:1 MY HEART IS INDITING A GOOD MATTER:
I SPEAK THE THINGS WHICH I HAVE MADE TOUCHING THE KING:
MY TONGUE IS THE PEN OF A READY WRITER

John 18:33 "Then Pilate entered into the judgment hall again, and called Jesus, and said unto him, Art thou the King of the Jews? 37 .... Thou sayest that I am a king. To this end was I born, and for this cause came I into the world, that I should bear witness unto the truth. Every one that is of the truth heareth my voice.

And Pilate saith unto him, "What is truth?"

Rather Pilate uttered this as a question or in irony cannot be told. Perhaps even mockingly but I rather doubt it in light of the dream seen by Pilate's wife concerning this man called Jesus. He waited not for any answer. It was more of a statement than a question. Many today are desire truth yet when truth stands saying I am the way the truth the life. Turning, without waiting for an answer uttering the cry, "what is truth?" Cynics, like Dioceses, walking up and down the day lit streets with a lit lantern looking for an honest man. People walking through out this life looking for truth. The path of life is lit with the son of righteousness but only for those who will receive the truth. Which part of the Holy Scripture are we to take as literal and which is to be taken figuratively? What is truth? At what point do we become fanatics? Or is the term better put, orthodox? What is religion and what is salvation?

Hebrews 2:3 "How shall we escape if we neglect so great salvation,"

2 Peter 3:9 " The Lord is not slack concerning his promise, as some men count slackness, but is longsuffering to us-ward, not willing that any should perish, but that all should come to repentance."

Because God holds back his hand of reprisal men feel that God does not see nor care what goes on in this ol earth. God no longer strikes men dead on the spot for infractions against his laws. No longer does He strike thousands dead because of a rebellious nature. Do not error beloved brethren, The hand of the Lord is stayed simply because he wants you to repent of your sins and live for him. Before I came to the knowledge of the truth, long before I had ever read the Bible, a false concept was formed in the imagination of my mind. I had heard about a God that would strike someone dead, a God that would heal miraculously, A God that sat upon the heavens and watched over man like a eagle ready to pounce on anyone that was guilty of any infraction. This fierce God, This God of judgment, stepped back one day, turned to his son and said, "take over son for I have tried my best to make them live for me but they won't. I give them one last chance through you, see what you can do." This second in command, the son, stepped forward and with out any type of reprisal, coaxes men to live for God. How far off can you be when you work out a plan of your own?

1 Tim 3:16 "God was manifest in the flesh."

John 14:8 "Philip saith unto him, Lord, show us the Father, and it sufficeth us. Jesus saith unto him, Have I been so long time with you, and yet hast thou not known me, Phillip?"

2 Cor 5:19 "To wit, that God was in Christ reconciling the world unto himself, Who was in Christ? God was in Christ reconciling the world to Himself. Jesus Christ was God manifest in the Flesh. How can you say that Bro. Johnson? I didn't. The apostle Paul did in writing to timothy in 1st timothy 3:16.

There is a way which seemeth right unto a man, but the end thereof are the ways of death. Man, unable to accept the plan of salvation laid down by God begins to form his own plan of salvation. A Vietnamese friend feels that he must spent time in hell to pay for his sins, even the sins of accidentally killing a piglet. Oh Vietnamese friend, if you find yourself in hell there is no atonement for sins there. Just eternal torment. Can't you see that Jesus Christ has paid for your sins? Can't you see there is the right way? The truth. And he turns, his head bowed, and walking slowly away, utters, what is truth?

1 John 3:1 "Here by perceive we the love of God, because he lay down his life for us:"

Mark 10:17 "And when he was gone forth into the way, there came one running, and kneeled to him, and asked him, Good Master, what shall I do that I may inherit eternal life? Thou knowest the commandments, Do not commit adultery, Do not kill, Do not steal, Do not bear false witness, Defraud not, Honor thy father and mother. And he answered and said unto him, Master, all these have I observed from my youth. Then Jesus beholding him loved him, and said unto him, One thing thou lackest: go thy way, sell whatsoever thou hast, and give to the poor, and thou shalt have treasure in heaven: and come, take up the cross, and follow me. And he was sad at that saying, and went away grieved: for he had great possessions.

Truth has it's repercussions. Here was one that just knew that he had done all that was possible to inherit eternal life. He kept the commandments from his youth. He came to the one in authority and asked the question. What is truth? Wasn't that what he asked? Speak to me true Jesus. What do I have to do to inherit eternal life? Tell me truth. Sad to say, he went away grieved because he had other gods before him. Didn't he? Possessions, many possessions. His life was in his possessions and not in Christ. There is nothing wrong with possessions as long as they don't possess you. Do they dictate your life? Push Christ out. Make him play second fiddle to some material object or god? Possessions or possessed?

Around the hem of the garment of the high priest that ministered in the Holy Place, were golden bells and pomegranates. Exodus 28:34 "And beneath upon the hem of it thou shalt make pomegranates of blue, and of purple, and of scarlet, round about the hem thereof, and bells of gold between them round about. And it shall be upon Aaron to minister: and his sound shall be heard when he goeth in unto the holy place before the LORD, and when he cometh out, that he die not." The High Priest had to be truthful to himself. His life depended upon it.

Hosea 4:6 "My people are destroyed for lack of knowledge: because thou hast rejected knowledge (translate that as truth if you would), I will also reject thee." This verse of scripture was written to the priests of the LORD God Almighty. "I will reject thee, that thou shalt be no priest to me: seeing thou hast forgotten the law of thy God, I will also forget thy children." The priests had departed from the law of God. They taught in their own way. People were going to hell because of a lack of the knowledge of God. Because of a lack of truth. We now live in a day of grace. No longer are we under the law of the sacrifices yet the principle remains. Jesus Christ has become our sacrifice, taking away our sins, putting His law in our hearts. Remember the man that came to Jesus asking, Master, which is the greatest of the commandments? Jesus answered, The first of all the commandments is, hear O Israel, the Lord our God is one Lord: And thou shalt love the Lord thy God with all thy soul, and with all thy heart and with all thy soul, and with all thy mind, and with all thy strength: this is the first commandment. And the second is like, namely this, Thou shalt love thy neighbor as thyself. There is none other commandment greater than these". Mk 12:29 "This is the law of grace. I will have mercy and not sacrifice." Later, Jesus told his disciples in John 13:34 "A new commandment I give unto you, that ye love one another, as I have loved you, that ye also love one another. By this shall all men know that ye are my disciples, if ye have love one for another." And John 14:21 "He that hath my commandments, and keepeth them, he it is that loveth me"...What commandments lord? The greatest commandments...

Jesus said that he came to fulfill the law not to take it away. He fulfilled the law by being nailed to the tree, the cross, and by dying for you and me. How can we escape if we neglect so great a salvation?

Our world is filled with Christian clichés, Born again, are you saved?, rapture, you might be too late, when I was in the world. Christianity, or the Christian group has its own nomenclature. Some is slang, most of it is. What in the world do these things mean? Questions, questions in your mind, questions that even when their answered they are still questions in your mind. Unsatisfactory answers given by those who are supposed to know. Is salvation blind faith and nothing else? You have to ignore the Spirit of truth to believe a lie and wind up in hell. Unanswered questions nagging at the door of reason in your mind. Thousands of different religions. Are there thousands of different ways to salvation? 1000 names of God. I think not. The Jews were so careful about the name of God they wouldn't even spell it let alone utter it. What happens when someone calls you by the wrong name? How do you feel about that? A thousand ways to salvation? Let Jesus answer this one.

Matthew 7:13-23 "Enter ye in at the straight gate: for wide is the gate, and broad is the way, that leadeth to destruction, and many therebe that go in there at: Because strait is the gate, and narrow is the way, which leadeth unto life, and few there be that find it." "Beware of false prophets, which come to you in sheep's clothing, but inwardly they are ravening wolves. Ye shall know them by their fruits. Do men gather grapes of thorns, or figs of thistles? Even so every good tree bringeth forth good fruit, but a corrupt tree bringeth forth evil fruit. A good tree cannot bring forth evil fruit, neither can a corrupt tree bring forth good fruit. Every tree that bringeth not forth good fruit is hewn down, and cast into the fire. Wherefore by their fruits ye shall know them. Not everyone that saith unto me, Lord, Lord, shall enter into the kingdom of heaven, but he that doeth the will of my Father which is in heaven. Many will say to me in that day, Lord, Lord, have we not prophesied in thy name? And in thy name have cast out devils? And in thy name done many wonderful works? And then will I profess unto them, I never knew you: depart from me, ye that work inequity."

Exodus 28:34 "And beneath upon the hem of it thou shalt make pomegranates of blue, and of purple, and of scarlet, round about the hem thereof, and bells of gold between them round about. And it shall be upon Aaron to minister: and his sound shall be heard when he goeth in unto the holy place before the LORD, and when he cometh out, that he die not. "

The high priest had to make atonement for the sins that he himself had committed before he could intercede for the children of Israel. Taking the blood of a bull and putting it upon the horns of the alter of sacrifice, pouring the blood of the sacrifice beside the bottom of the alter, taking the caul, the two kidneys and the fat upon them and offering them as a burnt offering, then the bulls flesh was taken outside the congregation and burnt with fire as an offering. Next he had to lay his hand upon the head of a ram while it was being slain. This offering was then burnt in total upon the alter of sacrifice. Jesus Christ is your sacrifice and you accept it by repentance, asking forgiveness for your sins. Next he had to wash at the brazen laver, which is the type of baptism,

Acts 2:38 says to "repent and be baptized in the name of Jesus Christ for the remission of your sins. the washing away of the filth of the flesh." Wearing the garments of the priesthood, the robe, with the bells and pomegranates, the ephod, the breastplate, the girdle or belt of the ephod, the hat and crown of righteousness, he then went into the holy place to offer up incense, which is a type of prayer, once this had all been accomplished, he then entered into the Holiest of Holies once a year to make intercession for the sins of Israel. Around his ankle was a rope that trailed behind him so that if there was any sin in his life or he felt that one of the ordinances wasn't necessary and skipped it, the presence of sin in the presence of God would cause the death of the high priest and the bells quit ringing. Don't think for a minute that you'll be able to stand before God with sin in your life. Sin separates. Sin puts you in the enemies seat. Sin divides. Sin destroys. Sin will see your soul in a lake of fire.

Hebrews 2:3 "How shall we escape if we neglect so great salvation," God is longsuffering to us-ward, not willing that any should perish, but that all should come to repentance." God is not slack. Try going in before the presence of God without fulfilling his requirements. Go ahead and do it your own way. The righteous will pull you out of the Holy Place by the rope tied around your ankle when the bells quit ringing. Friend of mine, My goal is heaven. If you know something about salvation that I don't know please tell me. I want to make it. Orthodox? I know of no other way. Holiness unto the Lord. I must be saved. I must be saved. I must be saved. I've studied the word of God.

I've poured over the scriptures. I've read and read and read. No where, I say Nowhere do I find in the scriptures where the gifts of God have been revoked from the church of the living God. From the body of Christ. Read in Romans 11:29 where Paul says, "For the gifts and calling of God are without repentance." This tells me that God will not take back that which he has given.

And Pilate looks in the eyes of Jesus, in the eyes of salvation, and asks, "What is truth?" It's easier to sell a lie than to give the truth away. People put little value upon that thing given to them. Jesus put no value on truth. Freely he gave to all men. Man is the one that puts the great value upon truth. Great prices are required for truth among men yet few even esteem it let alone seek it. Truth is something to be hidden among the stuff. Jesus put the value of his own life upon this message. Only he could lay down his life, no man could take his life away. He was without sin, there was no death in his bones. Giving up his life is the greatest example of second mile Christianity you'll ever find. "Master, how many times should I forgive my brother his sin against me, Seven times?" No, try 490 times. 490 is a good number to remember. And the rich young ruler ran up to Jesus and said, "Master what shall I do that I may inherit eternal life?" Do you really desire truth? Truth reigns supreme. Truth is the high priest's bells still ringing in the Holiest of Holies. Nothing Hid. Nothing covered. Just truth. Pure, unadulterated truth and the bells will keep on ringing. The bells, the pomegranates, the rope around the ankle all kept him honest and pure and righteous and obedient to the word of the Lord. The problem today is grace. God withholds judgment that grace may abound. That all may come to repentance. That all may find God. To thine's own self be true, read the word of God and get your questions answered. Manufactures put manuals in their equipment because they designed features in that you wouldn't know about. And they want you to take full advantage of the design of this piece of equipment. Software writers put manuals of instruction in their packages because you'll never figure out all the bells and whistles in their programs. God gave us the book of life because our salvation is so important to God that he didn't want it distorted by passing this message from man to man. Had the high Priest just left out one small part of the salvation pattern before he entered into the Holiest of Holies the bells would have stopped ringing. Aaron's sons, Nadab and Abihu offered up strange fire unto God, fire not taken from the alter, perhaps they just didn't feel it was important, after all fire is fire. Well God didn't feel that way. Fire went out from the LORD, and devoured them, and they died before the LORD." the LORD is not slack concerning his promises as some men count slackness, but is long suffering to us ward....We serve a holy God, A pure God, and the fear of the LORD is the beginning of all wisdom. Friend, the most difficult thing to do is to be honest with yourself. Put away the foolish pride that will condemn your soul to eternal torment. Salvation is the goal, salvation is the object of going to Church. Why go to church if you're not serious about your salvation? Don't play the hypocrite, quit fooling yourself. You are only fooling yourself. Keep the bells ringing. Serve God with a pure heart. Don't think that you have to serve God after the law of the old testament though, that's not what this message is about.

Colossians 2:8-16 "Beware, least any man spoil you through philosophy and vain deceit, after the tradition of men, after the rudiments of the world, and not after Christ. For in him dwelleth all the fullness of the Godhead bodily. and ye are complete in him, which is the head of all principality and power: In whom also ye are circumcised with the circumcision made without hands, in putting off the body of sins of the flesh by the circumcision of Christ: Buried with him in baptism, wherein also ye are risen with him through faith of the operation of God, who hath raised him from the dead. And you, being dead in your sins and the un-circumcision of your flesh, hath he quickened together with him, having forgiven you all trespasses: blotting out the handwriting of ordinances that was against us. which was contrary to us, and took it out of the way, nailing it to his cross, and having spoiled principalities and powers, he made a shew of them openly, triumphing over them in it. Let no man therefore judge you in meat, or in drink, or in respect of an holy day, or of the new moon, or of the Sabbath days:"

1 Peter 4:17 For the time is come that judgment must begin at the house of God: and if it first begin at us, what shall the end be of them that obey not the gospel of God? And if the righteous scarcely be saved, where shall the ungodly and the sinner appear?

2 Thessalonians 1:7-8 And to you who are troubled rest with us, when the Lord Jesus shall be revealed from heaven with his mighty angels, In flaming fire taking vengeance on them that know not God, and that obey not the gospel of our Lord Jesus Christ: Obey the gospel? What is the gospel of Christ? The gospel is the death burial and resurrection of Jesus Christ. How shall, how can I obey that? How can I obey the death, burial and resurrection of Jesus Christ? Does that even make sense? How do I obey the death of Jesus Christ? By repentance, A dying out towards sin. By repentance sin no longer has a death grip on your soul. Jesus Christ paid the price as your passover lamb on the cross. When you repent of your sin you accept his sacrifice, his death for your sins.

Romans 6:3 What shall we say then? Shall we continue in sin that grace may abound? God forbid. How shall we, that are dead to sin, live any longer therein? Know ye not, that so many of us as were baptized into his death? Therefore we are (that's present tense) we are buried with him by baptism into death: that like as Christ was raised up from the dead by the glory of the Father, even so also should we walk in newness of life. For if we have been planted together in the likeness of his death, we shall be also in the likeness of his resurrection: Knowing this, that our old man is crucified with him, that the body of sin might be destroyed, that henceforth we should not serve sin. For he that is dead is freed from sin.

Colossians 2:12 Buried with him in baptism, wherein also ye are risen with him through faith of the operation of God, who hath raised him from the dead.

those Jews asked Peter on the day of Pentecost, Men and brothern what shall we do?

Acts 2:38 Repent, and be baptized every one of you in the name of Jesus Christ for the remission of sins, and receive the gift of the Holy Ghost, for the promise is unto you and to your children and to all that are afar off, even as many as the lord our God shall call. Save yourselves from this untoward generation. Keep the bells ringing. ☐

FIRST BELIEVE   04/07/1991

PSM 45:1 MY HEART IS INDITING A GOOD MATTER:
I SPEAK THE THINGS WHICH I HAVE MADE TOUCHING THE KING:
MY TONGUE IS THE PEN OF A READY WRITER.

<u>**Hebrews 11:6**</u> "For he that cometh unto God must first believe that he is and that he is a rewarder of them that diligently seek him."

There is in this world many gods. People will believe in everything from Santa Clause to the Easter Bunny. There are lucky charms and rabbit's feet, four leaf clovers, leprechauns, and horseshoes. A myriad of different things to believe in, worship or bow down to. Some believe in the corporations they work for while others may worship a business of their own. Any thing that displaces God from your life has become and idol, a false god.

Some trust in economic structures or financial institutions, man made things that will eventually fail or collapse. All man made things, structures, organizations, or cultures will fail eventually. Man made structures left to themselves soon fall into disrepair and then back to the earth from which they came. Highways fall apart by the very nature of things.

There are in this world idols meant to represent things or gods not seen. Diana, goddess of the Ephesians supposedly fell from Jupiter in an egg. She was also known as Estartes to the Babylonians. Apollo's, mercury, Vulcan, Venus, Juno, Ceres, Vesta, Minerva, all gods, minor gods of the Greeks. When the apostle Paul visited Athens to preach Jesus Christ, his spirit was stirred within him for he saw that the whole city was given over to idolatry. The very street that he walked upon was lined with statutes of different gods, idols. These people worshiped the gods of wood, gods of fire, gods of iron, gods of water, gods of the sky, sensuality, gods of everything. Paul continued to preach the one true God to the disturbing of their whole city.

Then certain philosophers of the Epicureans, the Epicureans believed the world simply exists and that the only pleasures of life are to eat drink and be merry for tomorrow you will die and after that nothing, live for the moment, if it feels good do it, this isn't a new philosophy for this age, and of the Stoics, The stoics were fatalists who believed that no good would or was received from the hands of their gods, men form these two opposing groups, got together and encountered him.

"And some said, what will this babbler say? Some others, He seemeth to be a setter forth of strange gods: because he preached unto them Jesus, and the resurrection." You can follow along with this reading by turning in your Bible to the Book of Acts the 17th chapter and the 19th verse.

"And they took him, and brought him unto Areopagus, Areopagus, you see, was their supreme court, saying May we know what this new doctrine, whereof thou speakist, is?" "For thou bringist certain strange things to our ears: we would know therefore what these things mean. " (For all the Athenians and strangers which were there spent their time in nothing else, but either to tell, or to hear some new thing.) The Bible says of this type of people, they are ever learning yet not able to come to the knowledge of the truth.

Acts 17:22 "Then Paul stood in the midst of Mars hill, and said, ye men of Athens, I perceive that in all things ye are too superstitious." Or you are very religious. Jesus said it this way, "You strain at a gnat and swallow a camel."

Acts 17:23 "For as I passed by, and beheld your devotions, I found an alter with this inscription, to the unknown God." You were even careful not to leave out any god that might be offended at his omission. "Whom therefore ye ignorantly worship, him declare I unto you, the God that made the world and all things therein," Do you believe this? Do you believe that the one true God made all the heavens and the earth? If you don't, Genesis 1:1 doesn't apply to you. "In the beginning god made".. You'll not be judged for not believing in Jesus Christ, You'll not be judged for not repenting of your sins or being baptized in the name of Jesus Christ for the remission of your sins, you'll not be judged for not receiving the baptism of the Holy Ghost for you never got past the first verse in the Bible, God is, and he is a rewarder of them that diligently seek him.

Acts 17:24 "Seeing that he is Lord of heaven and earth, and dwelleth not in temples made with hands, Neither is worshipped with men's hands, that is, nothing that you can make, design, carve, or build will ever add to God. As though he needed any thing, seeing he giveth to all life, and breath, and all things, wouldn't it be strange to stand before the God that you've denied all your life, and have to proclaim him the builder and maker of all things?

Acts 17:26 "And hath made of one blood all nations of men for to dwell on all the face of the earth, and hath determined the times before appointed, and the bounds of their habitation, That they should seek the Lord, if haply, (like a blind man or a man groping in the dark), if haply they might feel after him, and find him, though he be not far from every one of us: For in him we live, (God is a spirit and fills all the heaven and earth our very existence, our very breath of life is drawn from Him), and move, and have our being, we move, live and draw our life from Him." He is the sum essence of our very life.

Acts 17:28 "as certain also of your own poets have said,"

> *"With Jove we must begin, nor from him rove,*
> *Him always praise, for all is full of Jove!*
> *He fills all places where mankind resort,*
> *The wide spread sea, with every shelt'ring port.*
> *Jove's presence fills all space, upholds this ball,*
> *All need his aid, his power sustains us all.*
> *For we his offspring are, and he in love*
> *Points out to man his labor above:*
> *Where signs unerring show when best the soil,*
> *By well-timed culture, shall repay for our toil."*
> *Aratus and Cleanthus Hymn to Jupiter*

For we are also his offspring. Forasmuch then as we are the offspring of God, we ought not to think that the Godhead is like unto gold, or silver, or stone, graven by art and man's device. And the times of this ignorance God winked at, but now commandeth all men every where to repent: Because he hath appointed a day, in the which he will judge the world in righteousness by that man whom he hath ordained, (Jesus Christ), whereof he hath given assurance unto all men, (if they accept him), in that he hath raised him from the dead." Isaiah 40:18 "To whom then will ye liken God? or what likeness will ye compare unto him? The workman melteth a graven image, and the goldsmith spreadeth it over with gold, and casteth silver chains. He that is impoverished that hath no oblation chooseth a tree that will not rot, he seeketh unto him a cunning workman to prepare a graven image, that shall not be moved. (Or shall not move). (It has no life). Have ye not known? Have ye not heard? Hath it not been told you from the beginning? Have ye not understood from the foundations of the earth? It is he that sitteth upon the circle of the earth, and the inhabitants there if are as grasshoppers, that stretcheth out the heavens as a curtain, and spreadeth them out as a tent to dwell in: that bringeth the princes to nothing, he maketh the judges of the earth as vanity. The wisdom of this world is foolishness with God. To whom will ye liken me, or shall I be equal? saith the Holy one. Lift your eyes on high, and behold who hath created all these things, Why sayest thou, O Jacob, and speakest, O Israel, My way is hid from the LORD, and my judgment is passed over from my God? " (God hasn't seen what I've done. God has slipped up and my record has fell between the cracks of the floor, he won't judge me because he forgot, or he didn't see). "Hast thou not known? hast thou not heard, that the everlasting God, the LORD the Creator of the ends of the earth, fainteth not, neither is weary?" There is no searching of his understanding. He giveth power to the faint, and to them that have no might he increaseth strength. Even the youth shall faint and be weary, and the young men shall utterly fall: "But they that wait upon the LORD shall renew their strength, they shall mount up on wings as eagles, they shall run and not be weary, and they shall walk, and not faint."

  Why, why would any one want to worship any god that couldn't live, didn't live, was created by their own hands, out of their own imaginations. That couldn't help in time of need, that couldn't strengthen the feeble knees that won't stop shaking or the hands that hang down, that can't heal, or deliver? Why? Why? Here is the almighty God that requires nothing of you but you, that is willing to go to lengths that tax our very humanity. There are gods that require all of your time. There are gods that require of you great, mighty things that are almost beyond your endurance. These gods give nothing, asking all of you. They are gods of stone, clay, mortar, wood, chrome, tin, paper, and lust. Who can endure? Who can run? Who can go? Where? Why? How? Cut them from wood. Give them eyes that don't see, Mouths that don't speak, ears that don't hear and hands that don't strengthen. Set them up. So the carpenter encouraged the goldsmith, and he that smoothed with the hammer, him that smote the anvil, saying it is ready for the soldering: and he fastened it with nails, that it should not be moved. So that it just won't fall over." Hand made gods that can't even stand on their own bases. Go ahead, be encouraged O god of wood stone or mortar. O god that is covered with gold. Answer my prayer now. Speak louder perhaps minds to heal, to save? Why? why won't you serve him? there are gods of the Nile river that require the first born to be thrown in to the river. There are gods that require your babies to pass through the fire. There are gods that require you he's went on a journey. Maybe you can call him up and leave a message on his answering machine. So Elijah went to King Ahab after three years of drought, he told the King to gather together the prophets of Baal, and the prophets of the groves on mount Carmel. There he asked the people of Israel, "How long halt ye between two opinions? If the LORD be God, follow him, but if Baal, then follow him. And the people answered not a word. Much like today. Then said Elijah unto the people, "I, even I only, remain a prophet of the lord, but Baal's prophets are 450 men. Let them therefore give us two bullocks,: and let them choose one bullock for themselves, cut it to pieces, lay it on wood, put no fire under it, and I will dress the other and lay it on wood and put no fire under it. You call on the name of your gods, and I will call on the name of the LORD. The god that answers by fire let him be God. And the people answered, It is well spoken. And they took and dressed the bullock and called on the name of Baal from morning until noon, saying O Baal hear us. But there was no voice, nor any that answered. And by your god. Ask help of it. They leaped upon the alter. And it came to pass at noon, that Elijah mocked them, saying, cry aloud: for he is a god, either he is talking, or he is pursuing, or he is in a journey, or peradventure he sleepeth, and must be awaked. And they cried aloud, and cut themselves after their manner with knives and lancets, till the blood gushed out upon them. No one would do such a thing today. Or would they? I remember a missionary who brought back pictures of people doing just this very thing, thinking that they could atone for their sins by the blood of their own sacrifice. these are supposed to be a Christian people. Totally ignorant of the scripture, they profess themselves to be just that. People! Jesus Christ has already done the work at Calvary. He shed his blood for the sins of the world. He shed his blood for your sins. Just accept it. It doesn't require penitence. It doesn't require self-flagellation. It doesn't require you to be brutally, literally nailed to the cross. All you need to do is repent of your sins, be baptized in the name of Jesus Christ, for it was his sin free sacrifice, his sin free blood that covers your sins and makes you pure, white as snow, and receive the Holy Ghost. This is from a giving God and not a god that requires great sacrifices from you. Just one sacrifice,

Romans 12:1 "that you present your bodies as a living sacrifice, Holy, acceptable unto God, which is your reasonable service. Well, these prophets of Baal screamed, and cut and danced clear up until the evening sacrifice." There was neither voice, nor answer, nor any that regarded. And Elijah said, People come near unto me. And he rebuilt the alter, took twelve stones, and with the stones he built an alter in the name of the LORD,

He made a trench about the alter, and put the wood in order, cut up the bullock, and laid him out upon the wood, and said, fill four barrels with water and pour it upon the sacrifice, and on the wood. Twelve barrels of water all total. Remember this was a time of intense drought. The alter, the sacrifice and the wood was drenched and the trench was full. And at the time of the evening sacrifice Elijah said, LORD God of Abraham, Isaac, and of Israel, let it be known this day that thou art God in Israel, and that I am thy servant, and that I have done all these things at thy word. Hear me, O LORD, hear me that thou art the LORD God, and that thou hast turned their heart back again." 63 words, no cutting, no screaming, no pleading, just 63 simple words. Then the fire of the LORD fell, and consumed the burnt sacrifice, and the wood, and the stones, and the dust, and the water that was in the trench. And when all the people saw it, they fell on their faces: and they said, the LORD, he is the God, the LORD he is the God. Does it take God consuming the sacrifice with fire to wake a nation? Will it take three years of drought to turn the heads of the people to the one true God? Will it take three years of tribulation such as the world has never known, where The four horsemen of apocalypse run through out the land. A white horse with a rider with a bow in his hand, no arrows just a bow. The antichrist bringing peace, the chief ruler of the federated kingdoms, The red horse with a rider that has power to take peace from the earth, Red, because of blood, and the sword because of war. Black horse, with a rider holding s a set of scales, A measure of wheat for a penny, a days wage, three measures of barley for a penny, all able bodied men will be a war. No one to till the land. Behold a pale horse, the rider is Death. Hell follows in the wake of this rider ready to swallow the victims of this war and famine. People will be beheaded for being Christian during this time. To talk of Christ during this time will be deadly for the speaker. The earth will reel to and fro as a drunk man, people will run to the rock and mountains crying fall on me. Hail, mingled with fire and blood, a third part of the trees and all green grass will be burnt up, a burning mountain will fall into the sea and a third part of the creature of the sea and a third part of the ships will be destroyed. Their blood will discolor a third part of the sea. A great burning star will fall from the heavens and poison the streams of fresh water, a third part of the sun, moon, and stars will lose a third part of their light, an angel will fly through the heavens announcing three woes that are to follow, an angel is given the key to the bottomless pit and then opens it, a smoke like cloud of locusts come out and cover the earth. They look like a combination of a horse, a man ,a woman, a lion, and scorpions. Their size isn't spoken of but they are to hurt and sting man. They have power to sting and torment but not to kill. Four angels are loosed which were bound in the river Euphrates, they are the leaders of a cavalry of 200 million. Horses with the body of a horse and the head of a lion, a tail like a serpent. Fire coming out of their mouths. a third part of men will be killed. These four angels had been prepared for the hour and day and month and year. This is an day hour month and year determined before hand, a long time ago, by God. On and on this book goes describing the time that is to come. Don't think that there will be a lasting peace in the Middle east. Don't think that this war is over yet. It's not. Only the first battle. I wish it were over entirely, but it's not. This is so harsh for a God of love. All this killing, hurting, burning. But,

Romans 11:22 tells us to "behold therefore the goodness and severity of God,"

2 Corinthians 6:2 "Behold, now is the accepted time, behold now is the day of salvation."

Hebrews 2:3 "How shall we escape, if we neglect so great salvation,?"

Isaiah 31:1 "Woe to them that go down to Egypt for help: Egypt is the type of the world system and order, and stay on horses, and trust in chariots, because they are many, and in horsemen because they are very strong, but look not unto the HOLY ONE of Israel, neither seek the LORD." My strength lies not in what I can do. My strength lies not in mine own knowledge. But my strength lies in my trust of the LORD God all mighty.

Proverbs 3:5 "Trust in the LORD with all thine heart, and lean not unto thine own understanding. In all thy ways acknowledge him, and he shall direct thy paths." David the shepherd King said in

Psalms 36:25 "I have been young, and now I am old, yet have I not seen the righteous forsaken, nor his seed begging bread." God takes care of those that claim Him to be their God. He's not capricious concerning his children. Whom do you serve? What or who is your god? If you seek the esteem of men , then your a man pleaser and their esteem becomes your idol. If you seek recognition, then recognition is your god. If you seek only friends, then they are your god. Man's ego is the fountainhead of all his own creation. From it flows the ideas that turn the wheels of creativity. The question is, would man be creative if, and only if, there was no one to please but God? Whatever your hands find to do, do as unto the Lord. Please God. We're all affected by esteem and recognition, I'm affected, I'd be a liar to say that I wasn't. There was one who wasn't affected, Jesus Christ. Jesus is totally approachable because he has nothing to prove and nothing to lose. This is the yardstick we're to measure ourselves with. Seek the face of God with all your heart, mind soul and strength.

WHERE TO FROM HERE   04/14/1991

PSM 45:1 MY HEART IS INDITING A GOOD MATTER:
I SPEAK THE THINGS WHICH I HAVE MADE TOUCHING THE KING:
MY TONGUE IS THE PEN OF A READY WRITER.

A cross, an empty tomb, an upper room. Where to from here? Lack of direction. No goals. A loss, or lack of vision. No direction for your life. Emptiness, disparity, discouragement, defeat, despondency, aggravation, anger. All lumped into one day, one month, one year, one life. Why Lord? Why hast thou madest me this way? You're the God of the universe, nothing is impossible for you, why don't you just touch me and make me into what you want me to be? You spoke the worlds into existence, Speak to me. Reprogram me, remake me, reshape me. Ah, there it is, the very reason you've been looking for. The potter saw a vision that was in the molded clay. Just a lump a clay thrown on the potter's wheel. Only in the mind of the potter is the pattern of the vessel. Only he has the vision. Wetted with the tears of compassion, the clay remains pliable for the hand of the potter. There are, in the house of the LORD, vessels of honor and vessels of dishonor. The difference is in the clay. Jesus which vessel am I? Will I be used of you? Or will I be rendered useless and cast into the fire never to be used again? Judas Iscariot was buried in the potter's field. This is the place where the potter threw away the broken, useless vessels and the clay that grew too hard to be sharpen anymore. Judas Iscariot, a vessel that refused to be sharpen by the hand of the potter. Cast off. Thrown into the potter's field, never to be used again, because of a hard heart. Where to from here? First a cross, then an empty tomb, then an upper room. Death thorough repentance of sins, a dying out to self, a dying to the hand of sin, a cross, then a burial in the waters of baptism buried with Him in baptism, In like manner as Christ was buried, and risen with him to walk in newness of life. An empty tomb. And then on the day of Pentecost in an upper room. The Power was given through the baptism of the Holy Ghost. You must have an upper room experience too. Tarry until ye be endued with power from on high. Then Go ye into all the world and preach the gospel, the death, burial and resurrection of Jesus Christ. The voice of God has spoken to our hearts but we have allowed the voice of discouragement and dismay overshadow the word of God written in our hearts and we like Peter go fishing. Jesus, their leader, crucified, resurrected, showed himself to the disciples as they stood in a closed room. Thomas had put his hand in the nail prints, had seen the torn side, had handled the risen Christ. All had seen him, talked with him, fellowshipped with him yet, There were together Simon Peter, and Thomas called Didymus, and Nathanael of Cana in Galilee, and the sons of Zebedee, and two other of his disciples, those that had walked with the King for three years. "Simon Peter, the one close to the Savior, saith unto them, I go a fishing. They say unto him, We also go with thee. They went forth, and entered into a ship immediately, and that night they caught nothing." Discouragement over the seeming failures in our life. Discouragement over what is actually God's hand shaping the rough edges off our walk with him. the things that hinder, the things that are not like him. The hand of the potter shaping us into vessels of honor. Vessels fit to be used in the house of the Lord. 500 seen Jesus Christ after the resurrection, Acts says brethren, Jesus taught and spoke to them that they should tarry in Jerusalem until they be endued with power from on high. But they had other things to do. Fields to plow, live stock to look after, wives they had married, houses and land to look after, fish to catch, I go a fishin. Discouragement with the way things were going. Discouragement because it just simply wasn't happening fast enough. Only 120 were left in the upper room. 120 faithful vessels looking for the promise of the Father. The Holy Ghost, Oh, how disappointed were the 380 when the power came. 5000 were added to the church the body of Christ. Miracles, wonders, signs, many other things were done and are done in the church. The voice of God has spoken to our hearts concerning the kingdom, given words of encouragement, words of life, but we turn ear to the demons of defeat and like Peter and the others, go fishin.

    On a hill far away stood an ol rugged cross. Jesus hung on that cross after preaching and teaching to thousands and tens of thousands. Twelve faithful followers even forsook him. Yet discouragement was a unknown garment to this lowly carpenter from Galilee. With a voice filled with tears, came the mandate, "Father forgive them for they know not what they do." Who Jesus those that drove the nails in your hands? The women that wept for you as you labored up the via del Rosa? No, My disciples for forsaking me. Discouragement? Here was one that had just spent, used up, given his whole life to die on a cross between two thieves. For a band of disciples that wouldn't even go to bat for him. Three years they walked the sandy shores of Galilee together.

For three years they shared every bite of bread. For three years they labored in the kingdom together. Betrayed with a kiss from one of the twelve. Denied vehemently by Peter. Railed upon, beaten, beard plucked out, nailed naked to a cross. What right have we to be discouraged? What right have we to be depressed? What right have we to say I go a fishin? Why art thou cast down oh my soul? Lift up the hands that hang down. Make strong the feeble knees. Without a vision my people perish. No vision. No goal. No direction. No dream. Life has past by swifter than a weavers shuttle. My life is over. The days of youth are past. There is nothing but death lingering in the wings for the curtain to be pulled. Sounds so bad. While there is breath there is hope. While there is Hope there is life. where there is life there is peace. where there is peace, God dwells. there is hope. There is Peace. There is life. Where there was a cross there was an empty tomb. Where there was a cross and an empty tomb there is an upper room. New Life comes out of an empty tomb.

Romans 8:28 "And we know that all things work together for good to them that love god, and to them who are called according to his purpose." Joseph, son of Jacob, youthful dreamer, dreamed a dream,

Genesis 37:5 "And Joseph dreamed a dream, and he told it his brethren: and they hated him yet the more. And he said unto them, Hear, I pray you, this dream which I have dreamed:" For behold we were binding sheaves in the field, and, lo, my sheave arose, and, behold, your sheaves stood round about, and made obeisance to my sheave. And his brethren said to him, Shalt thou indeed reign over us? or shalt thou indeed halve dominion over us?" He dreamed another dream, "And the sun and the moon and the eleven stars made obeisance to me." This was his father, his mother and his brothers bowing down to him. Joseph was sold into slavery to the Egyptians for twenty pieces of silver, lied upon by the wife of his master, locked in a prison to be forgotten, faithful to God, a model of a prisoner, a vision far back in his mind, a vision of the sun the moon and the eleven stars. Yet not discouraged, not cast down, still holding his head up. A faithful slave to Potifer, the one whose wife had lied upon him. "Why am I in prison?" Perhaps, just perhaps God was saving you from further temptation with Potipher's wife. Flee Joseph, but how can a slave flee? Flee Joseph, But how can he escape temptation? God will make a way where there seems no way. But prison? Yes even prison. Remember it was because of his righteousness not his unrighteousness that he was in prison.

1 Peter 3:14 But and if ye suffer for righteousness sake, happy are ye: and be not afraid of their terror, neither be troubled, verse 17 For it is better, if the will of God be so, that ye suffer for well doing than for evil doing.

Romans 4:12 "Beloved, think it not strange concerning the fiery trial which is to try you, as though some strange thing happened unto you: but rejoice, in as much as ye are partakers of Christ's sufferings, that when his glory shall be revealed, ye may be glad also with exceeding joy. 15 But let none of you suffer as a murder, or as a thief, or as an evildoer, or as a busybody in other men's matters."

Unrealized dreams, unfulfilled visions, cast down hopes. Across the paths of our minds comes the ghost of discouragement and dismay. The subtle voice of discouragement courses through the highways of my mind. Bringing blackness, doubt, and lack of self esteem. Then rises in my heart, indignity at being compromised by such a foe as this. Up screams the voice of dignity saying Satan get thee behind me. Utterly drive out the inhabitants of the land least their sin becomes yours. What destroyed the wisest man that ever lived, Solomon? He compromised his walk with God by worshiping the pagan gods of his wives. Don't you take wives or husbands of the children of Ammon. Drive them out of the land. Don't make a covenant with them. Don't make a covenant with the children of defeat. Don't make a covenant with the children of discouragement. They will destroy you. Lift up the hands that hang down, make strong the feeble knees. God told Abraham, Be holy and walk before me and I will make a covenant between me and thee, and will multiply thee exceedingly. With in Abraham was unrealized potential. With in you is great amounts of unrealized potential. There thrives within every child of God the ability to be what ever God would have you to be. What ever your hands find to do, do as unto the Lord. "I can do all things through Christ which strengtheneth me" Phil 4:13

Discouragement gnaws at the very foundation of my mind. Wearing me like a continual dripping. On and on the dripping goes. Day after day after day until my very resolution is nearly gone. Screaming, driving, crying, on and on it goes. Day after day after day after day. When, oh Lord will it let up? The hand of the potter changing the shape of the vessel to the vision which is in the potter's mind.

Romans 9:20 "Nay but, O man, who art thou that repliest against God? Shall the thing formed say to him that formed it, why hast thou made me thus? Hath not the potter power over the clay, of the same lump to make one vessel unto honor, and another unto dishonor?"

Isaiah 64:8 "But now, O LORD, thou art our father, we are the clay, and thou our potter, and we all are the work of thy hand. Arise, and go down to the potter's house, and there I will cause thee to hear my words. Then I went down to the potters house, and, behold, he wrought a work on the wheels. And the vessel that he made of clay was marred in the hand of the potter: So he made it again another vessel, as seemed good to the potter to make it. Then the word of the LORD came to me, saying, O house of Israel, cannot I do with you as this potter? saith the LORD. Behold, as the clay is in the potter's hand, so are ye in mine hand." There was a man named Saul of Tarsis. Tarsis is now called turkey. Saul, a Pharisee, a religious leader of the day. Saul who had sat at the feet of one of the two great teachers of the day. Saul, son of a rich Jewish family. Saul, who himself watched over the coats of those that stoned the first Christian martyr. Saul, who went about with a mandate to put in prison or kill, or maim or destroy or whatever he wished. Saul, who the scripture says

Acts 8:3 "made havoc of the church, entering into every house, and haling men and women committed them to prison." Saul, scattering abroad the whole church with his persecution. Who breathed out threatening and slaughter against the disciples of the Lord. Saul, who thought that he was doing the work of Jehovah, by persecuting these followers of Christ had a Damascus road experience. Journeying to Damascus to bring back to Jerusalem, those that worship in this way, was struck to the ground by an exceedingly great light and a voice from heaven said, "Saul, Saul, why persecutest thou me? It is hard for thee to kick against the pricks." Like an ox goaded with a sharp stick. Like an ox, dull, uncomprehending, stiff-necked, slow to respond to the gentle nudging, now prodded with a sharp stick, then jabbed, and jabbed again until the kicking stops or the ox turns. Saul, why do you kick against the prodding? Oh, God, does it take you knocking me down with a bright light to see your hand on my life? What is this voice of discouragement that blows you to and fro? Ever wind of adversity that comes along blows you off course. As I was doing dry wall on an addition upstairs in my home, I noticed little symmetric tracks in the plaster dust on the floor. Round and round they went. First one direction then another, against one object then another, turning, bumping, turning to bump again into the same object, round and round back and forth, no direction, no purpose, no goal, no leading had of God to direct, point, shape, and shine. Oh, God, am I like that bug? You knew me while I was in my mother's womb. You knew the plan, the direction you had for my life long long ago. Help me not to be a hard mouthed mule, not responding to the Master's hand. Help me to be a vessel of honor.

Help me to perceive the hand of the potter on my life. You must have direction for your life. Don't wonder to and fro in the hurricane years. The years without goals. Life is to short and precious to waste going round and round, round and round bumping into the same problems, the same lessons God is trying to teach you. I've told God, speak to me plain God, tell me what it is you want me to learn. I'm cautious, ever alert for repetitive lessons and situations in my life. God is using the ox goad to push me in the right direction for my life. Acts 9:4 "Saul, Saul, why persecutest thou me? And he said, Who art thou, Lord? And the Lord said, I am Jesus whom thou persecutest: it is hard for thee to kick against the pricks. And he trembling and astonished said, what wilt thou have me to do?" The right answer. LORD, what will you have me to do? Saul, stood before kings. Saul, now Paul, preached and taught throughout the civilized world. It cost him his family, It cost him his riches, It cost him his life. He said it this way,

Phil 3:8-11 "I count all things but loss for the excellency of the knowledge of Christ Jesus my Lord: for whom I have suffered the loss of all things, and do count them but dung, that I may win Christ, and be found in Him, not having mine own righteousness which is of the law, but that which is through the faith of Christ, the righteousness which is of God by faith: that I may know him, and the power of his resurrection, and the fellowship of his sufferings, being made conformable unto death, if by any means I might attain unto the resurrection of the dead." I count all things but dung. Paul had it. But for the excellency of the knowledge of Christ, threw it all away. Temporal. Temporary. Just for this life. Of no good in the next. You can't take it with you, but you can send it on ahead. Despondent one,

Phil 1:6 Paul says, "Being confident of this very thing, that he which hath began a good work in you will perform it until the day of Jesus Christ:" And in another place,

Heb 13:5 "Yea, I will never leave you nor forsake you even unto the end of this age."

I Tim 5:9 "For God hath not appointed us to wrath, but to obtain salvation by our LORD Jesus Christ, who died for us that whether we wake or sleep, we should live together with him. Wherefore comfort yourselves together, and edify one another, even as also ye do. "

The possibilities in Christ are unlimited. With God all things are possible, think not? Look at Noah, Gideon, Jonah, David, Solomon, Elijah, Elisha, Peter, James, John and the rest of the disciples. Time would prevent the mention of all the others. Men and women of Faith. Those who walked by and in faith.

Hebrews 11:32 says it this way, "And what shall I more say? For the time would fail me to tell of Gideon and of Barak, and of Samson, and of Jephthae, of David also, and Samuel, and of the prophets: Who through faith subdued kingdoms, wrought righteousness, obtained promises, stopped the mouths of lions, Quenched the violence of fire, escaped the edge of the sword, out of weakness were made strong, waxed valiant in fight, turned to flight the armies of the aliens. Women received their dead raised to life again: and others were tortured, not accepting deliverance, that they might obtain a better resurrection: and others had trial of cruel mockings and scourgings, yea, moreover of bonds and imprisonment: They were stoned, they were sawn asunder, were tempted, were slain with the sword: they wondered about in sheepskins and goat skins, being destitute, afflicted, tormented, (of whom the world was not worthy:) they wandered in deserts, and in mountains, and in dens and caves of the earth. And these all, having obtained a good report through faith, received not the promise: God having provided some better thing for us, that they without us should not be made perfect. Wherefore seeing we also are compassed about with so great a cloud of witnesses, let us lay aside every weight, and the sin which did so easily beset us, and let us run with patience the race the is set before us." A lack of vision will destroy you.

Proverbs 29:18 "Where there is no vision, the people perish:"

Acts 2:17 " And it shall come to pass in the last days, saith God, I will pour out of my spirit upon all flesh: and your sons and your daughters shall prophesy, and your young men shall see visions, and your old men shall dream dreams:" Perhaps we are like the blind man that Jesus healed, What do you see, ask he. I see men as trees walking. We have a blurred vision of what God wants for our lives. Maybe just maybe we need to get on our collective knees and seek the face of God to heal our blurred vision of what he has for our lives. The Lord bless and keep you until we meet again.

THE BIBLE   08/11/1991

PSM 45:1 MY HEART IS INDITING A GOOD MATTER:
I SPEAK THE THINGS WHICH I HAVE MADE TOUCHING THE KING:
MY TONGUE IS THE PEN OF A READY WRITER

The Bible, God's Holy Word for today. Written over a period of 1500 years by 40 different writers. Divided into two main divisions, The Old Testament and the New. A testament is a document disclosing the will of a departed person. It's a covenant or an agreement between two contracting parties. The Old Testament is the covenant agreement God made with man about his salvation before Christ came. The New Testament is the agreement God made with man about his salvation after Christ came. The Bible is composed of 66 books, 39 in the Old Testament, 27 in the New. The Old Testament has five books of law written by Moses. God dictated and Moses wrote. 2 Peter 1:21 "For the prophecy came not in old time by the will of man: but holy men of God spake as they were moved by the Holy Ghost." Twelve books of history. Five books of poetry. Five major prophets, and twelve minor. The New Testament has four books called the gospels, Matthew, Mark, Luke, and John. One book of history, the book of the Acts of the Apostles, the history of the church. Fourteen epistles written by Paul. Seven general epistles written by various writers and one book of prophesy, The Revelation of St. John the Divine. The writers of the Bible were of wide and diverse occupations, Moses, The writer of the first five books, was learned in all the wisdom of the Egyptians. Joshua, writer of the book of Joshua, was a valiant military captain. David, writer of many of the Psalms, was a shepherd boy turned king. Solomon, the wisest man that ever lived, was King David's son, penned Proverbs, Ecclesiastes, and the Song of Solomon. 1 Kings 4:32 tells me that Solomon spoke 3000 proverbs and his songs were a thousand and five. Daniel, the writer of the book of Daniel, was a captive, a Hebrew slave in Babylon, and then held the office of Prime minister of this country. Amos was a herdsman, Matthew, was a tax collector, Peter, a fisherman. Paul, a Pharisee, a persecutor of Christians until God got a hold of him on that Damascus road.

The writers of the Bible were of many varied occupations and experience. What a crew to write such a book. Every book is carefully dovetailed with each other. Words, penned by different men in different ages, many who never even saw each other. They never knew that others had written on the same subjects. Yet when these writings came together, not one contradiction could be found among them. What would happen if you were to take forty professionals, Doctors, lawyers, engineers, each in a different country and in a different age. Ask them, some how, to write on the same subject. To the Doctors, a cure for a disease. To the Lawyers, a point of law. Engineers, the design of a building or a bridge. No doubt, you'll have forty different opinions on each of these three subjects. There is seldom found any unity of thought on any subject written by men. Yet there is total unity between the books of the Word of God. There may have been many writers but only one author, God. Each writer had one thing in common with all the others. A direct connection with God. 2 Tim 3:16 All scripture is given by the inspiration of God. God breathed. Although their inspiration came from God each retained his individual style and personality. The Bible was written on three different continents, Europe, Asia, and Africa. Portions were written in the Wilderness of Sinai, others in Jerusalem, some in Babylon, in captivity, A few were written in a prison cell in Rome. One was written by an exile on the Isle of Patmos in the Mediterranean Sea. None used a typewriter or a word processor. Most were written on coarse paper with scratchy pens in dimly lit places. Gods message to mankind. For what purpose? What was the intent of this Book? To whom was it written and why? Is it true or just some collection of writings put together for some unknown purpose? Like the paintings on the cliff walls in Utah. Never, never has there ever been a book like this. Go ahead, search the libraries of the world for a book that compares with this one. You'll not find one. Every self help book written has found it's roots in the Bible. There is no new thing under the sun. God has authored a book for all seasons, for all purposes, for all occasions, for all situations. God breathed. Great is the word of God. Mighty are His words for mankind today. Will it work? Listen, in the story, "Mutiny on the Bounty", the mutineers had sank their ship. They landed with their native women on the lonely island of Pitcairn. Nine white sailors, six natives, ten women, and a girl of fifteen. One of the sailors knew how to distill alcohol, and the island became vice filled and drunken. Time passed and only one sailor was left along with some of the native women and their children. The survivor found a Bible among the chest taken off the Bounty. He began teaching the others, the native women, the Bible. His life was changed along with the lives of the others. In 1808 The United States ship Topaz visited an island that had a thriving community without whiskey, vice, crime, or insanity. The Bible had totally changed the life of this colony.

Psalms 119:130 "The entrance of thy words giveth light." Contained within the pages of the Bible are guide lines for every day living. How to treat your children, your neighbor, your wife, or husband. Guide lines for conduct, speech, business, interpersonal relationships, salvation. You need no other book. The Bible is complete in it's self. You'll find between the two covers, explanations, clarifications, and definitions of its self. God's word is true.

Psalms 12:6-7"The words of the Lord are pure words: as silver tried in a furnace of earth, purified seven times. Thou shalt keep them, O Lord, thou shalt preserve them from this generation forever."

The Bible proves in itself that it is true. But what of those that don't believe the Word of God is indeed the Word of God? What of the skeptic? How can the Bible be proven to be true? We can wait until the end of this age. Philippians 2:10 "That at the name of Jesus every knee should bow, of things in heaven, and things in earth, and things under the earth, and that every tongue should confess that Jesus Christ is Lord, to the Glory of God the Father." I'm telling you, there will be no doubters standing in the judgment at the end of this age. All will believe that the Bible is indeed the word of God. Discovery. The National Geographic magazine did a paper on ants. A man made a life's work out of the study of ants. One of his great discoveries was that almost all the ants, 95%, are female. Proverbs 6:6 tells me, "Go to the ant, thou sluggard, consider her ways, and be wise:" Consider her ways, not his. The Bible is written predominately, in the male gender. This was not a slip. Read on. "Which having no guide, overseer, or ruler, provideth her meat in the summer, and gathereth her food in the harvest." Three times her is used. Science is moving forward at such a rapid pace that present technology and learning are outdated and obsolete before it can be used or even learned by others. But the Word of God has never been proven incorrect by science or anything else. Over 250 different plants are spoken of in the Bible. Botanists claim every Biblical comment concerning their field, plants, is completely accurate. Many facts about animals, birds, insects, music, law, art, architecture and other studies have all been proven true as scientists verify their findings with the Bible. Mysteries of the body, the soul, natural things, like rain, water, clouds, thunder lightning, winds, evaporation, and others have been recorded in the Bible for thousands of years. We are still learning the facts concerning all these things. Where did the writers of the Word of God get their information? Divine inspiration. The one that set up this universe knows all about it. How many stars are there in the universe? (HI PAIR CUS) Hipparchus, the father of astronomy said 1,080. For three hundred years this was thought to be true. Galileo invented the telescope in the 1600's and this count fell to the way side. Countless millions, no, billions hang in the summer sky. Astronomers now say there are over 100 billion stars in our galaxy alone. It's impossible to get an accurate count. Sir James Jeans, the English mathematician and astrology professor, must have been reading his Bible when he made the statement there are as many stars as grains of sand on all the beaches of the entire world. Read

Jeremiah 33:22 " The Host of heaven cannot be numbered, neither the sand of the sea measured."

Man's historical records are full of mistakes but not the Word of God. Hundred of cities dating back thousands of years, but spoken of in the Bible have been located and identified. The Bible is the most reliable history book of all the ages. Every detail is accurate. Critics have held that the Creation and Flood events are only myths. The record of the flood in the Bible isn't the only written record of this catastrophe. Flood traditions have been found in every civilization of the world. All these flood traditions describe a complete destruction by water, a boat is the means of escape, and sin is the reason for the flood. If the flood was only a myth, how can this similarity between all these accounts be explained? They must all stem from a common event, the Genesis Flood. Bible prophecy, history before the fact. Fulfilled prophecies show the Word to be true. 333 prophecies were fulfilled during the life of Christ or by the life of Christ. the prophet Micah writing in the inspiration of the Holy Ghost, said

Micah 5:2 " But thou, Bethlehem Ephratah, though thou be little among the thousands of Judah, yet out of thee shall he come forth unto me that is to be ruler in Israel, whose goings forth have been from of old, from everlasting."

Isaiah 7:14 said, "Behold, a virgin shall conceive, and bear a son, and shall call his name Immanuel." Immanuel means God with us. Isaiah went on to say that he would be despised and rejected, also that he would be crucified on a cross.

Zechariah 9:9 Described his entry into Jerusalem "Rejoice greatly, O daughter of Zion, Shout O daughter of Jerusalem: behold, thy king cometh unto thee: he is just, and having salvation, lowly, and riding upon an ass, and upon the colt the foal of an ass." David tells of his betrayal by a friend, and the giving of gall and vinegar, of the cross, the piercing of His hands and feet, and the gambling of men for his garments. The price of his betrayal, thirty pieces of silver, the price of a slave, was prophesied. Jeremiah wrote of the return of the Jews to Israel, never have we seen such an in fluxing of people to their country of origin. This is happening today. Rather or not what is happening in the Saudi desert is prophecy, only time will tell.

In 1947 two shepherd boys searching for a lost goat, found instead, the Dead sea scrolls. One young lad had tossed a rock into one of the caves in the cliff. The a breaking jar was the answer to this rock throwing. Eight clay jars were found . One of them contained three leather scrolls hundreds of years older than any previously read. Other caves in the area were searched for more scrolls, fragments of 382 manuscripts were found. Every book, with the exception of Esther, of the Hebrew Bible, the one from which our Old Testament is translated was found among these fragments.

The Bible. Men and women have fought for it. Been crucified, imprisoned, flayed alive, stoned, beaten, persecuted, torn by savage beasts, run through with swords, speared, and all manner of evil over this thing called the Word of God. This book has survived longer, is owned by more, read by less than any other book in the whole world. The average person's knowledge of the Bible is sketchy at the most. No more than five of it's leading characters are known by many. Most don't know of it's origin or purpose. It's teachings are clear out of the picture. We all have a desire to know what God has to say to us. Why is it so easy to excuse ourselves from the reading of God's word? I think the enemy has devised all kinds of extra curricular activities just to keep us busy. Do nothing type of things. Make work. He fills our heads with nonsense, saying It's boring, it's hard to understand, it's wording is too difficult. If only he can keep us from being fed with the bread of life, or drinking from the streams of the living water, then he can deal us the death blow to our souls while we lay in weakness, unable to fend off the attacks of the Devil. Starved, sapped of our strength, a lack of faith brought about by staying too long away from the Lord's table of life. Would you go without food for a day? A week? A month? Only in rare cases does such a thing happen. We feed our flesh just as often as possible. But faith cometh by hearing , and hearing by the Word of God. Without faith it is impossible to please God. We cannot stand against the wiles of the Devil if we don't have faith in God's word. We can't put on the whole armor of God. The helmet of salvation, the breastplate of righteousness, the shield of faith, having our feet shod with the preparation of the gospel. I'm telling you, it's impossible to live for God without reading the words, the letters, the love letters or letters written in love to you. These are the instructions that you are to live your life with. This is not some Midsummer's Night Dream written by William Shakespeare in old English. This is a letter penned to you. To you, I say. These are the words of wisdom, of a father that loves his children. These are instructions to make your life better, easier, more abundant, fulfilled. The man carried his Bible to work every day. He read it at lunch time. One day he felt self conscience about carrying the Bible under his arm, down the isle at work, Then the thought came that these are letters written by God to him. Those who look on, have not had that privilege yet. He knew then that his lives' work was to transfer these letters to those who don't know the savior, making these letters, theirs also. Think on that. The words of the one that created everything around you. The Bible, Isn't that awesome? "I have a wonderful treasure, given to me above measure, and were going to travel, my Bible and I." (unk) From the first words in Genesis, In the beginning God, to the last words in Revelation, The grace of our Lord Jesus Christ be with you all. Amen. It's written to you, for you. there's encouragement, Trust in the Lord with all thine heart, lean not upon thine own understanding and he will give you the desires of your heart. there's chastisement, Ye have wearied the Lord with your words. But, encouragement is in the book, The Lord God is my strength, and he will make my feet like the hinds' feet, and he will make me to walk upon mine high places.

    The Bible will show you God's divine plan for your life. It's personal. As you read God's words, a verse will seem to be highlighted in your mind. It relates to some problem or situation your now going through. Or perhaps, something you've went through but didn't understand why. God speaks to us through his eternal word. As you become more and more familiar with God's word, these occurrences will happen more and more. Now you'll know that this is not accidental, You'll know that God is speaking to you. Suddenly, you'll be looking and listening and God will be showing and speaking, you'll have fellowship with God and he with you. There will be a relationship formed with God that you'd thought to be impossible. This is exactly the relationship that God wants for your life. This close relationship. God seeks to improve and perfect you so that all your ways please him. All the things that you read may not be what you want to hear. Hebrews 4:12 "For the Word of God is quick, and powerful, and sharper than any two edged sword, piercing even to the dividing asunder of soul and spirit, and of the joints and marrow, and is a discerner of the thoughts and intents of the heart." The word of God can take apart your thoughts and then divide them from your intents. There is a difference. It is very important that you respond to the gentle nudging of God. God will not let you just slip by. There's not any, just passing on to the next grade, in Christ. If there's something in your life that hinders your walk and fellowship with God and your fellow man, God'll not let you go on to the next lesson until you learn this one. He's not capricious in any thing. But especially where his children are concerned. Hebrews 12:7 "If ye endure chastening, God dealeth with you as with sons, for what son is he whom the father chastened not? But if ye be without chastisement, whereof all are partakers, then are ye fatherless, and not sons." it's easy to accept a verse of Scripture if it sounds appealing and promising, but difficult, it's the ones that correct us.

How would you like to be more intelligent then any of your instructors? Smarter then your enemies? Happy all the time? Success in all you do? Healthy and full of life? How would you like to enjoy Peace for the rest of your life? How would you like to have faith to believe God for everything? Super power to overcome temptation and sin? The Bible has promised that you can have every one of these things, IF you are willing.

Proverbs 4:4 "He taught me also, and said unto me, Let thine heart retain my words: keep my commandments, and live. Get wisdom, get understanding: forget it not, neither decline from the words of my mouth. Forsake her not, and she shall preserve thee: love her, and she shall keep thee." Wisdom is the principle thing, therefore get wisdom: and with all thy getting get understanding. and then Psalm 119:97 "O how love I thy law! It is my meditation all the day. Thou through thy commandments hast made me wiser than mine enemies: for they are ever with me. I have more understanding than all my teachers: for thy testimonies are my meditation. I understand more then the ancients, because I keep thy precepts. I have refrained my feet from every evil way, that I might keep thy word. I have not departed from thy judgments: for thou hast taught me." Joshua 1:8 "This book of the law shall not depart out of thy mouth, but thou shalt meditate therein day and night, that thou mayest observe to do according to all that is written therein: for then thou shalt make thy way prosperous, and thou shalt have good success." Psalm 1:2-3 "But his delight is in the law of the Lord, and in his law doth he meditate day and night, his leaf also shall not wither, and whatsoever he doeth shall prosper." 1 Timothy 4:15 "Meditate upon these things, give thyself wholly to them that thy profiting may appear to all" Visualize the scripture. Get a mental picture of each word in the verse. Expand the meaning of each key word in our mind. Personalize the scripture to you. Change the nouns and pronouns to make it personal. Mark 11:24 reads like this, "What things so ever you desire when you pray, believe that ye receive them, and ye shall have them." Now take it and make it to read like this in your mind "What things so ever I desire when I pray, I believe that I'll receive them, and I shall have them." Read the Psalms of David. Most of them are already in the first person. Put yourself in them. If you haven't yet been born into the family of God, why not? Drop us a line and we will help you to receive an understanding of God's word for your life, then you can receive the baptism of the Holy Ghost. Repent of your sins, be baptized in the name of Jesus Christ for the Remission of your sins, and ye shall receive the gift if the Holy Ghost for the promise is unto you and your children and to those afar off as many as the lord our God shall call.

WHAT SHALL A MAN GIVE?   08/25/1991

PSM 45:1 MY HEART IS INDITING A GOOD MATTER:
I SPEAK THE THINGS WHICH I HAVE MADE TOUCHING THE KING:
MY TONGUE IS THE PEN OF A READY WRITER

The message for this session is for the Church, for the individual, and for the unsaved. Some parts will be hard to understand to those who are not deeply involved with the word of God while other parts will be easily understood. The burden of the Lord was upon me as I wrote this message. The words are those that need to be said, said to each individual within the body of Christ today. So many are discouraged, cast down, giving up in the face of adversity when there is absolutely no need to do so. This message is not meant to discourage but to encourage the individual and the Church to reach for that mark, the high calling of Christ. To press on when your strength faith, to realize that Christ will put nothing on us we can't bear. Our strength come in realizing that we have nothing to be discourage or despondent about. If you're in the body of Christ, the battle is not yours but Christ's. Phil 4:13 "[I can do] all things through Christ which strengthened me." If indeed you believe the Word of God then the backside of this scripture is, "I can't do anything without Jesus. If this is the case, then it's the Lord's problem and not ours, for he's the one that has accomplished all the good in our lives. Its a clear case of being crucified with Christ. Gal 2:20 "I am crucified with Christ: nevertheless [I live], yet not I, but Christ liveth in me: and the life which I now live in the flesh [I live] by the faith of the Son of God, who loved me, and gave himself for me." Col 1:27 "[Christ in] you, the hope of glory:". With these thoughts in mind let us press on into the lesson.

Ezekiel 22:30 "And I sought for a man among them, that should [make up] the hedge, and stand in the gap before me for the land, that I should not destroy it: but I found none. "

1 Samuel 14:6 "And Jonathan said to the young man that bare his armor, Come, and let us go over unto the garrison of these uncircumcised: it may be that the LORD will work for us: for <there is> no restraint to the LORD to save by many or [by few]."

Individuality. God deals with and through individuals. The body of Christ, the Church, is made up of individuals doing for each other. The body is several parts but a whole being. There are in our body, different parts, a hand, a foot and so on, yet each is part of the whole. One cannot exist without the other. Oh, a person can live without a hand or a foot or even both hands or both feet, but try to live without a heart or head or brain. 1 Cor 12:27 "Now ye are the body of Christ, and members in particular."
1 Cor 12:21-27 "And the eye cannot say unto the hand, I have no need of thee: nor again the head to the feet, I have no need of you. {22} Nay, much more those members of the body, which seem to be more feeble, are necessary: {23} And those <members> of the body, which we think to be less honorable, upon these we bestow more abundant honor, and our uncomely <parts> have more abundant comeliness. {24} For our comely <parts> have no need: but God hath tempered the body together, having given more abundant honor to that <part> which lacked: {25} That there should be no schism in the body, but <that> the members should have the same care one for another. {26} And whether one member suffer, all the members suffer with it, or one member be honored, all the members rejoice with it. {27} Now ye are the body of Christ, and members in particular. Jesus Christ is the head if this body." There's only one head allowed per body otherwise the person will be called a freak. A hand is a hand and not a foot. The hand performs the functions of the hand and the foot the functions of the foot. The hand can't say: I'd rather be an eye. The foot can't say, I'd rather be a hand. God has given to the body of Christ, members with a diversity of talents, abilities, and ministries, set there for the edification of the body, for the saving of souls. 1 Cor 12:28 "And God hath [set some] in the church, first apostles, secondarily prophets, thirdly teachers, after that miracles, then gifts of healings, helps, governments, diversities of tongues." What's the key to being used of God? What single thing does God require of you to be used by him for the edification of the Body of Christ? Availability. It's the voice of Isaiah crying out, Here am I, send me. It's the little widow woman in 1 Kings making a cake for the prophet with the last of her flour and oil, It's Matthew getting up from the tax collector's table and walking after Jesus, It's Zachus climbing down out of that sycamore tree and making things right with the people, It's Peter and John forsaking the fisherman's nets for the Lord.
Ezekiel 22:30 "And I sought for a man among them, that should [make up] the hedge, and stand in the gap before me for the land, that I should not destroy it: but I found none." In the whole of the populated world, not a single solitary person to stand in the

gap for Israel, no one to make intercession for God's people. Who will go? Who will be available to make intercession? Who will do the menial tasks, the troublesome things that life is made up of? Where are the Stephens that are called out to wait on tables? Acts 6:1-6 And in those days, when the number of the disciples was multiplied, there arose a murmuring of the Grecians against the Hebrews, because their widows were neglected in the daily ministration. {2} Then the twelve called the multitude of the disciples <unto them>, and said, It is not reason that we should leave the word of God, and serve tables. {3} Wherefore, brethren, look ye out among you seven men of honest report, full of the Holy Ghost and wisdom, whom we may appoint over this business. {4} But we will give ourselves continually to prayer, and to the ministry of the word. {5} And the saying pleased the whole multitude: and they chose Stephen, a man full of faith and of the Holy Ghost, and Philip, and Prochorus, and Nicanor, and Timon, and Parmenas, and Nicolas a proselyte of Antioch: {6} Whom they set before the apostles: and when they had prayed, they laid <their> hands on them. Acts 6:8 "And Stephen, full of faith and power, did great wonders and miracles among the people." Here was a man, full of the Holy Ghost and power, waiting on tables, ministering to the needs of others. Yet in his ministering, waiting on tables, he found time to preach the word of God, the gospel, where ever he could find an ear. The ministry of helps didn't depress this man of God, it was part of his ministry. There's a great tragedy in measuring yourself with the works of others, with their walk with God. Scriptures tell us 2 Cor 10:12 "For we dare not make ourselves of the number, or compare ourselves with some that commend themselves: but they measuring themselves by themselves, and comparing themselves among themselves, [are not wise]." When Christian folk begin to look at one another, and each other's ministries, when you begin to become envious, desiring the works, the ministries, the glory of others, the snare is set, the trap is sprung, and the green color of envy and jealousy destroy any work that could have been accomplished through you. God has set a special ministry in your life that's yours alone. No one else can fill your shoes. There's people in your life that no one else, having the truth, will ever be in a position to influence. There's in your life, a certain talent that you alone possess. Bro Sams can't take your place, I can't take your place. No one can. The mantle rests upon only your shoulders. None else can wear it. no one else can bear your burden. God has set it upon your heart to do some thing, some ministry, some help. What do you lack to fulfill this talent? What is needed to prompt you into accomplishing this thing?

"Our doubts are traitors that make us lose the good we ought might win by fearing to attempt." **William Shakespeare**, *"Measure for Measure", Act 1 scene 4*

Fear stands in the way of many a noble enterprise. Fear of failure, fear of what others will say, fear of not doing the right thing. Let Joe do it, he knows how. But you see, God has set it upon your heart to accomplish this thing, this ministry, not Joe's. We can find all kinds of things for others to do, but when it comes to the things that are on our hearts to do. Well. One evangelist carried a map of a certain city around for a full year seeking someone to go to that city. Everywhere he preached, out came the map. Won't you go? Here is a city in need. You must go. No one would answer the preacher's call. God had called him to that city. No one else would do. He's the only one that would fit. No round pegs in square holes. God knows. Here was God telling Jonah to go to a city called Nineveh. Jonah didn't want to answer the calling of God. Only Jonah would do. Only Jonah could reach this dying city. The prophet ran for everything he was worth, chartered a boat and sailed for cities across the pond. A storm came and near destroyed the boat and everyone on it. Jonah spoke up and told the crew it was his fault they were in such trouble. They threw Jonah over the side to be eaten by a large fish. You all know the story of Jonah and the whale. Deep in the sea, darkness about him, stomach acids working on his flesh, Jonah found a place of repentance, an alter to the living God. Send me a man. Who will go? "Here am I Lord, send me." Jonah went and the city repented of the evil they did from the king to the lowest animal fasted. But if Jonah hadn't went. What if the prophet stayed in the belly of the fish? Where would Nineveh be? Who will go? Who will feel the burden for the lost and dying? Who will answer the Lord's call? Mat 25:14-26 "For <the kingdom of heaven is> as a man traveling into a far country, <who> called his own servants, and delivered unto them his goods. {15} And unto one he gave five talents, to another two, and to another one, to every man according to his several ability, and straightway took his journey. {16} Then he that had received the five talents went and traded with the same, and made <them> other five talents. {17} And likewise he that <had received> two, he also gained other two. {18} But he that had received one went and digged in the earth, and hid his lord's money. {19} After a long time the lord of those servants cometh, and reckoneth with them. {20} And so he that had received five talents came and brought other five talents, saying, Lord, thou deliveredst unto me five talents: behold, I have gained beside them five talents more. {21} His lord said unto him, Well done, <thou> good and faithful servant: thou hast been faithful over a few things, I will make thee ruler over many things: enter thou into the joy of thy lord.

{22} He also that had received two talents came and said, Lord, thou deliveredst unto me two talents: behold, I have gained two other talents beside them. {23} His lord said unto him, Well done, good and faithful servant, thou hast been faithful over a few things, I will make thee ruler over many things: enter thou into the joy of thy lord. {24} Then he which had received the one talent came and said, Lord, I knew thee that thou art an hard man, reaping where thou hast not sown, and gathering where thou hast not strowed: {25} And I was afraid, and went and hid thy talent in the earth: lo, <there> thou hast <that is> thine. {26} His lord answered and said unto him, <Thou> wicked and slothful servant, thou knewest that I reap where I sowed not, and gather where I have not strowed:" Talents can represent money, but here, in this message, they represent what the Lord God almighty has given to you in respect of the abilities, the ministries, the works that are placed in your hands. All through the word of God, one man would turn the tide of things. Sin entered into the world by one man and death by that sin. Yet one man led the Children of Israel out of Egypt. One man led them into the promise land. Life came by the blood of Jesus Christ, just one man. Give me a man for the hour, give me a watch word full of power. One man can turn the tide of opinion. One man can move mountains. One man can change the whole world. It's not the great that rise to the occasion, to stand in the gap, it's the everyday man or woman that is available. Heroes are made out of the necessity of the moment, not out of planning. Give me a man filled to overflow with God's Spirit. Give me a man filled with a God given vision. Give me man willing to go, to do, to be what God wants him to be. this man will turn what ever city town factory or place he is in, upside down for Jesus. Vision, vision, vision, Prov 29:18 "Where <there is> no vision, the [people perish]: Get yourself a vision of God's greatness, of his love, of Calvary. Pray for a burden, a consuming burden for His Church and it's work here on earth. Angels stand aside for the man with a consuming fire in his bones. God works through those who are willing. Those who will willingly pick up the mantle of responsibility, using the talents and abilities that God has given them. God works through those who answer like Samuel of old " 1 Sam 3:4 "Here <am> I."

    The world sits with bated breath waiting for the Antichrist to appear. Not as the antichrist but as the savior of society as we know it today. That man, the antichrist will rise up with the answers to the dilemma that hasn't yet appeared but is waiting on the horizon for the world conditions to be just right. It's like the creeping darkness of the twilight of evening when the shadows are absorbed in the ensuing darkness. Who will rise up to stay the hand of this Antichrist? Who will stand in the gap and make up the hedge? Who will answer the clarion call that rings across our day and hour?

2 Th 2:3-8 "Let no man deceive you by any means: for <that day shall not come>, except there come a falling away first, and that man of sin be revealed, the son of perdition, {4} Who opposeth and exalteth himself above all that is called God, or that is worshipped, so that he as God sitteth in the temple of God, showing himself that he is God. {5} Remember ye not, that, when I was yet with you, I told you these things? {6} And now ye know what withholdeth that he might be revealed in his time. {7} For the mystery of iniquity doth already work: only he who now letteth <will let>(restrains)(will restrain), until he be taken out of the way. {Who is this he? It's The body of Christ, the church of the living God}" What happens when the Church is taken out of the way and the Antichrist has a free hand? {8} "And then shall that Wicked be revealed, whom the Lord shall consume with the spirit of his mouth, and shall destroy with the brightness of his coming:" What restrains the coming of the man of sin the antichrist? The presence of the Christian.

The spirit of iniquity already works in the children of disobedience. Awake Christian awake. Awake and trim your lamp. Wipe the sleep out of your eyes, shake off the stiffness of sleep, There looms on the horizon the end time. Behold, the fields of wheat have already been harvested. Behold, the husbandman cometh, shake yourself before the atrophy of disuse robs you of your strength. Awake Zion, for the sleep of death knocks at your door. Prov 6:10 "<Yet> [a little sleep], a little slumber, a little folding of the hands to sleep:" The world awaits the man who will take this gospel to the far corners of the earth. No. it waits for the man who will go across the street and tell his neighbor about the good ness of the Lord. Missionaries can be found for there's something dramatic about one who would give up all and go to a far country and preach. There's a need for this, but those who feel it dramatic are usually screened out far before the opportunity to leave our fair shores is ever in sight. The need is here. The need is now. The need is for a man who will reach those his life touches. There are those who look on in disgust as the church sleeps. the voice of mockery rings loud and true in the evening shadows, If what they have is true, why don't they share it? Awake church of the Living God, Now is the appointed time, today if you'll hear his voice. If you want revival in your church, in the congregation you attend, draw a circle where you want it to begin, the circle doesn't have to be large, then step inside the circle and get on your knees. Don't leave the circle until your revived. Until your vision is renewed. Then the burden of the Lord God Almighty will sweep over your soul. The mantle of responsibility you shrugged off your shoulders for so long, again lets it's presence be known. Awake oh Zion Isa 52:2 "Shake thyself from the dust, arise, <and> sit down, O Jerusalem: loose thyself from the bands of thy neck, O captive [daughter of Zion]. For thus saith the LORD, Ye have sold yourselves for naught, and ye shall be redeemed without money." Awake, oh Zion, the church, the individual, the man, the woman, the child of God. Trim your lamps, let your light shin forth as the noonday sun. Remove the baskets you've hid your light under. There are those that know what you believe, they wonder at you. They wonder why you don't share it. Prayer and fasting will break the strangle hold the Devil has on your life. He's choked out the fruit of your life with weeds of inadequacy too long. The battles you fight are real, there's no doubt of that, but God is sufficient for every need. Awake oh child of the King, awake and shake off the lethargy. Stretch yourself as the sky, shake off the sleep of death. Your one talent you've kept hidden in the shadows. Your ashamed of what you suppose to be a meager offering. Hopefully, you think, the master will be pleased that you can return to him your one talent. He won't be pleased. With that one talent he's given you the ability to make it multiply. All of nature multiples. John 12:24 "Verily , verily, I say unto you, [Except a corn] of wheat fall into the ground and die, it abideth alone: but if it die, it bringeth forth much fruit." John 12:25 "He that loveth his life shall lose it, and he that hateth his life in this world shall keep it unto life eternal." It's the law of seed time and harvest. You've let the light of the multi talented ministries rob you of the good you might do. They've thrown across your path such a bright light that your one talent is swallowed up in their glory. Remember what Jesus said of the widow's two pennies Mark 12:44 "For all <they> did cast in of their abundance, but she of her want did cast in all that she had, <even> all her living."

    The sacrifice of this poor woman was more then all the sacrifice of the multi talented ones or the ones that have a more visible ministry. Song leaders wish they could preach. Preachers wish they could sing. Sunday school teachers wish they could lead song service, on and on it goes while the one with five talents envies the one with only one to control while the one with one talent wishes he had more. Paul said Phil 4:11 "Not that I speak in respect of want: for I have learned, in whatsoever state I am, <therewith> to be content." Heb 13:5 "<Let your> conversation <be> without covetousness, <and be> [content] with such things as ye have: for he hath said, I will never leave thee, nor forsake thee." You have one talent, be content to work with this talent to the best of Christ in you. You have two talents? Work them for everything you can. Make your one, two and your two, four, and your four, eight. . To the edifying of the body the church which Christ bought with his own blood. Work in your local assembly, work in the district, work in the nation, work in the world, do as your talent, or talents lead you. You can play the guitar yet there is no need for you to help in the local assembly because of the type of music doesn't fit in with the worship. There are other places to minister in. Go to the retirement homes, there are thousands who will be willing to allow you to minister to them in song and deed and lessons. Go to the highways and by ways and compel them to come in. Go to the court yards of our cites and villages, be a troubadour for the Lord. There is no limit to the ministries one talented persons can blossom in. We have limited our thinking with self imposed limitations to the structure called the church when in reality it is only a building. The church of the Living God does not dwell in buildings made with hands. We are the Church, the body of Christ. We are his temple not made with hands. We are his feet, his hands, his life here on earth. We have a passport, we're not of this land, we're ambassadors, strangers and pilgrims looking for a city whose builder and maker is God. Don't be discouraged, what ever you can do, be it humble or great, do unto the Lord. Sunday school teachers, pray and fast over your lessons, be the best you can be for it's for Christ. Cooks, cook and bake, and work in the ministry of helps. Cook as though you were preparing a meal for Jesus Christ himself for you are. Sunday school secretaries, treasurers, janitors, preachers, evangelists, what ever you do, put your all into it for these are the talents God has given you. Let your mind run wild with ways that you can accomplish your ministry. Preacher, just what are you doing sitting in the congregation on a Sunday? Judg 5:23 "Curse ye Meroz, said the angel of the LORD, curse ye bitterly the inhabitants thereof, because they came not to the help of the LORD, to the help of the LORD against the mighty." There's a ministry for you, but you'll never find it sitting. I don't have anywhere to preach, you say, Luke 14:23 "And the lord said unto the servant, Go out into the [highways] and hedges, and compel <them> to come in, that my house may be filled." There's a pulpit on every street corner, on every block, in every city. Go, and compel them to come in. Rom 11:29 tells you "For the gifts and calling of God <are> [without repentance]." Mat 25:24-26 "Then he which had received the [one talent] came and said, Lord, I knew thee that thou art an hard man, reaping where thou hast not sown, and gathering where thou hast not strowed: And I was afraid, and went and hid thy talent in the earth: lo, <there> thou hast <that is> thine. His lord answered and said unto him,

<Thou> wicked and slothful servant, thou knewest that I reap where I sowed not, and gather where I have not strowed:" verse 29 "For unto every one that hath shall be given, and he shall have abundance: but from him that hath not shall be taken away even that which he hath. And cast ye the unprofitable servant into outer darkness: there shall be weeping and gnashing of teeth." God is calling his Church. Awake oh Zion, awake the husbandman cometh. Rev 22:12 "And, behold, I come quickly, and my [reward] <is> with me, to give every man according as his work shall be." Salvation is full and free to who so ever will come unto Jesus. Repentance and baptism in the name of Jesus Christ for the remission of your sins and the infilling of the Holy Ghost are the requirements of salvation. James 2:17-18 "Even so faith, if it hath not works, is dead, being alone. Yea, a man may say, Thou hast faith, and I have works: show me thy faith without thy works, and I will show thee my faith by my works." Faith without works is dead. Though salvation is full and free, faith has the fruit of works. What talent has God placed in your hand? Why stand you here gazing up into the heavens? Put hands and feet on your talent and exercise your liberty in Christ. God is in your cheering section. Go for the big one.

We want to thank you for listening to the We Preach Jesus Ministries

MADE TO MORN   09/15/1991

PSM 45:1 MY HEART IS INDITING A GOOD MATTER:
I SPEAK THE THINGS WHICH I HAVE MADE TOUCHING THE KING:
MY TONGUE IS THE PEN OF A READY WRITER

Three verses of scripture which is needful to read in your hearing.

1 Pet 1:7-8 "That the trial of your faith, being much more precious than of gold that perisheth, though it be tried with fire, might be found unto praise and honour and glory at the appearing of Jesus Christ: Whom having not seen, ye love, in whom, though now ye see <him> not, yet believing, ye rejoice with joy unspeakable and full of glory:"

John 15:11 "These things have I spoken unto you, that my joy might remain in you, and <that> your joy might be full."

Man was not made to morn. The garden of Eden was a place of happiness, a place of tranquility, of peace. As long as man continued to obey God there was nothing in the garden that could cause him sorrow or morning. Remember, that man was created to live with God forever, never to grow old, but to remain at the perfection of his life. Eternal fellowship with God. The garden, was created for the joy of God and man. The flowers gave off their fragrance for his delight, The rivers flowed and spoke over golden sands. The trees gave their shade and fruits for the benefit of man. God had made human beings to be happy. Totally capable of happiness, in the right attitude, in the right element to be happy. Sin has brought sorrow, morning, and death to man kind. But, Jesus Christ has come to restore that which has been taken away by sin through the fall of Adam. Jesus Christ has come to restore that old joy that Adam knew in the garden as he walked with God in the cool of the day. This restored joy, though, is sweeter, deeper, than it would have been if it had never been lost. You'll never realize just what Christ has come to develop in you, until you've grasped what the joy of the Lord is. It's his wish that you be happy. He doesn't want you looking like an ol mule eating saw briers. When we've come to the place of perfection, not in this life but in the next, we'll be completely happy. As you learn to trust in Christ, the more your joy will be full. The more your joy is full the closer you are to heaven and it's perfection. It's Christ's will that his joy should remain in you, and that your joy should be full. Everything that Jesus spoke was meant to produce joy in you. John 15:11 "These things have I spoken unto you, that my joy might remain in you, and <that> your joy might be full." This whole fifteenth chapter of John, and even the chapter before, are instruction in truth, giving the meaning of truth, and telling your that knowing the truth you should have joy in it. Ignorance of the scriptures hides so much truth and joy from the average Christian. Wells of delight that might be drank from are hidden by ignorance of the scriptures. All things being equal, the well read Christian will be the happiest. John 8:32 "And ye shall know the truth, and the [truth shall] make you free." The truth can kill a thousand fears in the heart of the Christian that ignorance bred within him. What truth? The truth of the Love of God. The truth of the full atonement made by Christ. The truth of the eternal covenant, of the eternal faithfulness of God, The truth of God's relationship with his people or to his people. All these create in the heart of the Knowledgeable Christian comfort and solace. Don't be careless about the study of Scripture and with that scripture, doctrine. Study the word, be diligent, be instant in season out of season, seek and find, knock and it shall be opened to you. The more you read the word of God the more you'll walk with God and the closer you walk with Him the more your Joy will be full. Let the Holy Ghost, the Spirit of truth, lead you into all truth. Learn the mind of the Spirit of God. This Bible was written for you. Rom 15:4 "For whatsoever things were written aforetime were written for our learning, that we [through patience] and comfort of the scriptures might have hope." Make that personal: "For whatsoever things were written before were written for your learning, that you, through patience, and comfort of the Scriptures might have hope." For you. If you're, or if you become a student of the Word of God you'll find a good reason to rejoice in the Lord under all circumstances.

    Sometimes the words spoken by Jesus were words of warning to help that your joy might be full. Like in John 15:1-7 "I am the true vine, and my Father is the husbandman. {2} Every branch in me that beareth not fruit he taketh away: and every <branch> that beareth fruit, he purgeth it, that it may bring forth more fruit. {3} Now ye are clean through the word which I have spoken unto you. {4} Abide in me, and I in you. As the branch cannot bear fruit of itself, except it abide in the vine, no more can ye, except ye abide in me. {5} I am the vine, ye <are> the branches: He that abideth in me, and I in him, the same bringeth forth much fruit: for without me ye can do nothing. {6} If a man abide not in me, he is cast forth as a branch, and is withered, and men gather them, and cast <them> into the fire, and they are burned. {7} If ye abide in me, and my words abide in you, ye shall ask what ye will, and it shall be done unto you." You are branches of a vine and any vine dresser knows that a branch that doesn't bear fruit is cut off. Well, just what is so joy inspiring about this? Christ is telling me that if I don't bear fruit I'm to be cut off. These sharp words make you jerk back in astonishment and listen to the question ringing in your mind, "Am I bearing fruit?" Search your heart it's beneficial to your joy. God doesn't want you rejoicing in a false joy. One of presumption. So he takes a sharp knife of his word and cuts away that false joy so that the true joy can bear fruit in your life. Joy on any basis but truth prevents you from the true joy, and with that joy, rejoicing in the Lord. The scripture gives sharp cutting words of instruction that you may be sound in the faith, sound in the life of Christ. Built on the solid rock of Jesus and not some false hope conjured up by yourself. The pruning shears of Christ at work in your life and mine. Thank God when you can perceive his hand on your life. Christ goes on to say, even the branches that bear fruit will have to be pruned that they'll bear more fruit. This might seem unpleasant but Rom 5:3-5 says on a matter similar to this, "Knowing that tribulation worketh patience, And patience, experience, and experience, hope: And hope maketh not ashamed, because the love of God is shed abroad in our hearts by the Holy Ghost which is given unto us." It's a Jacob's ladder, with every rung placed by God at the right distance apart, it's a safe climb to make. There's nothing that Jesus said to you in warning, that doesn't guard against sorrow. It keeps you away from danger, always points you to the path of safety. Live by them. And they'll guide you into the happiest life you've ever known. True happiness comes to those who know their God and obey him. What harm can come to one who loves his neighbor as himself? What harm can come from obeying: Matt 7:12 "Therefore all things [whatsoever] ye would that men should do to you, do ye even so to them: for this is the law and the prophets." Or to those who follow this: Prov 15:1 "A soft answer turneth away wrath: but grievous words stir up anger."

    John 15:4 "Abide in me, and I in you. [As the branch] cannot bear fruit of itself, except it abide in the vine, no more can ye, except ye abide in me." Very humbling words. These words bring the truth of your commitment to Christ, right to the fore front. You have to feel completely dependent upon Christ, upon the power of the Holy Ghost, for your joy to be full. You need to be thankful when you read scriptures for the instruction or correction or warning or humbling, for they are intended to help your present and eternal joy in Christ. Woe be to the man or woman that when they read the scriptures they don't find instruction, correction, humbling or solace there. This person has things in their life they needs to be purged out if they're going to live for God. How do I purge these things out? Simply by repenting. Repentance is a turning away from the direction of life that opposes God. If you've never been baptized in the name of Jesus Christ for the remission of these sins then you need to call a man of God and have him baptize you in water in the name of Jesus Christ for the remission of your sins. Call and we'll see that you are baptize you in the name of Jesus Christ. The next thing you need, is to be filled with the Holy Ghost. This is the spirit of Christ in you, the hope of glory. Please give a great deal of importance to this matter. Your eternal destiny is at stake.

This chapter of John abounds with words of promise. John 15:7 "[If ye abide in me, and my words] abide in you, ye shall ask what ye will, and it shall be done unto you." Read that again slower, taste each word. Let it simmer in your mind a moment. If ye abide in me, and my words abide in you, ye shall ask what ye will, and it shall be done unto you. If is a mighty big word. If you live in Christ, and If his words live in you, your joy will be full, and you can ask what you will and you'll receive it. When you ask, you'll ask within the framework of the words that Jesus spoke. The gifts of the Spirit are love operated. That is, the gift of healing comes out of the heart of compassion, not out of want. Miracles are performed by those that see a deep need in the life of others and are not done for vain glory. There are more promises here. Are you tried beyond your strength? Are you depressed? Then listen to this: "These things have I spoken unto you that my joy might remain in you, and that your joy might be full." or Mat 6:34 "[Take therefore] no thought for the morrow: for the morrow shall take thought for the things of itself. John 14:1 "[Let not your] heart be troubled: ye believe in God, believe also in me." John 10:27-28 "[My sheep] hear my voice, and I know them, and they follow me: And I give unto them eternal life, and they shall never perish, neither shall any <man> pluck them out of my hand." Don't let all these scripture go to waste in your life. These are precious promises that God has given to you that you may prosper and grow. Also in the same book of John are words of principle. Precepts, signposts, that point out the road to joy. The ten commandments engraved by the finger of God upon tables of stone seem hard and cold but the precepts of Jesus Christ are tender and bring to you the joy of life. Obedience to these commandments will give you the highest joy.

"These things have I spoken that my joy might remain in you." Or that I might rejoice over you and rejoice in you, and being pleased with you, that your joy might be full. The obedient child is a pleasure to his parents. And the obedient child receives pleasure out of being obedient and doing the will of his father. He gets pleasure out of his father's pleasure. Jesus loves you beyond a shadow of a doubt but he isn't always pleased with your service to him or your walk in life. When his joy in your life is gone, so is your joy. If you have a heart that is true towards him, then he has joy in your response and he can rejoice with you and your joy will be full. "Enter into the joy of the Lord", goes the command to the faithful servant who was diligent with the talents given him. Many never enter into the joy of the Lord because they've never learned to be obedient. Because they've been self serving and buried the talent that the Lord has given them. Joy comes from doing. You, that have never found the Joy since you've received the Holy Ghost, you need to examine your walk with God. Look deep. Ask the Lord what he would have you to do with the talent you've been given. You who don't know what the talent or talents are, ask. Read the word of God, be diligent in your study. "Faith cometh by hearing and hearing by the word of God." This is the bread of life. "If ye abide in me and my words abide in you ye shall ask what you will, and it shall be done unto you." If you sporadically abide in Christ, there will be little pleasure in your walk. But if he is your companion in your life, then even a small reduction of your companionship with Christ would make you unhappy, if you feel connected to him like a branch to the stem, then you can delight in your fellowship with Christ. Fervent love pleases Christ but to the Church of Laodica who was luke warm he said in Rev 3:16 "So then because thou art lukewarm, and neither cold nor hot, I will [spue] thee out of my mouth." If you continue day by day to walk with God, and to abide in Christ, Christ will find joy in you and you'll find the reward of your service is, that your cup of joy will overflow. Is there any greater joy than to feel that your life is pleasing to God? Communion with the Lord of Glory is the only way to life eternal. Jesus has joy in us when we bring forth much fruit. John 15:8 "[Herein is my Father] glorified, that ye bear much fruit, so shall ye be my disciples." Are you bringing forth much fruit for the kingdom of God? Are you doing all you can for the kingdom of God? Jesus gave his all for you and you have received from him so very much. If you are giving your all then as Rom 12:1-2 says: "I beseech you therefore, brethren, by the mercies of God, that ye present your bodies a living sacrifice, holy, acceptable unto God, ÷<which is> your reasonable service. " All you can do, is but a little price to pay for what he has done for you. Christ is overjoyed at your bearing fruit. If you please Jesus, then your joy will be full. The key to peace, joy and happiness in the Lord is to be totally involve in the

Kingdom of God. There are no shot cuts to Christianity, and no short cuts to joy. If your life is not giving Jesus Joy then you don't have the joy in yourself. Little fruit equals little joy. Don't let the opinion of others hinder you from doing the work God, has put in your hands. Your joy is predicated upon your obedience to the call of God upon your life. The way to give pleasure to Jesus Christ is written in John 15:10-13 "If ye keep my commandments, ye shall abide in my love, even as I have kept my Father's commandments, and abide in his love. These things have I spoken unto you, that my joy might remain in you, and <that> your joy might be full. This is my commandment, That ye love one another, as I have loved you." He that walks carefully , obeying the commandment of the Lord, He that prays for a tender heart, a tender conscience, He that seeks to leave nothing undone, will have happiness and joy unspeakable rising up within his soul. This particular man or woman may not laugh a lot, but there is a joy that laughter simply would mock and be as the crackling of thorns under a pot. This person, when he lays his head upon a pillow at night, can say, "I've not been all that I wanted to be today, but I've done everything I could to be holy. I've looked after the Master's will in all that I've done this day." Here then, is a person that wakes in the morn with music in his heart. With in this person, is a wellspring of joy. Those around him know it for the waters of joy overflow and splash upon all that come in contact with his life. This man or woman is pleasing to Christ. His joy is full. This person loves the body of Christ. He'll never condemn anyone. He'll not find fault with the operation of the Church. He'll pray for those that find fault with the man of God and the operation of the local assembly. Do you know some one that hasn't been to church for a while? They used to come regular but some stone fell in the path they walked and tripped them up. Some snare laid in their way by the devil. When was the last time you prayed for them? When brothern come together for prayer, bring their name up for prayer. Don't be like the Pharisee in

Luke 18:10 "Two men went up into the temple to pray, the one a Pharisee, and the other a publican. The Pharisee stood and prayed thus with himself, God, I thank thee, that I am not as other men <are>, extortionist, unjust, adulterers, or even as this publican. I fast twice in the week, I give tithes of all that I possess." I suppose though, that some must maintain this facade in self defense of the evil that they do. Perhaps the Lord should open the closets of their lives and let their secret sins out in the open. Like God told Ezekiel the prophet about the leaders of Israel in Ezek 8:12 "Then said he unto me, Son of man, hast thou seen what the ancients of the house of Israel do in the dark, every man in the chambers of his imagery? for they say, The LORD seeth us not, the LORD hath forsaken the earth." God showed the prophet all that the leaders were doing, all that the people of this city were doing in the open, And he determined a purge was necessary for they had forsaken the God of Israel, so: Ezek 9:3 "And the glory of the God of Israel was gone up from the cherub, whereupon he was, to the threshold of the house. And he called to the man clothed with linen, which <had> the writer's inkhorn by his side, And the LORD said unto him, Go through the midst of the city, through the midst of Jerusalem, and set a mark upon the foreheads of the men that sigh and that cry for all the abominations that be done in the midst thereof." Does the things that are done by those around you at work cause you to groan within? Does the evil that fills the airways, sneaking in through the only opening it can, in to your living room, into the hearts of your children, does it bother you? Are you Christian? Does the pictures of children on milk cartons bother you? Then, perhaps if you had lived in the day of Ezekiel you would have been marked with the mark of that angel. But to the others who received not the sign of righteousness, not having the name of God written in their minds, Ezek 9:5 "And to the others [the angels of death] he said in mine hearing, Go ye after him through the city, and smite: let not your eye spare, neither have ye pity: Slay utterly old <and> young, both maids, and little children, and women: but come not near any man upon whom <is> the mark, and begin at my sanctuary Then they began at the ancient men which <were> before the house. Mine eye shall not spare, neither will I have pity, <but> I will recompense their way upon their head." God now withholds this type of judgment. Why? Because as it says in 2 Pet 3:9-10 "The Lord is not slack concerning his promise, as some men count slackness, but is longsuffering to us-ward, not [willing that] any should perish, but that all should come to repentance. But the day of the Lord will come as a thief in the night, in the which the heavens shall pass away with a great noise, and the elements shall melt with fervent heat, the earth also and the works that are therein shall be burned up." 1 Tim 5:24 "Some men's sins are open beforehand, going before to [judgment], and some <men> they follow after." Be sure your sins will find you out. 1 Pet 4:17 "For the time <is come> that judgment must begin at the house of God: and if <it> first <begin> at us, what shall the end <be> of them that obey not the gospel of God? And if the righteous scarcely be saved, where shall the ungodly and the sinner appear?" Humility before all is the only way to walk. Don't be as the Pharisee but be ye humble as the publican in the book of Luke 18:13 "And the publican, standing afar off, would not lift up so much as <his> eyes unto heaven, but smote upon his breast, saying, God be merciful to me a sinner." Jesus said it this way about these two, I tell you, this man [this publican] went down to his house justified <rather> than the other: for every one that exalteth himself shall be abased, and he that humbleth himself shall be exalted." Humility comes from falling upon the rock of Christ and being broken: Luke 20:18 "Whosoever shall [fall upon] that stone shall be broken, but on whomsoever it shall fall, it will grind him to powder." Jesus is that rock that your to fall upon. If you won't humble yourself through Christ there will come a time when you'll be humbled. The time at the end of this age when every knee shall bow and every tongue confess that Jesus is Lord.

      By what sign shall all men know that you follow after Christ? Is it a mysterious gift of speaking in some unknown language? Is it the laying on of hands so that the person might be healed? Is it some great and mysterious gift that God has bestowed upon you? No. It's simply that you love one another. This is the new commandment that Jesus gave us. That you love one another. Greater love hath no man than this that he gives his life for his friends. As Jesus gave his life for us, his friends, so we are to give our lives daily, in the shadow, no, in the light of what Christ has done for us. The great love chapter of the Bible says it this way 1 Cor 13:5-7 "Love doth not behave itself unseemly, seeketh not her own, is not easily provoked, thinketh no evil, {6} Rejoiceth not in iniquity, but rejoiceth in the truth, {7} Beareth all things, believeth all things, hopeth all things, endureth all things." How can you love your brother when your cutting him up? Look at 1 Cor 13. "Thinks no evil," doesn't feel good about evil things that have fallen on your brother, bears all sorts of iniquities that are done against him. on and on it goes. It takes the divine love of God dwelling in you to live in this manner. It takes the Holy Ghost the Spirit of Christ in you, to do this. You have to be born of the Water and the Spirit. Then, for the joy to continue in you, you must put a watch over your life. You must walk with diligence. you must be a careful care taker of God's planting in your life. Your thoughts, for as a man thinketh in his heart so is he, must be guarded, Paul said it in Phil 4:8 this way: "Finally, brethren, whatsoever things are true, whatsoever things <are> honest, whatsoever things <are> just, whatsoever things <are> pure, whatsoever things <are> lovely, whatsoever things <are> of good report, if <there be> any virtue, and if <there be> any praise, think on these things." Jesus Christ declared in John 16:27 "that the Father himself loveth you, because ye have loved me, and have believed that I came out from God." You should share the Joy Christ has, and you should make it your own also. You are to have intimate fellowship with the most holy, He is to be your constant companion. He is your friend, Henceforth I call you not servants, for the servant knoweth not what his Lord doeth: but I have called you friends, for all that I have heard of my Father I have Made known unto you. Jesus Christ is your personal friend. He's your divine companion, Soon you'll be dining with him at his table. No more are you to be a servant but a friend. His friend. Bro Kenneth Reeves of Granite City was coming out of a grocery store in Fairview Heights, headed towards his car. Praying, talking with the Lord as he walked he asked, "I have always desired to know how I rate with you Lord. Well, Lord, how do I really rate with you? Am I making it or where am I falling short? How do I really rate?" The sweetest words he had ever known came to him. "You are my friend." Others down through the ages have been called a friend of God but this function, this mandate, this commission, this privilege, is given to you and me that our joy might be full.

    For a copy of today's message, send a card requesting it to
The We Preach Jesus Ministries
PO Box 274
Eureka, Ill
Until next week,
Gen 31:49 "The LORD watch [between me and thee], when we are absent one from another."
    This is Bro Randy Johnson for the We Preach Jesus Ministries

MARRAGE   10/06/1991

PSM 45:1 MY HEART IS INDITING A GOOD MATTER:
I SPEAK THE THINGS WHICH I HAVE MADE TOUCHING THE KING:
MY TONGUE IS THE PEN OF A READY WRITER

There has been perhaps a great flux of marriages this summer. Time has found my wife and me in five different weddings this year. There is yet another wedding on the horizon. Weddings are fun to attend but hard to arrange. Costly beyond imagination. You who have daughters don't need to be made aware of this butchering of bank balances. Marriage though, is honorable and sanctified before God. It wasn't an accident that God used marriage to show the relationship between Christ and His Church. The first miracle Jesus ever performed was at a wedding. Weddings in the Bible were somewhat different then the ceremonies and celebrations of today. Ours are full of pomp and circumstance but theirs were carried to the extreme. In the book of Judges 14:2 is the story of a man called Samson. Samson had seen him a woman that he wished to marry and so told his mother and father. in the tenth verse his father went to the Philistines and made arrangements for the marriage. Sampson then set up the marriage feast. the Feast was to last seven days as the twelfth verse tells us. Seven days of feasting. Seven days devoted to a wedding banquet. Everything was laid aside for the wedding. If anyone was invited to the wedding and had a quarrel with another, he had to ask forgiveness before he could attend. It was to be a joyous occasion, no room for grudges. John 2:1-4 "And the third day there was a marriage in Cana of Galilee, and the mother of Jesus was there: {2} And both Jesus was called, and his disciples, to the marriage. {3} And when they wanted wine, the mother of Jesus saith unto him, They have no wine. {4} Jesus saith unto her, Woman , what have I to do with thee? mine hour is not yet come." For some people, the only time they ever go to church is to be married. Why is it that people want their marriages to be performed in a church? Why is it the only thing that they want God to bless in their lives is their marriage? Marriage can only be sanctified in Christ not just by Christ. A marriage can't be sanctified just because it was performed in some building or performed by some man having what ever semblance of Christ. The wedding between my wife and my self was performed by a minister that I knew from the time I worked at Dale's Ford sales. We hunted for several days to find this minister. We found him in Pekin and made arrangements to be married by this man. I liked him. It was a quiet ceremony nothing elaborate, simple and quiet. Just a few friends and relatives. Our honeymoon lasted for several years then our marriage fell apart. It was based on a church not God. It was performed by a minister in a church building but our marriage wasn't based on Christ. We wanted God's blessing on our marriage but not on our lives. We didn't understand who or what Christ was and is. Just young people who were ignorant of the ways of God. Marriage is honorable before God. Marriage was made in heaven by God for Adam and Eve in the garden. Marriage symbolizes the relationship of Christ to his Church. Our marriage didn't become sanctified before God until 1972 when we found our way to a alter of prayer. There we laid our sins before God for the Blood of Christ to cleanse us of. God took our lives and our marriage and made something of it. A sanctified marriage begins long before you get to the marriage alter. It must begin in the heart of the individual. Marriage is giving yourselves to one another. I mean giving. Mat 19:5-6 "For this cause shall a man leave father and mother, and shall cleave to his wife: and they twain shall be one flesh? Wherefore they are no more twain, but one flesh. What therefore God hath joined together, let not man put asunder." Eph 5:32-33 "This is a great mystery: but I speak concerning Christ and the church. Nevertheless let every one of you in particular so love his wife even as himself, and the wife <see> that she reverence <her> husband." There is no independence of the individuals in marriage. The two become one. There are no longer two individuals but one. Individuality is set aside, the two become of one mind, of one accord. So it is in Christ, your individuality and the individuality of Christ become melded into one identity, one in Christ. You take on the attributes of the one you love, you begin to act like him talk like him walk like him emulating every thing that you find in him that you like. Couples who have been together for a long time begin to actually resemble one another. I was reconciling my check book and couldn't help but see the resemblance between my signature and my wife's. Her's has began to look like mine. People who are in love with one another are that way you know. So it is to be with you and Christ, you're to take on the attributes of the one you love, you're to resemble him. This process can only come about if, and only if you spend time with him. The more time you spend the more you'll take on his attributes. What are the attributes of Christ Bro Johnson? Gal 5:22 "But the fruit of the Spirit is love, joy, peace, longsuffering, gentleness, goodness, faith, Meekness, temperance." 1 Cor 13:4-7 "Charity suffereth long, and is kind, charity envieth not, charity vaunteth not itself, is not puffed up, Doth not behave itself unseemly, seeketh not her own, is not easily provoked, thinketh no evil, Rejoiceth not in iniquity, but rejoiceth in the truth, Beareth all things, believeth all things, hopeth all things, endureth all things." My Lord and my God, what a mandate.

    The first marriage of the year was one of pomp and circumstance as my pastor's son was married. fancy dresses, tuxedos and long cars. A church house filled with friends and neighbors. Hundreds of people to watch this event take place. This was an open wedding for whosoever would come. Invitations were sent out to friends and relatives far and wide but only one was placed on the bulletin board for all to see. To the church family, your all invited to the wedding of my son Jeffrey Allan and so on. Reception following the ceremony at such and such. No RSVP. No response necessary. Even with all the to due, everyone was invited to the reception. I'm sure there was an intimate group that went to the pastor's home afterwards, but only those who were family or near family were invited to this supper. Only a few. Only a few. Mat 22:2-3 "The kingdom of heaven is like unto a certain king, which made a marriage for his son, And sent forth his servants to call them that were bidden to the wedding:" Ah, the beauty of the bride arrayed in white. Veil covering her face so the groom cannot see her until their pronounced husband and wife. The bridesmaids all arrayed in the finery of the day all in honor of the great event taking place. Tuxedos and patent leather shoes, ties, and cummerbunds, silk hankies, and see thru socks, flowers in the lapels, everyone dressed just right, every hair in the right place, hours have went into this ceremony, everything is just right, just right just right. The ushers have seated everyone in the right place, the white runner, never before walked on, is unrolled for the bride elect. The flower girl stands ready to cast rose pedals before her, everyone is poised, ready, ready for that certain music to begin, ready to stand, to turn and face the bride as she makes her way down the isle to the alter of love. There, there the organist begins to play the famous wedding march, The flower girl begins to spread the rose pedals before the bride, but wait, where is the beautiful dress? What's going on? Why is the bride wearing torn blue jeans? Why the sweat shirt? What's her problem? Don't she know what today is? Her fiancé paid, paid thousands for her wedding dress, why is she doing this to him? What is the matter with her? What a fiasco. Everything looked all right, it was all going according to plan then this. The disappointment is evident in the eyes of those who have went to great lengths to be here. Quickly though, they hide their disappointment least they put a damper on the ceremony. On she walks, slowly, her father to her side, to the alter, to the alter, to the alter. Who gives this woman to this man? Her mother and I. But the fiancé doesn't take his bride's slight without comment. He won't ignore what's going on. Through the hush comes his voice, Where's your wedding dress? With a defensive voice loaded with causticism she replies: "I decided to wear blue jeans and a sweat shirt instead." Discussed, frowning, shaking his head slowly from side to side, he turns away from her, with head bowed, he quickly walks out the door, never to return. His bride to be didn't want what love he had to offer. His bride to be, humiliated him before all his friends and loved ones. Scorning the wedding garments provide for her by her lover, she thought, she though, she though to provide her own. Too poor to provide her own wedding dress, too poor to set up the wedding feast, too poor to provide for her own needs, her future husband paid for the needs of the wedding. Your too poor to pay for your own sins. Jesus Christ your bridegroom had provided you with a robe of righteousness to wear before him, that your sins, your nakedness, your torn worn blue jeans, may be covered with the righteousness of the lamb of God. You'll not stand in the wedding of the Lamb of God clothed in your own righteousness. You must, You must wear the garment provided by Jesus Christ two thousand years ago when he died for your sins. Naked he hung on a tree that you might have everlasting life. How do you think you can make it to heaven any way but the way he has provided? You'll not stand in your own righteousness. You'll not.

    The wedding of my nephew was beautiful. What wedding isn't though. In the suburbs of Chicago, at a little Lutheran church made up of hand laid stones, with the light of the sun passing through stained glass windows coloring the wedding gown, They were married by a woman pastor with the essence of the poetry of love. The wedding feast was catered in a place specializing in banquets. Opulence everywhere you turned, a man to park your car, a waiter for your table. As you walked into the banquet hall, a man dressed in finery announced, Mr. and Mrs. Johnson and party. To the table you were led. A place card stated with finality, The Johnson party. Eleven places were set for we had sent back the card stating eleven in our party. RSVP by such and such date. You must reply to the request, are you coming or are you going to be rude? The invitation came because they, the future bride and groom, wanted your presence at the wedding. Your invited. Anything less is a slight to close people. To not reply to the invitation would be more than rude. Yes, we'll be coming. Thank you for requesting our presence at this blessed event. There will be eleven in our party. Thank you again for inviting us. Our car broke down so we rented a car for the wedding. No expense is to great for friends who are getting married. Spare not the fatted calf. Early in the morning of the wedding we leave for Chicago. Three cars in our entourage. It would have been good to go the night before but money is tight and we're doing all we can. A frantic drive of better than two hundred miles to be at a wedding, people have went farther than that to travel to a wedding but not on less money. No expense is too great for you to be in the wedding of the Lamb of God. No price is to large for you to obtain salvation, but you see the price has been paid, you don't have to rent anything to be there. Transportation is provided. All you have to do is accept the invitation. RSVP. We were directed to a table provided for eleven persons. Each family or group had a table. Only ten sat at a table set for eleven. One couldn't be there. Conspicuous in absence, ten sat where eleven should have been. The only thing that should keep you from a wedding is sickness or death. The absence of this one was poignant with meaning. There'll be places set at the marriage supper of the Lamb of God that won't be filled. Name tags set before the places. All who pass by will know who it is that is absent. Conspicuous in absence. How sad to have been invited to the wedding of the Lamb but you couldn't find the time to pray. How sad when it is all said and done to have your plate removed from the table. There goes your name tag. Even the chair is removed. The remaining ten soon fill in the vacant place. Ten where eleven should have been. Sad so sad. The saddest words of tongue or pen are these four words, it might have been. He might have made it. He could have made it. Luke 14:16-23 "Then said he unto him, A certain man made a great supper, and bade many: And sent his servant at supper time to say to them that were bidden, Come, for all things are now ready. {18} And they all with one <consent> began to make excuse. The first said unto him, I have bought a piece of ground, and I must needs go and see it: I pray thee have me excused. {19} And another said, I have bought five yoke of oxen, and I go to prove them: I pray thee have me excused. {20} And another said, I have married a wife, and therefore I cannot come. {21} So that servant came, and showed his lord these things. Then the master of the house being angry said to his servant, Go out quickly into the streets and lanes of the city, and bring in hither the poor, and the maimed, and the halt, and the blind. {22} And the servant said, Lord, it is done as thou hast commanded, and yet there is room. {23} And the lord said unto the servant, Go out into the highways and hedges, and compel <them> to come in, that my house may be filled." The invitation came, but all had something else to do. It may not be a team of oxen that keep you from Christ but it can be a wife, a husband, a piece of land, some thing you render to be more valuable then Christ. Acts 24:24 "And after certain days, when Felix came with his wife Drusilla, which was a Jewess, he sent for Paul, and heard him concerning the faith in Christ." Acts 24:25 "And as he reasoned of righteousness, temperance, and judgment to come, Felix trembled, and answered, Go thy way for this time, when I have a convenient season, I will call for thee." At a convenient season. There's no record of Felix ever finding that season to come to Christ. Trembling under the power of God, The Holy Ghost moving on him, Yet he never found time. I'm sure he would find the time now if he could. Bidden, but never came. Ten at a table for eleven. One missing, conspicuous in absence. You'll be missed. You already are. Each Church service I look for you. I'll know you when I see you. But you're never there. Your place is empty. Your name tag is still there. It's not too late to come, The wedding trumpet hasn't been blown yet, What does hinder your coming? Have you things that just need to be done? They'll be there tomorrow. This opportunity doesn't come often. And a great man made a wedding feast and bid many and they began to make excuse. Jesus Christ won't force anyone to be saved he's too much of a gentleman. What a shame to be bidden to the wedding feast of the Lamb of God and not have time to go. Rev 19:7-9 "Let us be glad and rejoice, and give honour to him: for the marriage of the Lamb is come, and his wife hath made herself ready. {8} And to her was granted that she should be arrayed in fine linen, clean and white: for the fine linen is the righteousness of saints. {9} And he saith unto me, Write, Blessed <are> they which are called unto the marriage supper of the Lamb. And he saith unto me, These are the true sayings of God." Who is the bride of Christ? Look to Eph 5:25-32 for in these verses Paul explains the attitude of Christ and the Church, his body through the attitude of a husband towards his wife, "Husbands, love your wives, even as Christ also loved the church, and gave himself for it, {26} That he might sanctify and cleanse it with the washing of water by the word, {27} That he might present it to himself a glorious church, not having spot, or wrinkle, or any such thing, but that it should be holy and without blemish. {28} So ought men to love their wives as their own bodies. He that loveth his wife loveth himself. {29} For no man ever yet hated his own flesh, but nourisheth and cherisheth it, even as the Lord the church: {30} For we are members of his body, of his flesh, and of his bones. {31} For this cause shall a man leave his father and mother, and shall be joined unto his wife, and they two shall be one flesh. {32} This is a great mystery: but I speak concerning Christ and the church." The bride of Christ is the church bought with his blood, washed clean, clothed in the righteousness of his sacrifice. Bought with his life given on a cross two thousand years ago. It doesn't matter if you believe and accept it or don't it's fact. Just as the planets hang in the evening sky, just as the sun gives it's light, it's fact. There will be no excuse at the judgment. You must have the wedding garment. Mat 22:11-14 "And when the king came in to see the guests, he saw there a man which had not on a wedding garment: And he saith unto him, Friend, how camest thou in hither not having a wedding garment? And he was speechless. Then said the king to the servants, Bind him hand and foot, and take him away, and cast <him> into outer darkness, there shall be weeping and gnashing of teeth. For many are called, but few <are> chosen." The custom was to provide long white robes to the guests of the feast. Any who wore not the robes was highly susceptible to punishment. The person without the wedding garment, his conduct was totally unacceptable for all he had to do was ask and the garment would have been given to him. Rev 19:7-9 "Let us be glad and rejoice, and give honor to him: for the marriage of the Lamb is come, and his wife hath made herself ready. {8} And to her was granted that she should be arrayed in fine linen, clean and white: for the fine linen is the righteousness of saints. {9} And he saith unto me, Write, Blessed <are> they which are called unto the marriage supper of the Lamb. And he saith unto me, These are the true sayings of God." Without holiness no man may see God. Holiness is the emblem of the saints of God. They took note that they had been with Jesus. There was something about these saints, this people of the name of Jesus, that you could feel, you could see it in their eyes feel it in their presence, understand it when they talked, you knew that they had been with Jesus. Now it's in prayer, in the study of the word of God, in the fellowship of his sufferings that you are with Jesus. The closer you look the better Jesus looks. Walking with the Lord in the cool of the day. There is no fear to them that wait upon the Lord. In the good times and in the bad, for they surely shall come, Isa 40:31 "But [they that wait] upon the LORD shall renew <their> strength, they shall mount up with wings as eagles, they shall run, and not be weary, <and> they shall walk, and not faint." Is it difficult for a wife to wait for her husband to provide? What more can she do? Will she undermine his position as the bread winner and go to work without his permission? Not the wife that is spoken of in the word of God for these two have become one and they don't war against each other.

    Then there was the wedding we attended where there were places set at the wedding reception where there weren't name tags placed in certain spots. This was done for those who were crash slugs unable to comprehend simple social graces such as sending back the little card with the number that would be in their party. I'm sure they felt like slugs. They had to feel small in the sight of all that had name tags by the plates. There won't be any extra places set in the wedding feast of the Lamb of God. This wedding will take place in heaven while the whole world reels to and fro like a drunk man. The earth will suffer tribulation such as the world has never seen. Fire, earthquakes, hail, storms, famine, bugs, disease, death, Rev 6:8 "and behold a [pale horse]: and his name that sat on him was Death, and Hell followed with him. And power was given unto them over the fourth part of the earth, to kill with sword, and with hunger, and with death, and with the beasts of the earth. Blessed <are> they which are called unto the marriage supper of the Lamb. On these people, the second death has no power. The second death will be for those who are cast into the lake of fire there to burn in torment for ever and ever. "

  Jesus spoke words of warning to those who were his Mat 25:1-13 "Then shall the kingdom of heaven be likened unto ten virgins, which took their lamps, and went forth to meet the bridegroom. {2} And five of them were wise, and five <were> foolish. {3} They that <were> foolish took their lamps, and took no oil with them: {4} But the wise took oil in their vessels with their lamps. {5} While the bridegroom tarried, Jesus has been gone almost two thousand years, they all slumbered and slept. {6} And at midnight there was a cry made, Behold, the bridegroom cometh, go ye out to meet him. {7} Then all those virgins arose, and trimmed their lamps. {8} And the foolish said unto the wise, Give us of your oil, for our lamps are gone out. You can't use someone elses' Holy Ghost consecration, it must be your own. {9} But the wise answered, saying, <Not so>, lest there be not enough for us and you: but go ye rather to them that sell, and buy for yourselves. {10} And while they went to buy, the bridegroom came, and they that were ready went in with him to the marriage: and the door was shut." 1 Cor 15:52 "In a moment, in the twinkling of an eye, [at the last trump]: for the trumpet shall sound, and the dead shall be raised incorruptible, and we shall be changed." There won't be time for you to get right you must be right and stay right to go in the rapture with Jesus. {11} "Afterward came also the other virgins, saying, Lord, Lord, open to us. " God closed the door of Noah's ark, Gen 7:16 "And they that went in, went in male and female of all flesh, as God had commanded him: and the LORD shut him in." and if God shut the door Rev 3:7 he that openeth, and no man shutteth, and shutteth, and no man openeth, "Then you or I cannot open the door {12} But he answered and said, Verily I say unto you, I know you not. {13} Watch therefore, for ye know neither the day nor the hour wherein the Son of man cometh. Be ye also ready for in the day that ye think not, the son of man cometh." God has bidden you to a wedding. What will you do with the invitation? The wedding garment is prepared for you even this day why do you hesitate? Righteous, peace and joy are yours in the Holy Ghost all you must do is ask and the Lord of the supper will give you garments of righteousness. Repent of you sins, gird up the loins of your minds ye doubled minded, be baptized in the name of the one that died for you, your to be his in marriage as the bride of Christ, who's name are you to take on? Why, the bridegroom's name of course, Jesus. And he will fill you with the Holy Ghost. Drop us a card at The We preach Jesus Ministries, PO Box 274 Eureka, Il and we will come and set up a Bible study right in the comfort of your own home. The word of God is powerful and life giving and it is a pleasure to teach you his truths. If you would like a copy of today's' message send a card to the We preach Jesus Ministries Po Box 274 Eureka Il, I'll be looking for you in church next Sunday so until next Sunday

Gen 31:49 The LORD watch between me and thee, when we are absent one from another. This is Bro Randy Johnson.

A MAJORITY OF ONE   10/20/1991

PSM 45:1 MY HEART IS INDITING A GOOD MATTER:
I SPEAK THE THINGS WHICH I HAVE MADE TOUCHING THE KING:
MY TONGUE IS THE PEN OF A READY WRITER

You have missed, never seen before, healings, troubles, miracles. Revival is here. revival of the Book of Acts church. This is the end times. Never before such as this. Joel 2:23 "Be glad then, ye children of Zion, and rejoice in the LORD your God: for he hath given you the former rain moderately, and he will cause to come down for you the rain, the former rain, and the latter rain in the first month." James 5:7 "Be patient therefore, brethren, unto the coming of the Lord. Behold, the husbandman waiteth for the precious fruit of the earth, and hath long patience for it, until he receive the early and latter rain."

Ezek 22:30 "And I sought for a man among them, that should make up the hedge, and stand in the gap before me for the land, that I should not destroy it: but I found none." God searches among us for a man or a woman that He can use to do his work upon the earth. But man feels insignificant for the battle that lies ahead. What man forgets is that God and man are a majority of one.

The significant number, one. Each and every person among us is an individual, one person, alone. Each has his or her own goals, ideals, morals, schemes, and dreams. My dreams are not your dreams, nor are your dreams mine. My goals are not your goals, and so it goes. Preach though we may, about being of one mind and accord such a task is near impossible to achieve. Very few such occurrences have happened down through time and history. One such time was in the Book of Acts 2:1 "And when the day of Pentecost was fully come, they were all with one accord in one place." You can be in one accord with a group but to be of one mind with each thinking the same thoughts, only can happen in Christ as his people lift up their hearts in worship. What happens when people of God are of one accord in worship and singing praises to our God?

Acts 2:2-4 "And suddenly there came a sound from heaven as of a rushing mighty wind, and it filled all the house where they were sitting. And there appeared unto them cloven tongues like as of fire, and it sat upon each of them. And they were all filled with the Holy Ghost, and began to speak with other tongues, as the Spirit gave them utterance." There were 120 people in that upper room, praying and worshiping God of one mind. This is only way people can be of one mind and accord, worship and prayer. Psa 34:3 "O [magnify the LORD] with me, and let us exalt his name together." You can worship, magnify the Lord and pray alone, but when two or more get together to exalt his name together, Heaven comes down and glory touches every soul. In the world we daily live in, out side of worship and prayer, such a thing as being of one accord is not a reality. A program that has recently been put into practice throughout industry in the United States, bases its existence on a thing called participative management. There are teams that arrive at a consensus of opinion among themselves. No voting is permitted, only an assumed agreement arrived at by the silence of the team members.

What in reality happens is that the stronger personalities simply exert their opinions upon the rest of the group. The decision though loses identification with it's originator. The group is not in one accord. It doesn't have one mind. It's the decision of the strong person of the group that's accepted, acquiesced to. Never have a people came together spontaneously of one mind and accord. We're not ants or bees or some other colony beings. We all strive along individual paths, hopefully to some common goal. (Believe me, there is room in the Body of Christ for individuality) for Rom 12:4 says "For as we have many members in one body, and all members have not the same office: So we, <being> many, are one body in Christ, and every one members one of another." 1 Cor 6:15 "Know ye not that your bodies are the members of Christ? 1 Cor 12:12 "For as the body is one, and hath many [members], and all the [members] of that one body, being many, are one body: so also <is> Christ." 1 Cor 12:18 "But now hath God set the [members] every one of them in the body, as it hath pleased him." 1 Cor 12:20 "But now <are they> many members, yet but one body." Eph 5:30 "For we are [members] of his body, of his flesh, and of his bones." Members' means plural. If we were to lose our individual identity then it would have been written as a singular member. Now are we a member of the body of Christ. Different, individual, separate in function, personality, and lives yet all members of the same body. The pleasing of our God and savior is the pathway. Heaven is our ultimate goal. There is nothing like living for God. We have a goal, an example that will always be the epitome, the high rock of our life, Jesus Christ. He's not some man made into a god, He is God gift wrapped in the flesh. Before us stands an open door where Christ has went before. Standing just beyond that open door is Christ beckoning us to come on.

"What can one person do?" The task is overwhelming. The burden great. I sought for a man to stand in the gap. Who will it be? Through out the Word of God there are many references to times when only one man or woman stood in the gap. Behind them, beside them stood no one. Alone, facing uncertainty, these stood, and filled the place, filled the gap and made up the hedge for the people. Individuals no different from you or me. They had families, goals, and desires just as we do, but when push came to shove, they stood. Necessity was laid upon them. David when no one would battle for the Lord stood in the gap. Nothing but a lad. Read it in

1 Sam 17:1 "Now the Philistines gathered together their armies to battle, and were gathered together at Shochoh, which <belongeth> to Judah, and pitched between Shochoh and Azekah, in Ephesdammim. And Saul and the men of Israel were gathered together, and pitched by the valley of Elah, and set the battle in array against the Philistines. And the Philistines stood on a mountain on the one side, and Israel stood on a mountain on the other side: and <there was> a valley between them. And there went out a champion out of the camp of the Philistines, named Goliath, of Gath, whose height <was> six cubits and a span. This man was near nine feet tall, the staff of his spear <was> like a weaver's beam, And he stood and cried unto the armies of Israel, and said unto them, Why are ye come out to set <your> battle in array? <am> not I a Philistine, and ye servants to Saul? choose you a man for you, and let him come down to me. {9} If he be able to fight with me, and to kill me, then will we be your servants: but if I prevail against him, and kill him, then shall ye be our servants, and serve us. {10} And the Philistine said, I defy the armies of Israel this day, give me a man, that we may fight together." He was laughing at the people of God. "The Philistine drew near morning and evening, and presented himself forty days. And David spake to the men that stood by him, saying, What shall be done to the man that killeth this Philistine, and taketh away the reproach from Israel? for who <is> this uncircumcised Philistine, that he should defy the armies of the living God?" 28 "And Eliab his eldest brother heard when he spake unto the men, and Eliab's anger was kindled against David, and he said, Why camest thou down hither? and with whom hast thou left those few sheep in the wilderness? I know thy pride, and the naughtiness of thine heart, for thou art come down that thou mightest see the battle. And David said, What have I now done? <Is there> not a cause?" One man defying the army of Israel, but one man, young may he be, standing up and saying "Is there not a cause?" A lad ready to go against the giant Goliath, just him and God a

majority of two. ø 1 Sam 17:37 "David said moreover, The LORD that delivered me out of the paw of the lion, and out of the paw of the bear, he will deliver me out of the hand of this Philistine. 42 "And when the Philistine looked about, and saw David, he disdained him: for he was <but> a youth, and ruddy, and of a fair countenance." "And the Philistine said unto David, <Am> I a dog, that thou comest to me with staves? And the Philistine cursed David by his gods. Then said David to the Philistine, Thou comest to me with a sword, and with a spear, and with a shield: but I come to thee in the name of the LORD of hosts, the God of the armies of Israel, whom thou hast defied." God and man a majority. Who can defy God? Who shall stand against Him? One man against a giant. One man against a nation. What can one man do? He can turn the tide of a nation. He can stop mighty rivers. Change the very coarse of history. One man with a vision is unstoppable. One man with a dream can build a nation. One man moving under the anointing of God can, it's unexplainable what you can do in Christ. I can do all things through Christ which strengtheneth me. Not I but Christ in me. God wants availability. God wants a man. Calvary stands calling all to the foot of the cross where you can give your life to the Lord of Glory. The master picks up your broken destitute life and begins to use it to shape a church, a body, a bride. Soon your life no longer resembles what it was when you tried to make it into what you wanted for your life. Nothing ever worked out as you wanted it to anyhow. Why not let the Lord finish a great work in you? Isn't it strange how that you can plan and plan and plan but your plans always go astray? Mine always did.

    It seems like God always had a man or woman for the time and hour. It was an individual moved upon by God. An individual not a whole nation or people. Look at the woman named Esther, a Jewish woman who was the wife of Ahasuerus king of all the land from India to Ethiopia. She was chosen to replace a rebellious wife that had shunned the kings' command. This command wasn't an unreasonable one, he simply wanted her to come into the presence with the crown royal so that he could show the people and the princes her beauty. These were a vast number of people that he had invited to a feast honoring all the princes and chiefs of the kingdom of Media and Persia. The king was mad beyond description, he asked the wise men who knew the people and the times what should be done to the queen for this rebellion. Give her royal estate to another, let her come no more before the king, replace her with another. My mind quickly rushes to the Song of Solomon the fifth chapter, Song 5:2-6 "I sleep, but my heart waketh: <it is> the voice of my beloved that knocketh, <saying>, Open to me, my sister, my love, my dove, my undefiled: for my head is filled with dew, <and> my locks with the drops of the night. I have put off my coat, how shall I put it on? I have washed my feet, how shall I defile them? {4} My beloved put in his hand by the hole <of the door>, and my bowels were moved for him. {5} I rose up to open to my beloved, and my hands dropped <with> myrrh, and my fingers <with> sweet smelling myrrh, upon the handles of the lock. {6} I opened to my beloved, but my beloved had withdrawn himself, <and> was gone: my soul failed when he spake: I sought him, but I could not find him, I called him, but he gave me no answer." Thank God, the Lord is merciful in his dealings with you and me. Time after time he calls for us to be in his presence so that he may show off the beauty of his bride but time after time, just like in the song, we're too late in answering our Lord's call. Only the presence, only the fragrance of his presence remains. The smell is on our hand, but not in our lives. Jesus Christ says Rev 3:20 "Behold, [I stand at] the door, and knock: if any man hear my voice, and open the door, I will come in to him, and will sup with him, and he with me." What greater joy could you have then intimate communion with the Lord of Creation? He calls, but hesitating, you stop, wait, think, then answer. Too late, he's gone and only the fragrance of his passing remains.

    Esther, the cousin of Mordecai who had been carried away, that is as a captive, by the Babylonians, was brought before the man that took care of the women for the king, and she found favor with him and he helped her and gave her the best place in the house. Twelve months it was before her turn came to go before the king. Twelve months of purification before she was fit to stand before an earthly king, yet we, in a moment, can be born anew and be purified by the blood of Jesus Christ and can stand before God clothed in a righteousness that even twelve months of purification, six of which are with the oil of myrrh and the other with things for the purifying of the women. How powerful do you think the blood of Christ is? It is a sin free blood that won't corrupt like the blood that is shed on the battle fields and in the slaughter houses throughout the land. This is the pure incorruptible blood of the Lamb of God that taketh away the sins of the world. Purifying is the flow that washes white as snow no other fount I know nothing like the Blood of Jesus. All the blood that was shed of the day of atonement couldn't take away the sins of the world. Though it flowed deep down the road, into the valley of Kidron, though the smoke of the sacrifices blacked the bright sun lit sky, though the stench of the corrupting blood fills the evening air, The man would come with his bullock or lamb, laying his hand upon the head of the animal to transfer his sins to this sin free beast, the priest would slay the beast as an sin offering, pushing the sins of the people ahead one more year until, until messiah would come and take away the sins of the world.

Heb 9:13-14 "For if the blood of bulls and of goats, and the ashes of an heifer sprinkling the unclean, sanctifieth to the purifying of the flesh: How much more shall the blood of Christ, who through the eternal Spirit offered himself without spot to God, purge your conscience from dead works to serve the living God?" Heb 10:4 "For <it is> not possible that the [blood of bulls] and of goats should take away sins." It was only possible to push them ahead to the time that Jesus hung on the Cross and died for your sins and mine. Some times words are such an understatement of the weightier matters of life. Words grouped together like, John 3:16 "For God so loved the world, that he gave his only begotten Son, that whosoever believeth in him should not perish, but have everlasting life". Or Rom 5:6 "For when we were yet without strength, in due time [Christ died] for the ungodly." Rom 5:8 "But God commendeth his love toward us, in that, while we were yet sinners, [Christ died] for us." Christ died for us. Four words that are so profound in context that they are almost impossible to comprehend. Unworthy of salvation. Unworthy of anything but death yet while we were yet sinners, Christ died for us. The only man in the history of the world that was without sin. The only man that could have lived forever because sin causes death and he was without sin. Just think that he could still be hanging on the cross today, two thousand years latter, because he was without sin and death had no hold over him. I'm telling you Christ was without sin. And because he was without sin, death had no dominion over him. He told Pilate

John 19:11 "Thou couldest have no power <at all> against me, except it were given thee from above: " Christ gave up the Ghost and died on the cross but not until he said It is finished. Those put in prison had the crime and the sentence written on a paper nailed to the door of their cell, when the sentence was completed, fulfilled, it was written across the page, It is finished. When Jesus Christ said It is finished, the crimes you have committed against God and man are covered with the Blood of Christ, contingent on your acceptance, and the debt is paid.

So Esther was purified in one year and brought before the king:

Est. 2:17 "And the king loved Esther above all the women, and she obtained grace and favor in his sight more than all the virgins, so that he set the royal crown upon her head, and made her queen instead of Vashti." There was an evil man in the kingdom named Haman. Haman set out to destroy all the Jews simply because Mordecai, Esther's cousin, wouldn't bow down to him. Haman didn't realize that Esther was a Jewish woman. Mordecai got wind of Haman's plan and sent word to Esther of this devilish scheme. Mordecai charged her that she should go in before the king and make request to him for the people. The law stated that no one should come before the king that was not bidden, except to whom he held out the golden scepter to. The penalty is death to those that transgress this law. She told him that the king hadn't called her in thirty days. Mordecai said Est 4:13-14 "Think not with thyself that thou shalt escape in the king's house, more than all the Jews. {14} For if thou altogether holdest thy peace at this time, <then> shall there enlargement and deliverance arise to the Jews from another place, but thou and thy father's house shall be destroyed: and who knoweth whether thou art come to the kingdom for <such> a time as this?" You are set for such a time as this. Enlargement and deliverance at the hand of one person. God and man a majority of one. Who knows whether you are come to the kingdom for such a time as this? What can one do? He can change the course of rivers, turn the tide of history, move mountains, give deliverance and enlargement to a people. What can one do? The next time you turn on your lights remember it was one man's vision that gave you light. The next time you use the phone, it was Bell's vision that gave you this part of your life. The next time your in a basketball game, or the civic center arena, look around, one man died to save all these people from their sins. One man, one woman. The Bible is full of people that turned the tide, stopped the avalanche, made things happen in the kingdom of God. Each, an individual not a team. God works with the individual. He may work with a people such as the Jews or the Gentiles but within that group it is the individual that takes precedence. Your sins cannot be blamed on a group. Your sins cannot be blamed on how you were raised or the opportunities or the lack of opportunities you have had. Your sins rest solely upon your own shoulders. What will you do with them? You must pay for your own sins irregardless of who or what you think caused you to sin. Keep that in mind please. You are an individual and God will deal with you, Rev 3:20 "[Behold, I stand] at the door, and knock: if any man hear my voice, and open the door, I will come in to him, and will sup with him, and he with me." If any man, not if any men. Make that feminine if it pleases you. If any woman not women. God deals with, speaks with the individual.

What can one do?

1 Sam 14:6 "And Jonathan said to the young man that bare his armor, Come, and let us go over unto the garrison of these uncircumcised: it may be that the LORD will work for us: for <there is> no restraint to the LORD to save by many or [by few]." Deu

32:30 "How should one chase a thousand, and two put ten [thousand to flight], except their Rock had sold them, and the LORD had shut them up?" God can use one to put a thousand men on the run. I tell you that God and one are a majority.

Judg 6:15 "And he said unto him, Oh my Lord, wherewith shall I save Israel? behold, my family <is> poor in Manasseh, and I <am> the least in my father's house." Judg 6:16 "And the LORD said unto him, Surely I will be with thee, and thou shalt smite the Midianites as one man." Gideon, one man that God used to free the Israelites from the bondage of the Midianites. Look at the man named Moses. Chosen by God to free the people from the bondage of Egypt. Moses was the adopted son of Pharaoh's daughter, chosen to be the next king of Egypt, trained in all the ways of the Egypt yet Heb 11:24-27 " when he was come to years, refused to be called the son of Pharaoh's daughter, Choosing rather to suffer affliction with the people of God, than to enjoy the pleasures of sin for a season, Esteeming the reproach of Christ greater riches than the treasures in Egypt: for he had respect unto the recompense of the reward. By faith he forsook Egypt, not fearing the wrath of the king: for he endured, as seeing him who is invisible." A vision given to him by God. A desire to save his own from Egypt. A willingness to give himself for others. Knowing that God and man can do anything together. A majority of one. What can one man do? What can one woman do? You've asked yourself this time after time. What does God want you to do? There's no stopping the man or woman that has a vision. you can do what God wants you to. I can do all things through Christ Jesus which strengtheneth me. Have you tried? If not why not? Step out by faith, lift up the hands that hang down, Don't let yourself be discouraged by what others say, God will help you do what he has set in your heart to do. You simply need to step out. You lack a vision? Are you filled with the Holy Ghost? Have you been baptized in the name of Jesus Christ for the remission of your sins? The promise is unto you and your family and to those that are afar off, even as many as the Lord our God shall call. God will set a vision in your heart. He will give you a purpose and a goal for your life. One is a significant number.

For a copy of this broadcast, send your name and address to
THE WE PREACH JESUS MINISTRIES
PO BOX 274
EUREKA, IL
We'll be watching for you next Sunday morning

Come on over to the First United Pentecostal Church at 3510 West Malone St in Peoria, ill or Visit the Pentecostals of Pontiac 101 Grove St, Pontiac Il

The Lord watch between thee and me while we're absent from one another. This is Bro Randy Johnson of the We Preach Jesus Ministries.

PROFOUND   10/20/1991

PSM 45:1 MY HEART IS INDITING A GOOD MATTER:
I SPEAK THE THINGS WHICH I HAVE MADE TOUCHING THE KING:
MY TONGUE IS THE PEN OF A READY WRITER

Rom 5:8 "But God commendeth his love toward us, in that, while we were yet sinners, [Christ died for] us."

One of the great difficulties in learning a language is the slang or clichés that each country uses in the expression of the individual ideas. Even different areas of each country have their own dialect and clichés. Even the deaf with their sign language have different dialects. The same sign may mean different things in various areas of the country. It's best that if you are to actually learn the language of a country to go there and speak the language for a year or so. We work with the Japanese in the facility that I labor in. It's interesting in that some want to learn the American version of English but others remain at arms distance with it. One even sends his daughter to ISU to take Japanese so that when he goes home she won't be behind in anything. Not Americanized that is. Time after time you can stump these men by using some nomenclature not understood or taught in their schools. Then it takes time to translate into English known to them what this particular expression means. We have in our language, many double meaning expressions. Sometimes though, an expression has been used for so long that it is totally outdated or it's meaning completely forgotten. Try explaining that to someone with terms that you both understand. Then take a time worn expression and bring it up to date for them. Difficult at best. But it does begin to make you think of what you are about to say. There is in the Word of God sentences that just seem to roll off a person's mind like water off of a duck's back. 1 Cor 12:3 "....no man can say that Jesus is the Lord, but by the Holy Ghost." That doesn't make sense at first light. You can stand around all day long and say that Jesus is Lord. Try it. See that didn't take anything extra to say that Jesus is Lord but when it comes to Jesus being Lord of your life that then is another matter all together. No man may call Jesus Lord of his life except when the Holy Ghost lives within him and directs his life. Then is Jesus Lord, totally Lord.   Deu 10:17 "For the LORD your [God <is> God] of gods, and Lord of lords, a great God, a mighty, and a terrible, which regardeth not persons, nor taketh reward:" God is God. That's easy to say but hard for many to realize. We easily recognize that the heavens were formed by the word of God, that all the beasts of the field are the handiwork of his hands. That God set the heavens in order, spoke them into existence. Touched this creature called man and breathed into him the breath of life. God is God is easy to say and recognize except when it comes to the every day life we live. It's easy to believe that you have your life in order that you have set the path for your feet and to an extent you have been permitted the options of doing so. God won't interfere with what you call your life, but, don't think for one minute the devil will allow you this option. As long as your a unrepentant hell bound sinner the devil will leave you nearly alone but the minute you decide to make God your God by allowing God to direct your footsteps you'll have the Devil's attention. God is God only and if you let him have full responsibility for your life regardless of what happens to it. Remember Job the man who suffered greatly he knew who God was and God was his God for he said in Job 13:15 "Though he slay me, yet will I trust in him:" God is God. He has all things in his power. All that is the creation of his hands. But to trust in God to direct your everyday life makes it possible for you to say that God is God of your life. God has given you everything that you have. Everything. Have you created your own air to breath? What, just what have you created? You may assemble certain compounds or put elements together but have you ever created an atom? Look at 1 Cor 4:7 "For who maketh thee to differ from another? and what hast thou that thou didst not receive? now if thou didst receive it, why dost thou glory, as if thou hadst not received it?" Rom 9:20 "Nay but, O man, who art thou that repliest against God? Shall the thing formed say to him that formed it, Why hast thou made me thus?" God is God and all things that happen unto me are by his hand. He allowed it to happen to create Christ in me. The Perfecting of my life, maybe there is something in my life that isn't like Christ and it must come out. God is God.

    Another set of scriptures that roll off the mind are the 3:16s of the New Testament, John 3:16 "For God so loved the world, that he gave his only begotten Son, that whosoever believeth in him should not perish, but have everlasting life."

    1 Tim 3:16 "And without controversy great is the mystery of godliness: God was manifest in the flesh, justified in the Spirit, seen of angels, preached unto the Gentiles, believed on in the world, received up into glory."

1 John 3:16 "Hereby perceive we the love <of God>, because he laid down his life for us: and we ought to lay down <our> lives for the brethren." Or the Golden rule that we all learned in school.

Mat 7:12 "Therefore all things whatsoever ye would that men should do to you, do ye even so to them: for this is the law and the prophets." This is a profound statement by the Lord of Glory. This is the law and the prophets. Hundreds of pages of laws and all the writings of the prophets summed up in one statement, "Whatsoever ye would that men should do to you, do ye even so to them." Or treat your neighbor as yourself. How can I ever express to you how profound these statements are? Maxwell Maltz, Dale Carnage, Earl Nightingale, all the self motivational writers and interpersonal relationship books are based on this very principle of fifteen words. How can my life be governed by one Book? The principles set forth by the word of God are timeless. This generation says it's outgrown the Word of God. Guess what friend, there has been other generations and nations that perceived they had out grown the principles set down by the Word of God. We stand now at an age when mankind is separating, purging even, the government of the land from the Bible principles that built this nation. No longer sacred are the truths set forth by the Word of God. Are you getting political? No, just sad and concerned over the bent of the nation. Is it wrong to leave what is right and has worked for centuries, to forge ahead on what is perceived to be new paths that are indeed not new but as old as time itself? There's a cry throughout the land for a drink of the well of salvation but who will dip for the water? How long will it be before religious freedom turns into freedom from religion? Even China realizes that the great nation of the United States of America was founded on religious principles. They want our people to come and teach Christianity. Their nation needs the individual motivation that Christianity brings. They need the principles of love your neighbor as yourself, and Deng knows it. You don't believe it? Try riding a bicycle in downtown Beijing, or anywhere in China for that matter. I saw a dead woman laying in the streets with everyone simply walking around her, avoiding the fact that she was indeed dead. they simply didn't want to get involved in the lengthy process that no doubt would have taken place if the had shown concern. Leave it for her family. Oh, they were courteous to the blue eyed long nose alright, but what a beautifully tired old nation. Old as time itself.

Russia wants religion to rebuild it's economic base, mean while America has a great flux of impostors leaving black marks on what is known to many as Christianity. The false prophets of this nation haven't done a whole lot of good for the reputation of the

Church. The world is on the brink of the seven year tribulation. The church stands poised for the next dispensation to be ushered in. Revival of first century Christianity is everywhere. The Book of Acts is being added to each day in the lives of the body of Christ. Revival is in the land.

The preacher preached. It wasn't this message but another that came across the pulpit. In the text of the message, the opening scripture was the most profound statement ever spoken by man, "Christ died for your sins." The great truths of life are not hidden in the deep sayings of man, but in the simple truths discovered while digging for the value of life itself. Christ died for your sins. Analyze this statement, dig around it like you would a newly planted tree. Water it with the tears of repentance would flow down your cheeks. Kneel beside this fantastic truth with bowed head and closed eyes. Christ died for your sins. Man, clear away the cobwebs of your mind, Christ died for your sins. If your listening to this at the close of your day take it to bed with you, ponder it, lay your head down with this thought ringing through your mind, Christ died for your sins. To some this is no more than foolishness to think that they have sins, to them, is foolishness. 2 Pet 3:5 "For this they [willingly] are ignorant of, that by the word of God the heavens were of old, and the earth standing out of the water and in the water:" Willingly ignorant that they might believe a lie and be eternally without salvation, damned to a devil's hell simply because of an unwillingness to believe that Jesus died for their sins. 1 Cor 1:27 "But God hath chosen the foolish things of the world to confound the wise, and God hath chosen the weak things of the world to confound the things which are mighty, 1 Cor 1: 18 "for the preaching of the cross is to them that perish foolishness, but unto us which are saved it is the power of God. {19} For it is written, I will destroy the wisdom of the wise, and will bring to nothing the understanding of the prudent. {20} Where <is> the wise? where <is> the scribe? where <is> the disputer of this world? hath not God made foolish the wisdom of this world? {21} For after that in the wisdom of God the world by wisdom knew not God, it pleased God by the foolishness of preaching to save them that believe. {22} For the Jews require a sign, In Mat 12:38-39 the religious leaders of Jesus' day sought a sign from Jesus "Then certain of the scribes and of the Pharisees answered, saying, Master, we would see a sign from thee. But he answered and said unto them, An evil and adulterous generation seeketh after a sign, and there shall no sign be given to it, but the sign of the prophet Jonas:" and the Greeks seek after wisdom: Luke 23:8 "And when Herod saw Jesus, he was exceeding glad: for he was desirous to see him of a long

<season>, because he had heard many things of him, and he hoped to have seen [some miracle] done by him." And Paul preaching to the group that sat on Mars Hill to hear some new thing that anyone might bring to them: Acts 17:22-33 "Then Paul stood in the midst of Mars' hill, and said, <Ye> men of Athens, I perceive that in all things ye are too superstitious. {23} For as I passed by, and beheld your devotions, I found an altar with this inscription, TO THE UNKNOWN GOD. Whom therefore ye ignorantly worship, him declare I unto you. {24} God that made the world and all things therein, seeing that he is Lord of heaven and earth, dwelleth not in temples made with hands, {25} Neither is worshipped with men's hands, as though he needed any thing, seeing he giveth to all life, and breath, and all things, {26} And hath made of one blood all nations of men for to dwell on all the face of the earth, and hath determined the times before appointed, and the bounds of their habitation, {27} That they should seek the Lord, if haply they might feel after him, and find him, though he be not far from every one of us: {28} For in him we live, and move, and have our being, as certain also of your own poets have said, For we are also his offspring. {29} Forasmuch then as we are the offspring of God, we ought not to think that the Godhead is like unto gold, or silver, or stone, graven by art and man's device. {30} And the times of this ignorance God winked at, but now commandeth all men every where to repent: {31} Because he hath appointed a day, in the which he will judge the world in righteousness by <that> man whom he hath ordained, <whereof> he hath given assurance unto all <men>, in that he hath raised him from the dead. {32} And when they heard of the resurrection of the dead, some mocked: and others said, We will hear thee again of this <matter>. {33} So Paul departed from among them." I Cor 1:23 "But we preach Christ crucified, unto the Jews a stumbling block, and unto the Greeks foolishness, {24} But unto them which are called, both Jews and Greeks, Christ the power of God, and the wisdom of God. {25} Because the foolishness of God is wiser than men, and the weakness of God is stronger than men. {26} For ye see your calling, brethren, how that not many wise men after the flesh, not many mighty, not many noble, <are called>: {27} But God hath chosen the foolish things of the world to confound the wise, and God hath chosen the weak things of the world to confound the things which are mighty, {28} And base things of the world, and things which are despised, hath God chosen, <yea>, and things which are not, to bring to nought things that are: {29} That no flesh should glory in his presence. {30} But of him are ye in Christ Jesus, who of God is made unto us wisdom, and righteousness, and sanctification, and redemption: {31} That, according as it is written, He that glorieth, let him glory in the

Lord." It's foolishness to the wise and not many wise, not many rich, not many mighty men will find it in their hearts to believe that Jesus died for their sins. Such a profound statement though, Christ died for your sins. Festus Agrippa cried out with a loud voice to Paul in Acts 26:24 at the gospel being preached to him, " Paul, thou art beside thyself, [much learning] doth make thee mad." Acts 26:25 "But he said, I am not mad, most noble Festus, but speak forth the words of truth and soberness. For the king knoweth of these things, before whom also I speak freely: for I am persuaded that none of these things are hidden from him, for this thing was not done in a corner. King Agrippa, believest thou the prophets? I know that thou believest. Then Agrippa said unto Paul, Almost thou persuadest me to be a Christian. And Paul said, I would to God, that not only thou, but also all that hear me this day, were both almost, and altogether such as I am, except these bonds."

"Much learning doth make thee mad." To the wise, foolishness.

2 Tim 3:7 "[Ever learning], and never able to come to the knowledge of the truth." Paul the apostle told Timothy in 2 Tim 4:3-4 that "For the time will come when they will not endure sound doctrine, but after their own lusts shall they heap to themselves teachers, having itching ears, And they shall turn away <their> ears from the truth, and shall be turned unto fables." People desiring to hear what they will that will soothe their conscience and salve their souls, so that they can turn and go back to the life of sin they desire in their hearts. But such a life is not salvation but self justification. This won't save the soul. Eternal salvation is the desire of my heart. I want to make it. I love Jesus and want to be with him forever. Jesus chose the simple things to confound those that think themselves to be wise. Remember the beginning of true wisdom is the fear of the LORD. The fact that Christ was indeed crucified, died and was buried for three days, arose and led captivity captive, ascended into the heavens to make atonement for your sins and mine, descended to walk with the disciples for some forty days, was seen of five hundred people at one time, ascended once again while the angels comforted the disciples with, Acts 1:11 "Ye men of Galilee, why stand ye gazing up into heaven? this same Jesus, which is taken up from you into heaven, shall so come in like manner as ye have seen him go into heaven." Poured out his Spirit upon the 120 in the upper room on the day of Pentecost, gave promise of the Holy Ghost to you and me in Acts 2:38 and walks with us day by day. This fact, this truth, has given to me a song that the angels can't sing. The angels of heaven can't even participate in this salvation plan. It's not for them, it's just for us. 1 Pet 1:12 "Unto whom it was revealed, that not unto themselves,

but unto us they did minister the things, which are now reported unto you by them that have preached the gospel unto you with the Holy Ghost sent down from heaven, which things the angels desire to look into." Rev 15:3 "And they sing the song of Moses the servant of God, and the song of the Lamb, saying, Great and marvelous <are> thy works, Lord God Almighty, just and true <are> thy ways, thou King of saints." What song? Exo 15:2 "The LORD <is> my strength and song, and he is become my salvation: he <is> my God, and I will prepare him an habitation, my father's God, and I will exalt him. What is this habitation that we are to prepare?" 1 Cor 3:16 "[Know ye not] that ye are the temple of God, and <that> the Spirit of God dwelleth in you?" God dwells in the temple, the temple that we prepare for him. How do we prepare the temple? By cleansing it of all sin through repentance and baptism in the name of Jesus Christ for the remission of our sins, Then with cleansed temple ready for the occupancy of God, the Spirit of God comes through the Eastern gate. The Lord fills the temple with his presence. You cannot sing a song properly until it becomes yours by experience. The song of Moses and the Lamb is a song of salvation and devotion unto the LORD. Make it your song also.

Profound statements of life are usually simple words such as these, Christ died for your sins. Rom 5:11 "Every year the high priest went into the Holiest of Holies, not without blood, to offer the blood of the atonement for the sins of the people." This blood couldn't atone for the sins of mankind though. It was a substitution blood, the blood of a bull, just a substitute to push their sins ahead until messiah should come. Push them ahead, forward looking ever forward to that day when this profound statement would echo through the sanctuary, Christ died for your sins. One day near two thousand years ago, a man gave his life for you and me. Not just a man but God gift wrapped in the flesh. It had to be a sin free man, one who had no sin, to make atonement for your sins and mine. Now we stand looking back to that time trying to understand, trying to comprehend how and why. By faith, we understand that the worlds were framed by the spoken word of God. Well by faith you'll have to understand, no, believe that this man, "if it be lawful to call him such", as Josephus said in Antiquities 18:3.3, actual came to seek and save the lost. Once you've made this faith call, you'll know beyond a shadow of a doubt, that Christ did come to seek and save you. You'll know, when the burden of sin is lifted from your shoulders that, Christ died for your sins. Christ died for you. But more than that, he's alive, the tomb is empty, the cross is empty, and my heart is full of rejoicing.

SOLD A BILL OF GOODS   11/03/1991

PSM 45:1 MY HEART IS INDITING A GOOD MATTER:
I SPEAK THE THINGS WHICH I HAVE MADE TOUCHING THE KING:
MY TONGUE IS THE PEN OF A READY WRITER

Gen 1:26 "And God said, Let us make man in our image, after our likeness: and let them have [dominion] over the fish of the sea, and over the fowl of the air, and over the cattle, and over all the earth, and over every creeping thing that creepeth upon the earth."

Mark 8:36 "For what shall it profit a man, if he shall gain the whole world, and lose his own soul?"

I don't know where the statement "sold a bill of goods" came from. I can well imagine that it came from someone that was sold just a bill of laden, just a bill of goods, a list of articles that was to be sent to a person or address. It was just a bill of goods, it had no substance except what was written on the bill. Someone no doubt bought just the bill of goods.

There was a time some six thousand or so years ago, when man, the only man, walked the face of the earth sin free. Adam and Eve had all they could ever want, eternal life for death had no hold on them as they were sin free, all the food for the picking they could ever want, continual fellowship with the Most High God, love one for another. Every tree in the garden was theirs for food except one. Gen 2:16-17 "And the LORD God commanded the man, saying, Of every tree of the garden thou mayest freely eat: But of the tree of the knowledge of good and evil, thou shalt not eat of it: for in the day that thou eatest thereof thou shalt surely die." They knew no evil, they didn't even know right from wrong for they had done no wrong in the eyes of God. Things were great, never could they be better. Everything was perfect until Eve walked alone in the garden. Passing by the forbidden tree a voice spoke to her,

Gen 3:1"Yea, hath God said, ye shall not eat of every tree of the garden? And the woman said unto the serpent, We may eat of the fruit of the trees of the garden: But of the fruit of the tree which <is> in the midst of the garden, God hath said, Ye shall not eat of it, neither shall ye touch it, lest ye die. And the serpent said unto the woman, Ye shall not surely die: For God doth know that in the day ye eat thereof, then your eyes shall be opened, and ye shall be as gods, knowing good and evil. It's the old play for the pride of the heart of the woman. Ye shall be as gods, knowing good and evil." Really what he was saying is that you would be of the same spirit as Lucifer . He thinks himself above what he ought, for he fell from a high place taking with him a third of the angels. This precipitated the battle that rages in the heavens and among mankind today. Gen3:6 "And when the woman saw that the tree <was> good for food, and that it <was> pleasant to the eyes, and a tree to be desired to make <one> wise," she was already using her own judgment, questioning the one that had created her from the rib of Adam. She took of the fruit thereof, and did eat, and gave also unto her husband with her, and he did eat. Why did Adam eat? The eternal question open to all sorts of speculation. Gen 3:7 "And the eyes of them both were opened, and they knew that they <were> naked, and they sewed fig leaves together, and made themselves aprons." So you see, not only did they make decisions for themselves, now knowing good from evil, but they decided they needed to be clothed. So, picking the most unsuitable plant they could have picked, they made clothes. 1 Tim 2:14 says, "And Adam was not deceived, but the woman being deceived was in the transgression." Regardless of who was or wasn't deceived, they sold the kingdom for folly. They were sold a bill of goods by the devil. After the transgression, it's true they knew good and evil but the kingdom passed to Satan, they lost fellowship with God, and now death had dominion over their lives. Death now reigned. Sold out for a bill of goods. In the day that thou eatest thereof thou shalt surely die. Soul death, now subject to ageing. The body began to die the moment they ate of the fruit of self-will. No longer could they walk with God in the cool of the day, no long were they a resident of the Garden of Eden. No longer did they have eternal life. Lost all to a whim. All they had was a piece of paper with a bill of goods written upon it. Mark 8:36 "For what shall it profit a man, if he shall gain the whole world, and lose his own soul?"

    The story goes of a man named Ezra. Israel had been in captivity by the Babylonians. God had moved on the heart of Cyrus to rebuild the temple in Jerusalem. Opposition came in the form of the occupants of the land around Jerusalem. They feared the Jews and what they could do if the worship was reestablished. After writing a letter condemning the Jews in their work, the work on the temple and the walls was halted for a long time. The building was re established under the reign of Darius the king. The worship was established all the rites observed and on the scene comes a man named Ezra.

Ezra 7:6 "This Ezra went up from Babylon, and he <was> a ready scribe in the law of Moses, which the LORD God of Israel had given: and the king granted him all his request, according to the hand of the LORD his God upon him." Ezra's job was to teach all of Israel the law of the LORD. He had prepared his heart to seek the law of the Lord, and do it, and to teach in Israel statutes and judgments. On came Ezra with the gold and silver and with the free will offerings of the people, to purchase and offer up bullocks, rams, and lambs upon the alter of the house of the LORD in Jerusalem for the people. Thousands of pounds of treasure were the responsibility of this man. Responsibility of establishing magistrates and judges were set upon the shoulders of this man. When all this had been accomplished in Jerusalem, there came the chief princes of Israel and said the Priests and Levites have not separated themselves from the people of the lands and are doing the abominations of the Canaanites, the Hittites, the Perizzites, the Jebusites, the Ammonites, the Moabites, the Egyptians, and the Amorites. They have taken of their daughters for themselves, and for their sons: so that the holy seed is mingled with the people of the land. When Ezra heard this thing, he tore his garments in grief, plucked off the hair of his head and beard, and sat down astonished. Why, you say, did he do this beard plucking in the streets? These were the leaders, the religious leaders of Israel who were to remain separated and not to marry out of their tribe because the lineage was to be perfect. The abominations of these people, the Canaanites, the Hittites, the Perizzites, the Jebusites, the Ammonites, the Moabites, the Egyptians, and the Amorites, were of such that it's not fit to mention them in this setting. These were the abominations they were doing. They had sold out for the pleasures of this world but Ezra was about to call them to task.

Ezra 9:4-8 "Then were assembled unto me every one that trembled at the words of the God of Israel, because of the transgression of those that had been carried away, and I sat astonished until the evening sacrifice. {5} And at the evening sacrifice I arose up from my heaviness, and having rent my garment and my mantle, I fell upon my knees, and spread out my hands unto the LORD my God, {6} And said, O my God, I am ashamed and blush to lift up my face to thee, my God: for our iniquities are increased over <our> head, and our trespass is grown up unto the heavens. {7} Since the days of our fathers <have> we <been> in a great trespass unto this day, and for our iniquities have we, our kings, <and> our priests, been delivered into the hand of the kings of the lands, to the sword, to captivity, and to a spoil, and to confusion of face, as <it is> this day. {8} And now for a little space grace hath been <showed> from the LORD our God, to leave us a remnant to escape, and to give us a nail in his holy place, that our God may lighten our eyes, and give us a little reviving in our bondage." And to give us a little reviving in our bondage. What an awe-inspiring statement. A little reviving in our bondage. What was the purpose of Jesus Christ? Luke 4:18 Jesus said: "The Spirit of the Lord <is> upon me, because he hath anointed me to preach the gospel to the poor, he hath sent me to heal the brokenhearted, to preach deliverance to the captives, and recovering of sight to the blind, to [set at liberty] them that are bruised," To set at liberty them that are bruised, to deliver the captives, to break the yoke of bondage wherewith sin binds every man woman and youth upon the face of the earth. What happens to that glorious liberty that Christ gives to you so freely do you run back to the same bondage that you were bound with? God help us for it is like a dog turning back to his vomit.

Gal 5:1 "Stand fast therefore in the liberty wherewith Christ hath made us free, and be not entangled again with the yoke of bondage." Why sell out for a bill of goods? Just an empty promise, one of no substance. Give us a little reviving in our bondage. They were under slave rules but God had set before them an open door. Instead of the release God had intended for them, they found a place to sin and with the sin, new bondage. They chose to sin.

Ezra 9:14-15 "Should we again break thy commandments, and join in affinity with the people of these abominations? Wouldest not thou be angry with us till thou hadst consumed <us>, so that <there should be> no remnant nor escaping? {15} O LORD God of Israel, thou <art> righteous: for we remain yet escaped, as <it is> this day: behold, we <are> before thee in our trespasses: for we cannot stand before thee because of this. "

The people repented of the evil they had done and put away the strange wives from themselves. The lineage of the priest hood was checked and purged and the land had revival. What is the desire of your heart? Is it for revival throughout the land? Do you desire revival in your heart? Is that the wish, the desire of your heart? The strange wives among us are the different idols put between God and yourself. What do you have that displaces God? What is so important in your life that you can't put it aside for God? Is it going fishing on a Sunday when you should be in the Lord's house worshiping? Maybe you like camping, I do, but not every weekend when you could be teaching others about the Lord of Glory. What are our strange wives? You know, you know for sure what they are. It's up to you to purge them out of your life. Don't be suckered into buying a bill of goods, God has the real thing for you. The real goods.

Israel was led by Moses, a man who didn't buy deception from the adversary, led by Moses right up to the river that separated the wilderness from the land of promise. Twelve men were sent over the river Jordan to see what the land was like. Back they came with reports of an abundance of the fruit of the land. And a report that they were as grasshoppers in comparison to the inhabitants of the land. Only two remembered how God had brought them out of Egypt. Only two didn't sell out to fear and unbelief. All the people except Joshua, Caleb, and Moses were afraid to go over into the land of promise. Doubters are do with outers. God told them that because of their unbelief, they wouldn't inherit the land of promise. All except these three were to wonder about in the wilderness until that generation all passed away. Forty years of God providing clothing, food, guidance, and water. Guided by a pillar of fire by night and a column of smoke by day. Told when to march when to stay, where to go. Forty years of graves left behind in the marching in the wilderness. Forty years to think about the promise land. Forty years to raise children in the nurture and admonition of the Lord. Fourth years of sacrifice so their children could enter into the promise, they themselves had rejected. Is it worth it? To reject the counsel of God against yourself? Heaping to yourself coals of fire? Don't you know that you're being sold a bill of goods? Don't be angry at these words for they are meant simply to make you stop and think about the direction your life is taking. What kind of friend would allow another to harm themselves? A right poor one. Oh that the two could have talked the other ten into believing in the Lord's promise. What pain and suffering could have been alleviated if, only if, they had believed. The twelve could easily have led the multitude into the land of promise. Ten against two are too great of odds for the people to believe. The voice of discouragement takes more than two to overcome. I imagine there were just a few that began to shout at the judgment of Jesus. Just a few shouting," Crucify him, crucify him." Soon the mob rule took over and the excitement of blood caused a multitude to shout, "crucify him, crucify him". Even though Pontius Pilate said, Why, I find no fault in him, he has done nothing. Caught in the tide of things. Washed along on the wave of the crowd. The individual didn't have a chance to stifle, to put down the shouting of the crowd. Sold out for a little excitement. We want to see a crucifixion today and we don't care who it is. Forget the healings, the bread and fishes, the word preached and taught in our streets, crucify him, crucify him. How many in Tienemmin square were caught up in the crowd, just curious about what was going on. In the wrong place at the wrong time. Death came to many who had nothing to do with the protest. Guilty by association. Oh, that I would have stayed home that day and watched it on the television.

There was a man named Achan who fought with Israel against Jericho. You know the story how they marched around the walls for seven days until the walls fell into the ground. Israel was told not to take any of the spoil of the city of Jericho for it is the Lord's. Josh 6:18 "And ye, in any wise keep <yourselves> from the accursed thing, lest ye make <yourselves> accursed, when ye take of the accursed thing, and make the camp of Israel a curse, and trouble it. But all the silver, and gold, and vessels of brass and iron, <are> consecrated unto the LORD: they shall come into the treasury of the LORD." Achan found among the destruction a garment, some silver and a wedge of gold. In his heart was a desire to keep them for himself, and he did. He buried them beneath the floor of his tent so that no one would know. Let me ask you, what good did his disobedience do him? He had the silver, gold and garments but he couldn't do anything with them. Could he wear the garment? No, because everyone would know where he got it. Where could he spend the silver and gold? Isn't it funny how a person will sell out for a bill of goods? About as funny as a heart attack. When it came time to take the next city of the land, not everyone was sent because the people that populated it were few, but: Josh 7:5 "And the men of Ai smote of them about thirty and six men: for they chased them <from> before the gate <even> unto Shebarim, and smote them in the going down: wherefore the hearts of the people melted, and became as water." Israel on the run because of the sin of Achan. Thirty-six men lost their lives because Achan sold out for a bill of goods. How many people do you influence? The responsibility of the lives of my children, my wife, my friends and who knows how many others lie upon my shoulders. God forbid that I should sell out like Achan. My strength is in the Lord and not in myself. I've found this to be true for like Paul said Rom 7:18 "For I know that in me (that is, in my flesh,) dwelleth [no good thing]: for to will is present with me, but <how> to perform that which is good I find not." What is the answer Paul to this dilemma of the war that is going on in my flesh? Rom 8:1 "<There is> therefore now no condemnation to them which are in Christ Jesus, who walk not after the flesh, but after the Spirit." Walk after the Spirit and not after the flesh. Desire holiness on your inward parts and you'll not fulfill the lust of the flesh.

Joshua fell on his face before the Lord in prayer, but God told him to get up for Israel had sinned. Joshua told the people to sanctify themselves and come before the

Lord in the morning. Israel marched past Joshua and when Achan came before him, Joshua said, "Give God the glory and confess your sin, what is it that you have done son?" And Achan said: Josh 7:21 "When I saw among the spoils a goodly Babylonish garment, and two hundred shekels of silver, and a wedge of gold of fifty shekels weight, then I coveted them, and took them, and, behold, they <are> hid in the earth in the midst of my tent, and the silver under it." I coveted them, and thirty-six men lost their lives because of his sell out. They took Achan and all that was his, and took them to the valley of Abhor, stoned them, and raised a pile of stones over him and all that he had. They buried him, his animals, his wife and children, and his wedge of gold, his shekels of silver and his Babylonian garment. Oh Achan, if only you had waited. When all the battles were over, they divided the spoils among all of Israel. You were too greedy. You had too big of eyes and because of it you lost all. You sold out for nothing. Don't have an aching for a wedge of gold, some silver and a garment. God will divide the spoils when the battles are over. Just a little bit longer and we will be on the other side of Jordan. Into the promise land, victorious in all that Christ wants us to be. Two desired recognition for what they hadn't done. Acts 5:1 "But a certain man named [Ananias], with Sapphira his wife, sold a possession," Acts 5:2 "And kept back <part> of the price, his wife also being privy <to it>, and brought a certain part, and laid <it>, at the apostles' feet." Acts 5:3 "But Peter said, Ananias, why hath Satan filled thine heart to lie to the Holy Ghost, and to keep back <part> of the price of the land?" Acts 5:4 "Whiles it remained, was it not thine own? And after it was sold, was it not in thine own power? Why hast thou conceived this thing in thine heart? Thou hast not lied unto men, but unto God. And Ananias hearing these words fell down, and gave up the ghost: and great fear came on all them that heard these things. And the young men arose, wound him up and carried <him> out, and buried <him>. And it was about the space of three hours after, when his wife, not knowing what was done, came in. And Peter answered unto her, tell me whether ye sold the land for so much? And she said, Yea, for so much. Then Peter said unto her, how is it that ye have agreed together to tempt the Spirit of the Lord? Behold, the feet of them, which have buried thy husband <are> at the door, and shall carry thee out. Then fell she down straightway at his feet, and yielded up the ghost: and the young men came in, and found her dead, and, carrying <her> forth, buried <her> by her husband." They had seen what Barnabas had done and the recognition received because of it. They desired the same but went about it all-wrong. Barnabas wanted only to help the cause of Christ so he sold and gave to the work. Ananias and Sapphira desired to keep back part and misrepresent what was left to be all. There wasn't any problem with them keeping part or all for it was theirs. The error was in deceiving the Holy Ghost. They thought they could keep part and present what was left as all and bask in the glory of the sacrifice. Their motive was all-wrong, they were sold a bill of goods. Just an empty promise with no substance. And it cost them their lives. Don't be sold a bill of goods. We're not ignorant of the devices of the enemy. God has shown to us the enemies' tactics. Sometimes it takes the Holy Ghost to snap us awake but never the less we're not ignorant of his ways. I've been suckered by his tricks many times. In Christ this isn't terminal. Do you love God? He loves you. Stumbling and falling are all part of learning how to walk in Christ. We all do it.

For the thousands that have sold out for a flash in the pan, there are thousands more that have stood fast in the face of adversity. Foxes Book of Martyrs is full of those that stood fast. Life here in the United States doesn't require us to make life and death decisions about living for God. Actually though, the easier the persecution the harder it seems to be to stand fast against the tide of the everyday. Esau sold his birthright to his brother for a bowl of porridge. He was hungry and he could only think of the present moment that he lived in. We have a birth right as children of the king, our flesh is a strong contender for the selling out of the kingdom. Eve, Achan, Judas Iscariot, Ananias and Sapphira, Esau, and Demas hath forsaken me having loved this present world. What these people sold remained only as a shimmering memory, vague, distant. Merely a shimmering glow upon the past days of their lives. Esau sought with much tears repentance but to no avail. There's no more record of Demas in the New Testament. Ananias is dead and so is his wife. Sold out for a little recognition. Achan sold out for a wedge of gold, a little silver and a stylish Babylonian garment. It all came to nothing. Merely a bill of goods. Empty, without substance. Moses, Joseph, Jeremiah, Paul the apostle, Peter, John, James, Stephen, All knew what it was they were selling out to. They saw the substance, they saw the vision, there was in their hearts a burning love of God that wouldn't stop. There wasn't a bowl of soup, or money, or a moment's pleasure that could turn their heads. They had a vision, a dream, and a love. Strength is found in adversity. Whose strength? The strength of the Lord God Almighty. When I am weak then am I strong for my strength is not of myself but of Christ in me. The way of the world is not free. It will cost you your soul. God has provided a way that you can abide in his strength. That is to abide in Jesus Christ. You can begin by repenting of your sins, then being baptized in the name of Jesus Christ for the remission of these sins, then the promise is yours, you shall receive the baptism of the Holy Ghost. This is Bro R Johnson of the We Preach Jesus Ministries.

    For a copy of today's message, send a card to
    The We Preach Jesus Ministries
    PO Box 274
    Eureka, IL

    We would like to invite you to the First United Pentecostal Church of Peoria
    3510 West Malone
    Peoria, ill
    Services begin on Sunday morning at 10 and 6:30 in the evening
    Wed services begin at 7:
    Or attend the Pentecostals of Pontiac
    101 E Grove St
    Pontiac, ill
    We'll be watching for you.
    The Lord watch between thee and me while were apart
    .

CONVENIENT CHRISTIANITY   11/17/1991

PSM 45:1 MY HEART IS INDITING A GOOD MATTER:
I SPEAK THE THINGS WHICH I HAVE MADE TOUCHING THE KING:
MY TONGUE IS THE PEN OF A READY WRITER

Mat 16:26 "For what is a man profited, if he shall [gain the whole] world, and lose his own soul? Or what shall a man give in exchange for his soul?"

What is the price of your soul? Is it the riches of the world or just the price of a fling? Who owns your soul? There's no neutral ground in this battle for your soul. You belong to one side or the other. God set the pace six thousand years ago in the Garden of Eden. Man had sold out his kingdom to the enemy. And the soul of man went along with this sale. The devil has taken the option on your soul, friend. But Jesus Christ has paid the price. Jesus Christ has offered you a blank check, signed, and waiting for your acceptance. Do you believe? Then receive what he has done for you.

Oh God that their eyes might be opened to the great battle that is going on for their soul. Oh that they might understand the final destination of the soul. Oh that they might come to a day of brightness a day of illumination, a day of restoration, a day of purchase. The purchase of their souls by the Lord God Almighty. Oh, that understanding would snap them out of this sleep unto death Oh that somehow, this message might move them unto you. There is within man an emptiness. A void. A desire for something that is unknown to him. Throughout his life, various things have been tried and rejected. The pathway of your life is littered with discarded things that wouldn't fill the void within. Tried, failed, and discarded. Some were barely used. Some are dented, torn, and worn, without paint, parts missing, but discarded just the same. You've tried it again and again yet it left you as empty as before. You tried it again, yet with the same results. You think, I'll try it once more maybe this time it will fill the void within. I don't know what your favorite thing was or is. I'm not even sure I know now what my favorite thing was. But I do know what will fill that emptiness of your soul. You do too, but you choose to ignore it. Why? Is this something price of your soul? Will you be sold for so little? Time and time again God has spoke to your heart. He's spoken in times of distress, word of comfort, words of solace when no other was around. You believe, yet you stop short. God is speaking to you right now. Isn't he? Go ahead and reach out, Touch the hem of his garment just like that woman that pressed through the crowd to reach Jesus.   Hear him say "Who touched me?" Healing is in that touch. That touch of faith. No other could cure her, no other can cure the hunger of your soul. No other can cure you. You've got to make it to take it. Softly Jesus looks into your eyes. Hear him when he says, "what is the price of your soul?" For what shall it profit a man if he shall gain the whole world and lose his own soul, The question is eternal. Behold, now is the day of salvation. Today, if you will not harden your hearts, this can be the day of your fulfillment, the day you find what you've been looking for.

  Look in Numbers 22: and see what the price of this mercenary prophet of convenience called Balaam was. The children of Israel had camped in the plains of Moab on this side of the Jordan river by Jericho. These people had a reputation of being fighters, or rather of letting God go before them and destroying the enemies of the soul. They were not warriors of convenience but people who had true faith in God. Here, in the plains of Moab was a king named Balak who opposed the children of Israel. Balak had seen what this people had done to the Amorites and he was sore afraid of what God would do to his people. Moab sent messengers to Balaam who lived near Pethor. "Behold, they said, there is a people who cover the face of the earth and they abide over near me. Come over here and curse them for they are to mighty for me and if I fight against them I might win and drive them out of this land: for I know that he whom you bless is blessed and whom you curse is cursed." These messengers brought the rewards of divination with them for Balaam. Balaam put them up for the night while he sought the face of God. Can you picture this? Here is a man asking God if he would like to curse the very same people he was protecting. These were supposed to be Balaam's people also. Though this man was a prophet of God he had absolutely no convictions. That's why the name of mercenary of convenience fits him well. So in seeking God about this matter God said, "What men are these with you?" God knew who these men were, Old Balaam wasn't daunted by this question, he just kept right on going, He couldn't see what was wrong with his line of thinking. He answered "Balak the son of Zippor, king of Moab, hath sent unto me, saying, Behold there is a people come out of Egypt, which coverth the face of the earth: come now curse me them, peradventure I shall be able to overcome them, and drive them out." God said unto Balaam, "Thou shalt not go with them, thou shalt not curse the people: for they are blessed." Well the next morning, before breakfast was even served, there Balaam was speaking to the princes of Moab saying, "Go home, for the LORD refused to give me leave to go with you." This sounds like this man has already sold out. He didn't say, "I'm not going to go and curse this people for they are blessed." No, what came out was, God won't let me go but if I can find a convenient time and convince God that I should, I still want to. The princes went back to Balak with this report. Balak sent back princes more and more honorable than they. Up the ante a bit and appeal to his pride. This is what they said to Balaam. "Let nothing, I pray thee, hinder thee from coming unto me: for I will promote thee unto a very great honor, and I will do whatsoever thou sayest unto me: come therefore, I pray thee, curse me this people." Nobleness must have rose up in the bosom of Balaam for the answer was, "If Balak would give me his house full of silver and gold, I cannot go beyond the word of the LORD my God, to do less or more." It really sounds like Balaam had some convictions until he opened his mouth too far. But, if you will stick around for the night I'll go see if God has maybe changed his mind. Balaam went with the chief princes and tried to curse the children of Israel but only blessings would come out. How goodly are thy tents, O Jacob, and thy tabernacles, O Israel! As the valleys are they spread forth, as gardens by the river's side, as trees of light aloes which the LORD hath planted, and as the cedar trees beside the waters. He shall pour the water out of his buckets, and his seed shall be in many waters, and his king shall be higher than Agag, and his kingdom shall be exalted. God brought him forth out of Egypt, he hath as it were the strength of an unicorn: he shall eat up the nations his enemies, and shall break their bones, and pierce them through with his arrows. He crouched, he lay down as a great lion: who shall stir him up? Blessed is he that blessth thee, and cursed is he that cursth thee." Balaam tried on every side to curse them. But no. Convection less, convenient scruples Balaam, He had sold out. The auctioneer's hammer had fallen. Going once, going twice, sold to an empty promise of esteem. Balaam couldn't curse the children of Israel but, he accomplished it through the women of the Midieanites and the children cursed themselves. Balaam's reward was short for Numbers 31:8 tells us, "And they slew the kings of Midian." "Balaam also the son of Beor they slew with the sword. And verse 15, And Moses said unto them, Have ye saved all the women alive? Behold, these caused the Children of Israel, through the counsel of Balaam, to commit trespass against the LORD on the matter of Peor," Balaam, prophet of esteem, prophet of convenience, sold out for nothing. Just a cheap mercenary who sold his soul to the highest bidder. For what shall it profit a man if he gain the whole world but lose his soul? Or what shall a man give in exchange for his soul? What did Balaam say? "If Balak would give me his whole house full of silver and gold, I cannot go beyond the word of the LORD my God," Great words flowing from an empty man void of convictions. He caused the people to be cursed. There was no record of his material reward except a sword.

Another, by the name of Achan, sold out for a wedge of gold, a goodly garment, and two hundred shekels of silver. Greed profited him nothing. For what shall it profit a man if he gain the whole world but lose his soul?

Solomon, he who spoke 3000 proverbs and wrote 1005 songs, Solomon, the wisest man that ever lived, author of the book of Proverbs, Author of the book of Ecclesiastes, Solomon the author of the Song of Solomon, A spiritual allegory of Christ and his Church. Solomon who built the great beautiful tabernacle unto the LORD, said, "And whatsoever mine eyes desired I kept not from them, I withheld not from my heart any joy, for my heart rejoiced in all my labor: and this was my portion of all my labor." Whatever was convenient Solomon did. Solomon, whom the Queen of Sheba came to see if all the reports she had heard of his wisdom and kingdom were true. King Solomon exceeded all the kings of the earth for riches and for wisdom. But king Solomon loved many strange women, together with the daughter of Pharaoh, women of the Moabites, Ammonites, Edomites, Zidonians, and Hittites, of the nations concerning which the LORD said unto the children of Israel, "Ye shall not go in to them, neither shall they come in unto you: for surely they will turn your heart after their gods: Solomon clave unto these in love." No convictions. And he had seven hundred wives, princesses, and three hundred concubines: and his wives turned away his heart. His heart was not perfect with the LORD as was the heart of his father David. No principles unless they were convenient. For Solomon went after Astoreth the goddess of the Zidonians, and after Milcom the abomination of the Ammonites. "And Solomon did evil in the sight if the LORD, and went not fully after the LORD, as did his father David. He built an high place for Chemosh the abomination of Moab and for Molech, the abomination of Ammon." Solomon sold out for women. Lots of women and they caused him to do abomination in the sight of the LORD. God never put his sanctification on more than one wife. He only made one woman for Adam, not a harem of 700. But this wasn't what caused Solomon's downfall. No it was his lack of conviction and principle that caused him to sin.

Judas Iscariot, who sold the Lord for the price of a slave. It surly couldn't have been the money. There was no prestige in what he did. Why, Judas? Why? And Judas went and hung himself. For what shall it profit a man if he gain the whole world but lose his soul? Or what shall a man give in exchange for his soul?

I do not wish to make you think that all have sold out for the material riches of this world or some measure of self-fulfillment. The scripture are full of those who stood fast in the face of adversity. Our own history is rich with those who stood fast on principles and convections. Even in this our day there are those who would not sell their principles at any price. The man that said everyone has his price never ran into a Christian on fire for God. But one of the things to beware of is the little prices that are offered every day. Small bids made for your soul made for your convections. They're not the big ones. Not the great ones, But the small foxes that spoil the vine, and thus the fruit of your walk with God. The big things, the large prices, aren't hard to resist but it's the everyday hum of the wheels that will destroy you. The tedium, the times that your not watching, the times that you've failed to pray for a while. The times that you lose sight of the goal the high mark the calling of the LORD, that you sell out for a bowl of porridge. Something to slake the hunger of the day. Remember. "For what shall it profit a man if he gain the whole world but lose his soul? Or what shall a man give in exchange for his soul?" Casual, convenient Christianity, empty and hollow, without substance or being, won't stand in the day of your adversity or temptation. Your Christian life has to be founded on the Principles of the Word of God. Any other foundation will be destroyed. 1 Cor 3:11 "For other foundation can no man lay than that is laid, which is Jesus Christ." Convection, morals, principles or convenient convections, convenient principles or convenient Christianity. The three little pigs has their story based upon the word of God. One built of hay or straw, another of sticks, but the third built with bricks. This church is based upon the apostles and the prophets with Jesus Christ being the chief corner stone. Jesus Christ is that rock that you can build upon. When the shaking comes. When the winds blow. When all hell breaks loose. You can stand in the knowledge that you are based on a foundation that will stand forever. The shaking is coming for

Heb 12:26-28 says: "Whose voice then shook the earth: but now he hath promised, saying, Yet once more I shake not the earth only, but also heaven. {27} And this <word>, Yet once more, signifieth the removing of those things that are shaken, as of things that are made, that those things which cannot be shaken may remain. {28} Wherefore we receiving a kingdom which cannot be moved, let us have grace, whereby we may serve God acceptably with reverence and godly fear:" What is the price of your soul? Is it convenience? Christianity is not convenient. Christianity is swimming against the tide. Upstream of the system of life. True Christianity may well cost you everything that you have. Convenience? I think not. Jesus Christ himself said, "Pick up your cross and follow me." That doesn't sound casual, or convenient. This is not some cross that you physically drag down the road behind you. This is not some cross, made of silver or gold and hanging from a chain around your neck. I have nothing against this but, this is a rough hand hewn cross that you daily find yourself crucified upon. Paul said , "I die daily." How? Gal 2:20 "I am crucified with Christ: nevertheless [I live], yet not I, but Christ liveth in me: and the life which I now live in the flesh [I live] by the faith of the Son of God, who loved me, and gave himself for me." The pathway of time that starts at the cross two thousand years ago, is littered with the bodies of the martyrs who gave their lives for this precious truth. First century Christianity had very few casual Christians. It began with the shedding of blood and it will end with the shedding of the same. John the Baptist lost his head for being the forerunner of Christ, Stephen was stoned simply because the people wouldn't stand for the truth, Peter and John were arrested simply for the healing God gave to a lame man. Many fell and the command of a man named Saul of Tarsis, James, the Brother of John, was slain at the command of Herod Agrippa I, Peter was put in prison but at the hand of an angel was led out, Paul, who was Saul, was beheaded in Rome, some were sewn into goat skins and set out for the lions, others run through with spears and swords, some were boiled in oil while others were burnt at the stake. Inquisitions, and accusations, tortures and killings. The Catacombs were their homes of safety, until Christianity was embraced by the Roman Government of the day. Before Long, Christianity became convenient. If you were to hold office in the government of the land, you had to proclaim Christianity. Melded together were Jewish, Christian and Pagan holidays. The Idea, make Christianity acceptable to everyone. God's desires for the church were left out of the decisions. Never fear. God has always had a remnant that hadn't bowed their knee to Baal. Rom 11:4 "But what saith the answer of God unto him? I have reserved to myself seven thousand men, who have not bowed the knee to <the image of> [Baal]."

Rom 11:5 "Even so then at this present time also there is a remnant according to the election of grace." Grace abounds in this present time so there are more than seven thousand that haven't bowed to the things of this world. That is, the lust of the eye, the lust of the flesh, and the pride of life. What is the price that you put on the Christianity that you live? How far would you go to defend your convictions, your morals, your principles? Are they a convenience? Have you ever heard anyone say, It's the principle of the thing.? They defend one principle held out in a set of standards but totally ignore another. It's just a convenient principle, not a real conviction. there's no such thing as convenient Christianity. It's simply convenient religion, not Christianity. Christianity requires only your life. You must turn over the keys to your kingdom. Christianity is a theocracy. It's a kingdom ruled only by one, Jesus Christ. There's no room for you and God to reign in your life. You must crucify the flesh, your soulish desires, daily. Peter left the fish nets to be a disciple of the Lord. Matthew left off collecting taxes, Paul was of a wealthy Jewish family, he left it all behind. There are no sacrifices made for Jesus that he doesn't see. Mark 10:29 "And Jesus answered and said, Verily I say unto you, There is no man that hath left house, or brethren, or sisters, or father, or [mother], or wife, or children, or lands, for my sake, and the gospel's, (30) But he shall receive an hundred fold now in this time, houses, and brethren, and sisters, and mothers, and children, and lands, with persecutions, and in the world to come eternal life." Does that mean that your to leave your wife or mother or children to serve God? I think the Bible will answer your question 1 Tim 5:8 "But if any provide [not for his own], and specially for those of his own house, he hath denied the faith, and is worse than an infidel." It shows that God sees all and will reward all your sacrifices. There are those who have been thrown out of their houses simply for embracing this precious truth. They didn't feel it was just a casual Christianity they were embracing. Why is it that people would rather have their children getting drunk than going to church? I don't understand. I wasn't raised in Church. My parents gave me a good Christian upbringing, instilled me with certain morals and convictions but I never knew who Jesus was until I was thirty years old. I would that I had known Jesus in the days of my youth, but not so. Nineteen years I've walked in this way. Nineteen of the best years of my life. Would I stand for him now? How could I do else? Against persecution, against fire, against all odds. But where the real battles come. Where the war is fought, where many perish day by day, in the everyday life, the nasty now now, how do I fare? Some men die by the sword, others perish in the flames, but most go down bit by bit playing little games. (unknown)

    Did you ever wonder what provoked Martin Luther to nail his ninety five thesis to the church door? Have you ever wondered what drove John Wesley? Have you ever wondered what makes a man give up a profitable occupation to struggle against all odds and build a congregation by giving of himself day by day? Have you ever wondered what causes a man, a rich man from a prominent family of Tarsis, to put it all aside and evangelize, the known world? Listen to his testimony of suffering. 2 Cor 11:21-29 "I speak as concerning reproach, as though we had been weak. Howbeit where in so ever any is bold, (I speak foolishly,) I am bold also. Are they Hebrews? so <am> I. Are they Israelites? so <am> I. Are they the seed of Abraham? so <am> I. Are they ministers of Christ? (I speak as a fool) I <am> more, in labours more abundant, in stripes above measure, in prisons more frequent, in deaths oft. Of the Jews five times received I forty <stripes> save one Thrice was I beaten with rods, once was I stoned, thrice I suffered shipwreck, a night and a day I have been in the deep <In> journeyings often, <in> perils of waters, <in> perils of robbers, <in> perils by <mine own> countrymen, <in> perils by the heathen, <in> perils in the city, <in> perils in the wilderness, <in> perils in the sea, <in> perils among false brethren, In weariness and painfulness, in watchings often, in hunger and thirst, in fastings often, in cold and nakedness. Beside those things that are without, that which cometh upon me daily, the care of all the churches. Who is weak, and I am not weak? who is offended, and I burn not?" Are you required to make this kind of a commitment? No, just to be willing. Your battles and mine come from the area of complacency, Ours is from the hum of the wheels on the pavement. It puts us to sleep. It's the everyday, humdrum, ho hum, type of a day that makes us nod our heads, our eyes go closed and our breathing is deep and regular. Sleep overpowers our walk with God and common complacency sets in. Awake Zion, awake. Trim your lamps. Make your light the brightest that you possibly can. Behold the bridegroom cometh. Listen, you can hear the sounds of his coming, Louder and louder each day. The newspapers proclaim it, the attitudes of the people proclaim it. Evil proclaims it. The Spirit shouts it in the messages you hear from day to day. Over to the side is a fallen angel saying

2 Pet 3:4 "Where is the promise of his coming? for since the fathers fell asleep, all things continue as <they were> from the beginning of the creation." Surly you have plenty of time. Who knows when Jesus is coming back for his people. Didn't he even say he didn't know? The body of Christ knows. You can feel it in the air. You can feel it everywhere. Something is in the air. What happens when Jesus comes back for his bride, the church? 1 Th 4:16-17 " For the Lord himself shall descend from heaven with a shout, with the voice of the archangel, and with the trump of God: and the dead in Christ shall rise first: {17} Then we which are alive <and> remain shall be caught up together with them in the clouds, to meet the Lord in the air: and so shall we ever be with the Lord."

Do you want to go when Jesus comes for his bride? Then Repent of the sins that you've done. Be baptized in the name of Jesus Christ for the remission of these sins, and he will give you the Holy Ghost. This is the Ernest of your inheritance. This is your seal of approval of the Holy Ghost.

This is bro Randy Johnson of the We Preach Jesus Ministries

THANKSGIVING   11/24/1991

PSM 45:1 MY HEART IS INDITING A GOOD MATTER:
I SPEAK THE THINGS WHICH I HAVE MADE TOUCHING THE KING:
MY TONGUE IS THE PEN OF A READY WRITER

There was, about this time of the year, a feast of Israel called the Feast of tabernacles. God had set this feast in order as a feast of thanksgiving. The children of Israel had journeyed out of a land of slavery. God had provided deliverance from this bondage at the hand of Moses. God had lead them across, no, through the Red sea. Set before them a pillar of fire at night and a pillar of cloud by day to guide them in the wilderness. God had provided clothing, food, water, and comfort.   God had delivered them from the hand of their enemies. He had given them the victory. They now occupied the land of promise that God had given to them. The fields had been plowed, planted, and harvested. The crops were plentiful. The barns full. There was no lack of food among the people due to the grace of God. Among this, in this, God set up a feast of Tabernacles, the "harvest home" celebration. The harvest was home where it should be. Feast of Tabernacles, to be observed at the end of the harvest and continue on for seven days. During this Feast of Tabernacles, the people dwelt in booths or arbors made up of the branches of palm trees and willows from the brook, to remind them of the palm trees of Elim, and the willows of Baboul. Elim was the second stop after the crossing of the Red Sea on dry ground. Elim had twelve wells and seventy date palm trees. Baboul, also known as Babylon not the one on the Tigris river but the one that was on the boundary between upper and lower Egypt. The feast of Tabernacles is the seventh of the feasts and the last. Seven is God's number of perfection. Six days God labored in the creation of the heavens and the earth. But on the seventh day he rested. Of the seven feasts God set in order, only four have been fulfilled. What I mean is, that in the Word of God there are types and anti types. In this particular instance each of the feasts relate to some special event that has taken place in the church since Christ came.   The first feast, the Passover feast, consisted of three individual festivities, the Passover, the unleavened bread, and the first fruits. Jesus Christ fulfilled these as our Passover lamb and also by being the first fruits of the resurrection from the dead. This feast happened about the time of the holiday known as Easter. His sacrifice provided a sin free life to pay for our sins. By paying the price of sin for us he provided the way that we might have everlasting life. Your sins, or the payment for your sins require of you the death of your soul. If it were otherwise, you and I would live forever. Sin, you see, is the willful disobedience of God. It matters not if it is REALIZED OR NOT. Sin consists of a multitude of things which boil down to the individual saying in his heart, "I will do what I want to. No one will tell me how to run my life." This attitude seems to be prevalent in this age we live in. Most never realize that they are in rebellion against God. There is no awareness of even the presence of God. Some aren't even aware of the hand of God in their lives. Some time in your life, God will, or has made him self known to you. It may have been in some hardship you have suffered through. Maybe it was in the death of a loved one. Or in some automobile wreck. God spoke to you, gave you comfort, and strength in this time of need. He also told you to draw near to him. Mat 11:29 "Take my yoke upon you, and learn of me, for I am meek and lowly in heart: and ye shall find rest unto your souls." It wasn't supposed to be just a one time touch of God, He wants you to draw near and learn of him. He has so much for you to do. Why tarry ye here gazing up into the heavens, looking for the God of glory? He's near to us all. He's not a God that can't be touched. You just need to reach out and touch him with your worship.

The first thanksgiving day in the United States was in 1621. The day was set aside by Gov William Bradford of the Plymouth Colony in gratitude for the first harvest in the New World. Thanksgiving day was set aside as a national holiday by Abraham Lincoln and was set for the fourth Thursday in November. It has become a time for feasting and fellowship. The memories of thanksgivings past are poignant and fresh in my memory. Grandma making her oyster dressing, the smells, the candy, the hustle and bustle in the kitchen as the preparations are finished up. The friends, the relatives, it's a creation of memories that last a lifetime. That the years cannot erase.

The scripture is inundated with references to offering up thanksgiving's

Psm 50:14 "Offer unto God thanksgiving, and pay thy vows unto the most High:" Psa 69:30 "I will praise the name of God with a song, and will magnify him with [thanksgiving]." Psa 95:2 "Let us come before his presence with [thanksgiving], and make a joyful noise unto him with psalms." Psa 107:22 "And let them sacrifice the sacrifices of [thanksgiving], and declare his works with rejoicing." Psa 116:17 "I will offer to thee the sacrifice of [thanksgiving], and will call upon the name of the LORD." Psa 147:7 "Sing unto the LORD with [thanksgiving], sing praise upon the harp unto our God:" Jonah 2:9 "But I will sacrifice unto thee with the voice of [thanksgiving], I will pay <that> that I have vowed. Salvation <is> of the LORD." 2 Cor 9:11 "Being enriched in every thing to all bountifulness, which causeth through us [thanksgiving] to God." Phil 4:6 "Be careful for nothing, but in every thing by prayer and supplication with [thanksgiving] let your requests be made known unto God." Col 2:6 "As ye have therefore received Christ Jesus the Lord, <so> walk ye in him:" Col 2:7 "Rooted and built up in him, and established in the faith, as ye have been taught, abounding therein with thanksgiving." Col 4:2 "Continue in prayer, and watch in the same with thanksgiving," Rev 7:12 "Saying, Amen: Blessing, and glory, and wisdom, and [thanksgiving], and honor, and power, and might, <be> unto our God for ever and ever. Amen." 2 Sam 22:50 "Therefore I will give [thanks] unto thee, O LORD, among the heathen, and I will sing praises unto thy name." 1 Chr 16:8 "Give [thanks] unto the LORD, call upon his name, make known his deeds among the people." And some seventy more references to thanksgiving in the scriptures. What is the mandate of the worshiper of God? To give thanks unto the Lord for all he has done. For salvation, for healing, for health, for forgiveness, for all that we have.

Colossians 1:12 "Giving thanks unto the Father, which hath made us meet to be partakers of the inheritance of the saints in light: who hath delivered us from the power of darkness, and hath translated us into the kingdom of his dear son: in whom we have redemption through his blood, even the forgiveness of sins: Who is the image of the invisible God, the first born of every creature: for by him were all things created, that are in heaven, and in the earth, visible and invisible, whether they be thrones, or dominions, or principalities, or powers: all things were created by him, and for him." The kingdom of this world is not the kingdom of God. This world, this system known as the world, is dominated by the prince of darkness. God didn't create this world to be under darkness but under the power of light. Not under the power of death but of life. Satan has set up his kingdom through man's flesh in the fall of a man called Adam. This creation, the first world, now in the hands of the adversary, is now known as the old creation. Nothing from this old creation can be transferred into God's new creation, the church, the body of Christ. Two rival realms now exist. No longer are we the children of darkness. He has delivered us and transferred us into the kingdom of God. Remember though, the things from the old can't enter into the new, God has to change us. John 3:6 says "that which is born of the flesh is flesh, and that which is born of the Spirit is spirit." and again in

1 Cor 15:50 "Now this I say, brethren, that flesh and blood cannot inherit kingdom of God, neither doth corruption inherit incorruption." And Matthew 9:16 "No man putteth a piece of new cloth unto and old garment, for that which is put in to fill it up taketh from the garment, and the rent is made worse. Neither do men put new wine into old bottles: else the bottles break, and the wine runneth out, and the bottles perish: but they put new wine into new bottles, and both are preserved. For us to inherit the Kingdom of God, God must make us a new creature in Christ by filling us with the Holy Ghost. That which is born of the flesh is flesh and will never be anything but flesh. That which is of the old creation can never pass into the new.

God wants you for himself, but not as you are, so he provided a way, a cross and a sacrifice on the cross, that we could die with him, and thus being dead we can rise to a newness of life a new creature in Christ, 2 Cor 5:17 "Therefore if any man be in Christ, he is a new creature: old things are passed away, behold, all things are become new." Now, with being a new creature in Christ, with a new nature and a new character, you can enter into the new kingdom and world, into the body of Christ.

The cross was the means that God used to bring an end to the old things by setting aside the old man, crucifying him on the cross with Christ. The resurrection is used to give all that is necessary for life in the new kingdom of Christ. Romans 6:4 "Therefore we are buried with him in baptism into death: that like as Christ was raised up from the dead by the glory of the Father, even so we also should walk in newness of life." The resurrection stands at the very beginning of the new creation. The cross ends life, and the resurrection begins life.

There now stands before you two worlds, the old and the new. In the old the adversary had absolute dominion. In the old creation you may have been a good man, but still the sentence of death hung over your head. It is the dividing barrier of the cross, , that God has made to be the way of escape from the old creation. God gathered up all of the old creation, the first man Adam, and hung it on the cross in the flesh of Jesus Christ. All that was of the old Adam was done away with. God then made a proclamation, "Through the cross, I have set aside all that is not of me, you who are of the old creation are included in that, you too have been crucified with Christ, all you must do is accept the sacrifice, repent and be baptized in the name of Jesus Christ for the remission of your sins and you shall receive the baptism of the Holy Ghost." Romans 6:3-4 "Know ye not, that so many of us as were baptized into Jesus Christ were baptized into his death? Therefore we are buried with him in baptism into death: that like as Christ was raised up from the dead by the glory of the Father, even so we also should walk in newness of life." Gal 6:14 "But God forbid that I should glory, save in the cross of our Lord Jesus Christ, by whom the world is crucified unto me, and I unto the world." No longer affected by the affection for the things of the world. You are delivered from this present evil world through death on the cross and burial by baptism. .

  1 Peter 3:21 " the like figure whereunto even baptism did also now save us (not the putting away of the filth of the flesh, but the answer of a good conscience toward God,) by the resurrection of Jesus Christ:" The answer of a good conscience toward God. there would be no need for an answer if God had said nothing, but he has spoken by way of the cross. By the cross, he told the world of the judgment of the old creation and of the old kingdom. The cross was not just an individual cross of Christ's but it is all inclusive, a Cross that includes us all. We are crucified with him, Crucified with Jesus Christ, the last man Adam,In his crucifixion, was wiped out all that was created by the first man Adam. What do you mean by this statement bro Johnson? Look to 1 Corinthians 15:20-22 "But now is Christ risen from the dead, and become the first fruits of them that slept. For since by man came death, by man came also the resurrection of the dead. For as in Adam all die, even so in Christ shall all be made alive." And Romans 5:12 "Wherefore as by one man sin entered into the world, and death by sin, and so death passed upon all men, for all have sinned:" And Romans 5:19 "For as by one man's disobedience many were made sinners, so by the obedience of one shall many be righteous." And 1 Corinthians 15:45-47 "And so it is written, The first man Adam was made a living soul, the last Adam was made a quickening spirit. Howbeit that was not first which is spiritual, but that which is natural, and afterward that which is spiritual. The first man is of the earth, earthly: the second man is the Lord from heaven." Made a quickening spirit. Or, made a life giving spirit. Death came by the first Adam and life came by the second Adam, Christ. In the first Adam came the end of spiritual kingdom God gave Adam. Then Adam sinned and gave this kingdom to Satan. But in Christ, the second Adam, a new kingdom is began. What then is the answer of a good conscience toward God? It's an answer to God's judgment on the old creation, The answer. I want to be baptized. Why? Because I need to be buried, Romans 6:4 "therefore we are buried with him in baptism into death: that like as Christ was raised up from the dead by the glory of the Father, even so we also should walk in newness of life." Baptism is connected with both

death and resurrection, but, it is neither death nor resurrection: it's the burial. Who are those that qualify for burial? The dead in Christ. So by asking for baptism I declare myself dead and fit only for burial. Unless you realize that your dead in Christ, and repented of your sins you'r batism is useless. You don't bury those that are not dead to the old world and it's sins. Baptism, you see, is not dying it's a burial. We go down into the water realizing that in Gods' sight, we are already dead. The question is simple, Christ has died, are you included there? The answer is just as simple, "Lord, I believe that Christ died for my sins and I want to be partaker in this death, Please forgive me of the sins that I have committed, I say yes to the death, burial and resurrection. There's an old world and a new, and between them there is a tomb. God has already crucified me with Christ, but I must buried. It says that I am no longer from the old world and I'm in the new kingdom of Christ. Baptism is no small thing. It means a definite break with the old way of life. Romans 6:2 "we who died to sin, how shall we any longer live therein?" If you are to continue in the old world, why be baptized? God forbid, How shall we that are dead to sin, live any longer therein? Baptism is a deep union between the believer and Christ. His death becomes ours. Our death and his is so closely identified that it is impossible to separate the two. God wrought this union. Baptism is our admission that the death of Christ, two thousand years ago, was all inclusive and power full enough to bring an end to everything in us that was not Christ like. More than that; it's the burial of the old man of sin.

I am baptized into his death, and resurrected with him. Romans 6:5 "For if we have been planted together in the likeness of his death, we shall be also in the likeness of his resurrection." We entered into his death but you see, the resurrection enters into us. 1Co 15:45-50 "And so it is written, The first man Adam was made a living soul; the last Adam *was made* a quickening spirit.

Howbeit that *was* not first which is spiritual, but that which is natural; and afterward that which is spiritual.

The first man *is* of the earth, earthy: the second man *is* the Lord from heaven.

As *is* the earthy, such *are* they also that are earthy: and as *is* the heavenly, such *are* they also that are heavenly.

And as we have borne the image of the earthy, we shall also bear the image of the heavenly.

Now this I say, brethren, that flesh and blood cannot inherit the kingdom of God; neither doth corruption inherit incorruption. "

It's the new heart of Ezekiel 11:19 "And I will give them one heart, and I will put a new spirit within you; and I will take the stony heart out of their flesh, and will give them an heart of flesh: "

God has cut off the old creation by the cross in order to bring in a new creation in Christ by the resurrection. The door to the old kingdom has been shut. We are translated into the kingdom of righteousness by Jesus Christ through the infilling of the Holy Ghost. My baptism was done as a burial and a washing away of sins that I had committed against God and man. Baptism is my testimony that I'm dead to the old world and risen up in newness of life through the quickening Spirit of the Holy Ghost. So, once we have been buried and resurrected we must present ourselves to Christ. Romans 6:12 "Let not sin therefore reign in your mortal body, that ye should obey the lusts thereof. Neither present ye your members as instruments of unrighteousness unto sin: but present yourselves unto God, as those that are alive from the dead and your members as instruments of righteousness unto God." and Romans 12:1 I beseech You therefore, brethren, by the mercies of God, that ye present your bodies a living sacrifice, holy, acceptable unto God, which is your reasonable service." This is not the consecration of the old man with his instincts and resources, the natural wisdom, strength and gifts, but the new man, as one alive from the dead. It is the outcome of knowing the old man was crucified with Christ.

I am no longer my own but Christ's. Real Christian life begins with knowing this, Because Christ is risen, we are alive unto God and not unto ourselves. We are the Lord's. We are his possession, bought with a price, redeemed by his blood. No longer our own. Not that we were actually our own. We were sin slaves to the devil, part of the old world, part of sin and bound to a dead man. If then we are in fact another's possession how can we dare squander an hour of our time, a penny of our money or any of our mental or physical strength? Holiness unto the Lord was the cry of the early Jews. Present your members as servants of righteousness unto sanctification. Give yourself wholly, completely to Christ: this is holiness. Separation unto the Lord. Sanctified unto God. Anointed with the Holy oil of the Holy Ghost. Set apart for God. You are altogether and completely his. This is a definite action just as reckoning or baptism. There has to be a day in your life when you give up ownership and put yourself in the hands of God. From that day forward, you belong to him. How are we to be consecrated? Not to a Christian work but to the will of God, to be and do what ever he wants us to do. If you are a Christian then God has a life all charted out for you, It may be anything from washing windows to who knows what. What ever he has for you to do you can be sure it will follow along with the written word. Our duty is to be consecrated to the will of God and do whatever God desires us to do. Paul said I have finished the course, Nothing would be more disheartening then to stand before God having sailed your own course when God had so much planed for you. Can you say as in

Romans 12:2 "And be not conformed to this world: but be ye transformed by the renewing of your mind, that ye may prove what is that good, and acceptable, and perfect, will of God." Do you want the will of God for your life? Does all your desires center around him? Can you truly say that the will of God is Good and acceptable and perfect to you? Your strong will has to go to the cross and you must give yourself wholly totally to the Lord. There's no way that God can be Lord of your life if he's not Lord of all of your life. Without reservation, not holding back even one little corner of our lives, not one little kingdom, we must present ourselves unto God. Are you willing? why resist God, it's much wiser to submit to him. Do you find that there are many things you dare not look into, pray about, or even think about because your in conflict with what God wants for your life? You can evade the issue but to do so will take you out of the will of God for your life. God is a perfect gentleman and won't force you to do anything your will decides you don't want to do. It's a good feeling to know that we are his. In this state there's a continual awareness of his presence. When ownership is established, then you'll do nothing in your own interest, for you are his totally and fully. Lev 22:29 "And when ye will offer a sacrifice of [thanksgiving] unto the LORD, offer <it> at your own will." Thanksgiving is worship and God is surly worthy of this. Turkeys, and hams, yams, and pies, friends and relatives all gather together for a time of feasting and fellowship. Let's remember just who started this thing called Thanksgiving. We have much to be thankful for even in light of layoffs and lock-outs. Life does not consist in the abundance of possessions unless your life is based upon material objects. Change your life's allegiance over to the rock of Ages and the storms of life won't have any lasting affect upon you.

THE LORD WATCH BETWEEN THEE AND ME WHILE WE'RE APART
THANK YOU FOR LISTENING TO RANDY JOHNSON OF THE WE PREACH JESUS MINISTRIES

RESOLUTIONS   12/29/1991

PSM 45:1 MY HEART IS INDITING A GOOD MATTER:
I SPEAK THE THINGS WHICH I HAVE MADE TOUCHING THE KING:
MY TONGUE IS THE PEN OF A READY WRITER

This is a time of the year when our minds turn to new beginnings. There is no better time to start afresh then at the first of the year. Now is the time for you to lay aside all the differences you've had with others and start a new. Wash it clean, start with a new slate, a clean record. This is the time to take the things that have troubled us throughout the year, write them on a slip of paper and burn these troubling thoughts in a bucket of fire. It works folks. This year, there is to be a series on the Body, Soul and Spirit that you'll find interesting and helpful in your walk with God. When one understands his spiritual make up it's easier to exercise control over the body. There is a series on prayer and worship that is needful to be taught. When I say series, I mean it will take more then one lesson to teach you about worship, and more then one for prayer, how many, I don't know, just that the subject is a large one and it will take some time to bring it to you. Forgiveness is a pertinent subject that will be covered. God is great and greatly to be praised. We sure appreciate being able to bring this broadcast to you, feeling that it indeed fills a void in your lives. God has been good in making it possible to bring this broadcast to you. It would be helpful if you would write us a note stating how, if indeed it has, this last 18 or so months helped you. This last year has seen the rise and fall of many. We've seen a war come and go. The breaking up of the republic of Russia and we are one year closer to the second coming of Jesus. How many days or years are left is unknown to the mind of man. God knows, and he alone knows when the last man woman or child will come to him for salvation and fulfillment. If we could just open our spiritual eyes and see into the heavens, I'm sure we would see a great host of heaven watching expectantly for the last trump when the Lord himself shall split he eastern sky and the dead in Christ shall rise out of the graves, then we which are alive and remain shall be caught up to meet them in the air, so shall we ever be with him.

Trouble on every hand. Fear of the things that are to come. Will Cat or won't they? What will Komatsu Dresser do? Will America become just a nation of service companies? Have we lost our manufacturing base? Is the trade agreement with Mexico going to do the same thing to us that our trade agreement with Canada did to them with the closings of Cat, Komatsu Dresser, and a multitude of others? Were will the next dollar come from? How are we going to make it through this generation? Will there even be a life for my children to live? Oh God, where have all the lilies gone? Pressure on every side. Stress, stress ,stress. Book shelves abound with books such as," HOW TO TURN YOUR STRESS INTO STRENGTH", HOW TO DEAL WITH STRESS" HOW TO QUIT WORRYING AND START LIVING." Yet on every side, the road of life is littered with the ones who couldn't cope with this rapidly changing world. Governments falling, companies closing doors. Marriages failing. Death, hell and destruction on every hand. Worry trouble fear and doubt nag at our every waking moment, Where is there peace and safety in this rapidly changing world? Life's stability is like standing on the beach and having the waves wash the sand out from under his feet. Like standing in mud or shifting sand.

In the last month, three of my acquaintances have underwent heart related difficulties. One had two heart attacks within the space of three hours. Another had a one. A great deal of blockage was found in the arteries feeding the heart. Another had terrific chest pains and was admitted for tests. What's going on? Just a fulfillment of scripture. Judgments of God? No, just misplaced trust concerning where your affections are directed. A man trusting in the arm of flesh is like a man accepting wise sayings from a fool. Scripture tells us Psa 146:3 "Put not your trust in princes, <nor> in the son of man, in whom <there is> no help." His breath goeth forth, he returneth to his earth, in that very day his thoughts perish." Psa 20:7 "Some <trust> in chariots, and some in horses: but we will remember the name of the LORD our God." Trust placed in anything or anyone except the Lord God Almighty is a misplaced trust.

Jesus Christ gave us some signs that we may know what time it is in the calendar of God. What time is it? "When shall the coming of the son of man be?" The disciples asked of Jesus in the book of Luke 21:6-37 "Jesus answered saying that the temple shall be torn down, not one stone left upon another." This happened in 70 AD when the Roman General Titus took Jerusalem. The disciples asked: "but when shall these things be? and what sign <will there be> when these things shall come to pass? {8} And he said, Take heed that ye be not deceived: for many shall come in my name, saying, I am <Christ>, and the time draweth near: go ye not therefore after them. {9} But when ye shall hear of wars and commotions, be not terrified: for these things must first come to pass, but the end <is> not by and by. {10} Then said he unto them, Nation shall rise against nation, and kingdom against kingdom: {11} And great earthquakes shall be in divers places, and famines, and pestilences, and fearful sights and great signs shall there be from heaven. {12} But before all these, they shall lay their hands on you, and persecute <you>, delivering <you> up to the synagogues, and into prisons, being brought before kings and rulers for my name's sake. {13} And it shall turn to you for a testimony. {14} Settle <it> therefore in your hearts, not to meditate before what ye shall answer: {15} For I will give you a mouth and wisdom, which all your adversaries shall not be able to gainsay nor resist. {16} And ye shall be betrayed both by parents, and brethren, and kinfolks, and friends, and <some> of you shall they cause to be put to death. {17} And ye shall be hated of all <men> for my name's sake. {18} But there shall not an hair of your head perish. {19} In your patience possess ye your souls. {20} And when ye shall see Jerusalem compassed with armies, then know that the desolation thereof is nigh. {21} Then let them which are in Judea flee to the mountains, and let them which are in the midst of it depart out, and let not them that are in the countries enter thereunto. {22} For these be the days of vengeance, that all things which are written may be fulfilled. {23} But woe unto them that are with child, and to them that give suck, in those days! for there shall be great distress in the land, and wrath upon this people. {24} And they shall fall by the edge of the sword, and shall be led away captive into all nations: and Jerusalem shall be trodden down of the Gentiles, until the times of the Gentiles be fulfilled. Israel had been trodden down of the gentile nations, that is it was under the rule of others, until it rose from the ashes in 1947 and again became a sovereign nation. Recognition was given to her by the United Nations and she was no longer was considered to be trodden down by the gentiles. {25} And there shall be signs in the sun, and in the moon, and in the stars, and upon the earth distress of nations, with perplexity, the sea and the waves roaring, {26} Men's hearts failing them for fear, and for looking after those things which are coming on the earth: for the powers of heaven shall be shaken. {27} And then shall they see the Son of man coming in a cloud with power and great glory. {28} And when these things begin to come to pass, then look up, and lift up your heads, for your redemption draweth nigh."

Verse 26 has the key to this great influx of heart attacks, "Men's hearts failing them for fear, and for looking after those things which are coming on the earth." Why? Because of fear of what tomorrow will bring and looking after the things that are already come. Jesus' answer to this dilemma is found in, Mat 6:19-34 "Lay not up for yourselves treasures upon earth, where moth and rust doth corrupt, and where thieves break through and steal: {20} But lay up for yourselves treasures in heaven, where neither moth nor rust doth corrupt, and where thieves do not break through nor steal: {21} For where your treasure is, there will your heart be also. {22} The light of the body is the eye: if therefore thine eye be single, thy whole body shall be full of light. {23} But if thine eye be evil, thy whole body shall be full of darkness. If therefore the light that is in thee be darkness, how great <is> that darkness! {24} No man can serve two masters: for either he will hate the one, and love the other, or else he will hold to the one, and despise the other. Ye cannot serve God and mammon. {25} Therefore I say unto you, Take no thought for your life, what ye shall eat, or what ye shall drink, nor yet for your body, what ye shall put on. Is not the life more than meat, and the body than raiment? {26} Behold the fowls of the air: for they sow not, neither do they reap, nor gather into barns, yet your heavenly Father feedeth them. Are ye not much better than they? {27} Which of you by taking thought can add one cubit unto his stature? {28} And why take ye thought for raiment? Consider the lilies of the field, how they grow, they toil not, neither do they spin: {29} And yet I say unto you, That even Solomon in all his glory was not arrayed like one of these. {30} Wherefore , if God so clothe the grass of the field, which to day is, and to morrow is cast into the oven, <shall he> not much more <clothe> you, O ye of little faith? {31} Therefore take no thought, saying, What shall we eat? or, What shall we drink? or, Wherewithal shall we be clothed? {32} (For after all these things do the Gentiles seek:) for your heavenly Father knoweth that ye have need of all these things. {33} But seek ye first the kingdom of God, and his righteousness, and all these things shall be added unto you. {34} Take therefore no thought for the morrow: for the morrow shall take thought for the things of itself. Sufficient unto the day <is> the evil thereof." "Seek ye first the kingdom of God." It's realizing that God is and is a rewarder of them that diligently seek him. It's realizing that you are a child of God and He will take care of you. It knowing that God will put nothing on you that He hasn't already made a way for you to bear it, or be victorious in. 2 Cor 3:4-6 "And such trust have we through Christ to God-ward: Not that we are sufficient of ourselves to think any thing as of ourselves, but our sufficiency <is> of God, Who also hath made us able ministers of the new testament, not of the letter, but of the spirit: for the letter killeth, but the spirit giveth life." We are not to bear our burdens alone. Jesus told us Mat 11:28-30 "Come unto me, all <ye> that labor and are heavy laden, and I will give you rest. Take my yoke upon you, and learn of me, for I am meek and lowly in heart: and ye shall find rest unto your souls. For my yoke <is> easy, and my burden is light."

We are not our own, we have been bought with a price. If indeed we are Christ's, then we are in his hands. Worry will accomplish nothing at all. Which of you by taking thought can add one cubit to your stature? Why cross a bridge that has never been built? Fight a battle that has never been set in array? So much of our lives has been spent in fruitlessly worrying and planning for what may come to pass. Take no thought for tomorrow or the trouble that it will bring , we have enough trouble today to fill our quota, why take on tomorrow's? the secret of inner peace is to know who holds the future. Not what the future holds. One of the beauties of heaven will be no more time. In short, you won't be worrying about yesterday and tomorrow for there won't be any such thing. Yesterday and tomorrow are finite terms that do not apply to eternity. Realizing that God has our future in his hands, that he does have a divine plan for our lives, and that he that began a work in your life is able to finish that work.

I get caught up in the worry cycle from time to time. It's hard to break the worry cycle because the idea that you have to worry about the future is deeply ingrained within this humanistic flesh. Years of training find it difficult to overcome worry. Suddenly, the realization that right now I can't do anything at all about the problem, calms the tight neck and wrinkled brow. I then put the entire thing in the hands of the Master of the storm, and he says Peace be still. The waves of doubt and discouragement are immediately beaten down by the glorious rain of his love. I am in his hands. It's Peter walking on the water.

Prayer is the key to calmness in the midst of the storm. It's a close relationship with Jesus that will keep you in the hard places of life. It's not a once in a life time thing. It's the everyday, continuous prayer life that will bring you through. It's not that your effective prayer will suffice, but it is that your faith in the operation of God wrought by your continual prayer and closeness with the savior that will accomplish the feat. A consistent communication with Jesus, not just in the cool of the day, or the heat of the battle, but the everyday communion with the savior. A set time coupled with a continual communication through out the day will bring you into a closeness with Jesus that even the den of lions won't sway. Careful for nothing. Don't have a care in the world for the things of the world or what they can do to you. Be careful for nothing, but in all things by prayer and fasting. Or don't take the burden of the cares of this life upon yourself, your heavenly Father knows what your needs are. The cares of this life will choke out all the seeds of righteousness and faith that God has planted in the fertile soil of your life. Jesus said it this way: Mat 13:18-23 "Hear ye therefore the parable of the sower. {19} When any one heareth the word of the kingdom, and understandeth <it> not, then cometh the wicked <one>, and catcheth away that which was sown in his heart. This is he which received seed by the way side. {20} But he that received the seed into stony places, the same is he that heareth the word, and anon with joy receiveth it, {21} Yet hath he not root in himself, but dureth for a while: for when tribulation or persecution ariseth because of the word, by and by he is offended. {22} He also that received seed among the thorns is he that heareth the word, and the care of this world, and the deceitfulness of riches, choke the word, and he becometh unfruitful. {23} But he that received seed into the good ground is he that heareth the word, and understandeth <it>, which also beareth fruit, and bringeth forth, some an hundredfold, some sixty, some thirty."

The Word of God is full of men and women that were not great in themselves but that had faith in the operation of God. Hebrews the eleventh chapter is sited as being the faith chapter of the Bible. In it is an impressive list of people that put total trust in God. These are those who were without coronary difficulties though if in themselves, had plenty to be concerned about. Remember that faith is putting your trust in God and his ability to perform all that he said he would perform. Heb 11:1-22 "Now faith is the substance of things hoped for, the evidence of things not seen. {2} For by it the elders obtained a good report. {3} Through faith we understand that the worlds were framed by the word of God, so that things which are seen were not made of things which do appear. {4} By faith Abel offered unto God a more excellent sacrifice than Cain, by which he obtained witness that he was righteous, God testifying of his gifts: and by it he being dead yet speaketh. {5} By faith Enoch was translated that he should not see death, and was not found, because God had translated him: for before his translation he had this testimony, that he pleased God. {6} But without faith <it is> impossible to please <him>: for he that cometh to God must believe that he is, and <that> he is a rewarder of them that diligently seek him. {7} By faith Noah, being warned of God of things not seen as yet, moved with fear, prepared an ark to the saving of his house, by the which he condemned the world, and became heir of the righteousness which is by faith. {8} By faith Abraham, when he was called to go out into a place which he should after receive for an inheritance, obeyed, and he went out, not knowing whither he went. {9} By faith he sojourned in the land of promise, as <in> a strange country, dwelling in tabernacles with Isaac and Jacob, the heirs with him of the same promise: {10} For he looked for a city which hath foundations, whose builder and maker <is> God. {11} Through faith also Sara herself received strength to conceive seed, and was delivered of a child when she was past age, because she judged him faithful who had promised. {12} Therefore sprang there even of one, and him as good as dead, <so many> as the stars of the sky in multitude, and as the sand which is by the sea shore innumerable. {13} These all died in faith, not having received the promises, but having seen them afar off, and were persuaded of <them>, and embraced <them>, and confessed that they were strangers and pilgrims on the earth. {14} For they that say such things declare plainly that they seek a country. {15} And truly, if they had been mindful of that <country> from whence they came out, they might have had opportunity to have returned. {16} But now they desire a better <country>, that is, an heavenly: wherefore God is not ashamed to be called their God: for he hath prepared for them a city. {17} By faith Abraham, when he was tried, offered up Isaac: and he that had received the promises offered up his only begotten <son>. {18} Of whom it was said, That in Isaac shall thy seed be called: {19} Accounting that God <was> able to raise <him> up, even from the dead, from whence also he received him in a figure. {20} By faith Isaac blessed Jacob and Esau concerning things to come. {21} By faith Jacob, when he was a dying, blessed both the sons of Joseph, and worshipped, <leaning> upon the top of his staff. {22} By faith Joseph, when he died, made mention of the departing of the children of Israel, and gave commandment concerning his bones. {34} By faith Moses, when he was born, was hid three months of his parents, because they saw <he was> a proper child, and they were not afraid of the king's commandment. {24} By faith Moses, when he was come to years, refused to be called the son of Pharaoh's daughter, {25} Choosing rather to suffer affliction with the people of God, than to enjoy the pleasures of sin for a season, {26} Esteeming the reproach of Christ greater riches than the treasures in Egypt: for he had respect unto the recompense of the reward. {27} By faith he forsook Egypt, not fearing the wrath of the king: for he endured, as seeing him who is invisible. {28} Through faith he kept the Passover, and the sprinkling of blood, lest he that destroyed the firstborn should touch them. {29} By faith they passed through the Red sea as by dry <land>: which the Egyptians assaying to do were drowned. {30} By faith the walls of Jericho fell down, after they were compassed about seven days. {31} By faith the harlot Rahab perished not with them that believed not, when she had received the spies with peace. {32} And what shall I more say? for the time would fail me to tell of Gedeon, and <of> Barak, and <of> Samson, and <of> Jephthae, <of> David also, and Samuel, and <of> the prophets: {33} Who through faith subdued kingdoms, wrought righteousness, obtained promises, stopped the mouths of lions, {34} Quenched the violence of fire, escaped the edge of the sword, out of weakness were made strong, waxed valiant in fight, turned to flight the armies of the aliens. {35} Women received their dead raised to life again: and others were tortured, not accepting deliverance, that they might obtain a better resurrection: {36} And others had trial of <cruel> mockings and scourgings, yea, moreover of bonds and imprisonment: {37} They were stoned, they were sawn asunder, were tempted, were slain with the sword: they wandered about in sheepskins and goatskins, being destitute, afflicted, tormented, {38} (Of whom the world was not worthy:) they wandered in deserts, and <in> mountains, and <in> dens and caves of the earth. {39} And these all, having obtained a good report through faith, received not the promise: {40} God having provided some better thing for us, that they without us should not be made perfect. "

    The tendency is for us to look upon these men and women as great people who excelled in their own strength. This is natural and we would raise monuments to their great achievements if it weren't for the fact that they simply weren't anxious about what God had told them. They had faith in the operation of God and simply knew that God would accomplish all that he said he would. In this, this simple statement, that God is, and he is able to finish the work that he began in your life, rests the secret of inner peace and freedom from a coronary. Do Christians have heart attacks? The answer to that is in the fact that we're not perfected yet. God's still working on us. Yes, Christians do have heart attacks, it's not easy to throw off years of training.

SHAKESPEAR AS YOU LIKE IT   09/06/1992

PSM 45:1 MY HEART IS INDITING A GOOD MATTER:
I SPEAK THE THINGS WHICH I HAVE MADE TOUCHING THE KING:
MY TONGUE IS THE PEN OF A READY WRITER

I have this close friend of mine that after growing up in the truth decided he no longer wanted to dwell therein. Namely, he backslid. He preferred the things of this world rather than the things of God. You ask how could one do such a thing? Perhaps out of discouragement or just a lack of understanding, nevertheless, he is gone from the Church. he's been to many countries, seen many things, met thousands of people yet he hasn't, at least he don't seem to, shown one sign of coming back to the Father's house. Just recently, he fell in love with this young lady that is of a different faith, one that isn't even Christian. that's no problem until the news came that he was receiving instruction in this pagan belief. Babylonian in origin. Yet predominate throughout the land. I was, I am crushed. He knows better. He understands how his friends feel about this total crashing to the other side of the battle. He's no better off then he was when he was a drunken souse yet there seems to be some sort of betrayal involved in this maneuver. The question comes crashing into my mind, Just what is it you want out of Christianity. Moreover what is it you want out of the umpteen thousand different faiths that crowd our land of the free and the home of the brave? Drive down any street in any city and you'll find one or more churches. All seem to bear the name of their founder or some variation of the such like. It's a variation of Shakespeare as you like it. How do you want to live for Christ? On a Sunday? On a Saturday? How about when ever you feel you need him? There's ham, Spam, chicken, lamb, hog, frog, turkey, dog, hair, bear, or buffalo rare. You name it it's available for your delight, consumption or hearing. On one side of the battle line there stands darkness, clothed in versions of respectfulness. Comes the reply of the uneducated in the ways of truth, "Some of the best people I know are witches." On the other side, carrying the banner of pure fanaticism, as the world would say, stands the true church today, still preaching the faith that once was delivered to the saints. What was it Jude said in the book by his name? Jude 1:3 "Beloved, when I gave all diligence to write unto you of the common salvation, it was needful for me to write unto you, and exhort <you> that ye should earnestly [contend for the faith] which was once delivered unto the saints For there are certain men crept in unawares, who were before of old ordained to this condemnation, ungodly men, turning the grace of our God into lasciviousness,{wanton lewd behavior} and denying the only Lord God, and our Lord Jesus Christ."

What was said of the early believers?   Acts 2:42 "And they continued steadfastly in the apostles' doctrine and fellowship, and in breaking of bread, and in prayers."

Well this young man said to me, "Does that preacher that baptized me still have the records?" "I need a copy of my baptism for the man of the cloth. He needs to know if I was ever baptized."

Why do you want to join this organization? So that I can marry this woman. What is it that you want out of a church? What is it that you want out of Christianity? Are you looking for a crutch? A wheelchair that you can be pushed around in? Are you looking for a cushy job, preacher? Maybe you can be a radio preacher and make lots of money, even get on TV. Go national and really give people the opportunity to be blessed in their giving. Your goals are distorted. Your of the earth earthly. You'll never get anything in the kingdom of God because you wish to fulfill the desires of your flesh. You don't even know what Christianity is all about. Christianity is keeping this broadcast alive in spite of the hardship it brings upon this flesh. But that's all right because God takes care of the problems. Christianity is fighting for truth in the face of overwhelming odds. Christianity is being nailed to a cross with a crown of thorns and a back that is so torn and bleeding that the ribs show through. Christianity is standing fast in the face of adversity. Christianity is being true to Christ. Read the whole book of James. What is it you want out of Christianity? There was a visitor that came to this certain church congregation. He went to the pastor and asked if it would be all right if he transferred to this location. The pastor, wise in years, perceiving this young man's intentions, he ask the young man if he was married. No, the young man replied. The pastor of this little flock let the young man know that his transfer wasn't to find a wife among these young ladies. What is you desire? What is the intention of your heart? Why did you go to church today? What is the real reason for your attendance? Is it to appease a troubled conscience? Is it to slake the guilt you feel in your heart? Does it make you feel righteous? Do you really know who Christ is and why he died? I used to think it would be a good idea if they had ash trays of the back of the pews, right near that little bracket that holds the song books and the communal wine. That was before I found out, that was before I found true Christianity. It's really strange the concepts that man can generate in the corners of his mind. Prov 14:12 "[There is a way] which seemeth right unto a man, but the end thereof <are> the ways of death." Jude 1:3 "Beloved, when I gave all diligence to write unto you of the common salvation, it was needful for me to write unto you, and exhort <you> that ye should earnestly [contend for the faith] which was once delivered unto the saints." Acts 2:42 "And they continued steadfastly in the apostles' doctrine and fellowship, and in breaking of bread, and in prayers." There is a way which seemeth right but friend of mine it is not the way of life. Jesus Christ himself said;

Mat 7:14 " strait <is> the gate, and [narrow <is> the way], which leadeth unto life, and few there be that find it." I'm here now telling you about the path that leads unto salvation. There is no need of you finding it. You need only listen, accept, repent of your sins, be baptized in the name of Jesus Christ for the remission of your sins and receive the Holy Ghost. What do you want out of the church? What is the desire of your heart? What do you expect from Christianity? What ideas do you have in your heart? Is it simply an arrangement of convenience? If that is the case then any congregation that lines the streets of any city will fulfill this requirement. Do you want companionship or fellowship? Are you looking for a place where nice people come together and play bingo? Or are you looking for the real things in life? Are you looking for salvation, a place to worship God in spirit and truth just like the word of God said it would be? A place where truth takes precedence over protocol. Where truth overrides the rules of any international organization. Where salvation is the main topic and how to live for God daily is taught each time you come together to worship the creator of the universe. Look no farther. Attend not another church. Don't wait another Sunday or Wednesday. The Pentecostals of Pontiac have the truth, The First United Pentecostals of Peoria have the truth and they're not hiding it.

I remember when this man, this Judas, received the baptism of the Holy Ghost. I have a picture of the great event. There he stood, tears of joy streaming down his face, eyes closed, hands uplifted, with a Holy glow on his face. Pure joy. True fellowship with the most high God. He's backslid now. he let his love affair with God die. He really didn't know how to keep the fire burning inside. Really it's quite simple to keep a close fellowship with God. You do just like you keep a friendship or a love affair with your spouse alive. You communicate with them. God wants your fellowship. God wants your friendship. He wrapped himself in flesh and bones. He walked the road of death for you. His sin free blood was shed for you. While he hung there, while the agony of death haunted every second, there stood about those that run to see blood shed, jeering, Mat 4:6 "And saith unto him, [If thou be] the Son of God, cast thyself down:" He who hung on the cross, this same Jesus who had said in the garden, Mat 26:53 "Thinkest thou that I cannot now pray to my Father, and he shall presently give me more than twelve legions of angels?" 72000 angels that would fight for him against the guards and priests. This same man hung there nailed to the cross, but the nails, you see, didn't hold him there. It wasn't death that kept him there. It wasn't that he was powerless to come down from the cross. It was the tremendous love he has for you and me that held him there. For with out the shedding of blood there is no remission of sin. Hebrews tells us that: Heb 10:4 "it is not possible that the blood of bulls and of goats should take away sins." Are you worried about your sins? You should be. But there is a more perfect sacrifice, Jesus Christ the righteous one. He who died and rose again. This was done for your purification that he should have fellowship with you.

What is it that you want out of the church? What is it that you seek after? Why do you attend at the congregation you do? Is it to worship in Spirit and truth? Can you stand truth? What will truth do to your life style? Truth can be a bitter pill to swallow. But friend what is the use of wasting time on a lie? A lie won't get you to heaven. It's an association of convenience. It's conviviality in the icon of Christianity.

"Hey," said this man," do you remember when I was baptized?" How could I forget? It was In Mobridge, South Dakota in the summer of 76. We were there working with the Indians trying to establish some ray of hope in their lives. We had a small church going in Jack Skibba's living room in the middle of town. The baptismal tank, which was a new stock watering tank, was set up in the dinning room with the pulpit right in front of it. The couch and chairs were pushed back against the walls to make room for the wooden folding chairs. Near 15 people, 8 of which were Indians, sat in that little service on that summer Sunday evening. A young Sioux Indian by the name of Stanley Bird desired to be baptized in the name of Jesus Christ for the remission of his sins. We baptized Stanley and after a period of worship asked if there were anyone else that would like to be baptized. This one who has forgotten what it was like to be born to truth, had inquired about baptism before. Remembering this was so, I asked him if he would like to be baptized tonight. We then put him under the water in the name of Jesus Christ just as the Apostles had done in the beginning of the church some two thousand years ago. Now this same one asks if I remember. How could I ever forget? "I need a letter to the priest explaining when and where I was baptized." Said this voice from the past. "Would you write it?" I struggled within my self. It was a battle for self-control. What should I do? I'm not going to write him a letter to make it easy for him to join this, this religion. Then it dawned upon me. My letter would do absolutely no good, for you see, he wasn't baptized just repeating the formula of Matthew 28:19, he was baptized in obedience of, in the name, in the name, in the name of the Father, in the name of the son, in the name of the Holy Ghost which is Jesus Christ.   Now the formula of Rome is, "I now baptize you in the name of the Father, and of the Son, and of the Holy Ghost." Col 2:8   "Beware lest any man spoil you through philosophy and vain deceit, after the tradition of men, after the rudiments of the world, and not after Christ." Tradition is what crucified Jesus Christ. Tradition is what stands in the way of so many thousands coming to Christ. Tradition blocks the path of light, stands in the way and resists all attempts of lost souls finding light. Mat 23:13   "But woe unto you, scribes and Pharisees, hypocrites! for ye shut up the kingdom of heaven against men: for ye neither go in <yourselves>, neither suffer ye them that are entering to go in."   Memory recalls a dream related to me by a preacher, and he spoke as this, "God had shown to me truth, but not wanting to lose my status in the church I was in, really not wanting to buck the tradition surrounding the style of worship I was a licensed evangelist in, I resisted this precious truth for several years. Then one night while in a deep tired sleep, the Lord came to me with a dream. In this dream I saw a man being in torment, pushing his way through a vast lake of fire up to his waist. I could tell he was casting forth all sorts of vile oaths, cussing if you please. I couldn't hear what he was saying, but I just knew he was doing this. He would push through for a while, he would stop, then reach down into this vast lake of shimmering fire, pull up this or that man, curse at him vehemently, then throw him back to his torment and walk on pushing through the fire. Three or four times this agitated man performed this same ritual. "Lord, I asked, What in the world is this man doing?" The answer came ringing back as chill as a late fall morning, "He's looking for the preacher that lied to him." I sat bolt upright, wide-awake, to the sobering revelation that I had condemned thousands to hell with my half truth. I fell on my face before God and wept, repenting and crying that I would have a chance to undo the harm that I had done. Never again would I resist truth. Never again would I preach the social gospel to the damnation of souls. God had given to me truth and I esteemed it lightly."

What is it that you want out of the church? What is it that you want out of Christianity? Josh 24:15 "And if it seem evil unto you to serve the LORD, choose you this day whom ye will serve, whether the gods which your fathers served that <were> on the other side of the flood, or the gods of the Amorites, in whose land ye dwell: but as for me and my house, we will serve the LORD." Hosea 4:6 "My people are destroyed for lack of knowledge: because thou hast rejected knowledge, I will also reject thee, that thou shalt be no priest to me: seeing thou hast forgotten the law of thy God, I will also forget thy children." Read that "My people are destroyed for a lack of truth: because thou hast rejected truth, I will also reject you, that you shall be no priest to me: seeing you have forgotten the law of thy God, I will also forget your children." This was written to the priests some five thousand of so years ago. They had turned aside to worship other gods and led the children of Israel to worship with them. They weren't blind to the truth but they willingly worshiped in error. What do you want? What is the desire of your heart for your children? Is it truth or just some semblance of truth? It's been said, "It's easier to sell a lie then to give the truth away." Is this where you stand in your walk with God? Surly you want all that God has for you. There stands before you an open door to truth, all you need to do is enter in. Examine yourselves to see if you are in the truth or not. Compare what you've been taught with what the Word of God says. Do you have to explain away passages of scripture to make your doctrine work? You might check your premise, I think it's showing. Salvation is the way, heaven is the goal. I want to make it. I can't think of anything worse than to have thought I was right, deceived in my self, because I was to bull headed to believe the word of God. If your salvation rests upon what some man says, you have more faith in a man than I have. I hope your faith won't let you down.

WASTED IS IT FOR NOTHING?   01/06/1991

PSM 45:1 MY HEART IS INDITING A GOOD MATTER:
I SPEAK THE THINGS WHICH I HAVE MADE TOUCHING THE KING:
MY TONGUE IS THE PEN OF A READY WRITER

Mark 14:3-9 "And being in Bethany in the house of Simon the leper, as he sat at meat, there came a woman having an alabaster box of ointment of spikenard very precious, and she brake the box, and poured it on his head. {4} And there were some that had indignation within themselves, and said, Why was this waste of the ointment made? {5} For it might have been sold for more than three hundred pence, and have been given to the poor. And they murmured against her. {6} And Jesus said, Let her alone, why trouble ye her? she hath wrought a good work on me. {7} For ye have the poor with you always, and when so ever ye will ye may do them good: but me ye have not always. {8} She hath done what she could: she is come afore hand to anoint my body to the burying. {9} Verily I say unto you, Where so ever this gospel shall be preached throughout the whole world, this also that she hath done shall be spoken of for a memorial of her."

[These are notes set up to preach to the folks in the Minonk church]

spikenard

Precious ointment,

worth more than 300 pence

Matthew 20:2 "And when he had agreed with the laborers for a penny a day, he sent them into his vineyard."

A pence = one penny.

one penny=A days wage.

This ointment was worth more than 300 days wages.

Almost one whole years' wage.

Very precious.

CHANEL 5

hope chest.

dowry.

savings.

Part of the future for this young maiden thought to be named Mary.

Disciples had indignation that this ointment was wasted.

Judas Iscariot was the instigator of this indignation.

Judas felt any sacrifice toward Jesus was wasted.

No amount of sacrifice toward Christ is ever wasted.

Mark 14:9 "Verily I say unto you, Wheresoever this gospel shall be preached throughout the whole world, this also that she hath done shall be spoken of for a memorial of her."

What was it the Lord wanted done with this story?

What did he intend for us to understand?

Mary took a year's wage and poured it over the Lord of Glory.

To Judas Iscariot, this was the epitome of waste,

To Judas pouring water over the master's head would have been waste.

Scripture don't say who she was

think it was Mary

anointing followed resurrection of Lazarus.

The family wasn't necessarily rich.

had no servants.

John 12:2 "There they made him a supper, and Martha served: but Lazarus was one of them that sat at the table with him."

Luke 10:40 "But Martha was cumbered about much serving,"

But Mary poured the whole thing,

three hundred penny worth of ointment,

wasn't this really too much?

Human reasoning says so.

Mark 14:4-5 "And there were some that had indignation within themselves, and said, Why was this waste of the ointment made? {5} For it might have been sold for more than three hundred pence, and have been given to the poor. And they murmured against her."

The word in their mouth was waste.

Waste means giving more than necessary.

Paying more then the object is worth.

Doing more then necessary,

expending some resource,

some strength,

something owned.

To not be conservative.

Taking longer than is necessary.

Too much for too little.

Waste.

the word is WASTE

The twelve thought it was waste.

Judas stands alone for He had never, ever, called Jesus Lord.

Judas Iscariot represents the world system of things.

The world thinks that serving Jesus is a waste.

Giving yourself to God is a waste.

People would just as soon see you go to Hell in a bushel basket as to see you waste yourself on Christ.

I've seen it.

I've felt it.

I've heard it.

bus children receive Holy Ghost

You've too much talent to be a Christian.

Why waste it?

I've an expensive tool that I loaned to another man to be used on racing engines.
Later, I needed it to work on Sunday school buses, so I went to him to pick it up.
To him, It seemed such a waste to use it on the Sunday school busses.

Why it could have been sold for three hundred pence.
Wasted, in the service of the Lord of Glory.

Talent for singing that they became famous among Christians.
the lure of being more famous drew them to sing country and western, or rock.
Soon they lost out with God, their talent wasted on pride.
Because scout said, "your talent is wasted."
Your talent is never wasted on God.
He is worthy
to be served.
to be praised.
He is worthy for me to live for Him.
What the world says doesn't matter.

The Lord says: Do not trouble her.
Men may say what they want, but we stand on the word of the Lord.
"It is a good work."
Nothing is too good for Jesus.
The Judas Iscariots don't cut much ice.
Their reaction don't affect us.

The rest of the disciples affect us much more.
The rest of the disciples make some difference in the course of our lives.
Whatthey say matters.
But It shouldn't.
And They should understand.

The disciples went along with Judas because

Matthew 26:8-9 "they had indignation, saying, To what purpose <is> this waste? {9} For this ointment might have been sold for much, and given to the poor."

Attitude?

Get all you can for as little as possible.

Something deeper here.

Is there someone that's telling you,

Your wasting your life by sitting and not doing much?

You ought to be helping in this or that.

Your talent would be much better used if you would work at this or that.

These people are concerned with use.

Everything should be used to it's fullest.

so should you.

But wait.

Why did Jesus say this story was to be preached where ever the gospel was preached?

Shouldn't the gospel,

prompt some sort of action similar to this?

The wasting of yourself on him.

The gospel is meant to produce the pouring out of self.

As Mary poured out all she had,

the person who worships the Lord God almighty should also.

God takes what you give him,

anoints it with his pleasure

and returns a blessing you cannot contain.

Luke 6:38 "Give, and it shall be given unto you, [good measure], pressed down, and shaken together, and running over, shall men give into your bosom. For with the same measure that ye mete withal it shall be measured to you again."

Mark 14:6-8 "And Jesus said, Let her alone, why trouble ye her? she hath wrought a good work on me. {7} For ye have the poor with you always, and whensoever ye will ye may do them good: but me ye have not always. She hath done what she could: she is come afore hand to anoint my body to the burying."

Beforehand.

There's a time coming
when you'll be called to a greater work for Christ
then your now doing.
A time when Jesus Christ will reign supreme.
A time called heaven.
not be called into inactivity,
retirement community,
sit on a cloud and strum a harp.
That's not how it reads folks.

Matthew 25:21 "His lord said unto him, Well done, thou good and faithful servant: thou hast been faithful over a few things, I will make thee ruler over many things: enter thou into the joy of thy lord."

Matthew 24:47 "Verily I say unto you, That he shall make him ruler over all his goods."

Luke 19:17 "And he said unto him, Well, thou good servant: because thou hast been faithful in a very little, have thou authority over ten cities."

Heaven won't be the end of working for Christ.
It's a new level.
The work for Christ will go on even after the end of this age.

Jesus said, "For ye have the poor with you always, but Mary is come to anoint my body to the burying."

whole lot more to this verse then first appears.

Matthew 25:21 "Thou hast been faithful over a few things, I will make thee ruler over many things."

Luke 19:17 "because thou hast been faithful in a very little, have thou authority over the cities."

What you have done on this side of the resurrection determines your reward beyond the resurrection.

Mary anointed Jesus beforehand,

No opportunity after the crucifixion.

By the time they arrived at the tomb, Jesus was already resurrected:

Luke 24:1 "Now upon the first day of the week, very early in the morning, they came unto the sepulcher, bringing the spices which they had prepared, and certain others with them. And they found the stone rolled away from the sepulcher."

The tomb was empty

Blessed are those that have poured themselves out for Christ in this life,

Opportunity to sacrifice for Jesus won't be available after our resurrection.

Every knee shall bow and every tongue confess that Jesus is Lord.

There won't be any distinction there.

Here we bow

but there all will bow.

But now if you're wise.

2 Corinthians 6:2 "(For he saith, I have heard thee in a time accepted, and in the day of salvation have I succored thee: behold, now is the accepted time, behold, now is the day of salvation.)"

Only one person succeeded in anointing the body of Jesus.

Our timing is extremely important.

What you are doing for the Lord is timely.

You who aren't doing,

Have your eyes been opened to see the preciousness of the one we preach about?

Have you come to the place where the most costly thing you own,

the dearest thing,

the most precious thing,

Is not too expensive for him?

You have the poor with you always,

Working for the good of the poor, for the good of the souls of men is necessary but not when it displaces Jesus.

this work is nothing compared with the work that is done for the Lord.

God has opened our eyes to his worth.

The world has it's values.

A seasons box ticket to a famous football teams home stadium cost a thousand dollars,

A famous painting cost a million,

A 66 427 Shelby Cobra auto cost 200 thousand,

A new boat cost 50k

But who dares call it waste?

How many pound of fish can you buy for the price of a fish finder?

Dare anyone call it waste?

No, waste is only used by the non-Christian in relationship to service for and to our Lord and God.

How precious is He really?

How precious is he to our souls?

When you realize just how precious He really is

nothing will be too good for him.

Everything you have to the most priceless possession will be poured out on him.

She has done what she could.

She has given her all to Christ.

She hath done a good work.

She kept nothing in reserve for a rainy day.

No Anninias and Saphria commitment

She kept nothing for herself.

She lavished all that she had on Him,

Come resurrection morn, there wasn't any reason for her to regret her extravagance.

She hath done what she could: she is come aforehand to anoint my body to the burying.

Jesus will be satisfied with nothing less then your doing what you could.

Not in physical effort,

but in a life lain at his feet.

Jesus' death was eminent when Mary poured out the ointment upon his head,

Today it's his crowning that's in view.

It's high time you broke the alabaster box of your heart,

Pour your life out for the Lord.

Do this and any house,

any place of business

will be filled with the fragrance of your sacrifice.

Spikenard seeds have to be crushed, broken into fine pieces.

Jesus said Luke 20:18 "Whosoever shall fall upon that stone shall be broken, but on whomsoever it shall fall, it will grind him to powder."

You must fall upon Christ and be broken

for that fragrance to burst forth.

Have you ever been around a Christian that there is just something different about them?

Really different from all the others?

really been brought through suffering,

gone through a deep experience with Christ.

been brought to the limitation of self

learned to be satisfied in the Lord and No where else.

There's that sweet savor of Christ in their lives.

You can smell it.

It's that same odor that filled the house in Bethany when Mary broke the alabaster box of spikenard and poured it over the head of Jesus.

There's nothing that moves Christ more,

than a pouring out of self for the sake of Christ.

It's the widow's penny of Mark 12:41

A days wages

All her living

It's the apostle Paul saying

of the Lord Jesus."

it's Paul saying to the church in Rome

Romans 9:2-4 "I have great heaviness and continual sorrow in my heart. {3} For I could wish that myself were accursed from Christ for my brethren, my kinsmen according to the flesh:"

It's Paul saying in

Philippians 1:21 "For to me to live is Christ, and to die is gain."

It's the fragrance of sacrifice.

Mary's fragrance never passes.

It only took one stroke to break the box

but her action,

Still abides even today.

Our lives have to touch others,

in this touch we impart the fragrance of our sacrifice.

Those that were in that room when Mary poured the ointment over Jesus' head,
They all smelt of Mary's sacrifice.
There was no way they couldn't have smelled of it,
It clung to them for days.
You seek, you long for some way that the Lord would use you.
Your life touches others but
You can't produce the proper fragrance without the breaking of everything,
You must lay even your most sacred possessions, at the feet of Jesus.
Then
God will use you to create hunger in others.
People will take note that you've been with Jesus.
People will smell the scent of Christ in you.
They will sense your suffering,
your closeness with the Lord,
They'll know that you move in Christ.
They can see that you belong to Christ.
This is a life that creates a hunger in others.
This hunger will provoke them to seek the fragrance
It'l provoke then
until divine revelation opens the door
and they walk into a fullness of life in Christ.
Such is the working of the Spirit.
There must be a sense of need.
For A hunger to be filled.
It can't be forced,
it can't be spoon fed,
or injected,
it has to be created,
and it can be created in others only by those who carry with them the fragrance of God,
the fragrance of the sacrifice.

Their words are that of the Shumimite woman of 2 Kings

I perceive that this is an holy man of God.
It wasn't what Elijah said
or what he did ,
but what he was.
See could see it.
She could feel it,
she could smell it.
The impression left
was the fragrance of God himself.
She could smell the fragrance.

And David longed, and said, Oh that one would give me drink of the water of the well of Bethlehem, which is by the gate!

His vocal thoughts were enough
three mighty men broke through the enemy lines and filled his desire.
And this for an earthly king.

You should seek to satisfy Jesus Christ and not to be troubled at the costs. there must be a willingness to yield,
    a breaking,
    a pouring out of everything to him,
    This fragrance will draw them out
    And spur them on to know the Lord.
    Oh to be wasted for Christ.

Jesus Christ put his seal of approval on Mary's action
It is a Basis of service for our Lord.
Pour out all you have,
your very self, on him:
it is enough.

Romans 12:1 "I beseech you therefore, brethren, by the mercies of God, that ye present your bodies a living sacrifice, holy, acceptable unto God, <which is> your reasonable service."

not a question of, "have the poor been helped yet?"
The question
Is the Lord satisfied with your sacrifice?
A thousand things that might be done.
A thousand ways to serve.
Souls are at stake.
Your precious to God.
So much so, that he gave his life for you,
That you might have life, and that more abundantly.
Crucified that you might be crucified with him
and in that death a burial with him in water
in the likeness of his death you might also
be resurrected with him in newness of life.

what fragrance do you leave?

Wasted, is it for nothing?

CORONARY THROMBOSIS   01/05/1992

PSM 45:1 MY HEART IS INDITING A GOOD MATTER:
I SPEAK THE THINGS WHICH I HAVE MADE TOUCHING THE KING:
MY TONGUE IS THE PEN OF A READY WRITER

This is a time of the year when our minds turn to new beginnings. There is no better time to start afresh then at the first of the year. Now is the time for you to lay aside all the differences you've had with others and start a new. Wash it clean, start with a new slate, a clean record. This is the time to take the things that have troubled us throughout the year, write them on a slip of paper and burn these troubling thoughts in a bucket of fire. It works folks. This year, there is to be a series on the Body, soul and spirit that you'll find interesting and helpful in your walk with God. When one understands his spiritual make up it's easier to exercise control over the body. There is a series on prayer and worship that is needful to be taught. When I say series, I mean it will take more then one lesson to teach you about worship, and more then one for prayer, how many, I don't know, just that the subject is a large one and it will take some time to bring it to you. Forgiveness is a pertinent subject that will be covered.   God is great and greatly to be praised. We sure appreciate being able to bring this broadcast to you, feeling that it indeed fills a void in your lives. God has been good in making it possible to bring this broadcast to you. It would be helpful if you would write us a note stating how, if indeed it has, this last 18 or so months helped you. This last year has seen the rise and fall of many. We've seen a war come and go. The breaking up of the republic of Russia and we are one year closer to the second coming of Jesus. How many days or years are left is unknown to the mind of man. God knows, and he alone knows when the last man woman or child will come to him for salvation and fulfillment. If we could just open our spiritual eyes and see into the heavens, I'm sure we would see a great host of heaven watching expectantly for the last trump when the Lord himself shall split he eastern sky and the dead in Christ shall rise out of the graves, then we which are alive and remain shall be caught up to meet them in the air, so shall we ever be with him.

Trouble on every hand. Fear of the things that are to come. Will Cat or won't they? What will Komatsu Dresser do? Will America become just a nation of service companies? Have we lost our manufacturing base? Is the trade agreement with Mexico going to do the same thing to us that our trade agreement with Canada did to them with the closings of Cat, Komatsu Dresser, and a multitude of others? Were will the next dollar come from? How are we going to make it through this generation? Will there even be a life for my children to live? Oh God, where have all the lilies gone? Pressure on every side. Stress, stress ,stress. Book shelves abound with books such as," HOW TO TURN YOUR STRESS INTO STRENGTH", HOW TO DEAL WITH STRESS" HOW TO QUIT WORRYING AND START LIVING." Yet on every side, the road of life is littered with the ones who couldn't cope with this rapidly changing world. Governments falling, companies closing doors. Marriages failing. Death, hell and destruction on every hand. Worry trouble fear and doubt nag at our every waking moment, Where is there peace and safety in this rapidly changing world? Life's stability is like standing on the beach and having the waves wash the sand out from under his feet. Like standing in mud or shifting sand.

In the last month, three of my acquaintances have underwent heart related difficulties. One had two heart attacks within the space of three hours. Another had a one. A great deal of blockage was found in the arteries feeding the heart. Another had terrific chest pains and was admitted for tests. What's going on? Just a fulfillment of scripture. Judgments of God? No, just misplaced trust concerning where your affections are directed. A man trusting in the arm of flesh is like a man accepting wise saying from a fool. Scripture tells us Psa 146:3 "Put not your trust in princes, <nor> in the son of man, in whom <there is> no help." His breath goeth forth, he returneth to his earth, in that very day his thoughts perish." Psa 20:7 "Some <trust> in chariots, and some in horses: but we will remember the name of the LORD our God." Trust placed in anything or anyone except the Lord God Almighty is a misplaced trust.

Jesus Christ gave us some signs that we may know what time it is in the dispensations of God. What time is it? When shall the coming of the son of man be? The disciples asked of Jesus in the book of Luke 21:6-37 Jesus answered saying that the temple shall be torn down, not one stone left upon another. This happened in 70 AD the Roman General Titus took Jerusalem. The disciples asked: but when shall these things be? and what sign <will there be> when these things shall come to pass? {8} And he said, Take heed that ye be not deceived: for many shall come in my name, saying, I am <Christ>, and the time draweth near: go ye not therefore after them. {9} But when ye shall hear of wars and commotions, be not terrified: for these things must first come to pass, but the end <is> not by and by. {10} Then said he unto them, Nation shall rise against nation, and kingdom against kingdom: {11} And great earthquakes shall be in divers places, and famines, and pestilences, and fearful sights and great signs shall there be from heaven. {12} But before all these, they shall lay their hands on you, and persecute <you>, delivering <you> up to the synagogues, and into prisons, being brought before kings and rulers for my name's sake. {13} And it shall turn to you for a testimony. {14}ø Settle <it> therefore in your hearts, not to meditate before what ye shall answer: {15} For I will give you a mouth and wisdom, which all your adversaries shall not be able to gainsay nor resist {16} And ye shall be betrayed both by parents, and brethren, and kinsfolk's, and friends, and <some> of you shall they cause to be put to death. {17} And ye shall be hated of all <men> for my name's sake. {18} But there shall not an hair of your head perish {19}ø In your patience possess ye your souls {20} And when ye shall see Jerusalem compassed with armies, then know that the desolation thereof is nigh. {21} Then let them which are in Judea flee to the mountains, and let them which are in the midst of it depart out, and let not them that are in the countries enter there into. {22} For these be the days of vengeance, that all things which are written may be fulfilled. {23} But woe unto them that are with child, and to them that give suck, in those days! for there shall be great distress in the land, and wrath upon this people. {24}ø And they shall fall by the edge of the sword, and shall be led away captive into all nations: and Jerusalem shall be trodden down of the Gentiles, until the times of the Gentiles be fulfilled Israel had been trodden down of the gentile nations, that is it was under the rule of others, until it rose from the ashes in 1947 and again became a sovereign nation. Recognition was given to her by the United Nations and she was no longer was considered to be trodden down by the gentiles. {25} And there shall be signs in the sun, and in the moon, and in the stars, and upon the earth distress of nations, with perplexity, the sea and the waves roaring {26} Men's hearts failing them for fear, and for looking after those things which are coming on the earth for the powers of heaven shall be shaken. {27} And then shall they see the Son of man coming in a cloud with power and great glory. {28} And when these things begin to come to pass, then look up, and lift up your heads, for your redemption draweth nigh.

Verse 26 has the key to this great influx of heart attacks, Men's hearts failing them for fear, and for looking after those things which are coming on the earth. Why? Because of fear of what tomorrow will bring and looking after the things that are already come. Jesus' answer to this dilemma is found in, Mat 6:19-34 Lay not up for yourselves treasures upon earth, where moth and rust doth corrupt, and where thieves break through and steal: {20} But lay up for yourselves treasures in heaven, where neither moth nor rust doth corrupt, and where thieves do not break through nor steal: {21} For where your treasure is, there will your heart be also. {22} The light of the body is the eye: if therefore thine eye be single, thy whole body shall be full of light. {23} But if thine eye be evil, thy whole body shall be full of darkness. If therefore the light that is in thee be darkness, how great <is> that darkness! {24} No man can serve two masters: for either he will hate the one, and love the other, or else he will hold to the one, and despise the other. Ye cannot serve God and mammon. {25} Therefore I say unto you, Take no thought for your life, what ye shall eat, or what ye shall drink, nor yet for your body, what ye shall put on. Is not the life more than meat, and the body than raiment? {26} Behold the fowls of the air: for they sow not, neither do they reap, nor gather into barns, yet your heavenly Father feedeth them. Are ye not much better than they? {27} Which of you by taking thought can add one cubit unto his stature? {28} And why take ye thought for raiment? Consider the lilies of the field, how they grow, they toil not, neither do they spin: {29} And yet I say unto you, That even Solomon in all his glory was not arrayed like one of these. {30} Wherefore , if God so clothe the grass of the field, which to day is, and to morrow is cast into the oven, <shall he> not much more <clothe> you, O ye of little faith? {31} Therefore take no thought, saying, What shall we eat? or, What shall we drink? or, Wherewithal shall we be clothed? {32} (For after all these things do the Gentiles seek:) for your heavenly Father knoweth that ye have need of all these things. {33} But seek ye first the kingdom of God, and his righteousness, and all these things shall be added unto you. {34} Take therefore no thought for the morrow: for the morrow shall take thought for the things of itself. Sufficient unto the day <is> the evil thereof. Seek ye first the kingdom of God. It's realizing that God is and is a rewarder of them that diligently seek him. It's realizing that you are a child of God and He will take care of you. It knowing that God will put nothing on you that He hasn't already made a way for you to bear it, or be victorious in. 2 Cor 3:4-6 "And such trust have we through Christ to God-ward: Not that we are sufficient of ourselves to think any thing as of ourselves, but our sufficiency <is> of God, Who also hath made us able ministers of the new testament, not of the letter, but of the spirit: for the letter killeth, but the spirit giveth life." We are not to bear our burdens alone. Jesus told us Mat 11:28-30 "Come unto me, all <ye> that labour and are heavy laden, and I will give you rest. Take my yoke upon you, and learn of me, for I am meek and lowly in heart: and ye shall find rest unto your souls. For my yoke <is> easy, and my burden is light."

    We are not our own, we have been bought with a price. If indeed we are Christ's, then we are in his hands. Worry will accomplish nothing at all. Which of you by taking thought can add one cubit to your stature? Why cross a bridge that has never been built? Fight a battle that has never been set in array? So much of our lives has been spent in fruitlessly worrying and planning for what may come to pass. Take no thought for tomorrow or the trouble that it will bring , we have enough trouble today to fill our quota, why take on tomorrow's? the secret of inner peace is to know who holds the future. Not what the future holds. One of the beauties of heaven will be no more time. In short, you won't be worrying about yesterday and tomorrow for there won't be any such thing. Yesterday and tomorrow are finite terms that do not apply to eternity. Realizing that God has our future in his hands, that he does have a divine plan for our lives, and that he that began a work in your life is able to finish that work.

    I get caught up in the worry cycle from time to time. It's hard to break the worry cycle because the idea that you have to worry about the future is deeply ingrained within this humanistic flesh. Years of training find it difficult to overcome worry. Suddenly, the realization that right now I can't do anything at all about the problem, calms the tight neck and wrinkled brow. I then put the entire thing in the hands of the Master of the storm, and he says Peace be still. The waves of doubt and discouragement are immediately beaten down by the glorious rain of his love. I am in his hands. It's Peter walking on the water.

    Prayer is the key to calmness in the midst of the storm. It's a close relationship with Jesus that will keep you in the hard places of life. It's not a once in a life time thing. It's the everyday, continuous prayer life that will bring you through. It's not that your effective prayer will suffice, but it is that your faith in the operation of God wrought by your continual prayer and closeness with the savior that will accomplish the feat. A consistent communication with Jesus, not just in the cool of the day, or the heat of the battle, but the everyday communion with the savior. A set time coupled with a continual communication through out the day will bring you into a closeness with Jesus that even the den of lions won't sway. Careful for nothing. Don't have a care in the world for the things of the world or what they can do to you. Be careful for nothing, but in all things by prayer and fasting. Or don't take the burden of the cares of this life upon yourself, your heavenly Father knows what your needs are. The cares of this life will choke out all the seeds of righteousness and faith that God has planted in the fertile soil of your life. Jesus said it this way: Mat 13:18-23 Hear ye therefore the parable of the sower. {19} When any one heareth the word of the kingdom, and understandeth <it> not, then cometh the wicked <one>, and catcheth away that which was sown in his heart. This is he which received seed by the way side. {20} But he that received the seed into stony places, the same is he that heareth the word, and anon with joy receiveth it, {21} Yet hath he not root in himself, but dureth for a while: for when tribulation or persecution ariseth because of the word, by and by he is offended. {22} He also that received seed among the thorns is he that heareth the word, and the care of this world, and the deceitfulness of riches, choke the word, and he becometh unfruitful.. {23} But he that received seed into the good ground is he that heareth the word, and understandeth <it>, which also beareth fruit, and bringeth forth, some an hundredfold, some sixty, some thirty.

The Word of God is full of men and women that were not great in themselves but that had faith in the operation of God. Hebrews the eleventh chapter is cited as being the faith chapter of the Bible. In it is an impressive list of people that put total trust in God. These are those who were without coronary difficulties though if they were to do so by themselves, had plenty to be concerned about. Remember that faith is putting your trust in God and his ability to perform all that he said he would perform. Heb 11:1-22 Now faith is the substance of things hoped for, the evidence of things not seen. {2} For by it the elders obtained a good report. {3} Through faith we understand that the worlds were framed by the word of God, so that things which are seen were not made of things which do appear. {4} By faith Abel offered unto God a more excellent sacrifice than Cain, by which he obtained witness that he was righteous, God testifying of his gifts: and by it he being dead yet speaketh. {5} By faith Enoch was translated that he should not see death, and was not found, because God had translated him: for before his translation he had this testimony, that he pleased God. {6} But without faith <it is> impossible to please <him>: for he that cometh to God must believe that he is, and <that> he is a rewarder of them that diligently seek him. Enoch's life was totally given over to God, he lived by faith in the realm of the spiritual.. {7} By faith Noah, being warned of God of things not seen as yet, moved with fear, prepared an ark to the saving of his house, by the which he condemned the world, and became heir of the righteousness which is by faith. ø Noah could have worried about where the substance would come from to build the ark, but it was God's responsibility to provide the materials and living for the man of God to accomplish the burden put upon his heart by God. . {8} By faith Abraham, when he was called to go out into a place which he should after receive for an inheritance, obeyed, and he went out, not knowing whither he went. {9} By faith he sojourned in the land of promise, as <in> a strange country, dwelling in tabernacles with Isaac and Jacob, the heirs with him of the same promise: He left prosperity and stability of the known behind for the promise of God. Anxiety could easily have been his bed mate.. {10} For he looked for a city which hath foundations, whose builder and maker <is> God. {11} Through faith also Sara herself received strength to conceive seed, and was delivered of a child when she was past age, because she judged him faithful who had promised. {12} Therefore sprang there even of one, and him as good as dead, <so many> as the stars of the sky in multitude, and as the sand which is by the sea shore innumerable. {13} These all died in faith, not having received the promises, but having seen them afar off, and were persuaded of <them>, and embraced <them>, and confessed that they were strangers and pilgrims on the earth. {14} For they that say such things declare plainly that they seek a country. ø{15} And truly, if they had been mindful of that <country> from whence they came out, they might have had opportunity to have returned.. {16} But now they desire a better <country>, that is, an heavenly: wherefore God is not ashamed to be called their God: for he hath prepared for them a city. {17} By faith Abraham, when he was tried, offered up Isaac: and he that had received the promises offered up his only begotten <son>. {18} Of whom it was said, That in Isaac shall thy seed be called: ø{19} Accounting that God <was> able to raise <him> up, even from the dead, from whence also he received him in a figure.. {20} By faith Isaac blessed Jacob and Esau concerning things to come. {21} By faith Jacob, when he was a dying, blessed both the sons of Joseph, and worshipped, <leaning> upon the top of his staff. {22} By faith Joseph, when he died, made mention of the departing of the children of Israel, and gave commandment concerning his bones. {34} By faith Moses, when he was born, was hid three months of his parents, because they saw <he was> a proper child, and they were not afraid of the king's commandment. {24} By faith Moses, when he was come to years, refused to be called the son of Pharaoh's daughter,. {25} Choosing rather to suffer affliction with the people of God, than to enjoy the pleasures of sin for a season, {26} Esteeming the reproach of Christ greater riches than the treasures in Egypt: for he had respect unto the recompense of the reward. {27} By faith he forsook Egypt, not fearing the wrath of the king:. for he endured, as seeing him who is invisible. {28} Through faith he kept the Passover, and the sprinkling of blood, lest he that destroyed the firstborn should touch them. He could have worried about the blood being effective. He could have worried about pharaoh killing him. He could have worried about a multitude of things, yet he had faith in God. How would you handle the responsibility of feeding and caring for a multitude of people? There was no anxiety attack here. He had to have faith in God, there simply wasn't any other way.. {29} By faith they passed through the Red sea as by dry <land>: which the Egyptians assaying to do were drowned. {30} By faith the walls of Jericho fell down, after they were compassed about seven days. {31} By faith the harlot Rahab perished not with them that believed not, when she had received the spies with peace. {32} And what shall I more say? for the time would fail me to tell of Gedeon, and <of> Barak, and <of> Samson, and <of> Jephthae, <of> David also, and Samuel, and <of> the prophets: {33} Who through faith subdued kingdoms, wrought righteousness, obtained promises, stopped the mouths of lions, {34} Quenched the violence of fire, escaped the edge of the sword, out of weakness were made strong, waxed valiant in fight, turned to flight the armies of the aliens. {35} Women received their dead raised to life again: and others were tortured, not accepting deliverance, that they might obtain a better resurrection: {36} And others had trial of <cruel> mockings and scourgings, yea, moreover of bonds and imprisonment: {37} They were stoned, they were sawn asunder, were tempted, were slain with the sword: they wandered about in sheepskins and goatskins, being destitute, afflicted, tormented, {38} (Of whom the world was not worthy:) they wandered in deserts, and <in> mountains, and <in> dens and caves of the earth. {39} And these all, having obtained a good report through faith, received not the promise: {40} God having provided some better thing for us, that they without us should not be made perfect.

    The tendency is for us to look upon these men and women as great people who excelled in their own strength. This is natural and we would raise monuments to their great achievements if it weren't for the fact that they simply weren't anxious about what God had told them to do. They had faith in the operation of God and simply knew that God would accomplish all that he said he would. In this, this simple statement, that God is, and he is able to finish the work that he began in your life, rests the secret of inner peace and freedom from a coronary. Do Christians have heart attacks? The answer to that is in the fact that we're not perfected yet. God's still working on us. Yes, Christians do have heart attacks, it's not easy to throw off years of training ingrained in the mind of man. I'm afraid our walk with God is similar to Peter's walking on the water in matt 14, we manage to walk by faith and then when the battles of life begin to wash upon our legs like the waves around Peter's feet, our gaze turns to the waves instead of Jesus. But remember, Peter had to get out of the boat to walk on the water, the rest of those boys stayed in the boat. It's time for you to get out of the boat and trust in God. Repent of your sins, by asking Jesus to forgive you of them, be baptized in the name of Jesus Christ for the remission of sins, and receive the gift of the Holy Ghost. The promise is unto you.

IF you enjoyed this broadcast and would like a copy, send your name and address to,

THE WE PREACH JESUS MINISTRIES
PO BOX 274
EUREKA, IL

WHERE IS THE PROMISE?   01/12/1992

PSM 45:1 MY HEART IS INDITING A GOOD MATTER:
I SPEAK THE THINGS WHICH I HAVE MADE TOUCHING THE KING:
MY TONGUE IS THE PEN OF A READY WRITER

I feel within me, an urgency. An urgency to proclaim, to warn, to compel, to broadcast far and wide, in light of the events already brought to light in this first month, no, week of 1992. We already knew about the European Economic Community being formed, this is not something that is just being sprung on the world in the last two years, but has taken more the a decade to bring to the fore front. But within the last year, Two Germanys' unite, Russia giving some semblance of independence to the Soviet states, now the news is filled with the two Koreas. All the world is behind the New World Order, and with that order, peace and safety. " 1 Th 5:1-4 "But of the times and the seasons, brethren, ye have no need that I write unto you. For yourselves know perfectly that the day of the Lord so cometh as a thief in the night. For when they shall say, Peace and safety, then sudden destruction cometh upon them, as travail upon a woman with child, and they shall not escape. But ye, brethren, are not in darkness, that that day should overtake you as a thief." I do not wish to be a harbinger of bad news, for it will only be bad news to those that don't believe, for the believer looks for a new heaven and a new earth wherein dwelleth righteousness." The whole key to the news is that first verse of 1 Th 5: "But of the times and the seasons, brethren, ye have no need that I write unto you." Paul is not talking about spring, summer, fall and winter but of the age we live in relationship to the second coming of Christ. 2 Peter 3: Explains this time relationship in further detail.

2 Peter 3:3 & 9 "Knowing this first, that there shall come in the last days scoffers, walking after their own lusts, and saying, Where is the promise of his coming? for since the fathers fell asleep, all things continue as they were from the beginning of the creation."But Verse 9 tells you why the Lord Hasn't come yet, " The Lord is not slack concerning his promise, as some men count slackness, but is long suffering to us-ward, not willing that any should perish, but that all should come to repentance." Verse 10 goes

on with how the Lord will come. Not with a great fan fair, or trumpets, or bands playing in the streets, "But the day of the Lord will come as a thief in the night, in the which the heavens shall pass away with a great noise, and the elements shall melt with fervent heat, the earth also and the works that are therein shall be burned up. Seeing then that all these shall be dissolved, what manner of persons ought ye to be in all holy conversation and godliness, looking for and hasting unto the coming of the day of God, wherein the heavens being on fire shall be dissolved, and the elements shall melt with fervent heat? Nevertheless we, according to his promise, look for new heavens and a new earth, wherein dwelleth righteousness." Where are we in the time table of God? The Word of God answers the question for Exo 20:11 says, "For in six days the LORD made heaven and earth, the sea, and all that in them is, and rested the seventh day: wherefore the LORD blessed the Sabbath day, and hallowed it." 2 peter 3:8 "But, beloved, be not ignorant of this one thing, that one day is with the Lord as a thousand years, and a thousand years as one day." Psalms 90:4 "For a thousand years in thy sight are but as yesterday when it is past, and as a watch in the night." There is always going to be troubles until the end of this age. No man knoweth the day nor hour, but we're not to be ignorant of His coming. How much time is left? I don't know. Surly the day is set before God circled in red. Every day brings us closer. Every hour brings us closer. How far do we have to go yet dad? Just a little farther down the road son. Seven days are in the creation week. Six days the Lord God worked on the earth and mankind, The seventh He rested. 2 peter 3:8 "But, beloved, be not ignorant of this one thing, that one day is with the Lord as a thousand years, and a thousand years as one day."

    Four thousand years of old testament history is gone, that's four days. 1992 years of the new testament age has already been spent, that's a little less than two days. That's five thousand nine hundred and ninety two years according to our calendar. That's five days and 23 hours and 50 minutes according to the figures. Ten minutes of the last day. Eight years till the end of the century. If you were relating this to a board six inches thick that you had to cut, only eight thousands of an inch remains to be cut. Revelations tells us there are seven years of tribulation to come. Subtract that from the eight years and that gives you one. It's no coincidence that the EEC is to come in to full power on January the 1st 1993, seven years before the end of the century. It's not a coincidence that the new world order is being harped by the powers that be. Revelations 13:17 Speaks of a mark that all must have to buy or sell, The EEC, the commonwealth of nations may not use anything but the trade dollar among themselves. A unified Europe. The whole world is aligning with her. It's a New World Order. There won't be any trade with the nations in the new world order unless you use the trade dollar. It's already here. "All the nations of the EEC must give up their sovereignty. The EEC reigns supreme. A bolt, nut or nail cannot depart from the design authorized by this cartels of nations. There will be not one single independent nation throughout the world, all will be co-dependent, all will be equal in trade, there will be no more trade deficits among the nations. This is not something from some science fiction book written by some noted author, this is the nasty now, now. This is not the United States of the world this is totally different, it is neither a democracy nor a republic, this will be a world ruled by a system, by one. If you want more information on the EEC write to The office of Community affairs, U.S. Department of Commerce, Washington , D.C. OR Brian Pallasch The American Society of Association Executives, Government affairs Division Washington, D.C. I don't know how close you've been paying attention to the tone of our leaders concerning our own national debt, but if I had any money, and I don't, it sure wouldn't be left in paper. What does all this mean? Given the errors in the calendars, and the changing from one type of calendar to another over the years, I'd say we're close to the second coming of the Lord when he will take his bride, the church, out of the world, to ever be with him, while the tribulation takes place.

After Jesus had given a lesson on what was to come to pass, the disciples were scratching their heads as to when these things would come to pass. So in Matthew 24:3 they asked Jesus privately, saying, "Tell us, when shall these things be? and what shall be the sign of thy coming? and the end of the world?"

Three questions were asked by the disciples here.

1. When shall these things be? That is, The destruction of the temple which was accomplished by the Roman general Titus in 70 ad.

2.What shall be the sign of thy coming? Or, How can we tell when you are coming back?

3. When shall be the end of the world? The consummation of this age?

When shall these things be? and what shall be the sign of thy coming? and the end of the world? Jesus went out and departed from the temple: and his disciples came to him for to show him the buildings of the temple. The temple was built of green spotted marble according to Lightfoot. Josephus said the stones were fifty feet long, twenty-four broad and sixteen thick. When shall this temple be put into utter destruction? Jesus said,

"Many shall come in my name saying I am the Christ, and deceive many. And ye shall hear of wars and rumors of wars: Nation shall rise against nation and kingdom against kingdom: famines, pestilences, and earthquakes, in divers places. Luke adds that there shall be fearful sights and great signs from heaven." Before the Roman general Titus took Jerusalem, these signs were given:

1. A star hung over the city like a sword and a comet continued in the sky for a whole year.
2. At the feast of the unleavened bread, at the ninth hour of the night, a great light shone about the alter and the temple, and this continued for half an hour.
3. At the same feast, a cow led to sacrifice brought forth a lamb in the midst of the temple.
4. The eastern gate of the temple which was made of solid brass, and very heavy, and could hardly be shut by twenty men, and was fastened by strong bars and bolts, was seen the sixth hour of the night to open of it's own accord.
5. Before sun setting there were seen, over all the country, chariots and armies fighting in the clouds, and besieging cities.
6. At the feast of Pentecost, when the priests were going into the inner temple by night to attend their service, they heard first an motion and noise, and then a voice, as a multitude, saying, let us depart hence.
7. One man, a country fellow, four years before the war began, and when the city was in peace and plenty, came to the feast of the tabernacles, and ran crying up and down the streets, day and night: "A voice from the east! A voice from the west! A voice from the four winds! A voice against Jerusalem and the temple! A voice against the bridegrooms and the brides! A voice against the people!" Though the magistrates endeavored by stripes and tortures to restrain him, yet he still cried, with a mournful voice, "Wo, wo, to Jerusalem!" And this he continued to do for several years together, going about the walls and crying with a loud voice: "Wo,wo to the city, and to the people, and to the temple" and as he added "Wo, wo to myself!" a stone from some sling of engine struck him dead on the spot!

(Josephus Wars of the Jews book 6 chapter 5 verse 3 and 4.) Josephus was a Jewish historian who wrote of the Jews. Another Tacitus a Roman Historian gives nearly the same account. These are not scripture but the history of the fulfillment of scripture. Not one stone was left upon another. Destruction was total. All that is left is the wailing wall. The Dome of the Rock now sits where the temple was built. Why did the people miss the signs of the destruction of Jerusalem? Why did they miss the coming of the messiah? In both cases the signs were clear as a winter night. 2 Th 2:11-12 "And for this cause God shall send them strong delusion, that they should believe a lie: That they all might be damned who believed not the truth, but had pleasure in unrighteousness." They were willingly ignorant. They chose to ignore the signs of both occurrences. Hopefully, in our sophisticated age that we live in, we to, won't chose to ignore the signs plainly written along the road of life. We're so sophisticated that we don't even need God to help us anymore. That's the same condition Israel was in. The Spirit of the Lord had long ago departed from the temple. No longer did it reside in the Holiest Place. The angels on the veil had even been replace with the signs of the Zodiac. Astrology was being worshiped instead of God.

Jesus said that, "All these are the beginning of sorrows." The beginning of travailing pains. These are only the first throws of what was to come. On and on goes the prophecy. Now we stand at a time of the fulfillment of the ultimate of prophecies: Jesus' second coming. Never has there been a time such as now. We've talked about the EEC. The one world government. The new world order. These are sign posts along the way for the Christian. Now is the appointed time. Today is the day of salvation. The Book of Revelation speaks of the terrible tribulation that is to come. the Book of Ezekiel says concerning "Gog, Magog, Meshech, Tubal, Persia, Ethiopia, Libya, Gomer, And Togarmah and many people with them." This is nearly the whole world. "Thou shalt ascend and come like a storm, thou, and all thy bands, and many people with thee. 38:2 And I will turn thee back, and leave but the sixth part of thee,(seventeen out of every hundred) and will cause thee to come up from the north parts, and I will bring thee upon the mountains of Israel: And I will smite thy bow out of thy left hand, and will cause thine arrows to fall out of thy right hand. Thou shalt fall upon the mountains of Israel, thou, and all thy bands, and the people that is with thee: I will give thee unto the ravenous birds of every sort, and to the beasts of the field to be devoured." This is a war to end all wars. So spoke the people in the early 1900s. WW1 The end of all wars.

WW2, most terrible of wars. The Persian gulf. Desert storm. The War in Lebanon, Wars and rumors of wars, earthquakes in various places, Pestilence and famine, evil men and seducers growing worse and worse. On and On the prophecies go. But the real object, the real subject is, where do you stand in Christ? Or where do you stand with Christ?

There is always going to be troubles until the end of this age. No man knoweth the day nor hour, but we're not to be ignorant of His coming. How much time is left? I don't know. Surly the day is set before God circled in red. Every day brings us nearer. Every hour brings us closer. As a child we would ask, How far do we have to go yet dad? Just a little farther down the road son. Seven days are in the creation week. Six days the Lord God worked on the earth and mankind, The seventh He rested. 2 peter 3:8 But, beloved, be not ignorant of this one thing, that one day is with the Lord as a thousand years, and a thousand years as one day.

Where are you in Christ? Jesus has a job for you to do. He knows you, he knew you before you were even born, and He has a plan for your life. It doesn't matter how young or how old you are. There is no retirement in the work of Christ. Not until the end. Then, friend, the benefits are out of this world. What is the overcoming sin in your life? The one that keeps knocking you down? The one that you just can't seem to overcome? Hebrews 12:1 Says, "Let us lay aside every weight, and the sin which doth so easily (easily, not with guile or force but easily) beset us (knock us off course), and let us run with patience the race that is set before us, looking unto Jesus the author and finisher of our faith, who for the joy that was set before him endured the cross, despising the shame, and is set down at the right hand of the throne of God." Romans 12:1 "I beseech you therefore, brethren, by the mercies of God, that you present your bodies a living sacrifice, holy, acceptable, unto God, which is your reasonable service."

Sacrifice, not the blood of bulls and goats not some lamb slain for your sins but present your selves and a living, continuing, ongoing, sacrifice, holy, acceptable, unto God, How Bro Johnson can I do this? Through day by day service, through worship, through loving with a Godly love the body of Christ His church which he bought with his blood when he died on that tree near two thousand years ago. Oh that Besetting sin, You've tried and tried to conquer it. Many time it has cast you down like the snare of the fowler, like a trap set in your way. It's a pit dug in the way, the road of your life. Disguised, covered over with leaves, twigs, and dust. Set to trip you up the first time your not looking. These are mountains in your life that you can't seem to climb. Well, hear the word of faith, Mark 11:22-23 "Have faith in God. He said, have faith in God," not in your ability to accomplish this mighty task, but have faith in God, for he is able to finish the work he started in your life. Phil 1:6 "Being confident of this very thing, that he which hath begun a good work in you will perform <it> until the day of Jesus Christ:" So, how then can I deal with the things in my life that continually overcome me? By this verse of scripture we are given instruction on how to deal with it. For verily I say unto you, That whosoever shall say unto this mountain, be thou removed and be thou cast into the sea, and shall not doubt in his heart, but shall believe that those things which he saith shall come to pass, he shall have whatsoever he saith.

What do you mean by that bro Johnson? Look at Mark the 11th chapter. Jesus and the disciples had just came from Bethany and went past a fig tree that had no figs upon it for the time of figs was not yet. Jesus then cursed the fig tree and it died from the roots. They all went on and took care of the business in Jerusalem and on the return trip passed by the fig tree. Peter, impetuous Peter, called to remembrance the fig tree saying "Master, behold the fig tree which thou cursed is withered away. Jesus answered unto him, Have faith in God. For verily I say unto you, That whosoever shall say unto this mountain, be thou removed and be thou cast into the sea, and shall not doubt in his heart, but shall believe that those things which he saith shall come to pass, he shall have whatsoever he saith." I think that Jesus cursed this fig tree for this particular spiritual application. The time of figs was not yet. So, this would indicate that the mountains in the lives of the disciples were the subject of this conversation. Whosoever shall say unto this mountain, be thou removed and be thou cast into the sea, and shall not doubt in his heart, but shall believe that those things which he saith shall come to pass, he shall have whatsoever he saith. You have spiritual mountains in your life that you can't overcome, speak to that mountain. Cast it into the sea. Have faith in God, doubting nothing, cast away that mountain in your life. And leave them there. I've told this story before, but it's application compels it's use again, In the late 1800s there were these two prospectors in Alaska. For years they had been together. Through long winters and short summers. Through cabin fever every winter, through all sorts of difficulties. Inseparable, would describe their relationship. Early one spring morning, after twenty five years together, Sam died. His partner Charley was devastated. How could he go on without Sam? Charley mechanically performed the necessary burial rituals by himself. There simply wasn't anyone else around to do it. He dug the grave deep and straight, near the stream the two had worked for gold so many years together. Covering Sam with his Hudson bay blanket, He bent down and put the gold pan over Sam's face to keep the dirt out. Charley then covered him up. With a broken heart filled with much sorrow, he returned to the cabin they had shared for so long together, heart broken, lost, desolate. In the corner, Sam's corner sat Charlie till long after the sun had gone down. Dragging himself off to bed, exhausted by the emotional strain, He fell asleep in his cloths on the covers. The first light of the breaking dawn of the new day hit Charlie square in his closed eyes. Rising, wiping the sleep from his sorrowful eyes, he shuffled to the cabinet to make coffee. Grabbing the pot he turned to the water, as he turned he caught a glimpse of Sam, sitting in his rocker, wrapped with his Hudson bay blanket, stone cold dead. What is this? Is my mind going? Shuffling over to where Sam sat, he reached out and touched him. Oh God, just what is going on? The coffee long forgotten, He Picked Sam up again and shuffled back to the grave to perform that same burial ritual over again. Twice, to bury so close a friend is twice devastated. Charlie shuffled back to the cabin to repeat the activities of yesterday. The day that friends are gone is long wearisome days. Charlie did what he could to keep busy. Night and then the morning came and Sam was again in his rocker, Charlie performed the same ritual again. Another night and morning and the same. Sam again in the rocker. Burial night and morning and Sam again. Charlie had lost it, every night he would go out and dig Sam up, bring him inside and sit him in the rocker. Charlie had lost all reality over the death of his friend. That besetting sin is like that. Take that sin, bury it deep. Put a marker on top of it, "here lies the sin that so easily beset Joe Dokes or Fred Jones or what ever your name is. And leave it buried. Speak to that mountain. Cast it far from you. Have faith in God that he is able to take care of it. Let it be said of you as it was of Jesus " The zeal of His Fathers house hath eaten him up." No better testimony could be said of you than this. No man can serve two masters. Bury that sin deep in the waters of salvation. Repent of your sin be baptized in the name of Jesus Christ for the Remission of your sins, and you shall receive the gift of the Holy Ghost. Speak to the Mountains in your life and do great and glorious things with the Lord of Glory.

THE APOSTLES   01/26/1992

PSM 45:1 MY HEART IS INDITING A GOOD MATTER:
I SPEAK THE THINGS WHICH I HAVE MADE TOUCHING THE KING:
MY TONGUE IS THE PEN OF A READY WRITER

Starting with this broadcast there is a new feature for you. It's called The Sounds of His Coming after the song of the same name, and it will deal with the events that are occurring around the world in relationship to prophecy. When something is seen or heard in the news, it will be brought to your attention and along with it an explain of how it relates to prophecy. Here is the sounds of his coming, Update Weds Jan 15, 1992 in the Peoria Journal Star, Front page, MONEY NETWORK ON LINE NEXT WEEK, This is concerning a state wide money network called by the same name. It will enable card holders to access their own bank accounts through seven different types of money machines across the country. Money Network card holders will have access to 3000 machines in Illinois and more than 35000 machines around the US. Future innovations will be the ability to use your ATM card for retail purchases. A cashless society. For the retailer, it means instant credit for your purchase. There will be no more kiting of checks. No more returned checks stamped insufficient funds. As the individual will not have any cash, nor will the retailer, robbery will be a thing of the past. The retailer will experience lower insurance premiums, or the next rate increase will be foregone, because of less risk due to the limited amount of cash he will have to deal with. Sound good? What is the negative side of a cashless society? He who operates the ATM system will have complete control over those who use it. Did you ever try to get cash out of an ATM when there was something wrong with your card? On a Saturday afternoon? How does all this relate to the Coming of Jesus Christ? Look to Rev 13:16-18 concerning the one called the Antichrist, "And he causeth all, both small and great, rich and poor, free and bond, to receive a mark in their right hand, or in their foreheads: And that no man might buy or sell, save he that had the mark, or the name of the beast, or the number of his name. Here is wisdom. Let him that hath understanding count the number of the beast: for it is the number of a man, and his number is Six hundred threescore and six." Before he that is called The Antichrist can make this demand of all who live on the earth, two things must happen, one is a computer system intelligent enough, fast enough, and large enough to manipulate the numbers of the population of the entire earth. I don't know if you are aware of the massive strides that have taken place in the computer industry in the last five years, but in the National Geographic of Oct 1982 the Japanese official Sozaburo Okamatsu of the Ministry for International Trade and Industry said, "Because we have only limited natural resources, we need a Japanese technological lead to earn money for food oil and coal. Until recently, we chased foreign technology, but this time we'll pioneer a second computer revolution. If we don't, we won't survive." He went on to state that they would have a prototype of a thinking computer by 1990, and a commercial product five years later. "It will be easy to use, By recognizing natural speech and written language, it will translate and type documents automatically. All you have to do is speak a command. If the machine doesn't understand, it will talk-ask questions. It will draw inferences and make its own judgments, based on knowledge of meanings as well as of numbers. It will learn too, by recalling and studying its errors." Shades of George Orwell in his book 1984. This is called artificial intelligence. The book of Revelations in the Bible calls it "The Beast." How urgent was this project? The Japanese ear marked 100 million for this eight year project, says a later reference. Sperry corp. committed 250 employees in 50 different AI projects, funding them with a commitment of 250 million dollars. This was in 1986. Computers have shrunk from room size to rack size to table top to portable to lap top to note book to palm top in just a few short years. Memories, that's what is needed to make the beast work, have increased in size numerically, exponentially. 64k was a big number ten years ago, now 64 meg is a nice number for today's 80486 desk tops. Chips are available with capacities that are beyond our imagination. The time is now. Enough for now.

    As I listened to the broadcast last Sunday, I wondered how many of you caught my mistake in about the middle of the broadcast? When I had a Sunday bus route we used to sing a song about Father Abraham having many sons. It went something like this, Father Abraham had many sons, and many sons had Father Abraham, I am one of them and so are you, so let's just praise the Lord. This very song precipitated this error. I said that Father Abraham put out our spiritual eye sight 5992 years ago. But in truth, it was Father Adam who took away our spirituality, our spiritual eye sight by allowing the flesh to dictate to the soul it's desires. You see, man is composed of a body, a soul, and a spirit. God formed Adam out of the dust of the earth, so the body is of the earth, earthly, 1 Cor 15:47 "The first man [that's Adam] is of the earth, earthy:" Made of the earth therefore of the earth. Gen 2:7 "And the LORD God formed man <of> the dust of the ground, and [breathed] into his nostrils the breath of life, and man became a living soul." God breathed the spirit of life into man, and the third part, the soul, was formed within a man. The spirit of man was meant for communication with God for it is of God and spiritual. The flesh was made for communication with the world or the earth as it is of the earth, earthly. The soul was meant to be sort of a liaison between the spirit and the flesh. When Adam decided to obey the dictates of the flesh in his supposed sacrifice for Eve, he was cut off from the spiritual side of man and became base or one who follows the dictates of the flesh. Always doing what pleases the body. No longer did Adam have spiritual eyes. Jesus Christ came to restore sight to our blinded eyes. When you or, if you've, decided to follow Christ by repenting of your sins, being baptized in the name of Jesus Christ for the remission of these sins, and receive the baptism of the Holy Ghost, then your spiritual sight will have been restored. The law of sin and death will no longer have dominion over you. You will see those things heavenly and begin to exercise a knowledge of the eternal. Please accept my apology for the error, it wasn't intentional.

Over the next several weeks I'd like to undertake a study of God's skilled craftsmen. My favorite has always been Paul the apostle. Paul, who himself said that he was an apostle born out of due season. Here was a man that had been taught by Jesus Christ himself, for Paul said in Gal 1:1 "Paul, an apostle, not of men, neither by man, but by Jesus Christ, and God the Father, who raised him from the dead," 1 Cor 15:8-10 "And last of all he was seen of me also, as of one born out of due time. For I am the least of the apostles, that am not meet to be called an apostle, because I persecuted the church of God. {10} But by the grace of God I am what I am: and his grace which was bestowed upon me was not in vain, but I labored more abundantly than they all: yet not I, but the grace of God which was with me. "

Each of the apostles had a distinct and individual ministry that followed along with their previous secular employment. Peter the fisherman. Mat 4:18 "And Jesus, walking by the sea of Galilee, saw two brethren, Simon called Peter, and Andrew his brother, casting a net into the sea: for they were fishers." Mat 4:19 "And he saith unto them, Follow me, and I will make you fishers of men." To Peter, Jesus gave the keys of the kingdom. The beginning, the entryway, the keys to the kingdom of heaven. Peter opened the door so that others could enter into the kingdom of heaven. Who was it that preached the first message on the day of Pentecost? It was Peter. Acts 2:14 "But Peter, standing up [with the eleven], lifted up his voice, and said unto them, Ye men of Judaea, and all <ye> that dwell at Jerusalem, be this known unto you, and hearken to my words:" Peter's ministry was the beginning of things. Three thousand souls received the word and were added to the church on that first day, the birth day of the church. Later, the church at Caesarea began when the Holy Ghost fell on Cornelius and his household. Peter was a pioneer ordained by God to make beginnings. Peter's message was salvation, salvation with the king and the kingdom in full view. His preaching placed emphasis upon salvation. He was truly an evangelist, and his burden was taking men alive just as a fisherman casts his nets into the sea and pulls in a draught of living fish. Jesus called him while he was casting his nets as a fisherman and so his ministry reflected his former occupation. I do not mean to infer that all our ministries will reflect our occupation at the time we came to Christ, it just simply a unique contrast, a peg to hang the studies of the apostles on. Next, comes the Apostle Paul. Totally different from Peter yet he too preached the gospel. There was no conflict between the ministries of Peter and Paul no more than there would be a conflict between Bro Sams and myself. their ministries were as different as ours are. Not that we comparer ourselves with these great men of God, but it illustrates a point. Gal 2 shows Paul's views the differences between their ministries and between themselves, These differences were geographical and racial and not personality problems: Reading from Gal 2:2-12 "But contrariwise, when they saw that the gospel of the un circumcision was committed unto me, as <the gospel> of the circumcision <was> unto Peter, (For he that wrought effectually in Peter to the apostleship of the circumcision, the same was mighty in me toward the Gentiles:) And when James, Cephas, and John, who seemed to be pillars, perceived the grace that was given unto me, they gave to me and Barnabas the right hands of fellowship, that we <should go> unto the heathen, and they unto the circumcision. Only <they would> that we should remember the poor, the same which I also was forward to do. {11} But when Peter was come to Antioch, I withstood him to the face, because he was to be blamed. {12} For before that certain came from James, he did eat with the Gentiles: but when they were come, he withdrew and separated himself, fearing them which were of the circumcision." Later initiated things, got them started, but Paul's task was to build, to construct. His task was to present the fullness of Christ. His was to bring all these into the fullness, into the body, perfecting them to be as Christ, a building fitly framed together. God isn't satisfied with his people just to become Christians and forever to sit in churches throughout the country, listening to sermons and taking up breathing space. God has this plan in view, that the Head, which is Christ, and his body, which is the Church, make up a new man called the Christ. You see, as one man ask of me at work, "If God is real, If Christ is real, then why hasn't he spoken to us in the last two thousand years?" To this man, and those around you, the only Christ they will ever hear or see, is you. 2 Cor 3:3 "<Forasmuch as ye are> manifestly declared to be the [epistle] of Christ ministered by us, written not with ink, but with the Spirit of the living God, not in tables of stone, but in fleshly tables of the heart." It's an awesome responsibility that, only in Christ, can we accomplish.   You see, you are the body of Christ. He is in you, perfecting you, bringing you to fruition, so that others might see Christ in you the hope of glory. We are his emissary, ambassadors if you please. 1 Cor 12:12 "For as the body is one, and hath many members, and all the members of that one body, being many, are one body: so also <is> Christ". Paul the master builder of 1 Cor 3:10 "According to the grace of God which is given unto me, as a wise master builder, I have laid the foundation, and another buildeth thereon. But let every man take heed how he buildeth thereupon." Building up a church, many congregations where ever he could find them. Building upon the foundation of Jesus Christ and not some foundation that would crumble under the stress of battle. Not just any building but one with the proper character and integrity. A master builder, one that handled the tools of his trade with the skill of a true craftsman. There are no cutting of the corners or inferior materials allowed in the building of God's temple. No substitutes. God has his People bonded together in love, framed and builded into a Holy temple, fitted to reveal and display the glories of Jesus Christ. This was Paul's ministry. All the lessons of his life, all his writings have this one end in view: that Christ might have the glorious Church that He died for.

at the last of Paul's ministry there were set backs and disappointments. In his letter to the Philippians Phil 2:21 "For all seek their own, not the things which are Jesus Christ's." And to Timothy he says of Asia: 2 Tim 1:15 "This thou knowest, that all they which are in Asia be turned away from me, of whom are Phygellus and Hermogenes." In revelations the first chapter, I'm afraid that all of the representative first churches had departed from his standard and were missing something of the divine purpose and intent.

Now is the time for John to come on the scene. He seemingly remained in the back ground until this appointed time.   But at this time, the apostle Paul had completed his earthly ministry and had went on to be with the Lord. the church needs a new, fresh distinctive emphasis to meet this new need. John's ministry is very different from Peter's or Paul's. John wasn't uniquely commissioned as Peter to begin something. The record shows that he was used at the beginning along side of Peter. He had not been entrusted in any particular distinctive way of making known the mysteries of the church. Doctrinally, he added nothing to Paul's revelation. With Paul, the things of God had reached a climax, an absolute, that couldn't be improved upon. Paul's concern is with the full realization of the plan of redemption and glory that had unfolded age by age, line upon line, here a little there a little, until in this special age of grace, it was made manifest in the birth death resurrection and exaltation of Jesus Christ. His burden was to present this plan in it's fullness, and to bring it to the full realization of his people, the church that Christ bought with his own body. His task was to express for the benefit of us all, something from the eternities now brought to light in time. For John to improve on this would have been inconceivable for it was that divine plan of God. How could one improve on what God has wrought? Why then, was there a need for a further ministry, the ministry of John? Because the enemy of our souls had entered into the house of God and caused God's own people to turn aside from the ways set down by Christ. Even those in Ephesus fell away. If you compare the epistle written by Paul to the church at Ephesus with that written in the book of Revelations, you can see something terrible had happened here. What then was John's ministry? To restore. The ministry of restoration. Nothing is said by John that is startlingly new or original. What distinguishes John's ministry is, his concern of bringing the people back to the position lost. John was called into discipleship while sitting on the shore with his brother, mending nets. So keeping in tune with the tenor of this lesson, John, with the ministry of restoration, is mending of fixing, restoring, bringing back to God's original plan. Peter first, with the ingathering of souls, Paul, the wise master builder, building according to the heavenly vision given to him by God, and then when failure threatened, we have John introduced to re-affirm that there is an original purpose still in view, and that it has never been abandoned. The original purpose and intent of God which he fully intends to fulfill, and will never be defected from. Three different ministries, all complementary to one another yet totally distinct from one another.

SALVATION   02/02/1992

PSM 45:1 MY HEART IS INDITING A GOOD MATTER:
I SPEAK THE THINGS WHICH I HAVE MADE TOUCHING THE KING:
MY TONGUE IS THE PEN OF A READY WRITER

I attempted to bring you a lesson of the Apostle Paul today. Yet I couldn't get past twelve minutes of the broadcast. Perhaps latter when I have more thoroughly study the life of the Apostles. Please be in prayer for Bro Sams and myself and our families.

In the book of Romans there's a division in the first eight chapters. From Romans 1:1 to 5:11 the subject is our sins. From Romans 5:12 to 8:39 the subject turns to sin. The first part deals with the sins committed before God by the Individual, while the second part deals with the sin principle at work inside of man. No matter how many sins you commit, it is provoked by the sin principle. You definitely need forgiveness from the sins you've committed but more than that you need deliverance from the sin principle dwelling within. Sin touches my conscience, but the sin power, the principle touches my life. You can receive forgiveness for your sins but you'll have no abiding peace of mind until you get deliverance from the sin principle within. When the light of Jesus Christ shines into my heart, the cry is for forgiveness, because of the awareness that my sins have been committed before and against Him. But once forgiveness of my sins is received, I discovered that not only has sins been committed before God but that there is something wrong inside. It's the nature of the sinner. There's a natural tendency to sin, it's a power inside that draws us to sin. When that power exercises it's strength, I sin. I again seek forgiveness. But the cycle repeats and sin is again committed. Sinning, forgiveness, sinning, and forgiveness, on and on it goes until the cycle is broken by death. I appreciate forgiveness but I want deliverance. I need the forgiveness, but I need deliverance from the sin nature that dwells inside. Total deliverance from what I am. And that deliverance comes from a new nature put within when you receive the Baptism of the Holy Ghost.

What then is the remedy? Here it is, it's The blood, the cross, and the new nature brought about by the infilling of the Holy Ghost.

In the first part of Romans there is reference to the blood of Christ, while 6:6 introduces us to our being crucified with Christ. The first part centers around the fact that the blood is shed for our justification through the remission of sins. Justification is to be vindicated, or just as if I'd never sinned. In the second part, the argument centers around the work of the Cross. By our union with Christ in his Death, burial, and resurrection by repentance, baptism and the infilling of the Holy Spirit, we become a new creature in Christ. The blood deals with what we have done. The cross deals with what we are while the Spirit deals with what we need to be. The blood covers our sins, The cross deals with our capacity to sin. We are crucified with Christ, which is the death of the flesh and the capacity to sin.

The problem of our lives being spotted no blackened by our sins must be delt with by the blood of Jesus Christ. The value of Christ's blood is clearly stated in Romans 5:8 "God commendeth his own love toward us, that, while we were yet sinners, Christ died for us. Much more then, being justified by his blood, we shall be saved from the wrath of God through him." How are we justified? Through his sin free blood.

Romans 3:24-26 "Being justified freely by his grace through the redemption that is in Christ Jesus: whom God hath set forth to be a propitiation through faith in his blood, to declare his righteousness for the remission of sins that are past, through the forbearance of God, to declare, I say, at this time his righteousness: that he might be just, and the justifier of him which believeth in Jesus."

You see, Sin enters as disobedience, and creates a separation between God and man. A wide gulf is fixed. God can no longer have fellowship with man. Who then is under the influence of sin? Romans 3:9 says that we are all under sin. So that sin in us, constitutes a barrier to fellowship with God. This barrier gives rise to a sense of guilt. Sin has provided Satan with grounds of accusation before God. Meanwhile our sense of guilt gives him grounds of accusation in our hearts, saying, "You've sinned, God'll have nothing at all to do with you".

To get us back into the fold, the body of Christ, Jesus had to do something with this threefold problem of sin, guilt, and Satan's accusation. Sin has to be delt with and is done with the precious sin free blood that Jesus shed on the cross. Guilt, next, has to be delt with and our guilty conscience is set at rest by the infilling of the Holy Ghost.

The blood of Christ operates on three fronts to remove us from the burden of sin, towards God, towards man and towards Satan. We need to recognize the value of the

Blood. It can't be emphasized enough. This is the first fundamental. The first step. The Prerequisite. We have to have a basic fundamental knowledge of the death of Jesus Christ as our substitute upon the cross for our sins. We have to have a clear understanding of the efficacy, the cleansing power, of the Blood of Christ, without this understanding, of Jesus' substitution death and the cleansing power of the blood, without this, there is no propitiation for our sins.

The blood is for the atonement and has to do with our standing with God. We need forgiveness for our sins, otherwise we'll come under judgments. And if judgment, then death. God doesn't overlook what we have done but the blood shed at Calvary covers this unrighteousness. God sees only the righteousness of Jesus Christ in this garment of righteous given to us by the blood. The blood is not for us but for God. it is not what value we place upon this precious blood but the value that God has placed upon it that matters. If we are to understand the value of the blood then we must accept the value placed upon it by God. Atone. Atonement. Webster says "to make expiation or amends for. To propitiate, appease, reconcile." reparation.

The one day that stands so prominently out in the Old Testament is the day of Atonement. Nothing explains the question of sin and the blood as well as the description of that day. In Leviticus 16 on the day of Atonement the blood was taken from the sin offering and brought into the Most Holy Place and there sprinkled before the Lord seven times. On this day, the sin offering was offered right in the open before all in the court of the tabernacle. But the LORD commanded that no man should enter the tabernacle but the High priest and that only once a year. It was this high priest alone who took the blood of atonement and going into the Holiest of Holies sprinkled this blood to make atonement for the sins of Israel. Why only the high priest? Because the high priest was a type of Jesus Christ in his redemptive work done on Calvary for your sins and mine. Hebrews 9:11,12 "But Christ being come an high priest of good things to come, by a greater and more perfect tabernacle, not made with hands, that is to say, not of this building, neither by the blood of goats and calves, but by his own blood he entered once into the holy place, having obtained eternal redemption for us." Only one act was performed in the Holiest of Holies, None but the high priest could draw near to it, one act, namely, the presenting of the blood of atonement to God. It was a transaction between the high priest and God, away from the eyes of those who were to benefit from it. God required it as such. The blood is therefore, not for ourselves but for God. Exodus 12:13 give the account of the shedding of the blood of a lamb, a Passover lamb, a lamb without spot or blemish, for Israel's redemption. The blood was put upon the doorposts and lintel, while the meat, the flesh of the lamb, was eaten inside the house, God said, "When I see the blood I will pass over you." The blood was not presented to God, not to man. The meat on the bones was for the man. The blood was put upon the door post and lintel where God would see but man wouldn't. The life is in the blood. That blood, Christ's blood, had to be poured out for me, for my sins. It was God's requirement that it be so. God is the one that requires the blood to satisfy his own righteousness. You see, God cannot tolerate sin. The blood of Christ, God manifest in the flesh, wholly satisfies by covering our sins with righteousness. God gave the requirements but he also gave the solution. There is a principle of the operation of God in this entire lesson. I can do all things through Christ Jesus which strengtheneth me. And simply that God won't put or require anything of you that He doesn't first give you the ability to perform.

Before you became a believer, your conscience was untroubled for the most part. You were dead in trespasses and sins. A dead man feels no pain nor the weight of sin., When a God awareness came upon you, your conscience was awakened and presented you with a real problem. The sense of sin and guilt can become so great that you can lose sight of the effectiveness of the blood. You should never be troubled that your sins are too large for the blood of Christ to cover. Martin Luther was down praying when the Devil came to him with a list of his sins. Luther asked him, "is that all of my sins". "No". and twenty some feet of written classified sins were unrolled. "Is that all of them." "Yes". "Well Write across them in big letters, Paid in full by the blood of Jesus Christ." Your sins are not too many or too large for the blood of Jesus Christ to cover. Repent of your sin, be baptized in the name of Jesus Christ for the remission of those sins and He will fill you with the Holy Ghost. Christ in you the hope of glory. We cannot estimate what the blood is for us. It doesn't work that way. The blood is first and foremost for God to see. We have to accept God's valuation of the blood. By accepting his valuation of the blood, we can find forgiveness and salvation. The debt has been paid. God is satisfied with the blood. Not according to our own valuation but according to His.

Hebrews 10:22 "Let us draw near with a true heart in full assurance of faith, having our hearts sprinkled from an evil conscience, and our bodies washed with pure water." Jeremiah 17:9 "The heart is deceitful above all things, and desperately wicked: who can know it?" Ezekiel 36:26 "A new heart also will I give you, and a new spirit will

I put within you: and I will take away the stony heart out of your flesh, and I will give you a heart of flesh. and I will put my spirit within you and cause you to walk in my statutes, and ye shall keep my judgments, and do them." the blood has satisfied God but it also has cleansed our conscience. God must do something more than cleanse our hearts for the heart is desperately wicked. It must be replaced. We don't clean up a shirt that is worn out and will become a rag. We replace it. the flesh is too dirty to clean and must be crucified with Christ. The work of God within us must be wholly new. Ezekiel 36:26 "A new heart also will I give you, and a new spirit will I put within you: and I will take away the stony heart out of your flesh, and I will give you a heart of flesh. and I will put my spirit within you and cause you to walk in my statutes, and ye shall keep my judgments, and do them." It just won't work without the Holy Ghost living, dwelling in you. It isn't written that the blood cleanses our hearts. Its work is not subjective in that way, but wholly objective, before God. Hebrews 10:22 "Let us draw near with a true heart in full assurance of faith, having our hearts sprinkled from an evil conscience, and our bodies washed with pure water."

    Having our hearts sprinkled from an evil conscience. "What is the meaning of this verse then, bro Johnson?" There was something between God and myself, an evil conscience. Whenever I sought to approach God, it reminded me of the barrier that stood between myself and him. But the blood removed this barrier and my conscience is cleared and the sense of guilt removed. I have no evil conscience towards God. A clear conscience void of offense, a heart of faith and a conscience clear of every accusation. These are essentials in dealing with God. An uneasy conscience makes for a shaky faith. We must know the up to date value of the Blood. Not that the blood has a valuation placed upon it by the stock market but that we must know God's value placed upon it every minute of our day. We are made near by the Blood. It never loses it efficacy. It never loses strength. My approach to God is never on my own merit. I approach God through his merit alone, and that by the blood, never through the thought that I've been extra nice today. Or that God owes me an audience for some great work that I've done. These count for nothing, nothing at all. I could not pay the price for one splinter from the tree that Jesus died upon, I come by way of the blood alone. It's a finished work. I can add nothing or take nothing away from it. I have nothing to do with it but accept God's valuation of it. I'm Dirt pure dirt, from the earth I came and to the earth I'll return, Thou art a worm o Jacob. What is man that thou art mindful of him? This is a work of Grace pure grace. Even though the temptation comes, making us to think that because

God has been dealing with us in a special way, because he has taken steps to bring to us something more of himself, that he has been teaching us the deeper lessons of the Cross, because of this he has set before us new standards, and we can only have a clear conscience when we reach these standards. A thousand times no! A clear conscience is never based upon some work that we have done. It's based on the work of Jesus Christ in the shedding of his blood. Today I've been a little better Christian. This morning I've read fifteen chapters of the Bible, so I can pray more effectively. Or maybe, Today, I'm depressed, I can't pray right now. Well just what is the basis of your approach to God? Is it the basis of your feelings? Or something far more secure, say, the blood of Christ? Keep in mind that, God looks at the blood. The unchangeable blood. the immutable blood. Therefore Your approach is always to be in boldness. Boldness given to you through the blood of Christ. It will never be, it can never be, through your own attainments. Whether you've had a good or bad day, whether you have sinned or not, your basis of approach is always the same, the blood of Christ. God's acceptance of that blood is the ground upon which you may enter into the Holiest of holies, there is no other.

What aspect does the blood have towards Satan? Rev 12:10 "And I heard a loud voice saying in heaven, Now is come salvation, and strength, and the kingdom of our God, and the power of his Christ: for the accuser of our brethren is cast down, which accused them before our God day and night." "The accuser of our brethren," The first chapter of Job shows Satan coming before God to accuse Job. Job 1:9 "Doth Job fear God for naught?" verse 11 and Satan says," Put forth thine hand now, and touch all that he hath, and he will curse thee to thy face." Adam's fall in the Garden of Eden this gave Satan a foothold with man. He had found a chink in the armor. A fracture in the rock. A place to get a toe hold in the sheer face of man's integrity. Now Romans 3:23 states the fact that, "All have sinned and come short of the glory of God." Set apart and estranged from God. Because of what man has done there is now inside a nature that renders God morally unable to defend man before Satan. It must be removed, this inward sin nature. The blood of Christ removes this nature in all who accept His sin free sacrifice. The blood effectively removes this great barrier and restores man's fellowship with God. This sin free man is now in favor with God and can face Satan without fear. 1 John 1:7 "But if we walk in the light, as he is in the light, we have fellowship one with another, and the blood of Jesus Christ his Son cleanseth us from all sin."   God is light and as we walk in the light with him, in spirit and truth, John 4:24 "God is a Spirit, and they that worship him must worship him in spirit and in truth,". The blood is able to cleanse us from every sin. There are no large or small sins. No black, red or white sins. No white lies or black lies, a lie is a lie so a sin is sin. No degrees of sin. Just sin and sin separates you from God, but the blood of Jesus Christ cleanses us from every sin. Since God sees all our sin in the light, and at our request for forgiveness, through the blood He forgives us of them, then what ground does Satan then have to accuse us before God? Romans 8:31 "If God be for us, who can be against us?" God simply points to Calvary and the blood that was shed for us. Romans 8:33 "Who shall lay any thing to the charge of God's elect? It is God that justifieth. Who is he that condemeth? It is Christ that died, yea rather , that is risen again, who is at the right hand of God, who also maketh intercession for us." Who shall separate us from the love of Christ?" The blood is sufficient. Christ having become a high priest....through his own blood, entered in once for all into the Holy place, obtaining eternal redemption for us. read it in Hebrews 9:11,12 He has been our high priest and Advocate for nearly two thousand years. He is the propitiation for our sins 1 John 2:1-2 "My little children, these things write I unto you, that ye sin not. And if any man sin, we have an advocate with the father, Jesus Christ the righteous: And he is the propitiation for our sins: and not for our's only, but also for the sins of the whole world." this does not mean that the sins of the whole world are automatically forgiven. They must ask forgiveness and believe in the cleansing value of the blood. God's valuation, not yours or mine.

"You've sinned, and you'll keep on sinning. You're weak, and God'll have nothing to do with you." This is the voice of the adversary accusing you in your conscience. Self sufficiency cause us to look within for some ground to dispel this thought. Without a proper answer, despair and depression at our helplessness overtakes our minds. Satan's greatest weapon of warfare is that he points to our sins and charges us with them before God and before our conscience. We accept his accusations and down we go. The big mistake is to think that you have some righteousness of your own. Your self sufficient. This desire for self righteousness is just the crack the devil needs to drive the wedge of doubt into our walk with God. Its' the old flanking movement. He gets you to look in one direction while he sneaks up on your backside and delivers the death blow. Until you learn to put absolutely no confidence in the flesh, for it is the very nature of flesh to sin, you'll not be able to be the Christian that you want to be. God is able to deal with our sins, but he can't, won't deal with the man under accusation, because this man is not trusting in the blood. It's work has already been done at Calvary. Christ is our advocate, but this man, this accused man, is siding with the accuser by listening to his lies. This man must recognize that he is unworthy of anything but death, only fit to be crucified. God alone can answer the accuser, not us. You shouldn't you try to answer the accuser with your good works. You must answer it as Martin Luther did. The blood of Jesus Christ paid for all my sins. His blood is sufficient for every sin. Our faith in the blood silences the charges of the devil and puts him to flight.

    Remember that you can do nothing in yourself, your faith has to be in the sin free blood that was shed for your sins and mine two thousand years ago. To accept this sin free sacrifice that Jesus has wrought, you must repent of your sins, turn from them, ask forgiveness, then be baptized in the name of Jesus Christ for the remission of your sins, and you shall receive the baptism of the Holy Ghost. It's a promise from God.

WHO CAN CONDEMN?   02/09/1992

PSM 45:1 MY HEART IS INDITING A GOOD MATTER:
I SPEAK THE THINGS WHICH I HAVE MADE TOUCHING THE KING:
MY TONGUE IS THE PEN OF A READY WRITER

Last week we covered how the Blood of Christ was shed for us and that the blood is for the atonement of the sins you and I have committed against God. The blood you see, satisfies God's requirement for holiness in us. The blood is for God and God alone. God values the blood in a way that you and I will not understand until we're with him. We further said, the blood operates on three fronts ,towards God ,man ,and Satan to relieve us from the guilt and burden of sin. The blood is for the atonement and has to do with our standing with God. God can see only the righteousness of Jesus Christ in the blood. The blood was not for us but for our standing with God. Therefore, Hebrews 10:22 says, "Let us draw near with a true heart in full assurance of faith, having our hearts sprinkled from an evil conscience, and our bodies washed with pure water. There was a barrier between God and myself caused by the sins I had committed. But the Pure sin Free blood of Jesus Christ has removed this barrier. My conscience is cleared and my sense of guilt removed. A clear conscience void of offense, a heart of faith, and a conscience clear of every accusation. Remember, A clear conscience is never based upon attainment or some work that we have done. It's based upon the work of Jesus Christ in the shedding of his righteous blood. God looks at the blood, the immutable blood, therefore your approach to God can always with boldness. The Blood has restored your fellowship with God. You are now in favor with God and you can face Satan without fear. 1 John 1:7 "But if we walk in the light, as he is in the light, we have fellowship one with another, and the blood of Jesus Christ his Son cleanseth us from all sin."   This is the answer THEN, Romans 8:31 "What shall we then say to these things? If God be for us, who can be against us? Who shall lay any thing to the charge of God's elect? It is God that justifieth. Who is he that condemneth? It is Christ that died, yea rather, that is risen again, who is even at the right hand of God, who also maketh intercession for us. Who shall separate us from the love of Christ? shall tribulation, or distress, or persecution, or famine, or nakedness, or peril, or sword?" The desire for self righteousness is the crack in our armor. This is all that Satan needs to drive a wedge of doubt into our walk with God. Don't let your drive for self sufficiency rob you of the glory that God has planned for your life. You mustn't put any confidence in the flesh, for it's very nature is to sin. We must have total faith and confidence in God. This includes believing in the cleansing power of the shed blood of Jesus Christ. the second lesson deals with the cross. The righteous blood is for forgiveness while the cross of Jesus Christ is for deliverance. The blood can wash away my sins but the old man remains. He needs crucified. The blood deals with the sin while the cross deals with the sinner. How many times have you tried to do the Christian thing? You tried with everything that was in you. Struggling and fighting to maintain a smile, say a kind word, just trying to be loving, but no, defeated, you must remember Romans 5:9 "Much more then, being now justified by his blood, we shall be saved from wrath through him." Lord, now I see. I can't do it in my own flesh. It's only by the blood and through death on the cross, being buried with Christ in the watery grave of baptism, through the resurrection by the Holy Ghost, that I can live, Galatians 2:20 "I am crucified with Christ: nevertheless I live, yet not I, but Christ liveth in me:" Through the infilling of the Holy Ghost you receive a new heart with the laws of God written in it.

2 Corinthians 5:17 "Therefore if any man be in Christ, he is a new creature: old things are passed away, behold, all things are become new." Now the word of God tells you: Romans 6:12 "Let not sin therefore reign in your mortal body, that ye should obey it in the lusts thereof" Romans 6:13 "Neither yield ye your members as instruments of unrighteousness unto sin: but yield yourselves unto God, as those that are alive from the dead, and your members as instruments of righteousness unto God." Romans 6:14 "For sin shall not have dominion over you: for ye are not under the law, but under grace." The twelfth verse said, "Let not," It's a clear case of willingness. A choice that must be made. Sin has no dominion over you for you are a new creature in Christ. Now there abides in your heart a willingness to serve God and not sin. Your frustration comes from trying to do it your way. Remember Proverbs 14:12 "There is a way which seemeth right unto a man, but the end thereof are the ways of death." There is the mandatory death on the cross. Romans 6:6 "Knowing this, that our old man is crucified with him, that the body of sin might be destroyed, that henceforth we should not serve sin." We have a more intimate position on the cross then the two thieves. They were crucified beside Jesus but we were crucified with him. Your life ends and begins at the cross

CHRIST IS MY FRIEND   02/23/1992

PSM 45:1 MY HEART IS INDITING A GOOD MATTER:
I SPEAK THE THINGS WHICH I HAVE MADE TOUCHING THE KING:
MY TONGUE IS THE PEN OF A READY WRITER

Have you ever had a friend that you just loved to be around? Jesus Christ will never take advantage of a relationship. He is a true friend that sticketh closer than a brother. Jesus won't let you down no matter how many times you may fail him. Mat 18:21 "Then came Peter to him, and said, Lord, how oft shall my brother sin against me, and I forgive him? Till seven times? Jesus saith unto him, I say not unto thee, until seven times: but until seventy times seven." If Jesus Christ expects you to forgive 70 times 7, then how much do you think he will forgive you? He won't even keep track. You've failed? Get up, dust yourself off. Ask Christ to forgive you and forgive yourself. Repent. That means, you won't do it again.

I'll tell you how wonderful Jesus is, Psms 103:13 "Just as a father has compassion on his children, so the Lord has compassion on them that fear Him." He takes our sins and puts them as far away as the east is from the west. Psm 103:12 "As far as the east is from the west , so far hath he removed our transgressions from us." This is not a license to sin. Galatians 5:13 says "..ye have been called unto liberty, only use not liberty for an occasion to the flesh, but by love serve one another." and 1 Pet 2:16 "As free, and not using your liberty for a cloak of maliciousness, but as the servants of God." Let the Word teach you how that Christ has freed us from the bondage of the law and of sin. Luke says that, Jesus stood in the synagogue on the Sabbath day and there was brought a book, the book of Isaiah, for him to read, and when he had opened the book and found the place where it was written. "The spirit of the Lord is upon me, because he hath anointed me to preach the gospel to the poor, he hath sent me to heal the broken hearted, to preach deliverance to the captives, and recovering of sight to the blind, to set at liberty them that are bruised, to preach the acceptable year of the Lord. And he closed the book, and gave it again to the minister, and sat down. And the eyes all of them that were in the synagogue were fastened on him. And he began to say unto them, This day is this scripture fulfilled in your ears." He had stopped reading Isaiah at a comma, and not a period. And that was the reason they all looked at him, waiting for him to finish the scripture reading. But, he said, "today is this scripture fulfilled in your ears." He proclaimed himself to be the messiah, the Christ.

The rest of the scripture read, "and the day of vengeance of our God, to comfort all that mourn, To appoint unto them that mourn in Zion, to give beauty for ashes, the oil of joy for mourning, the garment of praise for the spirit of heaviness, that they might be called trees of righteousness, the planting of the LORD, that he might be glorified." They were waiting for Jesus to finish the scripture reading. They all knew it so well. Instead, he spoke, "This day is this scripture fulfilled in your ears."

Jesus Christ came to heal the brokenhearted, The last part of the verse is for his second coming. He stopped at a comma because the rest of the Scripture would have carried us into the second coming of Christ, after this present age had come to an end. Now is the acceptable time. Now is the day of salvation.

Jesus came to heal the broken hearted.

Are you suffering?

To set a liberty them that are bruised.

Are you beaten and bruised by the trials and tribulations of today and by sin?

To preach deliverance to the captives.

Are you a slave to sin?

Are you a slave to what and who you are?

To preach the acceptable year of the Lord.

Every fiftieth year was the year of Jubilee. The year that every man received his possessions back and every man was returned to his own family. Isn't it strange that Pentecost is fifty days from the Passover, from Easter? The Holy Ghost was given on the day of Pentecost. The only liberty that has ever been given, is the spiritual liberty given by the Holy Ghost. In the year of the Jubilee, those that had been sold into slavery for payment of a debt were set free. The land that had to be sold went back to it's original owner, there wasn't such a thing as a foreclosure. God had given the land, not man, and God set it up so that a few wouldn't wind up with all. Fifty years and everything was restored to it's original owners. It was the great emancipation every fifty years. The acceptable year of the Lord. Jesus came to restore those that were sold into sin by the desires of the flesh. Sold on the auction block of sin. Romans 6:23 says "For the wages of sin is death," Sin has a price, a high price, a very high price. It's Death. Eternal death.

Forever death. I'm telling you, A Man can't bargain to sell his soul to the Devil, more than likely, it's already been bought for some meager price. The acceptable year of the Lord. This year could very well be the greatest year you have ever known, if. Child of God, to you he says, "The night is far spent, the day is at hand: let us therefore cast off the works of darkness, and let us put on the armor of light. Let us walk honestly, as in the day, not in rioting and drunkenness, not in chambering and wantonness, not in strife and envying, but put on the Lord Jesus Christ, and make not provision for the flesh, to fulfill the lusts thereof." Gal 5:1 "Stand fast therefore in the liberty wherewith Christ hath made us free, and be not entangled again with the yoke of bondage."

"The spirit of the Lord is upon me, because he hath anointed me to preach the gospel to the poor, he hath sent me to heal the broken hearted, to preach deliverance to the captives, and recovering of sight to the blind, to set a liberty them that are bruised, to preach the acceptable year of the Lord." "To set at liberty them that are bruised,"

Mat 12:20 says "A bruised reed shall he not break, and a smoking flax shall he not quench, till he send forth judgment unto victory." A reed, A single reed, a weak bruised reed. A state of weakness that borders on total spiritual death. Life deals us some very hard lessons

Most are to the heart, to the depth of our very soul. Some are killing wounds that take the life out of us, but they don't have to be. Jesus was despised and rejected of all men. I've never known that feeling, have you? You see though, Jesus had nothing to prove to anyone. We try to prove our worthiness to others and in doing so, we leave ourselves open for devastating blows to the ego. You don't need the acceptance of others, you need acceptance into the family of God. The body of Christ. You need to please God and not man. If indeed you do please God, no man can point a finger of accusation at you. None can cluck their accusing tongue at you. God or man? Whose servant are you? Please God and not man. The Lord Jesus wants you to succeed in all your endeavors. He will not break or crush you, He will gently, ever so gently heal your bruises. And a smoking flax shall he not quench. Flax was used as the wick in oil lamps. But after all the oil had been burnt out of the lamp, used up, the flax would continue to smoke. The lamp is your lamp to light the way for others to see Christ in you. The oil is the Holy Ghost which you receive when you repented of your sins and was baptized in to that Name above all names, Jesus Christ. If the oil has run out of your life, your flax will smoke, but Jesus won't put out your small smoking flame, He'll encourage you to seek the oil of the Holy Ghost by compassionate wooing. Jesus won't quench even the slightest amount of desire you have for salvation, friend. He will treat you with greatest tenderness you have ever known, encouraging you to seek after him. "A bruised reed shall he not break, and a smoking flax shall he not quench," "The spirit of the Lord is upon me, because he hath anointed me to preach the gospel to the poor, he hath sent me to heal the broken hearted, to preach deliverance to the captives, and recovering of sight to the blind, to set a liberty them that are bruised, to preach the acceptable year of the Lord. "But the fruit of the Spirit is Love, joy, peace, longsuffering, gentleness, goodness, faith, meekness, temperance: against such there is no law. And they that are Christ's have crucified the flesh with the affections and lusts." Does that say anything to you?

The apostle Peter, close to the Lord, part of the inner circle, one that was quick to let the Lord know that he would stand with him even to the end. Good ol Peter, Cephas, the rock, the one that got out of the boat to walk on the water. The fisherman. Good ol Peter. Jesus said, "Whom do men say that I am?" Peter said, "Thou art the Christ." later "Peter answered and said unto him, though all men shall be offended because of thee, yet will I never be offended." Jesus said unto him, "Verily I say unto thee, That this night, before the cock crow, thou shalt deny me Three times. Peter said unto him, Though I should die with thee, yet will I not deny thee." That night, the very same night, Peter slept while Jesus prayed, And he cometh unto the disciples, and findeth them asleep, and saith unto Peter, "What, could ye not pray with me one hour?" He then went back to prayer And he came and found them asleep again: for their eyes were heavy. And he left them, and went away again, and prayed the third time, it was this night that Jesus was captured in the Garden of Gethsemane. Then, all the disciples forsook him, and fled. And they that had laid hold on Jesus led him away to Caiaphas the high priest, where the scribes and the elders were assembled. But Peter followed him afar off unto the high priests palace, and went in, and sat with the servants, to see the end....Now Peter sat without in the palace: and a damsel came unto him, saying, Thou also wast with Jesus of Galilee. But he denied before them all, saying, "I know not what thou sayest." And when he was gone out into the porch, another maid saw him, and said unto them that were there, "This fellow was also with Jesus of Nazareth." And again he denied with an oath, "I do not know the man." And after a while came unto him the that stood by, and said to Peter, "Surely thou also art one of them, for thy speech betrayed thee." Then began he to curse and to swear, saying, "I know not the man." And immediately the cock crew. And Peter remembered the word of Jesus, which said unto him, "Before the cock crow, thou shalt deny me thrice." And he went out, and wept bitterly. Have you ever failed Jesus to the point that you've went and wept bitterly? Thoroughly discussed with yourself? Discouraged by your actions? I think that Peter probably spent the next three days with his face hidden from all.(Mark 16:7) Later, after Jesus was resurrected and seen of Mary Magdalene and the other Mary, the young man in the sepulcher. And the angel said to them to go and tell the disciples and Peter what they had seen. The next time you read of Peter was on the first day of the week in Luke 24:12 "Then arose Peter, and ran unto the sepulcher, and stooped down, and beheld the linen clothes laid by themselves, and departed, wondering in himself at that which was come to pass. Later in John, Peter, Thomas, Nathanael, the sons of Zebedee, and two other disciples went fishing. Fished all night and caught nothing. When morning was come, Jesus stood on the shore: but the disciples knew not that it was Jesus. then Jesus saith unto them, Children have ye any meat? They answered No. And he said unto them, Cast your net on the right side if the ship, and ye shall find." The first to recognize that it was Jesus was Peter. He didn't walk on the water this time. He dove in and swam to the Lord of Glory. After they were done eating the fish that Jesus had prepared for them, Jesus turned to Peter, Simon, son of Jonas, "lovest thou me more than these?" "Yea Lord, thou knowest that I love thee." "Feed my sheep." He saith it him again the second time, "Simon son of Jonas, lovest thou me?" "Yea lord, thou knowest that I love thee." He saith unto him, "Feed my sheep." He saith unto him the third time, "Simon son of Jonas, lovest thou me?" Peter was grieved because he said unto him the third time Lovest thou me? "Lord thou knowest all things: thou knowest that I love thee." "Feed my sheep. Verily verily I say unto thee, when thou wast young thou girdest thyself, and walkest whither thou wouldest: but when thou shalt be old, thou shalt stretch forth thy hands and another shall gird thee, and carry thee whither thou wouldest not." Peter turned and saw John asking Jesus "which is he that betrayeth thee? And what shall we do with him?" Jesus said "If I will that he tarry till I come, what is that to thee?" Peter denied, bitterly denied Jesus yet Jesus delt with him with compassion that is unheard of in our lives. Peter, lovest thou me more than these? I don't know what that does to you friend but I want to weep. Peter denied Christ, yet he was forgiven. Backsliders, Come home to Jesus. Young men and women, Older folks, children, come back to the Father's house. This is revival folks.   Isaiah 53:2 "For he shall grow up before him as a tender plant, and as a root out of dry ground: he hath no form nor comeliness, and when we shall see him, there is no beauty that we should desire him. He is despised and rejected of men, a man of sorrows, and acquainted with grief: and we hid as it were our faces from him:"

John 21:25 "And there are also many other things which Jesus did, the which, if they should be written every one, I suppose that even the world itself could not contain the books that should be written. "

Galatians 5:22 "The Fruit of the Spirit is love, joy, peace, longsuffering, gentleness, goodness, faith, meekness, temperance." In this person there is no malice. There is absolutely no hard feelings for anyone in your heart. You believe what ever anyone tells you. You do not loose your temper at anyone. On and on this list goes. Only with the Holy Ghost alive and well in your life can you live this kind of life. How would it feel if you didn't have any hard feelings? Peter, full of failures, full of denials of Christ, full of self seeking, is like the story of many of our lives. Just can't seem to make the grade that we have set for ourselves. You think that you are unworthy of any consideration by Jesus Christ. Well, he didn't come to seek and save those that didn't need or want him. That didn't need his help. The worst thing that could have ever been said was the statement that "God helps them that help themselves." If you can help yourself then why do you need God? Only when you quit struggling in your own power and rely upon the Lord will he help you out of your troubles. It's hard to realize that the greatest part of the troubles we have are of our own creation. We've been taught throughout our lives that you got yourself into trouble, get yourself out. Some times it's like chewing fat, the more you chew the bigger it gets. Troubles are that way, They just keep growing the more we worry over them. Responsibility, you broke it you fix it. All our lives we've been taught, your responsible for your own actions. You broke it, you fix it. That's good, we must be responsible to live in society. It's necessary to be responsible for your actions. What kind of society would it be if we were to blame everyone else for our own ignorance? One where every thing you buy has a disclaimer of responsibility for misuse on it. "Do not intentionally concentrate fumes." "May be hazardous to your health." "Do not place hands or feet under mowing deck" "Cigarette smoking may be hazardous to your health." "The manufacture cannot take responsibility for any misuse intended or accidental." We must have responsibility for our own actions. You'll stand before God and give an account for your actions. You'll have no one to argue your case then. But with our own children, now, today, we wouldn't hesitate to help our children out of trouble. Or maybe, it should be put, Help them while they are in their troubles. Give them support, counseling, encouragement. We are a delight to our heavenly Father.

He is more careful about His children then we could ever be. Why don't you just lean back into His arms and let Him take over? Let him strengthen you in your time of trouble. He wants to.

Jesus had told the disciples to get into a ship and to go to the other side of the sea while he, Jesus, sent the multitude away. Mat 14:23 "But the ship was now in the midst of the sea, tossed with the waves: for the wind was contrary. And in the fourth watch of the night Jesus went unto them, walking on the sea. And when the disciples saw him walking on the sea, they were troubled, saying It is a spirit, and they cried out for fear. But straightway Jesus spake unto them saying, Be of good cheer, it is I, be not afraid." The storms of life have your ship about ready to sink? Darkness is all about you? You think that you're in the boat alone? Then the voice comes soft and sweet, "Be of good cheer, it is I." And Peter answered him and said, "Lord, if it be thou, bid me come unto thee on the water." And he said, "Come." When the storms of life rage, then will come the times of closeness with Jesus, when you of your own will and intent could never do what Jesus would help you to do. "Master if it be thou, bid me come unto thee on the water." And when Peter was come down out of the ship, he walked on the water, to go to Jesus. But when he saw the wind boisterous, he was afraid, and beginning to sink, he cried, saying, "Lord save me." And immediately Jesus stretched forth his hand, and caught him, and said unto him, "O thou of little faith, wherefore didst thou doubt?" Just think there were twelve on that boat but only Peter got out and walked on the water. Was Peter impetuous, or doubting his own ability, or just in love with the Savior? We need some of that out of the boat faith in Christ. There's something to be said for just doing, just trusting to the Lord, without figuring if it will happen or not. I know there was a grin on Jesus' face when Peter got out of the boat. Like a father with a child's first step. Wherefore dist thou doubt? Jesus was happy that Peter got out of the boat. Peter began to sink, Jesus grabbed him. Get the point. If your walking on the waters by faith and you begin to sink through self doubt, I can't, I can't, Jesus will rescue you, your there by faith in the operation of God. But the only thing that keeps you from walking by faith is your unbelief, your doubt in your ability to trust in God. You either don't believe that God will regard your prayers, or you simply don't think God hears you. I understand that I've been there. Unworthy of consideration. Unworthy of a second glance. Unworthy of forgiveness. Unworthy of Calvary. Unworthy of the Master's touch. "Just as I am without one plea, but that thy blood was shed for me and that thou bidd'st me come to thee *Charlotte Elliott* 1835 just as I am Friend, It's not because we're worthy of the blood of Christ. It's not because we deserve salvation. It's not because of righteousness of our own doing. No, It is simply because of the Grace of God. Grace, not worthiness. Grace, not because we deserve it. Grace, free grace. Anything other than free grace isn't grace at all. You fell. You've slipped. You were Christian and you've sinned. Well, while your laying face down in the mud crying about your failure, think how it would be if every child that ever tried to walk, stayed down when he fell. No one would walk would they? Push yourself up to your knees, ask God to forgive you for your indiscretion. Get up and carry on. Look, the time is very short. The rapture is at hand. The master says "Arise, my love, my fair one, and come away." the winter of your desolation is past, spring is here, life has come again to you. Reach out like that woman with the issue of blood, all her money spent on a cure, now reaching out to touch the hem of the garment of the Master. Healing is in that touch. Lift up the hands that hang down, and the feeble knees, and make straight paths for your feet. Jesus wants to be your ever present help in time of need. Your rock in a weary and desolate land. Your rose of Sharon. Your lily of the valley of your life. Yea though I walk through the valley of the shadow of death. Life is that valley. Let the shepherd of your soul guide you around the thorns and rocky places of life. Jesus loves you like no other person could ever love you. Lift up your hands right now and call on him. Jesus, Jesus, Jesus. He needs no explanation. He knows. Just acknowledge him. "Master, if it be thou, bid me come. Help master I'm drowning." Feel his hand slip into yours. Feel the load being lifted? Jesus I love you.

THE HOLY GHOST   03/01/1992

PSM 45:1 MY HEART IS INDITING A GOOD MATTER:
I SPEAK THE THINGS WHICH I HAVE MADE TOUCHING THE KING:
MY TONGUE IS THE PEN OF A READY WRITER

Rom 5:5   And hope maketh not ashamed, because the love of God is shed abroad in our hearts by the Holy Ghost which is given unto us.

Rom 8:9   But ye are not in the flesh, but in the Spirit, if so be that the Spirit of God dwell in you. Now if any man have not the Spirit of Christ, he is none of his.

The Christian has absolutely nothing to boast of. Forgiveness and salvation was given as a gift, we can neither add to nor take anything away from this gift.

At the very center of the Christian's life there lives an experience known as the infilling of the Holy Ghost, The baptism of the Spirit. Without the love of God in your hearts, you'll never fulfill the plan that Christ has for your life. there's more, much more to IT then just being baptized. Much more than making a profession of faith. More than a handshake or signing a card.

Romans 5:5 " And hope maketh not ashamed, because the love of God is shed abroad in our hearts by the Holy Ghost." and Romans 8:9 "But ye are not in the flesh, but in the Spirit, if so be that the Spirit of God dwell in you. Now if any man have not the Spirit of Christ, he is none of his." the love of God is shed abroad in our hearts by the Holy Ghost, without the indwelling spirit of Christ you can have neither the Love of God in your heart nor can you have salvation. "Now if any man have not the Spirit of Christ, he is none of his." God doesn't give his gifts at random, or in an arbitrary manner. The Holy Ghost is given freely to whosoever will but on a definite basis. To receive the Baptism of the Spirit, you must know upon what grounds it may be received.

The old Testament saints were not so favored as we are. They desired to look into what we are freely given now. The Spirit of God was not freely given to whosoever would in the Old Testament times. In this day and age it's easy to take lightly the infilling of the Holy Ghost. There are hundreds of thousands of people who have received the in filling of the Holy Ghost. Once you have received the Holy Spirit, you'll understand just how precious a blessing this experience actually is. Just think, we can receive the same Spirit that just rested upon Moses, David, Samuel, and Elijah. We become as David's mighty men of valor, we become chosen servants of God. We join the ranks of the Old testament Prophets as chosen servants. The value of this Gift is without measure. No mere human can put a value upon something as precious as this. Once you realize the value of this gift of God, and see your need for it, you'll not hesitate to receive the Holy Ghost.

Upon what basis has Jesus Christ poured out his Spirit upon all men? What does it take to be baptized with his Spirit? How can you receive this Holy Ghost? Turn to the book of the Acts of the Apostles 2:32-36 "This Jesus hath God raised up, whereof we all are witnesses. Therefore being by the right hand of God exalted, and having received of the Father the promise of the Holy Ghost, he hath shed forth this, which ye now see and hear. For David is not ascended into the heavens: but he saith himself, the Lord said unto my Lord, Sit thou on my right hand, until I make thy foes thy footstool. Therefore let all the house of Israel know assuredly, that God hath made that same Jesus, whom ye have crucified, both Lord and Christ." Jesus Christ was exalted and at the right hand of God, the hand of power, and there, received of the Father, the promise of the Holy Ghost, {not having received the Holy Ghost for Jesus Christ's spirit is the Holy Ghost, but receiving the promise.} Keep in mind that the Holy Ghost had never been given to any one before that faithful day near two thousand years ago, the day of Pentecost. Always before, it was the anointing of the Holy Ghost it was never the infilling or indwelling. The promise Jesus Received of the Father is this infilling of the body of Christ. John the Baptist had the Holy Ghost from his mother's womb but this was not this same infilling that took place on the day of Pentecost. Because Jesus Christ is exalted, the Holy Ghost is given. Who is the Spirit or Holy Ghost? In John 14:6 Jesus says, "I am the way the truth and the life: no man cometh unto the Father, but by Me." and in verse 16 "And I will pray the Father, and he shall give you another comforter, that he may abide with you forever," Jesus says here, that he would pray the Father and he would send the Comforter, that you can dwell with God forever. The other side of this verse is, without the Comforter you'll be in eternity without God. Jesus goes on in verse 17 to say, "Even the Spirit of Truth," who is the Truth? In verse 6, Jesus says I am the truth. Going on, "Even the Spirit of Truth, whom the world cannot receive," WHY Not? "because it seeth him not, neither knoweth him: but ye know him, for he dwelleth with you, and shall be in you." Who dwelt with the disciples? Jesus did. Jesus goes on to say, "I will not leave you comfortless:" what do you mean Lord? I will not leave you as orphans, I will come to you. Who is the comforter Lord? Look at verse 26. "But the comforter, which is the Holy Ghost." The Holy Ghost is the comforter. The Holy Ghost is the spirit of Truth. The Holy Ghost is the Spirit of the resurrected Christ. The spirit of Christ in you. The hope of glory. Because Jesus died on the cross for you, there is available to you, forgiveness for your sins: because Jesus Christ was buried and rose from the grave, from the dead, you can be buried with him in baptism, and you can receive newness of life through the resurrecting Spirit of the Holy Ghost. 1 Cor 15:44-46 "It is sown a natural body, it is raised a spiritual body. There is a natural body, and there is a spiritual body. And so it is written, The first man Adam was made a living soul, the last Adam <was made> a quickening spirit. Howbeit that <was> not first which is spiritual, but that which is natural, and afterward that which is spiritual." Born of the flesh, natural, and as the first man Adam subject to death because of sin, you die with Christ on the cross and the old Adam is buried as a dead man with Christ only to be resurrected as a new man in the second Adam which was and is a quickening, life giving, Spirit. Because Jesus has been exalted, you can receive the Holy Ghost. All of this is because of him and what he has done for you. None of this great holy work is based upon your merit. All of it is based upon Jesus' death burial and resurrection and upon the pure unmerited favor called grace. The infilling of the Holy Ghost is not based on any human merit but upon Christ's exaltation. Acts 2:36 "Therefore let all the house of Israel know assuredly, that God hath made that same Jesus, whom ye have crucified, both Lord and Christ." Therefore, connects together verse 33 with verse 36.."Acts 2:33 Therefore being by the right hand of God exalted, and having received of the Father the promise of the Holy Ghost, he hath shed forth this, which ye now see and hear. he hath shed forth this, which ye now see and hear." verse 36 Therefore Let all the house of Israel know assuredly, that God hath made him both lord and Christ, this Jesus whom ye have crucified." This outpouring of the Spirit, which you have both seen and heard, {there is a visible and audible indication that one has received the Holy Ghost} . This outpouring of the Spirit, which you have both seen and heard, proves that Jesus of Nazareth whom ye crucified is now both Lord and Christ. The promise was made back some 800 years before the day of Pentecost in Joel 2:28 and spoken of in Acts 2:16 17 "But this is that which was spoken of by the prophet Joel, And it shall come to pass in the last days, saith God, I will pour out my Spirit upon all flesh: and your sons and daughters shall prophecy, and your young men shall see visions, and your old men shall dream dreams: And on my servants and on my handmaidens I will pour out in those days of my Spirit, and they shall prophesy:" What happened on that faithful day 2000 years ago? What did Peter mean when he said ,"that which you see and hear"? What sign followed these believers when they received the Holy Ghost? Acts 2:4 "And they were all filled with the Holy Ghost, and began to speak with other tongues, as the Spirit gave them utterance." Acts 10:45-46 "And they of the circumcision which believed were astonished, as many as came with Peter, because that in the gentiles also was poured out the gift of the Holy Ghost. For they heard them speak with tongues, and magnify God. Then answered Peter, Can any man forbid water, that these should not be baptized, which have received the Holy ghost as well as we?" and Chapter 11:15 still speaking of these people, "and as I began to speak, the Holy Ghost fell on them, as on us at the beginning." Acts 19:2-6 " He said unto them, Have ye received the Holy Ghost since ye believed? And they said unto him, We have not so much as heard whether there be any Holy Ghost. And He said unto them, Unto what then were ye baptized? And they said, Unto John's baptism. then said Paul, John verily baptized with the baptism of repentance, saying unto the people, that they should believe on him which should come after him, that is on Christ Jesus. When they heard this, they were baptized in the name of the Lord Jesus. And when Paul had laid his hands upon them, the Holy Ghost came upon them, and they spake with tongues, and prophesied." What are the requirements for you to receive forgiveness of your sins? What do you have to do to obtain forgiveness? Child of God, do you have to walk from Roanoke to Peoria on your hands and knees? Do you have to carry a cross with a wheel on it from Springfield to Chicago? Do you have to make a trip to Jerusalem and crawl on your knees from Pilate's Judgment hall to the place of the skull, Golgotha, where Christ was crucified, to receive forgiveness for your sins? Must you give all your riches to those in need, do penitence, and kiss a ring to obtain forgiveness for your sins? No friend of mine, the price has been paid, there is nothing you can pay or do to earn or get forgiveness. It's free. What must I do to receive the gift of the Holy Ghost? How were you justified? Simply by accepting the fact that the Lord had done everything. The baptism of the Holy Ghost comes the same way. Put your faith in the fact that the Lord has already done it. The whole question is one of faith. As soon as you see Jesus Christ on the Cross, you'll know that your sins are forgiven, likewise, as soon as you put Jesus Christ on the throne of your life, the Holy Spirit will be poured out upon you. the basis of receiving the Holy Ghost is not how much you fast and pray and wait and seek, but the veneration, the exaltation of Christ in your life. the Spirit is not given on the basis of who we are but of what Christ is. Suppose a person desires to find salvation. You explain to them the way of salvation and the person prays, "Lord, I believe that you have died for me and you can blot out all of my sins. I believe you will forgive me." do you have any confidence in this type of prayer? Shouldn't it be as this, "Jesus, thank you for forgiving me of my sins. You have died for me. My sins are gone. Thank you Jesus." Praise is the key to the heart of God. Thanksgiving is the garment of the righteous. You want the Holy Ghost? Praise Him for your salvation and for the Holy Spirit. The work has been done. It is called a Gift. You just receive a gift you don't beg for it. The Spirit has been poured out because Jesus has been Glorified. No single person, need to agonize over receiving the baptism of the Holy Ghost for the Spirit is already given. Keep in mind that Jesus cannot be made Lord for he is already Lord. But you need to make him the Lord of your life. It is a question of faith by revelation. When your eyes are opened that the Spirit is already given because Jesus has already been glorified, then your prayer will turn to praise and you'll receive the baptism of the Holy Ghost. All of God's spiritual gifts come by way of a definite basis. There are conditions that have to be fulfilled before reception is possible. In God's word, the book of Acts the second chapter the thirty eighth and ninth verses, "Repent and be baptized every one of you in the name of Jesus Christ for the remission of sins, and ye shall receive the gift of the Holy Ghost. For the promise is unto you, and to your children, and to all that are afar off, even as many as the lord our God shall call."

Four things; two conditions and two gifts.
1. repentance,
2. baptism,
3. forgiveness,
4. and the Holy ghost baptism.

The first condition, repentance, a change of mind. You thought the world was a good, pleasant, and attractive place, but now you know better. Once you thought sin was fun, but now you know different, Once you thought Godly things to be boring. But now you find them in high esteem. This is repentance, it's a changing of your mind, it's a turning around from the way of death. Actually, that repentance is available for you is in it's self a great gift. Baptism is the second condition. Baptism is faith in action. James 2:20 "But wilt thou know, O vain man, that faith without works is dead?" verse 17 "Even so faith if it hath not works, is dead, being alone." Baptism is a washing away, a burying of the old man and his sins with him. God offers you two things if you fulfill these two conditions. What does hinder your answer? A forgiven sinner is different from a ordinary sinner, and a consecrated Christian is very much different from an ordinary Christian. I'm not sure there is such a thing as an unconsecrated Christian only time will tell. Can you even be Christian without consecration? This isn't some vow that you take or form of worship that you study. The true issue is the lordship of your life. You can't bargain with God. There are no tradeoffs in this thing called Christianity. You can't be, what God wants you to be when your in charge of your own life. The real issue is, the spirit filled, Spirit led, Christian life cannot be realized with out the Holy Ghost baptism, the Spirit of Christ living in you. You can live a good life, you can be Christian in you behavior, deportment and manners but when you stand before Christ, what will be his judgment of your life? Will his words be? "Enter in thou good and faithful servant," or will they be, "depart from me for I never knew you." Your life assurance is easy to obtain. Repent of your sins and be baptized in the name of Jesus Christ for the remission of your sins and you will receive the baptism of the Holy Ghost. For the promise is unto you and your children and to those that are afar off, even as many as the Lord our God shall call.

This is Bro. Randy Johnson for the We preach Jesus Ministries may the Lord God Almighty show you and fill you with the Baptism of the Holy Ghost. You have never experienced true love until you experience divine love.

Bro Sams and I would like to invite you to the First United Pentecostal Church of Peoria Illinois located at 3510 West Malone Street in Peoria and the United Pentecostal Church 101 grove street of Pontiac, Illinois.

This last week has seen a great youth revival at the Peoria Church. Jesus Christ ministered in the preaching of the Word of God. Such a wonderful presence of God was made known. Now God fills all of heaven and earth so HE is everywhere at once, but He reveals, makes known his presence on special occasions with such a feeling of love as you have ever known. Pure, unadulterated love, untouched by the frailties of humanity. Pure, 100%, not 99.44, but 100% pure. I wish all of you could have been there to be blessed of the Lord God Almighty. It would give Bro Sams and Myself pleasure to hear from those who enjoy this broadcast. Just drop us a card at the We Preach Jesus Ministries PO box 274 Eureka, Ill . If you want a copy of this or any of the messages preached during the last year, just say so.

We're praying for you folks. we hope that this and the other broadcasts will be of some help to you in your daily quest for the life that Jesus lived. That's why we do this broadcast for you, and you only. It is our sincere desire to see you all filled with the Baptism of the love of God and living freely in the hop of Christ's coming for his church. the Lord watch between me and thee, when we are absent from one another. This is Randy Johnson for the We preach Jesus Ministries.

THE DIVIDING LINE   02/16/1992

PSM 45:1 MY HEART IS INDITING A GOOD MATTER:
I SPEAK THE THINGS WHICH I HAVE MADE TOUCHING THE KING:
MY TONGUE IS THE PEN OF A READY WRITER

Colossians 1:12 "Giving thanks unto the Father, which hath made us meet to be partakers of the inheritance of the saints in light: who hath delivered us from the power of darkness, and hath translated us into the kingdom of his dear son: in whom we have redemption through his blood, even the forgiveness of sins:" God has delivered us from darkness, from the power of darkness, into his marvelous light. No longer are we the children of darkness. He has delivered us and transferred us into the kingdom of God. Things from the old kingdom cannot enter into the new. John 3:6 says "that which is born of the flesh is flesh, and that which is born of the Spirit is spirit." Looking in at

1 Cor 15:50 "Now this I say, brethren, that flesh and blood cannot inherit kingdom of God, neither doth corruption inherit incorruption." Matthew 9:16 "No man putteth a piece of new cloth unto and old garment, for that which is put in to fill it up taketh from the garment, and the rent is made worse. Neither do men put new wine into old bottles: else the bottles break, and the wine runneth out, and the bottles perish: but they put new wine into new bottles, and both are preserved." How can we inherit the kingdom of heaven? God has to make us a new creature in Christ by filling us with the new wine which is the Holy Ghost. It's not a question of are we good or bad but the question is are we flesh, which is of the old kingdom and cannot inherit incorruption, or are we Spirit, the new kingdom in Christ for which the kingdom was created. That which is born of the flesh is flesh and will never be anything but flesh. The old creation, fleshly and corruptible, can never pass into the new or spiritual Kingdom which is the basis of true incorruptibility.

When the realization comes that God is seeking a new creation, one totally new, then it will dawn in your heart that you can bring absolutely nothing from the old life into this new incorruptible kingdom. Especially the old man of flesh. God wants you for himself, but not as you are. He provided a way, a cross and a sacrifice on the cross, that we could die with him, and thus being dead we can rise to a newness of life as a new creature in Christ, 2 Cor 5:17 "Therefore if any man be in Christ, he is a new creature: old things are passed away, behold, all things are become new." Now, with a new nature and character, you can enter into the new kingdom , the body of Christ.

The cross was the means that God used to bring an end to the old things, setting aside the old man, by crucifying him on the cross with Christ. The resurrection is used to give all that is necessary for life in the new kingdom of Christ. Romans 6:4 "Therefore we are buried with him in baptism into death: that like as Christ was raised up from the dead by the glory of the Father, even so we also should walk in newness of life." The cross wiped out everything not of God and the resurrection stands at the very beginning of the new creation. The cross ends the old, and the resurrection begins the new.

Now there stands before you two worlds, the old and the new. In the old the Devil, through the flesh, or more over fleshly desires and lusts, had absolute dominion over you and you did the works of the flesh. Righteousness was not in you, not a part of your make up. In the old creation, as the old creature, the sentence of death hung over your head because, the wages of sin are death. And because of the corruptible nature of the sinful old man, and that all that is in heaven is pure, nothing from the first creation can cross over to the second and better creation. Nothing can pass beyond the cross. It's this dividing barrier, this separation between the old and new, that God has made to be the way, the only way, of escape from the old creation. Mat 7:13 "Enter ye in at the strait gate: for wide <is> the gate, and broad <is> the way, that leadeth to destruction, and many there be which go in thereat:" Mat 7:14 "Because strait <is> the gate, and narrow <is> the way, which leadeth unto life, and few there be that find it." God gathered up all of the old creation, the first man Adam, and hung it on the cross in the flesh of Jesus Christ, so that all of the old Adam would be done away with. God then made a proclamation, "Through the cross, I have set aside all that's not of me, those who are of the old creation are included in this, but, you also have been crucified with Christ, if you'll just accept the sacrifice, repent and be baptized in the name of Jesus Christ for the remission of your sins and you shall receive the baptism of the Holy Ghost." Repentance is a dying out to the desires of the flesh Gal 5:19-21 "Now the [works of the flesh] are manifest, which are <these>, Adultery, fornication, uncleanness, lasciviousness, Idolatry, witchcraft, hatred, variance, emulations, wrath, strife, seditions, heresies, Envyings, murders, drunkenness, revellings, and such like: of the which I tell you before, as I have also told <you> in time past, that they which do such things shall not inherit the kingdom of God." Gal 2:20 "I am crucified with Christ: nevertheless I live, yet not I, but Christ liveth in me: and the life which I now live in the flesh I live by the faith of the Son of God, who loved me, and gave himself for me." If indeed I am crucified with Christ and by faith I understand this, then how is the old man buried? Romans 6:3-4 "Know ye not, that so many of us as were baptized into Jesus Christ were baptized into his death? Therefore we are buried with him in baptism into death: that like as Christ was raised up from the dead by the glory of the Father, even so we also should walk in newness of life." Baptism is intimately associated with salvation, read Mark 16:16 "He that believeth and is baptized shall be saved." It's not baptismal regeneration but baptismal salvation. Salvation from this world system. Baptism is our burial and through this burial, the world system is left behind along with the old man. Gal 6:14 "But God forbid that I should glory, save in the cross of our Lord Jesus Christ, by whom the world is crucified unto me, and I unto the world." I'm no longer affected by the affection for the things of the world. I'm no longer driven by the desires thereof. The world is crucified unto me and I unto the world.

  1 Pet 3:20 "When once the longsuffering of God waited in the days of Noah, while the ark was a preparing, wherein few, that is, eight souls were saved by water." Peter writes of eight souls that were saved through water by entering into the ark. Noah stepped by faith out of the old corrupt world system into a new world. Eight souls were saved. Not that they didn't drown but that they were saved out of the old corrupt world system of things. This is salvation. 1 Peter 3:21 "The like figure whereunto even baptism doth also now save us." The aspect of the cross is figured into your baptism. You are delivered from this present evil world through death on the cross, burial by baptism, and resurrection by the Spirit of the Holy Ghost. It's simply obeying the Gospel which is the death burial and resurrection of Jesus Christ. It's baptism into the death of Christ, you go down in the water and your world goes down with you. When you come up out of the water in Christ, your old world is dead. It's clear that baptism is greater than just getting wet, or a profession of faith. Baptism relates to the death, burial, and resurrection of Jesus Christ and has both worlds in view.

  1 Pet 3:21 "The like figure whereunto <even> baptism doth also now save us (not the putting away of the filth of the flesh, but the answer of a good conscience toward God,) by the resurrection of Jesus Christ:" The answer of a good conscience toward God. there would be no need for an answer if God had said nothing, but he has spoken by way of the cross. By the cross, he told the world of the judgment of the old creation and of the

old kingdom. The cross was not, is not, an individual cross of Christ's but it includes you and me. We are crucified with him, Crucified with Jesus Christ, the last man Adam, and in him, in his crucifixion, was wiped out all the death and corruption that was attributed to the first man Adam when he brought death through his willful sin. Look at 1 Corinthians 15:20-22 "But now is Christ risen from the dead, and become the first fruits of them that slept. For since by man came death, by man came also the resurrection of the dead. For as in Adam all die, even so in Christ shall all be made alive. And Romans 5:12 "Wherefore as by one man sin entered into the world, and death by sin, and so death passed upon all men, for all have sinned:" And Romans 5:19 "For as by one man's disobedience many were made sinners, so by the obedience of one shall many be righteous." And 1 Corinthians 15:45-47 "And so it is written, The first man Adam was made a living soul, the last Adam was made a quickening spirit. Howbeit that was not first which is spiritual, but that which is natural, and afterward that which is spiritual. The first man is of the earth, earthly: the second man is the Lord from heaven." Made a quickening spirit. Or, made a life giving spirit. Death came by the first Adam and life came by the second Adam, Jesus Christ. In the first Adam back at the beginning, came the end of God's kingdom in relationship with man. Adam sinned and gave the kingdom, the world system, over to Satan. But in Christ, the second Adam, a new kingdom is began over which sin and death have no power. What then is the answer of a good conscience toward God? It's the answer to God's judgment on the old creation, That answer is, I want to be baptized because I have been crucified with Christ and therefore am dead to this world system of things, dead to the law of sin and death, and I need to be buried. Because Romans 6:4 says, "therefore we are buried with him in baptism into death: that like as Christ was raised up from the dead by the glory of the Father, even so we also should walk in newness of life." and I can't be resurrected until I'm buried. Baptism is connected with both death and resurrection, though in itself, it is neither death nor resurrection: it is a burial. Who are those that qualify for burial? The dead in Christ. So by asking for baptism I declare myself dead. Unless you realize that your dead in Christ by repenting of your sins, you have no right to be baptized. You don't bury those that are not dead to the old world and it's sins. Baptism is not dying it's a burial. We go down into the water realizing that in God's sight, we're already dead. The question set before you is simple, Christ has died, are you included there? The answer is just as simple, "Lord, I believe that Christ died for my sins and I want to be partaker in this death, Please forgive me of the sins that I have committed, I say yes to the death and burial that you have committed to me." God has consigned you to death and the grave, the watery grave of Baptism in the name of the one who was crucified for you, Jesus Christ. There's an old world and a new, and between them there is a cross, a tomb, and a resurrection. God has already crucified me with Christ, but I must be consigned to the tomb. Baptism confirms God's death sentence of the Cross. It shows that I am dead to the old world and that I belong to the new kingdom of Christ. Baptism is no small thing. It's a definite break with the old way of life. Romans 6:2 "we who died to sin, how shall we any longer live therein?" But, If you are going to continue in the old world, why be baptized? God forbid, How shall we that are dead to sin, live any longer therein? Baptism is a intimate union between the believer and Christ. His death becomes ours. His burial becomes ours. Our death and his are so closely identified that it would be impossible to separate the two. It's A God wrought union. Baptism's our admission that the death of Christ powerfull enough to bring an end to everything in us that wasn't Christ like.

    I am baptized into his death, and resurrected with him. Romans 6:5 "For if we have been planted together in the likeness of his death, we shall be also in the likeness of his resurrection." We entered into his death but the resurrection enters into us. The resurrection is the quickening spirit of 1 Cor 15:47. Towards the death of Christ, it was I in Christ, but with the resurrection, the emphasis is Christ in me. He has become the quickening, life giving, Spirit.

    God has cut off the old creation by the cross in order to bring in a new creation in Christ by the resurrection. The door to the old kingdom has been shut and we are translated into the kingdom of righteousness by Jesus Christ through the infilling of the Holy Ghost. My baptism was done as a burial and a washing away of sins. Baptism is my testimony that I'm dead to the old world and risen up in newness of life through the quickening Spirit of the Holy Ghost. So, once we have been buried and resurrected we must present ourselves to Christ in consecration. Romans 6:12 "Let not sin therefore reign in your mortal body, that ye should obey the lusts thereof. Neither present ye your members as instruments of unrighteousness unto sin: but present yourselves unto God, as those that are alive from the dead and your members as instruments of righteousness unto God." and Romans 12:1 "I beseech You therefore, brethren, by the mercies of God, that ye present your bodies a living sacrifice, holy, acceptable unto God, which is your reasonable service." This is not the consecration of the old man with his instincts and resources, the natural wisdom, strength and gifts, but the new man, as one alive from the dead. This is the definition of the point where consecration begins, this is the origin, the beginning point. This is not the consecration of something from the old creation but that which has passed through the death, burial, and resurrection. 2 Cor 5:17 "Therefore if any man be in Christ, he is a new creature: old things are passed away, behold, all things are become new." The presenting of Romans 12:1 is the outcome of knowing the old man was crucified with Christ. Knowing your sins are forgiven and washed away by the blood of Christ, reckoning yourselves to be dead in Christ, and presenting yourselves to God as a living sacrifice, is the divine order of living for God. I am no longer my own but Christ's.

Real Christian life begins with knowing this, Because Christ is risen, we are alive unto God and not unto ourselves. We are the Lord's. We are his possession, bought with a price, redeemed by his blood. We are no longer our own. This is not intended to lead you to believe that we were ever our own, but we were slaves to the works of the flesh, part of the old world, bound to a dead man. If then, we are in fact another's, how can we dare squander an hour of our time, a penny of our money or any of our mental or physical strength? Holiness unto the Lord was the cry of the early Jews. Present your members as servants of righteousness unto sanctification. Give yourself wholly, completely to Christ: this is holiness. Separation unto the Lord. Sanctified unto God. Anointed with the Holy oil of the Holy Ghost. Set apart for God. The Old Testament priest hood was initiated by the anointing oil being poured over the head of the candidate for priesthood. This was done publicly so that all could know that this man was set apart for God. Sanctified, anointed. Exclusively reserved for the LORD. Presenting yourself to God represents this very same thing. He fills you with the Holy Spirit of Promise. You are altogether and completely hisThere has to be a day in your life when you give up ownership and put yourself in the hands of God. From that day forward, you belong to him. This doesn't mean that you then become a preacher or missionary or that you take a vow of poverty. There are many that fill pews today that have never given themselves to the Lord of Glory. They haven't consecrated themselves to him. It's their own uncrucified natural feelings and faculties doing what they feel is the work of God. Matthew 7:21-22" Not everyone that saith unto me, Lord, Lord, shall enter into the kingdom of heaven, but he that doeth the will of my Father which is in heaven. Many will say to me in that day, Lord, Lord, have we not prophesied in thy name? And in thy name have cast out devils? And in thy name done many wonderful works? And then will I profess unto them, I never knew you: depart from me, ye that work iniquity."

These have cast out devils and done many works in the name of Christianity yet Jesus calls them workers of inequity. . Oh, they have in name and deed but really haven't ever met the savior. How then are we to be consecrated? Not to a Christian work but to the will of God, to be and do what ever he wants us to do. I don't mean to infer that every man that fills a position on the mission field or that fills a pulpit is unconsecrated. If you are a Christian then God has a life all charted out for you, It may be anything from washing windows to mowing the church lawn to who knows what. What ever he has for you to do you can be sure it will follow along with the written word. Our thing is to be consecrated to the will of God and do whatever he desires you to do. Paul said 2 Tim 4:7-8 "I have fought a good fight, I have finished <my> course, I have kept the faith: Henceforth there is laid up for me a crown of righteousness, which the Lord, the righteous judge, shall give me at that day: and not to me only, but unto all them also that love his appearing." I have finished the course, Nothing could be more disheartening then to stand before God having sailed your own course when God had so much planed for you. Can you say as in Romans 12:2 "And be not conformed to this world: but be ye transformed by the renewing of your mind, that ye may prove what is that good, and acceptable, and perfect, will of God." Do you want the will of God for your life? Do all your desires center around him? Can you truly say that the will of God is Good and acceptable and perfect to you? Your strong self will must go to the cross and you must give yourself wholly, totally, to the Lord. There's no way that God can be Lord of your life if he's not Lord of all of your life. Without reservation, not holding back even one little corner, one little kingdom, of our lives, we must present ourselves unto God. This'll take many adjustments to your life. Are you willing? why resist God, it's much wiser to submit. Are you in conflict with what God wants for your life? You can evade the issue but the cost is high. To do so, will take you out of the will of God for your life. God's a perfect gentleman and He won't force you to do anything your will decides you don't want to do. It's a good feeling to know that we are his. There's a continual awareness of his presence when you know your his. When ownership of your life is established, you'll do nothing in your own interest, for you know you are his. As Servants? No. On my den wall, there's a scripture that has helped me in time of need, John 15:15-16 "Henceforth, I call you not servants, for the servant knoweth not what his Lord doeth: but I have called you friends, for all things that I have heard of my Father I have made known unto you. Ye have not chosen me, but I have chosen you, and ordained you." Friend, not servant. You need to earnestly covet the best gifts.

This is Randy Johnson of the We Preach Jesus Ministries

INADEQUATE   12/16/1992

PSM 45:1 MY HEART IS INDITING A GOOD MATTER:
I SPEAK THE THINGS WHICH I HAVE MADE TOUCHING THE KING:
MY TONGUE IS THE PEN OF A READY WRITER
1364

NOTE: This appears to be set up in my preaching notes format. Evidently, I preached this message to some congregation, somewhere.

Gal 2:19-20   "For I through the law am dead to the law, that I might live unto God. I am crucified with Christ: nevertheless I live, yet not I, but Christ liveth in me: and the life which I now live in the flesh I live by the faith of the Son of God, who loved me, and gave himself for me."

RIGHTEOUSNESS NOT OURS

IF OURS=SELF RIGHTEOUSNESS

SELF RIGHTEOUSNESS=I'M RIGHT YOUR WRONG

NO SPACE FOR WHO'S RIGHT AND WHO'S WRONG IN CHRIST

IN MARRAGE

OUR RIGHTEOUSNESS ARE THE GARMENTS OF CHRIST

OUR OWN GARMENTS = ADAM AND EVE IN GARDEN

UNSATISFACTORY TO COVER OUR SINFULLNESS

WE WERE NAKED
WHO TOLD YOU?

MUST WEAR THE RIGHTEOUS GARMENTS OF CHRIST

BRIDE WEARING LEVI 501

MY RIGHTEOUSNESS IS NOT MINE BUT CHRISTS

BY SAME LOGIC

I CAN DO NOTHING IN SELF

BUT

Phil 4:13 "I can do all things through Christ which strengtheneth me."

I AM INADEQUATE

IM NOT ADEQUATE FOR THE JOB, THE TASK, SET BEFORE ME

NO SUFFICENCY, STRENGTH, TALENT, ABILITY, NOR DESIRE

NOT SMART, NOT INTELLEGENT, I AM CHRIST'S

LIKE PAUL

Rom 7:15 "For that which I do I allow not: for what I would, that do I not, but what I hate, that do I."

Rom 7:18-19 "For I know that in me (that is, in my flesh,) dwelleth no good thing: for to will is present with me, but <how> to perform that which is good I find not. For the good that I would I do not: but the evil which I would not, that I do."

Rom 7:22-25 "For I delight in the law of God after the inward man: But I see another law in my members, warring against the law of my mind, and bringing me into captivity to the law of sin which is in my members. O wretched man that I am! who shall deliver me from the body of this death? I thank God through Jesus Christ our Lord. So then with the mind I myself serve the law of God, but with the flesh the law of sin."

PAUL TEMPERS WITH

Rom 8:1 "<There is> therefore now no condemnation to them which are in Christ Jesus, who walk not after the flesh, but after the Spirit."

TAKE LIBERTY TO SIN

WHO SHALL DELIVER ME?

DESIRES=CHRIST CENTER

PIVOT POINT OF LIFE

LIFE SHORT SEASON

James 4:14 "Whereas ye know not what <shall be> on the morrow. For what <is> your life? It is even a [vapour], that appeareth for a little time, and then vanisheth away."

1 Chr 29:15 "For we <are> strangers before thee, and sojourners, as <were> all our fathers: our days on the earth <are> as a shadow, and <there is> none abiding."

Isa 38:12 "Mine age is departed, and is removed from me as a shepherd's tent: I have cut off like a weaver my life: he will cut me off with pining sickness: from day <even> to night wilt thou make an end of me. "

LIFE IS SHORT THREE SCORE AND TEN

TENACIOUSLY BRO BRAYLAND MAN IN OTHER BED

(This Bro Brayland was in the hospital and the pastor and I went to pray for him. In the other bed was an elderly man on virtual life support holding on to what little life he had. He would never have any quality of life again.)

SEEMED SO LONG FROM 16

FROM 50 SO SHORT

WHERE HAVE THE YEARS GONE THE DREAMS, THE PLANS

Eccl 12:1 "[Remember] now thy Creator in the days of thy youth, while the evil days come not, nor the years draw nigh, when thou shalt say, I have no pleasure in them,"

7K YEARS

ETERNITY

NO WAY TO RELATE TO ETERNITY

LONG HOME

Eccl 12:5 "Also <when> they shall be afraid of <that which is> high, and fears <shall be> in the way, and the almond tree shall flourish, and the grasshopper shall be a burden, and desire shall fail: because man goeth to his long home, and the mourners go about the streets:"

THREE SCORE AND TEN

AND THEN

WE MUST HAVE LIFE IN CHRIST

JESUS CHRIST IS THE SUM TOTAL AND ESSANCE OF OUR LIFE

OUR STRENGTH, OUR ROCK IN A WEARY LAND, OUR SHIELD AGAINST THE BATTLES OF LIFE

OUR TOWER, OUR CITY OF REFUGE

OUR LIFE IN CHRIST IS A CONTINUAL LERNING PROCESS

JESUS IS DILIGENT PARENT

HERE IS AN A

AN A

AN A

UNTIL WE LEARN A

OR UNTIL WE ARE RAPTURED OR DIE

LEARN A

THEN HERE IS A B

THROUGHT THE WHOLE ALPHABET OF LIFE

ALPHA THROUGH OMEGA A THRU Z

ENOCH UNDERSTOOD THE SECRET OF THE STAIRS

HE LEARNED HIS LESSONS WELL

HE KNEW WHERE HIS STRENGTH CAME FROM

JESUS CHRIST IS THE SUM TOTAL AND ESSENCE OF OUR LIVES OUR EXISTANCE

OUR SUFFICIENCY IS IN CHRIST

1 Cor 4:7 "For who maketh thee to differ <from another>? and what hast thou that thou didst not receive? now if thou didst receive <it>, why dost thou glory, as if thou hadst not [received] <it>?"

WHAT HAVE YOU CREATED?

ASSEMBLE NOT CREATE

THOUGHTS, IDEAS, SENTENCES

ALL ARE GIFTS FROM GOD

LIFE IS A GIFT

CONTROL DESTINY

DON'T DIE

ONLY TWO SIDES IN THIS BATTLE OF LIFE

NO DEMILITARIZED ZONE, NO NEUTRAL GROUND

ONE SIDE OR OTHER ONLY CHOICE YOU HAVE

HOW THEN CAN WE LIVE?

IN CHRIST

BY ENTERING INTO HIS DEATH

CRUCIFIED WITH CHRIST

Rom 6:6-11 "Knowing this, that our old man is [crucified with] <him>, that the body of sin might be destroyed, that henceforth we should not serve sin. For he that is dead is freed from sin. Now if we be dead with Christ, we believe that we shall also live with him: Knowing that Christ being raised from the dead dieth no more, death hath no more dominion over him. For in that he died, he died unto sin once: but in that he liveth, he liveth unto God. Likewise reckon ye also yourselves to be dead indeed unto sin, but alive unto God through Jesus Christ our Lord."

NOW NO LONGER UNDER LAW OF SIN AND DEATH

LAW NOT GONE BUT YOU ARE

YOU NO LONGER LIVE, YOUR DEAD IN CHRIST

CHRIST LIVES IN YOU

Gal 2:20 "I am crucified with Christ: nevertheless [I live], yet not I, but Christ liveth in me: and the life which I now live in the flesh [I live] by the faith of the Son of God, who loved me, and gave himself for me."

IF I THEN ENTER IN TO HIS DEATH SO ALSO MUST I HIS BURIAL

Rom 6:4 "Therefore we are [buried with] him by baptism into death: that like as Christ was raised up from the dead by the glory of the Father, even so we also should walk in newness of life."

Col 2:12 "[Buried with] him in baptism, wherein also ye are risen with <him> through the faith of the operation of God, who hath raised him from the dead."

NOW YOU ARE DWELLING IN THE PROMISE

YOU WERE CRUCIFIED, BURIED AND RECEIVED NEW LIFE THROUGH THE HOLY GHOST

YOU HAVE RECEVIED THE EARNEST OF YOUR INHERITANCE AND TASTED OF THE HEAVENLY

NOW NOT YOU THAT LIVES BUT CHRIST

AND IF CHRIST THEN YOU HAVE NOTHING OF WHICH TO BOAST

BY THE SAME

NOTHING TO BE ASHAMED OF

I HAVE BEEN CRUCIFIED

I'M DEAD

ANY GOOD THING THAT COMES FROM THIS FLESH KNOW TO YOU AS R JOHNSON IS OF GOD

I HAVE BEEN CRUCIFIED

I'M DEAD

THE LIFE I LIVE IS CHRIST

NOTHING PERSONAL TO BOAST OF

CONVERSELY

IF IT IS CHRIST THAT LIVES, AND HE DOES

AND

Phil 4:13   "[I can do] all things through Christ which strengtheneth me."

I CANNOT BE INTIMIDATED BECAUSE IT IS NOT I BUT CHRIST

I KNOW IN WHOM I BELIEVE

PETER OUT OF BOAT

KNEW JESUS AND HIS WORD

WALKED ON THE PROMISE

UNTIL BEGAN BELIEVING IN SELF AND SANK

EVEN THEN HELP ME

YOU ARE NOT SUFFICENT IN YOUR SELF TO DO ANYTHING FOR CHRIST

TAINTED WITH FLESH

COME UP AND LETS DO SOME WALKING ON THE WATER TONIGHT

THERE ARE THINGS CHRIST WANTS YOU TO DO

YOU HESITATE

THINK YOU INADIQUATE

YOU ARE BUT HE ISN'T

STEP OUT OF THE BOAT

THE MASTER CALLS YOU COME

LORD IF IT BE THOU BID ME COME

DON'T HESITATE AT THE VOICE OF THE MASTER

YOU KNOW HIS VOICE

COME

THE HOPE OF THE BELIEVER   02/07/1993

PSM 45:1 MY HEART IS INDITING A GOOD MATTER:
I SPEAK THE THINGS WHICH I HAVE MADE TOUCHING THE KING:
MY TONGUE IS THE PEN OF A READY WRITER

[NOTE: The broadcast cost had risen completely out of sight. There were new owners of the radio station and the cost of the one hour broadcast was prohibitive. We cut the broadcast down to two 15 minute spots. Latter I would relinquish my 15 minutes to S Sams making it much easier on him.]

At the onset of this broadcast, I'd like to invite all of you to Peoria's First United Pentecostal Church for a revival beginning Feb 12, 13, 14.

2 Peter 3:13 "Nevertheless we, according to his promise, look for new heavens and a new earth, wherein dwelleth righteousness."

2 Peter 1:4 "Whereby are given unto us exceeding great and precious promises, that by these ye might be partakers of the divine nature, having escaped the corruption that is in the world through lust."

1 John 2:25 "And this is the promise that he hath promised us, even eternal life."

John 14:1 "Let not your heart be troubled: ye believe in God, believe also in me. In my Father's house are many mansions: If it were not so, I would have told you. I go to prepare a place for you."

The hope of the Christian, a home that will abide for ever.

This is trying to use finite terms to describe the infinite. Abide and forever are terms predicated upon time. Time is a measure of something that God has put in eternity strictly to deal with man. Eternity stretches from who knows to who knows. In the midst of this God set a period, called time, that he would deal with man. One week of time. Six days to take out a bride for His name, one day to rest.

Exodus 31:17"...For in six days the LORD made the heaven and earth, and on the seventh day he rested and was refreshed."

2 Peter 3:8 "But, beloved, be not ignorant of this one thing, that one day with the Lord is as a thousand years, and a thousand years as one day."

The Old Testament covers four thousand years of history, the time since Christ is to cover two thousand years. Six thousand years of the history of man on this earth.

How do the fossils, Hieroglyphics, sedimentary layers, rock composition, and all the prehistoric artifacts fit into this time plan? They are pre time, prehistoric. Time was set in eternity for this age. Those things were before time. We attempt to measure eternity with time. Eternity cannot be measured with time. The infinite cannot be compared to the finite. Apples and oranges are both fruit, yet we don't say, Give me two dozen apples of oranges, nor can it be said, there are three hundred thousand years of eternity..

There is within man, an intuition that he was meant to be with God. God desires for us to dwell in perfect harmony with the divine plan set in heaven. Every creature, except man, dwells within this plan of God. In the bush near the bedroom window, sits four sparrows, overstuffed feather balls, secreted away against the blowing wind. Sparrows, protected against the storm of the day. Why, do they stay tucked away? Because they trust God to provide comfort and protection for them. They dwell in harmony with God.

Matthew 10:29 "Are not two sparrows sold for a farthing? And one of them shall not fall to the ground without your Father. But the very hairs of your head are all numbered. Fear ye not therefore, ye are of more value than many sparrows."

God has given unto man the opportunity to erase the differences that have become the separating factor between God and man.

By providing a sacrifice, the sacrifice, by coming to earth in the form of a man, Jesus Christ, living a sin free life, being crucified, as a covering for the sins of our self will, he has broken down the middle wall of partition.

Ephesians 2:12 "That at that time ye were without Christ, being aliens from the commonwealth of Israel, and strangers from the covenants of promise, having no hope, and without God in the world: But now in Christ Jesus ye who sometimes were far off are made nigh by the blood of Christ. For he is our peace, who hath made both one, and hath broken down the middle wall of partition between us, having abolished in his flesh the enmity, even the law of commandments contained in ordinances, for to make in himself of twain one new man, so making peace, and that he might reconcile both unto God in one body by the cross, having slain the enmity thereby:"

Strangers from the covenants. Having no hope. Without, looking within. Cold, dejected, absolutely without hope. Now, reconciled by the sacrifice, making peace, reconciled unto God. No enmity between God and man. At peace by the sacrifice of Jesus Christ our savior. The ultimate gift.

John 15:13 "Greater love have no man then this, that a man lay down his life for his friends."

Colossians 2:13 "And you, being dead in your sins and the uncircumcision of your flesh, hath he quickened together with him, (Christ being risen from the grave) having forgiven you all trespasses (by the sinless sacrifice of Jesus Christ), Blotting out the handwriting of ordinances that was against us, which was contrary to us, and took it out of the way, nailing it to his cross,"

The Christian is not under the laws of thou shalt, thou shalt not for God hath put His laws in our hearts. We now have an overwhelming desire to do the will of God.

Hebrews 8:10 "... I will put my laws into their mind, and write them in their hearts: and I will be to them a God, and they shall be to me a people."

No longer does sin have dominion over this flesh. No longer do you have to be bound to sin. No longer do you have to fulfill the desires of the flesh. God has broken that bondage of sin. God has given to you spiritual liberty.

Romans 6:14 "For sin shall not have dominion over you, for ye are not under the law, but under grace."

Verse 17 "But God be thanked, that ye were the servants of sin, but ye have obeyed from the heart that form of doctrine which was delivered you, Being then made free from sin, ye became the servants of righteousness."

You now have freedom from the guilt ridden consciousness of sin in your life, you now have a closeness with God. Your fear is gone, only to be replaced by perfect love.

1 John 4:18 "There is no fear in love, but perfect love casteth out fear: because fear hath torment. He that feareth is not made perfect in love."

So then, first, God hath taken away our sins. Second, He hath freed us from the bondage of sin and death. Third, no longer are we moved by the desires of the flesh, but as our hope rest in Christ, we are moved by the desires of our Father. The Word of God being our guide, our map to take us through this strange and weary land.... We are now pilgrims and strangers in a foreign country. We carry passports that identify us to the heads of states and magistrates as citizens of that heavenly home. Fourth, by taking away sin, the sinful nature, and the guilt of sin, He has broken down any separation between God and man. Perfect love replaces the fear that dwelt in our hearts.

2 Peter 1:4 "Whereby are given unto us exceeding great and precious promises, that by these ye might be partakers of the divine nature, having escaped the corruption that is in the world through lust."

2 Peter 3:13 "Nevertheless we, according to his promise, look for new heavens and a new earth, wherein dwelleth righteousness."

John 14:1 "Let not your heart be troubled: ye believe in God, believe also in me. In my Father's house are many mansions: If it were not so, I would have told you. I go to prepare a place for you."

1 Corinthians 15:50 "Now this I say, brethren, that flesh and blood cannot inherit the kingdom of God, neither doth corruption inherit incorruption. Behold, I shew you a mystery, We shall not all sleep, but we shall be changed, In a moment, in the twinkling of an eye, at the last trump: for the trumpet shall sound, and the dead shall be raised incorruptible, and we shall be changed. For this corruptible must put on incorruption, and this mortal must put on immortality."

1 Thessalonians 4:13 "But I would not have you ignorant, brethren, concerning them which are asleep, that ye sorrow not, even as others which have no hope. For if we believe that Jesus died and rose again, even so them also which sleep in Jesus will God bring with him. For this we say unto you by the word of the LORD, that we which are alive and remain unto the coming of the Lord shall not prevent them which are asleep. For the Lord himself shall descend from heaven with the voice of the archangel, and with the trump of God: and the dead in Christ shall rise first: Then we which are alive and remain shall be caught up together with them in the clouds, to meet the Lord in the air: so shall we ever be with the Lord."

The hope of the Christian, the rapture, the great catching away. This body will be changed into the likeness of the body Jesus had when he arose from the grave. A glorified body, for this flesh that we now have is corruptible. Take the life out of it, and it rots. This corruptible body cannot stand in the presence of God. We cannot inherit the eternal with this finite flesh. 1 Cor 15:50 "Behold, we shall all be change, in a moment, in the twinkling of an eye, in an instant, this corruptible will take on incorruption, and death is swallowed up in victory."

1 Corinthians 15:55 "Oh death, where is thy sting? Oh grave, where is thy victory?"

What kind of body did the LORD have? What was this glorified body he arose from the grave with?

In the book of Luke the 24th chapter there walked two of Jesus' disciples on the road to Emmaus. They were talking about all that had transpired during the last several days, As they talked,

Luke 24:15 "And it came to pass that while they communed together and reasoned, Jesus himself drew near, and went with them. But their eyes were holden that they should not know him."

Jesus hid his identity from them. As they walked on, he ask them of these things they were speaking of. When they had told him what they knew concerning the events of the preceding days he rebuked them.

Luke 24:25 "Then he said unto them, O fools, and slow of heart to believe all that the prophets have spoken: Ought not Christ to have suffered these things, and to enter into his glory? And beginning at Moses and all the prophets, he expounded unto them in all the scriptures the things concerning himself."

Still he did not reveal himself unto them. Not until they sat at dinner.

Verse 30 " And it came to pass, as he took bread, and blessed it, and break it, and gave to them. And their eyes were opened, and they knew him, and he vanished out of their sight."

How that God has given unto man the opportunity to put aside, no, erase the differences that have become the separating factor between God and man.

By providing a sacrifice, the sacrifice, by coming to earth in the form of a man, Jesus Christ, living a sin free life, being crucified, as a covering for the sins of our self will, he has broken down the middle wall of partition.

And how that, the Christian is not under the laws of thou shalt, thou shalt not for God hath put His laws in our hearts. The Holy Ghost filled Christian has an overwhelming desire to do the will of God, to please the Father.

And that God has put his laws in our heart so that it is our desire to do the will of God: Hebrews 8:10 "... I will put my laws into their mind, and write them in their hearts: and I will be to them a God, and they shall be to me a people."

No longer does sin have dominion over this flesh. No longer do you have to be bound to sin. No longer do you have to fulfill the desires of the flesh.

And how that flesh and blood cannot inherit the kingdom: 1 Corinthians 15:50 "Now this I say, brethren, that flesh and blood cannot inherit the kingdom of God, neither doth corruption inherit incorruption. Behold, I show you a mystery, We shall not all sleep, but we shall be changed, In a moment, in the twinkling of an eye, at the last trump: for the trumpet shall sound, and the dead shall be raised incorruptible, and we shall be changed. For this corruptible must put on incorruption, and this mortal must put on immortality."

1 Thessalonians 4:13 "But I would not have you ignorant, brethren, concerning them which are asleep, that ye sorrow not, even as others which have no hope. For if we believe that Jesus died and rose again, even so them also which sleep in Jesus will God bring with him. For this we say unto you by the word of the LORD, that we which are alive and remain unto the coming of the Lord shall not prevent them which are asleep. For the Lord himself shall descend from heaven with the voice of the archangel, and with the trump of God: and the dead in Christ shall rise first: Then we which are alive and remain shall be caught up together with them in the clouds, to meet the Lord in the air: so shall we ever be with the Lord."

The hope of the Christian, the rapture, the great catching away.

We also spoke of how that this body must be changed into the likeness of the body Jesus had when he arose from the grave. A glorified body, Behold, we shall all be change, in a moment, in the twinkling of an eye, in an instant, this corruptible will take on incorruption, and death is swallowed up in victory.

1 Corinthians 15:55 "Oh death, where is thy sting? Oh grave, where is thy victory?"

What kind of body does our Lord have?

In the book of Luke the 24th chapter there walked two of Jesus' disciples on the road to Emmaus. They were talking about all that had transpired during the last several days, As they talked, well

Luke 24:15 "And it cane to pass that while they communed together and reasoned, Jesus himself drew near, and went with them. But their eyes were holden that they should not know him."

Jesus had hid his identity from them. As they walked on, he ask them of these things they were talking of. When they had told him what they knew concerning the events of the preceding days he rebuked them.

Luke 24:25 "Then he said unto them, O fools, and slow of heart to believe all that the prophets have spoken: Ought not Christ to have suffered these things, and to enter into is glory? And beginning at Moses and all the prophets, he expounded unto them in all the scriptures the things concerning himself."

Still he did not reveal himself unto them. Not until they sat at dinner.

Verse 30 " And it came to pass, as he took bread, and blessed it, and break it, and gave to them. and their eyes were opened, and they knew him, ÷and he vanished out of their sight"

Later, as the disciples were gathered to gather, the story was told how that Jesus had indeed arisen and had spoke with the two. While they yet stood together.

Luke 24:36 "And as they thus spake, ÷Jesus himself stood in the midst if them, and saith unto them, Peace be unto you. But they were terrified and a frightened, and supposed that they had seen a spirit. And he said unto them, Why are you troubled? and why do thoughts arise in your hearts? Behold my hands and feet, that it is myself: handle me and see, for a spirit hath not flesh and bones as you see me have."

They were in a room. John says the doors were closed for fear of the Jews, and suddenly, Jesus appears in their midst. Frighten? I think so. But here look at these scriptures. One, he can hide himself from the recognition of others. Two, he can eat if he so chooses. Three, he can appear and disappear as he so wills. Solid walls and doors have no hold over him. Death has no hold over him. Four, he knows the thoughts and intents of their hearts. The beautiful part is that we will be like unto him.

1 John 3:2 "Beloved, now are we the sons of God, and it doth not yet appear what we shall be: but we know that, when he shall appear, we shall be like him, for we shall see him as he is."

1 Corinthians 13:12 "For now we see through a glass, darkly, but then face to face: for I know in part, but then shall I know even as also I am known."

Now we look at puzzling reflections in the mirror. Indistinct yet there is some things we can discern. But after we receive our glorified body, then as face to face. there will be no puzzling reflections, only clearness.

The hope of the believer, all the trials and troubles of this life will be laid to rest. No longer subject to the limitations of this ol mortal body. We now have received the Ernest of our inheritance. The Holy Ghost. Just a very small portion of the glory the believer will receive. Just a token of God's sincerity in this endeavor.

What else is there Bro Johnson?

During the seven years of coming tribulation, we will be secreted away with Jesus for the marriage feast. Then comes the thousand years when the Devil will be bound and cast into the bottomless pit,

Revelations 20:1 " And I saw an angel come down from heaven, having the key of the bottomless pit and a great chain in his hand. And he laid hold on the dragon, that old serpent, which is the devil, and Satan, and bound him a thousand years. And cast him in the bottomless pit, and shut him up, and set a seal upon him, that he should deceive the nations no more, till the thousand years should be fulfilled: and after that he must be loosed a little season."

Verse 6 "Blessed and holy is he that hath part in the first resurrection: on such the second death hath no power, but they shall be priests of God and of Christ and shall reign with him a thousand years."

The image of a bunch of people flying around on clouds is a figment of someone's' imagination. There will be things that need to be done. Look to the parable Jesus spoke of the faithful servant.

Matthew 25:14-30 paraphrased "To one of his servants he gave five talents, to another he gave two, to another he gave one. The one who received five invested and the five grew to ten. the one with the two invested and it grew to four, the one that recited one buried it and then brought it back to the master. To the servant who now had ten he said, "Well done, thou faithful servant: thou hast been faithful over a few things, I will make thee ruler over many things: enter into the joy of the lord. The same thing was said to the four talent man. But the one talent man was unprofitable and was cast away from the master.

The point is that the servants that were faithful in that the LORD gave them were given more responsibility. Understand?

there is a city whose builder and maker is God, that the redeemed will live in. Look to Revelation the 21 chapter the first through the 27th verse.

{ALL OF THIS SCRIPTURE WAS NOT READ ON THE RADIO}

Rev 21:1-21 "And I saw a new heaven and a new earth: for the first heaven and the first earth were passed away, and there was no more sea. {2} And I John saw the holy city, new Jerusalem, coming down from God out of heaven, prepared as a bride adorned for her husband. {3} And I heard a great voice out of heaven saying, Behold, the tabernacle of God <is> with men, and he will dwell with them, and they shall be his people, and God himself shall be with them, <and be> their God. {4} And God shall wipe away all tears from their eyes, and there shall be no more death, neither sorrow, nor crying, neither shall there be any more pain: for the former things are passed away. {5} And he that sat upon the throne said, Behold, I make all things new. And he said unto me, Write: for these words are true and faithful. {6} And he said unto me, It is done. I am Alpha and Omega, the beginning and the end. I will give unto him that is athirst of the fountain of the water of life freely. {7} He that overcometh shall inherit all things, and I will be his God, and he shall be my son. {8} But the fearful, and unbelieving, and the abominable, and murderers, and whoremongers, and sorcerers, and idolaters, and all liars, shall have their part in the lake which burneth with fire and brimstone: which is the second death. {9} And there came unto me one of the seven angels which had the seven vials full of the seven last plagues, and talked with me, saying, Come hither, I will show thee the bride, the Lamb's wife. {10} And he carried me away in the spirit to a great and high mountain, and showed me that great city, the holy Jerusalem, descending out of heaven from God, {11} Having the glory of God: and her light <was> like unto a stone most precious, even like a jasper stone, clear as crystal, {12} And had a wall great and high, <and> had twelve gates, and at the gates twelve angels, and names written thereon, which are <the names> of the twelve tribes of the children of Israel: {13} On the east three gates, on the north three gates, on the south three gates, and on the west three gates. {14} And the wall of the city had twelve foundations, and in them the names of the twelve apostles of the Lamb. {15} And he that talked with me had a golden reed to measure the city, and the gates thereof, and the wall thereof. {16} And the city lieth foursquare, and the length is as large as the breadth: and he measured the city with the reed, twelve thousand furlongs. The length and the breadth and the height of it are equal.

{17} And he measured the wall thereof, an hundred <and> forty <and> four cubits, <according to> the measure of a man, that is, of the angel. {18} And the building of the wall of it was <of> jasper: and the city <was> pure gold, like unto clear glass. {19} And the foundations of the wall of the city <were> garnished with all manner of precious stones. The first foundation <was> jasper, the second, sapphire, the third, a chalcedony, the fourth, an emerald, {20} The fifth, sardonyx, the sixth, sardius, the seventh, chrysolyte, the eighth, beryl, the ninth, a topaz, the tenth, a chrysoprasus, the eleventh, a jacinth, the twelfth, an amethyst. {21} And the twelve gates <were> twelve pearls: every several gate was of one pearl: and the street of the city <was> pure gold, as it were transparent glass."

This THE Hope of the Christian. A new city the New Jerusalem. The city of God. An eternal home.

This is Randy Johnson of the WE PREACH JESUS MINISTRIES.

Thank you for listening.

DISPARE   02/21/1993

PSM 45:1 MY HEART IS INDITING A GOOD MATTER:
I SPEAK THE THINGS WHICH I HAVE MADE TOUCHING THE KING:
MY TONGUE IS THE PEN OF A READY WRITER.

Do you suffer from a Lack of direction. No goals. A loss, or lack of vision. Emptiness, disparity, discouragement, defeat, despondency, aggravation, anger. Has all this been lumped into one day, one month, one year, one life. Why Lord? Why hast thou madest me this way? You're the God of the universe, nothing is impossible for you, why don't you just touch me and make me into what you want me to be? You spoke the worlds into existence, Speak to me. Reprogram me, remake me, reshape me. The potter saw a vision that was in the molded clay. Just a lump a clay thrown on the potter's wheel. Only in the mind of the potter is the pattern of the vessel. Only He has the vision. The clay is wetted with the tears of compassion. The clay remains pliable for the hand of the potter. Where to from here? First a cross, then an empty tomb, then an upper room. Death comes thorough repentance of sins, a dying out to self, you share the cross of Jesus Christ. Then you enter into Jesus' burial by being buried with Him in baptism, In like manner as Christ was buried, and risen with him to walk in newness of life so we also enter into Christ. Tarry until ye be endued with power from on high. Then go ye into all the world and preach the gospel, the death, burial and resurrection of Jesus Christ. the voice of God has spoken to your heart but you have allowed the voice of discouragement and dismay overshadow the word of God. Like peter you go a fishin. The crucified, resurrected Jesus showed himself to His disciples as they stood in a closed room. Thomas had put his hand in the nail prints, had seen the torn side, and had handled the risen Christ. All had seen him, talked with him, fellowshipped with him yet, Simon Peter, the one closest to the Savior, saith unto them, I go a fishing. They say unto him, We also go with thee. You have discouragement over the seeming failures in your life. Discouragement over what is actually God's hand shaping the rough edges off your walk with him. The rough edges are the things that are not like Him. The hand of the potter shaping us into vessels of honor fit to be used in the house of the Lord. 500 seen Jesus

Christ after the resurrection. Jesus had told them to tarry until they be endued with power from on high. But they had other things to do. Fields to plow, live stock to look after, wives, houses and land, fish to catch. Discouragement because it just simply wasn't happening fast enough. Only 120 were left in the upper room. 120 faithful vessels looking for the promise of the Father. 5000 were added to the church that day. Miracles, wonders, signs, many other things were done and are done in the church. The voice of God has spoken to our hearts concerning the kingdom, given words of encouragement, words of life, but we turn ear to the demons of defeat and like Peter and the others, go a fishin.

Jesus hung on a cross after preaching and teaching to thousands even tens of thousands. His twelve faithful followers forsook him. Yet discouragement was a unknown garment to this lowly carpenter from Galilee. With a voice filled with tears, came the mandate, "Father forgive them for they know not what they do." Who, Jesus, those that drove the nails in your hands? "No, My disciples for forsaking me." Discouragement? Here was one that had just spent, used up, given his whole life to die on a cross between two thieves. For a band of disciples that wouldn't even go to bat for him. Three years they walked the sandy shores of Galilee together. For three years they shared every bite of bread. For three years they labored in the kingdom together. Betrayed with a kiss from one of the twelve. Denied vehemently by Peter. Railed upon, beaten, beard plucked out, nailed naked to a cross. What right have we to be discouraged? What right have we to be depressed? What right have we to say I go a fishin? Why art thou cast down oh my soul? Lift up the hands that hang down. Make strong the feeble knees. Without a vision my people perish. No vision. No goal. No direction. No dream. Life has past by swifter than a weavers shuttle. My life is over. The days of Youth are past. There is nothing but death lingering in the wings for the curtain to be pulled. Sounds so bad. While there is breath there is hope. While there is Hope there is life. Where there is life there is peace. Where there is peace god dwells. there is hope. There is Peace. There is life. Where there was a cross there is an empty tomb. Where there was a cross and an empty tomb there is an upper room. New Life comes out of an empty tomb.

Romans 8:28 "And we know that all things work together for good to them that love god, and to them who are called according to his purpose." 1 Peter 3:14 "But and if ye suffer for righteousness sake, happy are ye: and be not afraid of their terror, neither be troubled, verse 17 For it is better, if the will of God be so, that ye suffer for well doing than for evil doing." Romans 4:12 "Beloved, think it not strange concerning the fiery trial which is to try you, as though some strange thing happened unto you: but rejoice, in as much as ye are partakers of Christ's sufferings, that when his glory shall be revealed, ye may be glad also with exceeding joy. 15 But let none of you suffer as a murder, or as a thief, or as an evildoer, or as a busybody in other men's matters."

Unrealized dreams, unfulfilled visions, cast down hopes. Across the paths of our minds comes the ghost of discouragement and dismay. The subtle voice of discouragement courses through the highways of our minds. The subtle voice brings blackness, doubt, and a lack of self esteem. There rises in my heart, indignity at being compromised by such a foe as this. Up screams the voice of faith saying Satan get thee behind me. Don't make a covenant with the children of defeat and discouragement. They will destroy you. Lift up the hands that hang down, make strong the feeble knees. God told Abraham, Be holy and walk before me and I will make a covenant between me and thee, and will multiply thee exceedingly. Within Abraham was unrealized potential. Within you and I are greats amounts of unrealized potential. There thrives within every child of God the ability to be what ever God would have you to be. What ever your hands find to do, do as unto the Lord. "I can do all things through Christ which strengtheneth me." Phil 4:13

Discouragement gnaws at the very foundation of my mind. Wearing me like a continual dripping. On and on the dripping goes. Day after day after day until my very resolution is nearly gone. Screaming, driving, crying, on and on it goes. Day after day after day after day. When oh Lord will it let up? Num 21:17 "Then Israel sang this song, Spring up, O well, sing ye unto it:" There sprang up within my soul, a well of faith pushing back the darkness. My strength is in the Lord. He is my rock, my strong tower of refuge. He it is that is my shield and strength. Now, I can see the hand of the Potter. It shapes our faith to trust in the strength of the Lord. Isaiah 64:8 "But now, O LORD, thou art our father, we are the clay, and thou our potter, and we all are the work of thy hand." The trials of life fall on the just and the unjust. We have a refuge, the Lord God Almighty. There was a man named Saul of Tarsus. Saul, son of a rich Jewish family. He who watched over the coats of those that stoned the first Christian martyr. He went about with a mandate to put in prison or kill, or maim or destroy whoever he wished. Saul made havoc of the church, entering into every house, and haling men and women committed them to prison. He scattered abroad the whole church with his persecution.

He Who breathed out threatenings and slaughter against the disciples of the Lord. Saul thought he was doing the work of Jehovah by persecuting the followers of Christ. Journeying to Damascus to bring back to Jerusalem bound, those that worship in this way, he was struck to the ground by an exceedingly great light and a voice from heaven said, Saul, Saul, why persecutest thou me? It is hard for thee to kick against the pricks. Like an ox goaded with a sharp stick. Like an ox, dull, uncomprehending, stiff-necked, slow to respond to the gentle nudging, now prodded with a sharp stick, then jabbed, and jabbed again until the kicking stops or the ox turns. Saul, why do you kick against the prodding? Oh, God, does it take you knocking me down with a bright light to see your hand on my life? What is this voice of discouragement that blows you to and fro? Ever wind of adversity that comes along blows you off course.

In the dry wall dust on the floor were little symmetric tracks. Round and round they went. First one direction then another, against one object then another, turning, bumping, turning to bump again into the same object, round and round back and forth, no direction, no purpose, no goal, no leading hand of God to direct, point, shape, and shine. Oh, God, am I like that bug? You knew me while I was in my mother's womb. You know the plan, the direction you have for my life. Help me not to be a hard mouthed mule, not responding to the Master's hand. Help me to be a vessel of honor. Help me to perceive the hand of the potter on my life. You must have direction for your life. Don't wonder to and fro in the hurricane years. The years without goals. Life is to short and precious to waste going round and round, round and round bumping into the same problems, the same lessons God is trying to teach you.

THE LONELY GOD   02/21/1993

PSM 45:1 MY HEART IS INDITING A GOOD MATTER:
I SPEAK THE THINGS WHICH I HAVE MADE TOUCHING THE KING:
MY TONGUE IS THE PEN OF A READY WRITER.

There was a time, when God, out of a desire to love, created a creature who had his attributes. Created with an ability to reason, created with an ability to create. A free moral agent who could make decisions based upon a power of reason. Created with an ability to love. God spoke and the earth was formed out of nothingness. But when it came to this special creation, man, Genesis 2:7 "And the LORD God formed man <of> the dust of the ground, and breathed into his nostrils the breath of life, and man became a living soul." This then, was God's ultimate creation, made just a little lower than the angels. A creature that could love and be loved. This was man.

This lonely God put together man for fellowship unhampered by the walls and shackles of sin. He created him with understanding, compassion, wisdom and knowledge. Man could understand and love God.

God sat this ultimate creation, in the most beautiful garden ever created. And the Lord God said, "Of every tree if the garden thou mayest freely eat: But of the tree of the knowledge of good and evil, thou shalt not eat of it: for in the day that thou eatest thereof thou shalt surely die." God created man to live forever. This brain would never be full. This body was designed to regenerate itself, never grow old. What causes man to age? What brings death to our door? It wasn't planned this way. It was to be eternal fellowship with God. Walking in the cool of the day.

God, out of compassion for his creation, said "It is not good that the man should be alone, I will make him a help for him". God caused a deep sleep to come over this man Adam: and he took one of man's ribs and made a woman. From Adam's side, God took the rib. From under the arm of protection, close to his heart. The serpent, that Ol Devil, Satan saw in Eve's heart something not like God. Playing on this, he said to Eve, "Yea, hath God said, ye shall not eat of every tree of the garden? God had provided life, a garden, abundance, everything that Eve could ever want, but the lust of the eye, the lust of the flesh, and the pride of life wanted the forbidden. And the woman said unto the serpent, "We may eat of the fruit of the trees of the garden: But the tree which is in the midst of the garden, God hath said, Ye shall not eat of it, neither shall ye touch it, lest ye die." She misquoted God and the devil knew he had her. God had told Adam not to eat of this fruit. Genesis 2:17 But of the tree of the knowledge of good and evil, thou shalt not eat of it: for in the day that thou eatest thereof thou shalt surely die. God didn't say a word about touching this fruit, just eating it. This was Eve's downfall. Her lust allowed Satan the wedge he needed to split Eve from fellowship with God, and once Eve, then having struck a mighty blow to the heart of Adam, Adam fell, and the kingdom fell away from him. Eve said "ye shall not eat of it, neither shall ye touch it, least ye die." Satan then called God a liar and told the woman she wouldn't die. Why did Adam's love for Eve surpass his love for God? Who knows, but, it did. The tree was put there for a choice. Adam had to have a choice, will you love me or thee? That was Adam's choice. Adam and Eve became as gods knowing good and evil. Adam and Eve sinned. Fellowship with the Most High was broken. God cannot, will not walk with sin. Sin separates. That which was free, the unshackled fellowship with God, now would cost much.

    Adam and Eve tried to cover their nakedness discovered by their new knowledge of good and evil with fig leaves sewn together. Fig leaves could not cover their sin. It would take a blood sacrifice, an innocent life 4000 years in the future to cover their sin, the sinless sacrifice of Jesus Christ. And they heard the voice of the LORD God walking in the garden in the cool of the day. Nothing could have been more beautiful than to hear the voice of God in the cool of the day. Nearly every time God spoke to man from here on it would be in judgment or in the heat of the battle. Not until Jesus Christ came would God speak out of love. And Adam and his wife hid themselves from the presence of the LORD God amongst the trees of the garden. Sin has caused shame to put up a wall between you and your God. Go ahead and hide Adam! Hide yourself Adam, because you sure can't hide your sin from God. The mind of man rationalizes nearly every wrong. What have you done Adam? Why the fig leaves? We were naked God. Who told you that you were naked? Did you eat of the tree? The woman you gave me sheeeeeeeeeee----. Eve was deceived but Adam was not. God knew what Adam did,. He was asking Adam if Adam knew. Adam just rationalized. And the LORD God called unto Adam, and said unto him, where art thou? Do you really know where you are Adam? Death came by the sin of Adam.

The ground was cursed, thorns and thistles came into being, man must sweat to earn his bread, and death was pronounced upon mankind. Romans 5:12-19 "Wherefore, as by one man sin entered into the world, and death by sin, and so death passed upon all men, for that all have sinned: (For until the law sin was in the world: but sin is not imputed when there is no law. Nevertheless death reigned from Adam to Moses, even over them that had not sinned after the similitude of Adam's transgression, who is the figure of him that was to come. (Jesus) But not as the offense, so also <is> the free gift. For if through the offence of one many be dead, much more the grace of God, and the gift by grace, <which is> by one man, Jesus Christ, hath abounded unto many. {16} And not as <it was> by one that sinned, <so is> the gift: for the judgment <was> by one to condemnation, but the free gift <is> of many offences unto justification. {17} For if by one man's offence death reigned by one, much more they which receive abundance of grace and of the gift of righteousness shall reign in life by one, Jesus Christ.) Therefore as by the offence of one <judgment came> upon all men to condemnation, even so by the righteousness of one <the free gift came> upon all men unto justification of life. {19} For as by one man's disobedience many were made sinners, so by the obedience of one shall many be made righteous."

The worst consequence was that man was cut off from the presence of God. He ejected man from the garden of Eden. God then made coats of skins to cloth the nakedness of his Beloved creation. Innocent blood had to be shed to cover their sins. I wouldn't have done that. I would have done what God said to do. Yet each day your given a choice, just as Adam, and day after day you fail to. How do I fail? Examine yourselves, I say. Have you done what God has told you to do? Do you put other things ahead of God? Adam did. He made the decision to be a god to himself. Instead of trusting God to tell him right from wrong, he decided to do the judging. Of all the creatures that walk, fly, crawl, or swim, man is the only one out of tune with God. Think on this. Does God provide the birds with food? The deer in the timber? The fish in the river? Do they do as God directs them? Sure they do, and God gets glory from this order. When man decides to follow the will of God, it's joy unspeakable and full of glory. Just think, here is a man with a will of its own, surrendering to God.

God' with love abounding, set a plan in action whereby man could be justified in God's sight and be in his presence without being consumed. "And I will put enmity between thee and the woman, and between thy seed and her seed, it shall bruise thy head, and thou shalt bruise his heel." The enmity? The savior of the world, Jesus Christ.

On and on time went, God continued to deal with man, hoping for those that would return His love. From time to time there were those who loved God beyond life itself.

Divine love reaches across the gulf of sin and plucks from hell the person who would love God with all their heart, mind, soul, and strength. God then sets them on their feet, cloths them in garments of righteousness, and sets a new heart in place of an old stony one. He then writes his laws upon the tablets of their hearts. The Old heart, full of murder, lies, dissimulation, and evil is gone. Fellowship with divinity is restored. fellowship with God just as Adam had in the beginning.

Would you desire to know God as Adam did? You can. Really you can.

About The Author

Randy Johnson is an author, speaker, and seminar teacher. With 73 years experience in life and a Masters degree from The School of Hard Knox, he loves sharing his insights on Christian Living where ever a willing ear is found. Randy started his writing early in life and has amassed a large amount of manuscripts covering fiction, science fiction and Christian living. We hope to provide you with the opportunity to share his collection.

From The Desk

I began my ministry in May of 1972. Barb and I owned a Shell Station at the bottom of Germantown Hills. As part of the work we did, washing Cat proving ground cars on Sunday afternoon was t was late in the evening that I sent Barb up the hill to pick up another car. She had to go to the guard house to return the keys and sign out another car. Samuel Sams was working second shift security. Barb went in, gave Sam the keys, signed out the next car and left. Samuel liked to talk to the LORD on his rounds of the building and he felt heavy conviction for not witnessing to Barb. The next car Barb signed out gave him the opportunity to tell her about salvation. He asked her if she knew she was going to heaven.

Barb had doubts about her condition in Christianity and told him so. He spoke to her about repentance, baptism in the name of Jesus Christ, and the infilling of the Holy Ghost with the evidence of speaking with other tongues. Tuesday night found us on the third pew, left hand side. Barb and I repented, got baptized in the name of Jesus Christ, received the gift of the Holy Ghost and have been living in Joy ever since. We took up teaching teens, having a bus ministry, deacon, preaching, teaching, witnessing, cleaning the church, mechanic work on the buses, doing what ever was needed.

I love to share what God has done in my life. I love to encourage others to live for Him. Teaching, preaching, ministering, and just plane fellowship. During one of the trips to Minonk to record the Sunday message, I physically felt the Mantel of God drop on my shoulders. Since then, God has used me to minister in many different and sometimes strange ways. A deep faith in God has given me Joy throughout my life with Him.

It is with great joy that I share with you my file cabinet.

Jer 29:11 For I know the thoughts that I think toward you, saith the LORD, thoughts of peace, and not of evil, to give you an expected end.

INDEX

A

A MAJORITY OF ONE 10/20/1991 212
ANCILLARY 10/07/1991 25

B

BELIEVE 11/25/1990 2959 11/11/1990 46

C

CHRIST IS MY FRIEND 02/23/1992 317
CONVENIENT CHRISTIANITY 11/17/1991 237
CORONARY THROMBOSIS. 01/05/1992 282

D

DIRECT ACCESS 02/10/1991 96
DISPARE 02/21/1993 360

F

FIRST BELIEVE 04/07/1991 162
FOR PROFIT   11/11/1990 40

H

HOLY GHOST 03/01/1992 3167 325

I

I WAS BLIND BUT NOW I SEE 02/24/1991 110
INADEQUATE 12/16/1992 340

M

MADE TO MORN   09/15/91...194
MARRAGE 10/06/1991 203

P

PORTRAIT 1 01/06/1991 71
PORTRAIT 2 01/20/1991 78
PORTRAIT 3 01/27/1991 83
PORTRAIT 4 04/07/1991 88
PROFOUND 10/27/1991 221

R

RESOLUTIONS 12/29/1991 255

S

SALVATION   02/02/1992 306
SHAKESPEAR AS YOU LIKE IT 09/06/1992 263
SOLD A BILL OF GOODS 11/03/1991 228
SPEAK TO THE MOUNTAIN   02/03/1991 103

T

THANKSGIVING   11/24/1991 246
THE APOSTLES 01/26/1992 3273 300
THE BAPTISM OF THE HOLY GHOST 12/16/1990 59
THE BELLS KEEP RINGING   3/31/1991 154
THE BIBLE 08/17/1991...177
THE DIVIDING LINE   02/16/1992 332
THE GREATEST LOVE STORY EVER TOLD   08/19/1990 9
THE HOPE OF THE BELIEVER 02/07/1993 350
THE LESSON OF CHRISTMAS   12/23/1990 65
THE LONELY GOD 02/28/1993 364
THE PROMISE PART 1   12/08/1991...128
THE PROMISE PART 2   12/15/1991...138
THE PROMISE PART 3   12/22/1991...146
THERE'S ROOM IN THE BOAT   12/02/1990 52
TOO LITTLE FOR THE LAMB   03/03/1991 117

W

WASTED IS IT FOR NOTHING?   01/06/1991 269
WHAT SHALL A MAN GIVE?   08/25/1991 185
WHEN ORDINARY BECOMES EXTRAORDINARY   11/04/1990 31
WHERE IS THE PROMISE?   01/12/1992 291
WHERE TO FROM HERE? 04/14/1991...170
WHO CAN CONDEMN?   02/09/1992 314